Théophile Gautier, Orator to the Artists
Art Journalism of the Second Republic

LEGENDA

LEGENDA, founded in 1995 by the European Humanities Research Centre of the University of Oxford, is now a joint imprint of the Modern Humanities Research Association and Routledge. Titles range from medieval texts to contemporary cinema and form a widely comparative view of the modern humanities, including works on Arabic, Catalan, English, French, German, Greek, Italian, Portuguese, Russian, Spanish, and Yiddish literature. An Editorial Board of distinguished academic specialists works in collaboration with leading scholarly bodies such as the Society for French Studies and the British Comparative Literature Association.

MHRA

The Modern Humanities Research Association (MHRA) encourages and promotes advanced study and research in the field of the modern humanities, especially modern European languages and literature, including English, and also cinema. It also aims to break down the barriers between scholars working in different disciplines and to maintain the unity of humanistic scholarship in the face of increasing specialization. The Association fulfils this purpose primarily through the publication of journals, bibliographies, monographs and other aids to research.

Routledge
Taylor & Francis Group

LONDON AND NEW YORK

Routledge is a global publisher of academic books, journals and online resources in the humanities and social sciences. Founded in 1836, it has published many of the greatest thinkers and scholars of the last hundred years, including adorno, einstein, Russell, Popper, Wittgenstein, Jung, Bohm, Hayek, Mcluhan, Marcuse and Sartre. Today Routledge is one of the world's leading academic publishers in the Humanities and Social Sciences. It publishes thousands of books and journals each year, serving scholars, instructors, and professional communities worldwide.

www.routledge.com

Théophile Gautier, Orator to the Artists

Art Journalism in the Second Republic

❖

JAMES KEARNS

Routledge
Taylor & Francis Group

LONDON AND NEW YORK

2007

First published 2007 by Modern Humanities Research Association and Routledge

2 Park Square, Milton Park, Abingdon, Oxfordshire OX14 4RN
52 Vanderbilt Avenue, New York, NY 10017

Routledge is an imprint of the Taylor & Francis Group, an informa business

First issued in paperback 2020

ISBN: 978-1-904350-88-0 (hbk)
ISBN: 978-0-367-60459-2 (pbk)

CONTENTS

For Janie, Joe, and Paul, without whom...

ACKNOWLEDGEMENTS

I should like to express my sincere thanks to the University of Exeter for the generous period of study leave which enabled me to research and write this book and to the School of Modern Languages in the University for its financial support towards the research costs involved. What I owe past and present students of Gautier will be obvious throughout the pages that follow, but I should particularly like to thank the colleagues with whom I currently have the pleasure of working on the forthcoming eight-volume edition of Gautier's Fine Arts Salons to be published by Champion in Paris (Wolfgang Drost, Marie-Hélène Girard, Stéphane Guégan, Sandy Hamrick, Francis Moulinat, and Karen Sorenson), for their knowledge of Gautier and for the generosity and good humour with which they share it.

I am very grateful to the editorial department of the Service Culturel of the Musée d'Orsay, which, in the context of research collaboration with the University of Exeter, generously contributed illustrations of four works in its collection, and to Émilie Janvrin (The Bridgeman Art Library), Guillaume Assié (Musée Fabre, Montpellier), and Patrice Schmidt (Musée d'Orsay) for the kindness and efficiency with which they provided the illustrations.

Finally, I express my sincere thanks to the editorial staff at Legenda, particularly Ritchie Robertson, Graham Nelson and Polly Fallows, whose consideration, patience and efficiency have made the production of this book so much more agreable an experience than it might otherwise have been.

J.K.
Exeter, May 2007

ABBREVIATIONS

BSTG   *Bulletin de la Société Théophile Gautier*

Corr.   Théophile Gautier, *Correspondance générale*, ed. by Claudine Lacoste-Veysseyre, 12 vols (Geneva and Paris: Droz, 1985–2000)

MLR   *Modern Language Review*

PC   *Poésies complètes de Théophile Gautier*, ed. by René Jasinski, 3 vols (Paris: Nizet, 1970)

RCN   Théophile Gautier, *Romans, contes et nouvelles*, dir. by Pierre Laubriet, 2 vols (Paris: Gallimard, Bibliothèque de la Pléiade, 2002)

RDM   *Revue des deux mondes*

RMN   Éditions de la Réunion des musées nationaux

Note: In quoting from Gautier's art journalism I have retained the orthography of the period as it was practised, not always consistently, by Gautier (or his typesetter on *La Presse*), for instance, plurals in *-ans*, *-ens*, whose modern form would be *-ants*, *-ents* (enfans/enfants), omission of circumflex accents (from *grace*, *ame*). I have, on the other hand, corrected what were obviously typing errors. In quoting from correspondence of the period, I have retained the original idiosyncratic spelling and punctuation.

LIST OF ILLUSTRATIONS

INTRODUCTION

Gautier Then and Now

> Faites donc encore une fois entendre à l'autorité la voix des artistes qui se
> désolent, vous qui êtes leur orateur et qui les soutenez si noblement.
>
> Letter: Pradier to Gautier, 1848[1]

In 1847, Théophile Gautier wrote three versions of a piece of publicity for his own
Salon de 1847, which had initially appeared between 30 March and 10 April 1847
as a series of eleven articles in the Parisian daily *La Presse*, of which he was the art
and theatre critic, but which was about to be published in book form by Hetzel. It
was the first of only two of his reviews of the Paris Fine Art Salon to be published
during his lifetime (the other was his *Abécédaire du Salon de 1861*) and, as the three
versions indicate, he gave quite careful thought to the contents of this publicity:

> Il vient de paraître chez l'éditeur Hetzel, sous un format commode et portatif,
> une appréciation du Salon de 1847 par Mr Théophile Gautier, l'un de nos
> premiers critiques d'art. Les pages de Mr Théophile Gautier sont une vraie
> galerie de tableaux. Il ne se contente pas de louer ou de blâmer, il met les pièces
> du procès sous les yeux du lecteur. Son style est si net et d'un coloris si vif qu'il
> peut lutter contre la peinture. Nul doute que ce Salon n'ait autant de succès en
> livre qu'en articles; chaque artiste de réputation ou de mérite trouvera son nom
> dans ces pages bienveillantes et consciencieuses où tous les efforts sont appréciés
> et tous les avenirs pressentis.

> Le Salon de 1847 par Mr Théophile Gautier vient de paraître en volume chez
> l'éditeur Hetzel. Le critique de *La Presse* écrit avec une brosse et son encrier
> est une palette. Quand les tableaux lui manquent à l'Exposition, il en fait lui-
> même et décore les murailles du Louvre de chefs-d'œuvre absents. Bien des
> peintres en lisant ses pages auront envie de crever leurs toiles car ils y verront le
> dessin et la couleur qu'ils n'y ont pas mis. Mr Théophile Gautier est un critique
> enthousiaste qui cherche plus les beautés que les défauts. Son Salon est comme
> une espèce d'anthologie de l'exposition car il n'y parle que des bonnes choses.
> Avoir son nom dans ce livre est un honneur, la plus dure critique c'est de n'y
> être pas cité.

> Depuis Diderot et ses fameux Salons, personne n'a parlé des arts avec plus de
> feu et d'enthousiasme et l'on peut dire aussi avec plus de connaissance de cause
> que Mr Théophile Gautier. Il a appliqué à la critique toutes ses qualités de
> poète; son Salon de 1847 qui vient de paraître à la librairie de Hetzel n'est pas
> une sèche appréciation plus ou moins juste; c'est la transposition dans un autre
> art des chefs-d'oeuvre de cette année. Les toiles et les marbres de nos meilleurs
> artistes revivent dans ces pages à la fois si pittoresques et si colorées. La place de
> ce petit livre est marquée dans toutes les bibliothèques d'artistes, d'écrivains et

de gens du monde. Le Salon tel que l'a écrit Mr Gautier, où ne manque pas un nom illustre ou méritant, sera comme le livre d'or de l'Exposition.[2]

Though there is no evidence that Hetzel made use of what Gautier sent him, the three versions appear designed to provide the publisher with a choice of material from which to select whatever appeared the most suitable. Each is slightly longer than its predecessor and with each the self-promotion is cranked up a notch. In the first Gautier is 'un de nos premiers critiques d'art', by the third he is the successor to Diderot; in the first, the book is assured the same success as the original articles, by the third, it is the exhibition's 'livre d'or'. In all three the emphasis is on Gautier's mastery of the art of painting with words but from one to another we find variations in the features and objectives targeted. In the first there are the convenient portable format, the presentation of exhibits which provides the reader with the means to become his own art critic, and the closing allusion to the Salon review's speculative role in the art market. In the second, Gautier's mastery of verbal painting puts the artists in their place, overturns, where appropriate, the Salon jury's decisions, and clears out the exhibition's time-consuming dross, leaving the reader free to concentrate on the most important works and issues. In the third, the review becomes a sought-after *objet de luxe* in its own right, one that no self-respecting artist, writer, investor, or member of the *beau monde* would wish to be without. Together the three versions cover many of the aspirations felt by producers and consumers of the French nineteenth century's most important art event.

In 1847 Gautier had been art and theatre critic on *La Presse* for over a decade so it is hardly surprising that by then the language of publicity held no secrets for him. His three self-evaluations present the job specification of the art journalist from the point of view of someone who in 1847 surveyed the profession from the summit. As we shall see, Émile de Girardin, the founder and owner of *La Presse*, had already recruited Gautier for his new venture prior to its launch on 1 July 1836. He appreciated his critic's talents enough to pay handsomely for them for almost nineteen years until, on the eve of the Paris Universal Exposition of 1855, Gautier abandoned *La Presse* in favour of *Le Moniteur universel*, the French government's *journal officiel*, which offered enhanced prestige and even better financial terms than those *La Presse* could provide (and, so rumour had it, the promise of a government appointment as inspector of fine arts).[3] Yet the clearest sign of Gautier's position in the field of fine art in 1847 was the importance the artists themselves attached to it. His correspondence is littered with their requests for a favourable mention in his review for their work or that of a colleague, pupil, family member, or acquaintance and with invitations to visit the studio for a preview of work that was about to leave for the Salon. If in private these artists felt uneasy about his descriptions of their work, they were evidently prepared to run the risks involved in order to benefit from the oxygen of publicity that he could provide. At a time when the Salon was becoming less effective in providing an institutional basis for the artist's career, each version of Gautier's prospectus for his own *Salon de 1847* reasserted the importance of his art journalism as an intermediary between artists and buyers, public and private. In the chapters that follow we shall see examples of the ways in which he put his skills to use during the short-lived but pivotal era of the Second Republic.

In the increasingly competitive business of art in mid-nineteenth-century France, however, his position did not go unchallenged. Invited to write a piece for *L'Artiste* on the critics' response to the Salon of 1849, an artist who chose to remain anonymous began with Gautier:

> Théophile Gautier n'a eu qu'un tort, mais un tort qui a duré du commencement à la fin de son Salon. Ç'a [*sic*] été de prendre un encensoir d'or et de jeter de l'encens à pleines bouffées aux coloristes comme aux dessinateurs, aux tableautins comme aux tableaux sérieux. Théophile Gautier, le génie du paradoxe, est trop passionné pour s'arrêter à l'expression un peu froide de la raison: tout ce qu'il touche devient or et pourpre. Dès qu'il entame un tableau on y voit rayonner le soleil espagnol. Aussi, d'après lui, tout a le prisme, tout a le mirage, tout est beau. Il croit peut-être complaire à tous les artistes, mais en flattant tous les artistes il déplaît à tous les artistes. Qui sait! si on y regardait d'un peu plus près on trouverait peut-être bien un grain de raillerie souveraine dans son encens. Constatons d'ailleurs que Théophile Gautier ne parle que des vrais artistes. Il en fait à trop bon marché de grands artistes, mais il laisse de côté les médiocres.[4]

The article continued in much the same vein, and Gautier's fellow *salonniers*, it has to be said, fared little better. For the anonymous artist they were all guilty of equating judgement with personal taste, for they all appeared to be finding it increasingly difficult to contain the growing individualism of contemporary art within established categories and hierarchies. The fact that they knew what they liked did not compensate in his view for the sense of disorientation that this was causing for the public interested in such matters. What Gautier liked, he said, was to say nice things about everybody, which defeated the purpose. Admittedly, his reviews were a pleasure to read but they were indiscriminate, uncritical, inconsequential. Their one redeeming feature was that he at least always knew who the true artists were and did not waste his time and that of his readers on the mediocre.

This last point supported Gautier's assessment of his own reviews, but for the most part the anonymous artist described as weaknesses the very features of Gautier's art criticism that he in his self-evaluation had described as strengths. From the outset of his career in art journalism, he had preferred to praise rather than to criticize.[5] As we shall see, he was prepared to make exceptions, but generally he preferred to offset sharp criticism with encouragement, even occasionally an apology.[6] Equally, we shall see that his praise or blame was not dependent on the artist's allegiance, perceived or real, to one or other of the two major factions, those of the *dessinateurs* and *coloristes*, whose opposition was thought to structure the art of the period, and that he was equally unstinting in his devotion to the two artists identified then and since as the leaders of these two supposed factions (Ingres and Delacroix, respectively).[7] In his theory of art as microcosm, all great art was a law unto itself, to be approached on its own terms and merits, whether or not such flexibility exposed the critic to lazy, shallow labels such as 'le génie du paradoxe'.[8] Gautier's fondness for Spanish references and analogies was an easy target (easier certainly than thinking about the use he made of them) but at least the anonymous author's closing remark was more to the point. With so many artists taking part in the Salon, there was bound to be an element of the random and arbitrary in the choices the *salonnier* made of the work to be reviewed, but Gautier's alertness to the key artists and issues of the period was indeed a strong feature of his art criticism. In his Salon reviews he referred on average to about 3% of the artists exhibiting and only about 1% were the subject of an extended commentary.[9] The vast majority were overlooked, sentenced to what Gautier called 'la plus dure critique'.

The criticisms levelled against Gautier's art journalism took on greater significance when repeated, even if privately to begin with, by less anonymous voices. The best-known example is that of Delacroix in his diary entry of 17 June 1855. Usually truncated and taken out of context, his comments are worth quoting in full (with the familiar truncated elements italicized):

> Gautier a fait plusieurs articles sur l'École anglaise: il a commencé par là. Arnoux, qui le déteste, m'a dit chez Delamarre que c'était une flatterie de sa part pour le *Moniteur,* dans lequel il écrit. Je veux bien, pour moi, lui faire l'honneur d'attribuer à son bon goût cette espèce de prédilection marquée tout d'abord pour des étrangers; cependant ses remarques ne m'ont nullement mis sur la trace même des sentiments que j'exprime ici. C'est par la comparaison avec d'autres tableaux dans lesquels on croit admirer chez nous des qualités analogues qu'il fallait avoir le courage de faire ressortir le mérite des Anglais; je ne trouve rien de cela. *Il prend un tableau, le décrit à sa manière, fait lui-même un tableau qui est charmant, mais il n'a pas fait un acte de véritable critique; pourvu qu'il trouve à faire chatoyer, miroiter les expressions macaroniques qu'il trouve avec un plaisir qui vous gagne quelquefois,* qu'il cite l'Espagne et la Turquie, l'Alhambra et l'Atméïdan de Constantinople, *il est content, il a atteint son but d'écrivain curieux, et je crois qu'il ne voit pas au delà.* Quand il en sera aux Français, il fera pour chacun d'eux ce qu'il fait pour les Anglais. *Il n'y aura ni enseignement ni philosophie dans une pareille critique.*[10]

The context omitted in the truncated version was that of the Paris Universal Exposition of 1855. Gautier's collaboration on the *Moniteur universel* brought with it diplomatic and political considerations, associated with the international nature of the event, which, as author of the quasi-official account of the art work on show there, he was obliged to take on board.[11] Judging by Delacroix's note, Louis d'Arnoux interpreted the precedence given in Gautier's review to British art over that of the French school as an example of him currying favour with the regime (presumably because by reviewing the British art first, Gautier had ensured that his very positive comments on it would coincide with Napoleon III's visit to London in April 1855, a visit itself designed to prepare for that of Victoria and Albert to Paris later that year).[12] Delacroix was both more generous and more critical of Gautier than Arnoux appears to have been: more generous in the sense that he was prepared to attribute the order in which Gautier had presented the British and French work to a welcome openness on the critic's part to the art of other national schools; more critical in the sense that he believed Gautier's comments on British art illustrated fundamental weaknesses as an art critic rather than merely alleged subservience to new political masters.

From Delacroix's point of view, for Gautier to assume in the proper manner the responsibility of writing on British artists, he would have had to compare their achievements with those of their French counterparts by explaining the technical and material issues that arose when artists from different national traditions addressed similar developments (such as changing forms of realism, trends in landscape art, or the growth of genre painting). Instead, Gautier had developed his own system for creating verbal illusions of paintings, a form of transposition which resulted in a related but different product. Given the Gautier treatment, the painter's performance was obscured by the extraneous material and energy of the writing, its firework display of fashionable exotic reference and analogy (Spanish again), admittedly brilliant and entertaining but lacking precision and instruction. Delacroix's comments express what would become the long-standing assessment of Gautier as the 'failed painter who, both in his criticism and his poetry, contented himself with producing pretty word-pictures'.[13] They did not of course prevent Delacroix expressing his gratitude a few weeks later when Gautier did come to the French paintings on show in the Universal Exposition and Delacroix read his homage to his own work (*Corr.*, VI, 168). Gautier's eulogy was merely the latest episode in the campaign he had already waged for nearly two decades in *La Presse* on behalf of Delacroix. A few days earlier, Ingres had also responded graciously, albeit with his characteristic feigned humility, to Gautier's lavish praise (ibid., p.165).[14] The two most famous French painters of the first half of the century, who scarcely agreed on anything, agreed that his art journalism was a double-edged sword. As if in response to Delacroix's opinion (which he was well placed to know), Baudelaire subsequently singled out Gautier's analysis of the British painting in the Universal Exposition of 1855 as a particularly good example of the power of empathy that in his view distinguished Gautier's art criticism, but it was Delacroix's version of his critical methods that prevailed.[15]

Even allowing for these serious misgivings on the part of practising artists, the posthumous collapse of the reputation of 'l'écrivain le plus autorisé et le plus populaire en matière de critique d'art', as the journalist and fellow *salonnier* Albert de la Fizelière called him,[16] implied wider-ranging antagonisms. The professional trajectory that took Gautier from opposition to the art institutions of the July Monarchy, via support for the Second Republic's art policy, to quasi-official status as art critic to the Second Empire, exposed him to accusations of political detachment, opportunism, or servility in the intensely politically charged context of mid-nineteenth-century French art. His long association with *La Presse* may have been prejudicial to him through contamination by the powerful hostility felt for Girardin within conservative and republican opinion alike,[17] but his association with *Le Moniteur universel* (and, by implication as much as in reality, with the imperial regime's ruling elites) was more damaging in the longer term for it ensured that, after his death in 1872, his reputation fell in the backwash of the Second Empire's ignominious collapse. Compounding this political disgrace, the modernist tradition, which demonized journalism as the antithesis of literary modernity, relegated Gautier to the rank of a minor poet, while ensuring that Baudelaire's art criticism basked in the reflected glory of *Les Fleurs du mal*. Despite the fact that Baudelaire stated in 1859 that Gautier's art journalism had educated a whole generation — it had certainly educated Baudelaire, who, as we know, was already reading it in *La Presse* by 1838, if not before[18] — and that Mallarmé celebrated in

Toast funèbre 'le *Voyant* qui, placé dans ce monde, l'a regardé, ce que l'on ne fait pas',[19] Gautier was placed in quarantine from the early stages of the Third Republic. His refusal to embrace the forward march of history as exemplified by the work of Courbet and Manet was a red rag to Zola, who resorted to the 'génie du paradoxe' cliché to justify liquidation of Gautier's legacy.[20] Other contemporary cultural and academic heavyweights weighed in with similar enthusiasm.[21] The result was that when Gautier's art journalism was discussed at all, it tended to be dismissed as a model of descriptive commentary rendered obsolete by technological advances in the production of images and/or by the anti-descriptive emphasis of modernist art history and criticism. It survived largely in the form of decontextualized short extracts used to provide nineteenth-century local colour for modern blockbuster exhibitions of key figures or periods in French art. The lack of modern critical editions of Gautier's art journalism, long assumed to be of insufficient merit in terms of either literary or art history to warrant the intellectual and economic investment involved, compounded his relegation.

The impact of this relegation lasted for almost the first hundred years following his death. Yet the categorization of Gautier as a minor poet and spokesman of *l'art pour l'art* scarcely begins to account for his position in the French literary field during the period 1830–70. It also helped to sustain a hopelessly inadequate history of French art criticism dominated by the *grands écrivains critiques d'art* type of account, in which status within the literary canon secured de facto (or excluded in Gautier's case) a similar status within art criticism.[22] But these reductive accounts of his writing also had implications for French art history itself. For much of the nineteenth century the Salon was the single most important regular exhibition of contemporary art in Europe. Any French artist who aspired to a successful career in painting or sculpture during that period produced art for the Salon. Any historian working on French art during the period cannot avoid referring to the Salon. Yet the history of the institution itself during this period has never been written. Expressed schematically, this history is that of the forms of engagement and circuits of meaning into which its key participants were drawn: the state, which managed the institution, with all that this implied for such issues as patronage, delegation, censorship; the artists, for whom the Salon was a key factor in the management of their careers; the critics, through whom the relationship between the history of the Salon and the development of the press was conducted; and the public, for which the Salon played a significant role in the development of an urban bourgeois culture and social life. In all these areas of a hitherto unwritten history of French nineteenth-century art, Gautier was an indispensable witness and in this respect certainly more important, it must be said, than Baudelaire.

Almost a century after his death, Gautier's art criticism was finally the subject of a serious general study by Michael Spencer, who analysed his contribution towards what the author called 'an aesthetic of individualism'.[23] In 1982 it was followed by another informed and sympathetic study, in which Robert Snell located the legacy of Gautier's art criticism in the Nordic idealism and poetic mysticism of the Symbolist and Aesthetic movements.[24] Both accounts were constrained, however, by the critical approach adopted, which sought primarily to position Gautier's art writings in relation to those of Diderot and Baudelaire. In addition, despite the real merits of these studies in establishing Gautier's art literature as a serious object of study, their authors also created a few myths of their own, notably, as far as this present study is concerned, that his critical acumen as an art journalist declined from the late 1840s and that his support for the Second Republic was opportunistic or self-destructive.[25] The creation of the Société Théophile Gautier and its Bulletin gave new impetus to the revision of the history of Gautier's engagement in the visual arts, notably through publication of the papers of the 1982 conference *Théophile Gautier: l'art et l'artiste* (in *BSTG*, 4.1–2). In 1992 Wolfgang Drost's outstanding edition of Gautier's review of the Salon of 1859, and in 1994 Marie-Hélène Girard's excellent anthology of selected extracts from Gautier's Salon reviews, showed the importance of having modern editions of his complete Salons and untruncated commentaries on individual artists.[26] In 1997, the major exhibition *Théophile Gautier: la critique en liberté*, organized at the Musée d'Orsay by Stéphane Guégan, showed the progress made in restoring Gautier to his proper place in French nineteenth-century literary history.[27]

Faced with the vast amount of art journalism that Gautier wrote during a professional career spanning forty years, my own approach has been to focus on a specific period, that of the Second Republic from the revolution of February 1848 to the coup d'état of December 1851. In what will be the first study of his entire art journalism during this period, I shall analyse the range of issues with which he engaged and the efforts he made to maintain the fixed points of his aesthetic system while adapting it to meet the new situation arising from the change of regime. In this respect, as we shall see, the short-lived Second Republic was as pivotal a phase in the fine arts as it was in other areas of French national life, for the new administration and its supporters in the wider art community had ambitions to achieve major reform of the art institutions. These ambitions derived in part from grievances against specific features of July Monarchy policy (the creation, for example, of the Musée Historique at Versailles in 1833 and the Musée Espagnol in the Louvre in 1838 was attacked by opponents of the regime as the pursuit of self-serving dynastic priorities at the expense of long-overdue investment in the Louvre and in the provincial museums), but they were also a response to the changes taking place in France since the revolution of 1830 (the growth of supply and demand in the French art market, the extension of literacy, stimulating and stimulated by the industrialization of the press from 1836, with its corollary, the emergence of art journalism). In the fine arts as in politics, the Second Republic stood in principle for an extension of the franchise, in this case for access of a wider public to the products of the higher cultural forms. It hoped to trigger a second renaissance in public art by commissioning the decoration of the places of congregation and exchange needed by a more open, democratic society. It wanted to remove what it saw as the dead hand of official neoclassicism from control of the Academy, the École des Beaux-Arts, and the annual Salon. In the very short term it also wanted new symbols of the republic with which to present a reassuring image of a confident, secure, and modern regime. As we shall see, the so-called art-for-art's-sake Gautier had supported most of this since the mid-1830s and he wasted no time in saying so again in the spring of 1848. He would soon have no illusions about the extent to which the achievements failed to match the ambitions but he was never less than a critical friend to the Republican regime.

For the majority of artists, the essential issue was that of the Salon. As I have said, in the mid-nineteenth century this annual or biennial exhibition largely determined the manner in which artists organized their careers, but by that time the forms of state patronage and management of the event had become increasingly problematic from their point of view. On 21 August 1791, when the deputies in the National Assembly abolished the professional corporations, they could in theory have chosen, in accordance with the liberal principles for which the revolution had been fought, to disengage the State entirely from the management of the fine arts, leaving artists to exhibit their work when, where, and how they chose. Such, however, was the consensus both within and outwith the artistic community that the fine arts were too important to be left to artists alone that they decided instead to transfer the responsibility for organizing the event held in the Salon Carré of the Louvre (hence its name) from the ancien régime's Académie Royale de Peinture et de Sculpture to a directorate of the Département de Paris within the Ministry of the Interior and to extend to all artists, French and foreign, access to the exhibition hitherto reserved for members of the Academy.[28] By 1798 the artists had successfully petitioned for the creation of a jury whose role was to ensure that standards were maintained in the wake of this decision to widen access (and, as we shall see, fifty years later this need for a *jury d'admission* would be firmly back on the agenda). During the Empire and Restoration the number of artists exhibiting in the Salon grew steadily, but from the artist's point of view this development increased the risk of damaging the Salon's effectiveness as a showcase through which to achieve professional advancement, and the event was not held often enough during this period to offset this perceived reduction in the quality of contact between artists and potential patrons, public or private.[29] In the wake of the Revolution of 1830, artists petitioned Louis-Philippe for the Salon to be held annually and for the jury to be elected by the artists themselves. The Academy had no interest in seeing an event to which it had lost its control over access forty years earlier being held more frequently, and it particularly had no interest in seeing the management of the Salon jury falling into wider hands. The king, presumably trying to please everyone, granted one of the artists' requests — royal approval of the annualization of the Salon was formally granted in October 1833 — and refused the other, delegating to the Academy the responsibility for the management of the Salon jury.[30] The two decisions pulled in opposite directions. The first met the artists' hopes of increased opportunities to show their work in what was by then the most important regular exhibition of contemporary art in Europe; the second frustrated these hopes by giving a narrowly-based professional organization the means to restrict access to the Salon on the basis of criteria widely believed to be retrograde and self-serving. By 1847 opposition to the jury's decisions had led to widespread demand for reform, so much so that the attack on the jury had become an annual ritual with which many *salonniers*, including Gautier, began their reviews. But it had also led artists to pursue alternative strategies for showing their work which freed them from the forms of censorship or self-censorship created by the Salon jury. Gautier's contributions to these debates will feature prominently in the chapters that follow.

During the Second Republic Gautier published in *La Presse* reviews of the Salons of 1848, 1849, and 1850–51 (a total of 49 articles of, on average, 3000 words each), a series of seven articles on Paul Chenavard's proposed decorations for the Panthéon, nine on French museums, two on the government's competition for a figure of the Republic, three on the Indian pavilion in the Universal Exhibition of Crystal Palace, two on the Manufactures Nationales of Beauvais and the Gobelins, and a dozen on a range of art topics in *La Presse* and other periodicals (some of which, notably *L'Artiste*, managed by his friend Arsène Houssaye, reprinted extracts of articles already published in *La Presse*). By following his account of what he saw as the achievements and failures of the short-lived Republican phase of the management of the fine arts, we shall, I hope, free his art journalism from the simplistic art-for-art's-sake commonplaces to which it has been for so long reduced. Faced with regime change in 1848 he sought to use his hard-earned authority in the French artistic field to teach the lessons of the developments that had been taking place since 1789 in the organization, production, and reception of the French fine arts and to set out what he thought was the correct path for French art in the modern age. During this period the Salon remained the centrepiece of the French state exhibition system, the basis of the artist's career trajectory, and the benchmark of achievement. One chapter of this study will therefore be devoted to Gautier's analysis of each of the three Salons of these years, while other chapters will chart his response to the major art events and debates taking place outside and between these Salons. In each, we shall see examples of what Pradier called the oratory of Gautier's art journalism and it is with the Gautier–Pradier relationship in 1848 that we shall begin.

Notes to the Introduction

1. Letter from the sculptor James Pradier to Gautier, in Théophile Gautier, *Correspondance générale*, ed. by Claudine Lacoste-Veysseyre, 12 vols (Geneva and Paris: Droz, 1985–2000), III (1988), 362–63 (henceforth *Corr.*). The editor dated the letter 'fin juillet–début août 1848'.

2. The manuscript containing the three versions forms part of the Fonds Hetzel in the manuscript department of the Bibliothèque Nationale de France and was published for the first time by Claudine Lacoste in 'Théophile Gautier juge de lui-même', *Bulletin de la Société Théophile Gautier* (henceforth *BSTG*), 11 (1989), 156–60.

3. Girardin's letter to Gautier on learning of his departure for the *Moniteur* was a model of controlled fury. 'S'il est vrai qu'on vous ait promis une place d'Inspecteur des Beaux Arts, vous acquererez un titre de plus à cette nomination quand le gouvernement saura que la préférence donnée par vous au Moniteur sur la Presse vous y a fait perdre votre feuilleton de théâtre et que le feuilleton qui doit paraître demain mardi sera le dernier que les lecteurs de la Presse y liront' (letter of 2 April 1855 in *Corr.*, VI, 140–41). The post of fine arts inspector never materialized.

4. Un artiste qui n'a pas exposé, 'Salon de 1849: critique de la critique', *L'Artiste*, 15 September 1849, pp. 177–80 (p. 177).

5. In 1833, in his first Salon review, he wrote: 'Le génie en France n'est guère qu'un thème à calembours [*sic*]; notre public est dénué de cette puissance admirative qui fait les grands artistes; la louange est un fouet plutôt que la critique, et elle fait galoper un homme bien plus vite dans la carrière que ne ferait un sarcasme. Il faut se sentir admiré pour produire largement et librement ce qu'on a dans le cœur et la tête' ('Salon de 1833', *La France littéraire* (March 1833), 139–66 (p. 141)).

6. The following example from his review of Lehmann's *Océanides* shown in the Salon of 1850–51 is characteristic: 'nous sommes sévère à l'endroit de M. Lehmann, parce que nous aurons tout à l'heure l'occasion de lui donner, pour ses portraits, des éloges sans restriction' (*La Presse*, 1 March 1851).

7. This reductive account of the art of the first half of the nineteenth century in terms of the struggle between neoclassical *dessinateurs* led by Ingres and Romantic *coloristes* led by Delacroix has had a long and fruitful life in French art history. It was of course a rerun of the earlier opposition between the *Poussinistes* and *Rubénistes* which had divided the French Academy during the late seventeenth century. See Bernard Teyssèdre, *Roger de Piles et les débats sur le coloris au siècle de Louis XIV* (Paris: Bibliothèque des arts, 1965); Jacqueline Lichtenstein, *La Couleur éloquente: rhétorique et peinture à l'âge classique* (Paris: Flammarion, 1989); Andrew Carrington Shelton, 'Ingres versus Delacroix', in *Fingering Ingres*, ed. by Susan Siegfried and Adrian Rifkin (Oxford: Blackwell, 2001), pp. 76–92; James H. Rubin, 'Delacroix and Romanticism', in *The Cambridge Companion to Delacroix*, ed. by Beth S. Wright (Cambridge University Press, 2000), pp. 26–47.

8. Justifying his support for painters within each of the *paysage de style* and *paysage naturel* groups, Gautier said: 'La critique, dont le devoir est de tout comprendre, peut, sans se contredire, accepter des points de vue en apparence si contradictoires' (*Exposition de 1859*, ed. by Wolfgang Drost (Heidelberg: Carl Winter, 1992), p. 184).

9. These figures represent a snapshot of the Salons of 1848, 1849, and 1850–51, with which we shall be concerned.

10. *Delacroix, Journal 1822–1863*, ed. by André Joubin, rev. by Régis Labourdette (Paris: Plon, 1996), pp. 515–16.

11. Maxime Du Camp wrote to Gautier on 19 April 1855: 'Tu as quitté la Presse et tu es entré tout à fait au Moniteur. Tu représentes donc pour la masse du public l'opinion officielle du gouvernement sur l'art et la littérature [...] Ton article sur les embellissements de Paris te pose comme très Bonapartiste [...]' (*Corr.*, VI, 144–45). Gautier's article on Haussmann's transformation of Paris had appeared in the *Moniteur* of 16 April 1855.

12. See in this respect my article 'Gautier et la peinture allemande à L'Exposition Universelle de 1855', in *Gautier et l'Allemagne*, ed. by Wolfgang Drost and Marie-Hélène Girard (Siegen: UniverSi-Verlag, 2005), pp. 217–39.

13. See David Kelley, 'Transpositions', in *Artistic Relations: Literature and the Visual Arts in Nineteenth-Century France*, ed. by Peter Collier and Robert Lethbridge (New Haven and London: Yale University Press, 1994), pp. 178–91 (p. 178).

14. Two years later, Ingres thanked Gautier for 'le charmant et trop aimable article que vous avez fait dans l'Artiste au sujet de ma petite nymphe [*La Source*]', which was 'comme tout ce qui sort de votre plume touché de main de maître plein de bienveillance et de Poésie' (*Corr.*, VI, 284, letter of 2 February 1857). Coming from Ingres, praise for benevolence and poetry could only be a back-handed compliment.

15. Of the Universal Exposition, Baudelaire posed the rhetorical question: 'qui donc parla le premier et qui parla le mieux de cette école anglaise, que les plus instruits parmi le public ne pouvaient guère juger que d'après quelques souvenirs de Reynolds et de Lawrence? [...] Qui sut immédiatement britanniser son génie?' ('Théophile Gautier', in *Œuvres complètes*, ed. by Claude Pichois, 2 vols (Paris: Gallimard, Bibliothèque de la Pléiade, 1976), II, 123). Support for Gautier's art writing came from an unfamiliar source in late 1850, when the artist Charles Porion, who, it must be said, has left little trace in French nineteenth-century art history, summarized the qualities that in his view set Gautier apart in contemporary art journalism: 'Vos critiques font seules loi, non seulement parce qu'elles sont les seules vraies, savantes et spirituelles, mais encore parce qu'en touchant toujours juste & ferme; elles sont courtoises & comme un type de l'esprit français, dont votre plume a seule aujourd'hui la tradition' (*Corr.*, IV, 278). Porion was asking a favour (a mention in Gautier's Salon review for the two copies of Velasquez that the government had commissioned from him) and we would do well to make allowance for that. Nevertheless, his remarks seem to me to get closer to the strengths of Gautier's critical language than many others.

16. Quoted by Constance C. Hungerford in *Ernest Meissonier: rétrospective* (Paris: Éditions de la Réunion des musées nationaux (henceforth RMN), 1993), p. 40. Hungerford herself states that Gautier 'était le plus lu et le plus influent' of the art critics of the day (ibid.).

17. In the conservative press of the July Monarchy, Girardin had powerful enemies who never forgave him for the way in which his transformation of the press from 1836 had challenged their position. Republicans generally despised his naked personal ambition but, more specifically, those grouped around *Le National* still hated him in 1848 for the duel in which twelve years earlier he had killed Armand Carrel, founder of the newspaper in 1830 and for whom the republican opposition in the mid-1830s had had great hopes. See Pierre Pellissier, *Émile de Girardin, prince de la presse* (Paris: Denoël, 1985), pp. 113–15.

18. See Baudelaire, 'Théophile Gautier', pp. 123–24). For Baudelaire's early reading of *La Presse*, see *Lettres inédites aux siens*, ed. by Philippe Auserve (Paris: Grasset, 1966), and Baudelaire, *Salon de 1846*, ed. by David Kelley (Oxford: Clarendon Press, 1975), p. 44. A recent anthology entitled *Charles Baudelaire–Théophile Gautier: Correspondances esthétiques sur Delacroix*, ed. by Stéphane Guégan and Karine Marie (Paris: Éditions Olbia, 1998), which brings together in chronological order the texts of both poets on the painter, shows how Baudelaire's sense of Delacroix's modernity was related to Gautier's writings on the painter during the decade preceding Baudelaire's Salon of 1846.

19. See Mallarmé, *Œuvres complètes*, ed. by Bertrand Marchal, 2 vols (Paris: Gallimard, Bibliothèque de la Pléiade, 1998–2003), I, 1173.

20. 'Aucune idée nouvelle apportée, aucune vérité humaine de quelque profondeur, aucune prescience de l'évolution des siècles, rien que des symphonies exécutées sur des lieux communs qui courent nos ateliers et nos cabinets d'artistes depuis 1830. Toute l'œuvre écrite ou parlée de ce poète a été une gymnastique étourdissante sur le terrain du paradoxe' (*Documents littéraires, études et portraits* (Paris: G. Charpentier, 1881), pp. 137–38). Commenting on the 'scandal' of Gautier's attacks on Manet, Paolo Tortonese rightly wondered why Gautier's attacks on Racine had not provoked similar outrage: 'Parce que l'histoire littéraire nous apprend que s'opposer à Racine au XIXe siècle, c'est s'inscrire dans l'évolution en cours, c'est aller dans le sens de l'histoire [...] Si nous étions plus historiens et moins historicistes, la gaffe sur Manet devrait être moins choquante que celle sur Racine' (in 'Gautier classique, Gautier romantique: considérations en marge de l'exposition Gautier au musée d'Orsay', *BSTG*, 19 (1997), 75–94 (p. 84)).

21. In his introduction to the Folio edition of Gautier's *Voyage en Espagne* (Paris: Gallimard, 1981), Patrick Berthier quotes Edmond Scherer's 1885 description of Gautier as 'l'écrivain le plus étranger qui fut jamais à toute conception élevée de l'art aussi bien qu'à tout emploi viril de la plume' and Faguet's comment two years later that Gautier was 'un homme dépourvu d'idées, de sensibilité, d'imagination'.

22. By way of examples, neither François de Hérain, in *Les Grands écrivains critiques d'art* (Paris: Mercure de France, 1943), nor François Fosca, in *De Diderot à Valéry: les écrivains et les arts visuels* (Paris: A. Michel, 1960), mentions Gautier.

23. Michael Clifford Spencer, *The Art Criticism of Théophile Gautier* (Geneva: Droz, 1969).

24. Robert Snell, *Théophile Gautier: A Romantic Critic in the Visual Arts* (Oxford: Clarendon Press, 1982).

25. Spencer stated that 'the formulation of any value judgement had largely disappeared [from Gautier's art criticism] by the 1850s' and that there were two art journalists in him, the second of whom 'composed blatantly insincere, progressive dithyrambs to celebrate the 1848 revolution, frequently accepted help in the writing of his articles and [...] in the latter years of his life praised all and sundry with benign indifference' (pp. 101–02); Snell: 'The year 1848 was, for Gautier as for Baudelaire, a genuine trauma and a watershed; if it drove Baudelaire to a further awakening of his powers, it struck a decisive blow to Gautier's confidence in his own modernity' (p. 185).

26. *Exposition de 1859*, ed. by Drost; *Théophile Gautier, Critique d'art: extraits de Salons (1833–1872)*, ed. by Marie-Hélène Girard (Paris: Séguier, 1994). Drost, in 'Pour une réévaluation de la critique d'art de Gautier' (*Cahiers de l'Association Internationale des Études françaises*, 55 (2003), 401–21), and Giraud in the introduction to her anthology put forward the case for a re-evaluation of Gautier's contribution to French nineteenth-century writing on the visual arts. Both are currently co-ordinating the first complete edition of Gautier's Salon reviews, to be published in Paris by H. Champion in eight volumes from 2009.

27. In following Gautier's art journalism through the years of the Second Republic, we shall also encounter that of other important commentators of the period whose work deserves to be better

known (Louis Clément de Ris in *L'Artiste*, Prosper Haussard in *Le National*, Frédéric de Mercey in the *Revue des deux mondes*, to name but a few).

28. See Pierre Vaisse, *La Troisième République et les peintres* (Paris: Flammarion, 1995), pp. 95–96.

29. Between 1795 and 1802, the Salon had been held annually (with the exception of 1797), under the Consulate and Empire it became biennial but under the Restoration it was held only six times (in 1814, 1817, 1819, 1822, 1824, and 1827/28). As far as the increase in the number of exhibits during this period is concerned, the underlying trend is clear: 1798, 536; 1808, 802; 1819, 1702; 1827/28, 1834. See Patricia Mainardi, *The End of the Salon: Art and State in the Early Third Republic* (Cambridge University Press, 1993), p. 18.

30. Léon Rosenthal, *Du Romantisme au réalisme* (Paris: H. Laurens, 1914; repr. Paris: Éditions Macula, 1987), p. 36.

CHAPTER 1

Orator to the Artists:
Gautier and Pradier in 1848

Cher Théophile,

Faites donc encore une fois entendre à l'autorité la voix des artistes qui se désolent, vous qui êtes leur orateur et qui les soutenez si noblement. Le salon est fermé et point encore de nouvelles d'acquisitions par le Ministre l'an passé c'était la disette qui était la cause de la rentrée de nos ouvrages qui dorment encore dans nos ateliers aujourd'hui c'est la république qui ne s'en soucie guère qui gâche et avale tout...

Montpellier, désirant avoir ma statue de Nissia pour son Musée j'ai prié le ministre de la prendre pour le prix qu'il voudrait mes dépenses seulement point de réponse, un silence mortel règne dans ce misérable Ministère qui devrait songer que nous n'avons même plus la liste civile pour nous aider, pauvres arts relégués avec la police pourquoi cette administration n'est-elle pas avec sa soeur les lettres j'en suis avili et le courage me manque /.

votre tout affectionné

J. Pradier

This letter to Gautier from the Swiss-born French sculptor James Pradier, from which the title of this study is taken, was one of a number he wrote during the first summer of the Second Republic to draw attention to his financial plight and that of artists in general. The annual Salon had closed its doors at the beginning of July and Pradier was trying to secure the sale to the State, for the museum in Montpellier, of one of the works he had shown there, his marble statue *Nyssia* (Figure 1.1).[1] Gautier had good reason to be interested in the statue's destination since Nyssia was the heroine of his short story of 1844, *Le Roi Candaule*, a brief extract of which was quoted in the Salon catalogue as the source for the work.[2] He was not by any means the only one whose support Pradier sought to enlist that summer in his efforts to achieve the sale. Others included Hugo, who, like Gautier, was a long-standing friend, and Charles Blanc, Directeur des Beaux-Arts since the beginning of April that year and, as such, responsible in the Republican administration for the commission and purchase of art works. Since that year more than ever the government was taking an active interest in the fine arts, Pradier for good measure also contacted Antoine Sénard and General Louis Cavaignac, who, in the view of the National Assembly, 'avaient bien mérité de la patrie' during the bloody events of 23–26 June 1848 and had been duly rewarded for the key parts they

Fig. 1.1. James Pradier, *Nyssia*, 1848, Montpellier, Musée Fabre
© Musée Fabre, Montpellier Agglomération, cliché Frédéric Jaulmes

played in the brutal suppression of the insurrection that week with promotion to the posts of Minister of the Interior and Président du Conseil respectively.[3] With this level of support, it was perhaps not surprising that Pradier's efforts soon paid off. On 19 August Charles Blanc informed him that the State, in the person of the Minister of the Interior, had agreed to purchase *Nyssia* for ten thousand francs and to authorize its transfer to the museum at Montpellier.[4]

It is not known whether Gautier responded to Pradier's request to intervene on his behalf,[5] but what is clear is that, as a target for recruitment to the sculptor's sales drive alongside France's two most powerful politicians (albeit briefly), its most senior arts administrator, and its greatest living poet, Gautier was in distinguished company. In Pradier's designation of him as orator to the artists, allowance must of course be made for self-serving flattery, but as a description of Gautier's status in art journalism by that time, as an indicator of the speculative value his name had acquired, this quasi-official title was close to the mark. By then he had been France's best-known art journalist for over a decade, during which time he had given artists ample evidence of his loyalty, support and willingness to use his art journalism to further their professional interests. He knew the French fine arts system, its administrative structures and key personnel, he knew his art history, ancient and modern, he was familiar with the materials and processes of the visual arts, with the language of the studios and the tricks of the trade. Writing for the newspaper created by one of the most powerful figures in the French press of the nineteenth century, he combined erudition and exceptional verbal facility and range in ways well attuned to the new reading public that had emerged during the July Monarchy. The change of regime triggered by the revolution of 1848 created challenges and opportunities for the skills he had acquired and for the relationships he had nurtured since beginning to write art criticism in the early 1830s.[6] These skills and relationships, the part they played and the purposes to which they were put during the Second Republic, will be the subject of what follows.

To introduce the issues involved, we may continue our annotation of Pradier's letter to Gautier. In the summer of 1848 Pradier was fifty-two years old and had a long and distinguished career behind him. He had followed the French path of competitions and promotions to the summit of his profession: 1813, winner of the Grand Prix de Rome for sculpture; 1827, member of the Académie des Beaux-Arts and Professor at the École des Beaux-Arts; 1828, Légion d'honneur, promoted to the rank of Officer six years later. His work had been regularly accepted by the juries of the Paris Fine Art Salons from 1819 onwards and he had secured a steady stream of commissions and sales from both the Bourbon and the Orleanist administrations.[7] If in 1848 Pradier needed a concerted and high-powered campaign to enable him to translate his long-established professional eminence into the hard currency of a sale, what can it have been like for the others, those with less of a career behind them or with less access to the people who mattered? What could the immediate future hold for them?

One F. de Lagenevais, in his review of the Salon of 1848 for the fortnightly Orleanist *Revue des deux mondes*, had an answer of sorts to that question, but one which would have brought little comfort to Pradier. Referring to artists in general he wrote:

> La crise financière leur sera sans doute fatale: le niveau de fer qui pèse sur tant
> d'existences doit briser le pinceau et l'ébauchoir dans la main de plus d'un
> homme de talent. Les jours difficiles vont commencer. Les encouragemens que
> les particuliers accordaient aux artistes, et qui ne sont que l'emploi du superflu
> que bien peu possèdent aujourd'hui, vont leur manquer. Les nombreuses
> médiocrités qui vivaient de ce superflu sont donc condamnées à périr; n'ayant
> pas foi dans l'art, elles le délaisseront et se réfugieront dans d'autres carrières
> plus profitables. Les vrais artistes lui resteront seuls fidèles dans ces jours
> d'épreuves et partageront ses destinées. Le sort de ces hommes dévoués devra
> inspirer à l'état une juste sollicitude.[8]

F. de Lagenevais was a pseudonym for Frédéric de Mercey, who in 1840 had been
appointed chef de bureau in the Fine Arts division of the July Monarchy, and who
had, in a seamless transition, retained the same responsibilities under the Second
Republic. One of his tasks was to read the begging letters from artists which,
during the summer of 1848, were arriving on his desk in greater numbers than
ever and to make recommendations to Charles Blanc on the choice of artists to
receive commissions and art works to be purchased. His comments were, therefore,
an assessment by one of the most senior managers in the Fine Arts administration
of the likely impact on the fine arts of the financial difficulties that the country
was experiencing in the months following the revolution. As a good Orleanist
economic liberal and social conservative, he believed that with private buyers
abandoning the art market in droves, its collapse would at least have the beneficial
effect of persuading the 'numerous mediocrities' within the artistic community to
look for other careers. If those of weak vocation went to the wall, the state would be
in a better position to support artists of talent and achievement more deserving of its
munificence. This final comment might have been expected to improve Pradier's
morale, but in his letter to Gautier he clearly despaired of the government's will
and means to sustain the market during a period of crisis. As Pradier knew well and
as we shall see, state patronage of the arts was an issue close to Gautier's heart, one
which had already featured prominently in his art journalism that year.

Among artists and within the arts media, there was no shortage of support for
Pradier's grim assessment of the position in which artists found themselves by the
summer of 1848. While recognizing the good will, 'stérile il est vrai (faute sans
doute de l'argent)', of the Bureau des Beaux-Arts, *L'Artiste* published on 1 June an
extract of a petition, allegedly 'signée d'un grand nombre d'artistes', stating that
painters were having to sell their palettes and sculptors their knives at the very time
the government was creating four posts of inspector of provincial museums at an
annual cost of twenty-four thousand francs each — the usual story, in other words,
of jobs for the bureaucrats while the artists starved.[9] A fortnight later in the same
journal an anonymous editorial accused the administration of having betrayed the
artists' support for the republic and of treating them with the sort of mistrust that
was directed at the workers in the doomed *ateliers nationaux*:

> Les ateliers, où la misère et le désespoir ont élu leur domicile, ce sont pour
> la plupart les ateliers de peinture et de sculpture. Il y a là des douleurs qui
> se cachent et qui n'espèrent plus en la République. Et pourtant les artistes
> ont crié: *Vive la République* avec tout l'accent du cœur, quelques-uns avec des

armes triomphantes. Plus d'un artiste républicain en est à se rappeler avec un sentiment de reconnaissance le temps où il allait fumer à Vincennes quand M. de Montpensier, après lui avoir acheté un tableau, l'y appelait en toute liberté, égalité et fraternité; car M. de Montpensier était un démocrate de la république des arts, si on le compare aux parvenus de la veille qui traitent les artistes comme les ouvriers des ateliers nationaux, c'est-à-dire comme une canaille inquiétante suivant leur expression.[10]

These were the artists whom Gautier in euphoric mode had urged to seize the time and realize the vision of a democratic Republic of the Arts. 'Si vous le voulez', he had told them, 'que seront à côté du nôtre les siècles tant vantés de Périclès, de Léon X et de Louis XIV. Un grand peuple libre pourra-t-il moins pour l'art qu'une petite ville de l'Attique, un pape et un roi?'[11] Within hours of coming to power the Provisional Government appeared to have given itself the means of its ambitions through its annexation of the Civil List, whose remit, including the budget for the purchase and commission of art works shown in the annual Salon, had been removed from the defunct Maison du Roi and placed under the jurisdiction of the Ministry of the Interior, henceforth to be accountable to an elected National Assembly.[12] Yet here was the government being accused only three months later of succeeding only in rehabilitating in the eyes of artists the royal patronage of the arts under the July Monarchy (the duc de Montpensier was Louis-Philippe's fifth son and the château de Vincennes his official residence), such was its betrayal of even its own supporters among the artists.[13] The money formerly spent on the arts via the Civil List seemed to have vanished down the black hole of public finances.[14] As someone who had cultivated his connections with the royal family and entourage during the July Monarchy to secure commissions and sales, Pradier felt the loss of the Civil List keenly, as his comment to Gautier shows. Gautier felt it too, but because he, unlike Pradier, supported the republic.[15]

The loss of the Civil List was just one of the potential resources threatened, as far as Pradier was concerned, by government incompetence and inertia. Another was a strategy he had been pursuing since the early 1840s, when he had begun to cultivate relationships with curators and local artists, writers, and dignitaries in his home region of Provence, so as to broaden his market base and reduce his dependence on the increasingly competitive Parisian market for commissions and sales.[16] This objective had taken on greater urgency in 1847, when Clésinger's *Femme piquée par un serpent* had caused a sensation in the Salon. Gautier in particular had been very enthusiastic, a sure warning sign for Pradier.[17] It is clear that he felt threatened by the newcomer whose voluptuous nude appeared so much more audacious in its modernity than his own hitherto very marketable synthesis of antique and modern nudes.[18] In 1848, Clésinger's follow-up, *La Bacchante*, accompanied by another very positive Gautier commentary, had confirmed the threat.[19] At a time when few sculptors could afford to work in the noble materials of marble or bronze except to order, Pradier had assumed the financial risk of sculpting his *Nyssia* directly in marble without a buyer lined up in advance.[20] He would therefore have been anxious at the best of times to conclude the sale of the work, but with the emergence of a powerful rival in Paris combined with the dire straits in which the market for sculpture found itself, he was willing to let *Nyssia* go at cost price ('mes dépenses seulement', as he told Gautier) in order to protect his efforts to promote the sale of his work in his native Provence. The longer the delay, the more frustrated he became with 'ce misérable Ministère'.

Finally, Pradier was also dismayed by the government's reorganization of the Fine Arts administration in the weeks following the change of regime. On 18 March a decree clarifying the legal position created by Ledru-Rollin's annexation of the Civil List on 24 February announced: 'Les musées du Louvre, du Luxembourg, de Versailles, les galeries des anciennes résidences royales et palais du gouvernement, sont distraits de l'administration de la liste civile pour rentrer dans les attributions du ministère de l'Intérieur.'[21] These museums and galleries had formerly been attached to the Maison du Roi, and since the Salon was held in the Louvre, the organization of the event and the purchase by the authorities of work presented there had also been in the remit of the royal household.[22] The Second Republic regrouped all the attributions of the fine arts within three divisions of the Ministry of the Interior (one division having jurisdiction over the museums and (ex-)royal residences, another over the theatre, the third over what it called the visual and contemporary arts). The one attribution this ministry had held formerly but which it now transferred to the Ministry of Public Instruction was that of literature. Instead of a new combined Ministère des Arts et des Lettres which many had hoped to see in 1848, the visual arts were separated from literature and were, as Pradier tendentiously put it, 'relégués avec la police'.[23] Artists petitioned the National Assembly 'sur la nécessité de transférer l'administration des Beaux-Arts du ministère de l'Intérieur à celui de l'Instruction publique' but to no avail.[24] In July the Société Libre des Beaux-Arts did the same, with the same result.[25] Pradier evidently shared the view of the petitioners that the association of the arts and public instruction within a single ministry would increase the status of both, whereas in a Ministry of the Interior responsible for the management of many of the urgent political issues of the day, they would be, in the words of the petition, the object of only 'une attention distraite et une protection négligente'. In particular, the fact that business relating to the Salon, and, notably, to the state purchase of work exhibited there, had not been administratively united with its sister art ('avec sa sœur les lettres') located in the Ministry of Public Instruction was unlikely to further the cause of art patronage, public or private, to which both he and Gautier, for different reasons, attached such importance.[26]

In 1848 Gautier had begun his review of the work on show in the Salon with a powerful appeal for government investment in sculpture:

> A part quelques bustes et quelques travaux de peu d'importance, c'est le gouvernement seul qui, jusqu'ici, a soutenu ce bel art, le plus idéal et le plus réel à la fois de tous les arts; ce legs divin de la Grèce, ce beau reste du paganisme, qui a sauvé le monde de l'invasion définitive de la barbarie chrétienne et gothique, et défendu l'œuvre de Dieu contre les longs fantômes émaciés, les draperies en suaire, et les physionomies cadavéreuses d'un ascétisme mal entendu.[27]

The collapse of the ancien régime had placed the 'divine legacy' at the mercy of the cold winds of change. The eighteenth-century aristocracy had bought sculpture to furnish their châteaux and grounds but the nouveaux riches who had replaced them from 1789 did not consider sculpture when they were investing in the nineteenth century's status symbols and *objets de luxe*, preferring instead racehorses, expensive clothes, and English silverware:

> La sculpture est dans une excellente voie, et on doit lui en savoir gré; car le public n'est pour rien dans ses progrès. En aucun temps une nation de trente-cinq millions d'hommes n'a consommé moins de marbre ou d'airain: une statue est un luxe auquel les plus riches même ne songent guère en France, et tel qui paie vingt mille francs un cheval de course, une parure, un service d'argenterie anglaise, n'aura jamais l'idée d'acheter un marbre à Pradier ou un bronze à David [d'Angers].[28]

It was in this context of an appeal to the government to sustain through difficult economic times investment in the work of sculptors of the stature of Pradier and David d'Angers (as well as for the obvious reason of his own part in the creation of *Nyssia*) that he had devoted his longest and most prominent commentary on sculpture that year to Pradier's work.[29] For over a decade he had promoted what he saw as Pradier's sculptural equivalent of his own commitment to an authentic pagan ideal of beautiful form, untrammelled by Christianity's fear of the erotic and the natural.[30] Both considered the nude to be the very source of art and, for the representation of the female nude in particular, sculpture was the ideal medium and the medium of the ideal.[31] Nor was this celebration of the nude as the model of the *beau idéal* confined to conservative or traditional standpoints.[32] Pradier's synthesis of antique and modern nudes was for Gautier a marriage of naturalism and style designed to revitalize a pagan ideal of beauty for the modern age and to rescue sculpture from what he considered to be the debased neoclassicism of the Empire and Restoration, enslaved by rules formulated by Émeric-David in 1805.[33] Extending the series of large female nudes inaugurated by his *Psyché* in the Salon of 1824, Pradier's adaptation in *Nyssia* of a key moment of *Le Roi Candaule* reinforced an artistic and professional alliance between sculptor and critic already well established in the public mind.[34]

In the five-paragraph commentary on *Nyssia*, the reader reaches Gautier's description of the statue only in the fourth, for the author himself and his short story are the subject of the first three. In the first, he quoted the extract on which Pradier has performed his *transposition d'art*, so that the reader might better appreciate the quality of the performance. In the second, he explained that his aim in *Le Roi Candaule* had been to 'rendre sérieusement ce que le bon La Fontaine a travesti de manière grotesque et bouffonne, en son style marotique', alerting the reader to his story's lineage and presenting to his own advantage his relationship to the canonical predecessor.[35] In the third, he craved his readers' indulgence while he savoured for a moment the pleasure of seeing these 'quelques lignes signées de notre nom obscur' carved in marble by such a distinguished exponent of the *style antique*, lightening the tone with the knowingly false modesty of an author whose name was anything but obscure. Having prepared in these ways the reader's receptivity for what follows (and filled up a useful number of column inches in doing so), he finally turned his attention to Pradier's version of Nyssia's exposure to Gygès's gaze:

> Nyssia vient de laisser tomber son dernier voile; elle se tient debout dans sa

chaste nudité de statue, et Gygès, de l'ombre où il est tapi, peut juger à quel point l'enthousiasme de Candaule avait raison. Ce corps divin, suprême effort de la nature jalouse de l'art, développe ses belles lignes avec ces ondulations harmonieuses, et ces balancemens rhythmés, musique de l'œil, que les sculpteurs grecs savaient si bien entendre. Un des pieds porte sur un pavé de mosaïque dont les nuances sont indiquées en tons affaiblis, et semble un flocon de neige sur un bouquet; l'autre fait ployer à peine la plume d'un moelleux coussin, et tous deux ont des orteils si élégants, des doigts si délicatement effilés, des ongles si parfaits qu'ils paraissent n'avoir jamais foulé que l'azur du ciel ou la pourpre des roses. Les bras élevés au-dessus de la tête font ruisseler des torrens de cheveux sur un dos charmant qu'ils cachent, hélas! en partie; opulence regrettable! Le bout d'une de ces mèches vagabondes va se désaltérer aux parfums d'une longue cassolette placée à côté de la figure, et d'un goût plus grec qu'asiatique. La tête penchée un peu en avant et l'œil déjà inquiet semble, comme par un pressentiment de pudeur, chercher dans l'ombre le profane regard de Gygès.

This description begins in Gautier's short story at the point at which Gygès's 'profane gaze' fulfils Candaule's ambition to reveal his wife's naked body to another. It ends with Pradier's statue, which, according to Gautier, shows Nyssia's anxious gaze seeking out the intruder.[36] Between story and statue the musical analogy underlines the shared aesthetic finality of the verbal and visual arts. In the process of transposition from one art to the other, accessories are transformed to meet sculpture's three-dimensional requirements and constraints. The statue contains no item of clothing just fallen from her body and the text no soft cushion on which to rest her foot; in the story there is no cassolette other than the *trépieds* consigned to obscurity by the light's blinding focus on Nyssia's body, but in the sculpture, the cassolette (more Greek than Asian, as Gautier noted, despite the story's location) provides a support against which Nyssia stands and which the waves of her flowing hair reach. There is no reference to her hair at the moment in the text Pradier has chosen to present but he can hardly avoid emphasizing an attribute which has been such a powerful factor in Candaule's desire to exhibit his wife to a third party.[37] Gautier's Nyssia does not pose; on the contrary she seeks to hide her nakedness, hurrying to the bed, 'comme toute honteuse d'être si belle', arms crossed to hide her breasts. Pradier's Nyssia cannot avoid posing. The idealized nude pose was an essential element of the language of classical sculpture and Nyssia strikes one of the most familiar of all such female poses, that of the *jeune femme à sa toilette*, arms raised over her head to gather up her hair in a movement which exposes her frontally more fully to the spectator's gaze, in defiance of what Baudelaire called the 'enormity' of her prudery in Le Roi Candaule.[38] As if to attenuate this infidelity to his text, Gautier ends the paragraph by returning to Gygès's 'profane gaze' and to what Gautier claims is Pradier's success in capturing the essential psychological element at this point in the unfolding drama, Nyssia's 'œil déjà inquiet', her instinctive fear that she is being watched and which, in Le Roi Candaule, is described in the seconds preceding the fall of the final item of her clothing.[39] The implication is that through this alleged instinctive fear, Pradier rescues Nyssia not only from the vacant, detached stare of classical sculpture but also from the accusation that she was just another Pradier nude and Le Roi Candaule no more than a convenient pretext.[40] Many critics were not convinced and found Pradier's Nyssia expressionless.[41]

Having described the process of transposition, Gautier turned in his final paragraph to the significance of the aesthetic and spiritual equivalences between the textual and sculpted Nyssias. In the text, desire's active agent, surrogate to the passive spectator, Gygès, is the light in the darkened room which abandons the other precious objects to focus its attention exclusively on Nyssia's body, slipping across her 'exquisite forms' and enveloping them in a timid kiss; in the sculpture, it is what Gautier calls the music of the eye, as the Greek sculptors had understood it and as Pradier, their representative in the modern age, has perpetuated it:

> Cette figure brille, comme tout ce que fait Pradier, par un mélange de style antique et de réalité moderne, d'où l'étude n'exclut pas la pureté; les jambes et les cuisses de sa Nyssia ont les lignes sévères du marbre et la tendreté de la chair; les genoux surtout sont admirables pour leur modelé fin, souple et savant. L'anatomie la plus consciencieuse n'y ôte rien à la grâce et à la morbidesse; les passages des aines au ventre, les lignes serpentines du torse, les attaches de la gorge, le sein lui-même, détaché et mis en relief par le mouvement des bras, ont cette beauté placide, cette perfection sereine qui caractérisent le talent de Pradier, un des plus complets tempéramens de sculpteur qui se soient peut-être produits depuis le siècle de Périclès.

The visual music of Pradier's line and modelling sublimates the sensuality of Nyssia's precisely eroticized body. In her grace, delicate skin, sinuous lines, and perfectly shaped breasts pushed forward by the movement of the arms, she remains chaste in her nudity, serene in her beauty, in perfect equilibrium between the ideal and the natural, between ancient and modern forms of the nude. It is the same lesson that, only months later, Ingres would administer in his *Vénus anadyomène* (see below, pp. 76–79). Gautier's description reproduces this disciplined embrace of the natural by the ideal. Presented at the outset so as to frame the forms he is about to describe, the antique returns in the final clause in the homage to the classical age and to Pericles, its exemplary exponent. At the paragraph's central point, the technical term *morbidesse* (defined by Littré as signifying in painting and sculpture 'mollesse et délicatesse des chairs dans une figure') identifies the formal practice whose mystique seduces the connoisseur while it blinds the lay reader with science. As Pradier transposed Gautier's heroine, so the sculptor's *Nyssia* would return the compliment, joining the series of 'purs modèles, dont nous avons tâché de rappeler dans nos vers et notre prose les blanches images en les colorant du léger incarnat de la vie', notably in three of the poems on which he worked in the autumn of 1848, published in the *Revue des deux mondes* of 15 January 1849 and incorporated in the *Émaux et camées* of 1852: 'Affinités secrètes', 'Le poème de la Femme', and 'Symphonie en blanc majeur'.

Gautier's powerful support for Pradier in the Salon may well have appeared all the more significant for the sculptor on account of the fact that while his own efforts to achieve a productive relationship with the Republican regime had been almost entirely unsuccessful, Gautier found himself, in the aftermath of the revolution of February 1848, closer than ever before to the most highly placed officials in the arts administration. Not only had he probably known Charles Blanc and Frédéric de Mercey for years by then,[42] but more recently he had also been associated with Philippe-Auguste Jeanron (appointed Directeur des Musées Nationaux within hours of the February revolution) and Frédéric Villot (appointed Curator of Paintings in the Louvre on Jeanron's recommendation) through the group which had met from March 1847 at the home of the painter Fernand Boissard de Boisdenier, another friend of Gautier's, to plan a campaign for reform of the Salon.[43] Another indication of Gautier's highly placed contacts at this time is the fact that, about the same time as Pradier was writing to him, Delacroix was urging Préault, the leading Romantic sculptor of the day, to contact Gautier to enlist his support for Delacroix's campaign on behalf of Villot's plans to reorganize the Louvre's national collections.[44] Pradier would certainly have been very conscious of the fact that Gautier had well-established professional contacts with people whom the revolution had propelled into positions of power within the arts bureaucracy and might reasonably have reckoned on these contacts compensating for his own shortcomings in this area.

In French literary history for much of the final two-thirds of the nineteenth century and since, Gautier has been so firmly associated with *l'art pour l'art* that the compatibility between his commitments in the fine arts and those of the Republican administration in 1848 has tended, when considered at all, to be dismissed as opportunism or expediency.[45] I hope to show that though an element of these cannot of course be discounted, the compatibility was real and not new in February 1848. This might have been recognized earlier but for another firmly held idea, namely that Gautier was ruined financially as a result of the revolution of that year. We have already seen one allusion to this by Gautier himself in his comment on the impact on his finances of the temporary closure of *La Presse*, but there exists more recent and more authoritative support for this impact: 'La situation politique, les troubles qui suivent le rétablissement de la République, le marasme économique ruinent Gautier, qui va connaître de grands embarras.'[46] There is no doubt that Gautier was financially embarrassed in the summer of 1848 and his support for the republic would indeed be surprising if such accounts of its 'ruin' of him were true, but they are not. Unlike his father, who really had been ruined by political revolution when in July 1830, as a supporter of Charles X, he had backed the wrong side,[47] Gautier had by 1848 been demonstrating for more than a decade that he was quite capable of ruining himself financially, without any help from political events.[48] However much he earned, his income never seems to have kept pace with his expenditure, despite the fact that by the end of the July Monarchy he was one of the most highly paid cultural journalists in France, a position reinforced in the days preceding the revolution by his promotion to the post of *directeur du feuilleton littéraire* on *La Presse*.[49] In 1848 he earned more from his journalism than ever before. We know this from the statement of his earnings provided by the newspaper's administrator, Claude Rouy (see the Appendix, pp. 181–82).[50] Rouy described *La Presse* as Gautier's 'bonne mère nourrice' and its owner, Émile de Girardin, was openly scathing about what he saw as Gautier's chronic inability to manage his financial affairs, given that he was paying him annually, as Girardin put it in 1847, 'plus que ne reçoivent les présidents de chambre de la première cour royale du royaume'.[51] It is true that on 25 June Gautier's income from *La Presse* was abruptly cut off when the newspaper was closed down following Girardin's description in the previous day's edition of Cavaignac's assumption of emergency powers as a quasi-dictatorial 'régime du sabre',[52] but the ban was short-lived and at the time even Gautier recognized that his real financial problems lay elsewhere: 'Je travaille le plus que je peux mais les billets vont plus vite que les feuilletons et ces deux mois de suspension [the closure of *La Presse*] m'ont achevé' (*Corr.*, III, 368). The 'billets' were the promissory notes of the French nineteenth-century credit system of which Gautier, as his correspondence amply shows, made far more use than was good for him.[53] The income his articles earned him was more often than not already 'promised' in this judicial sense before he had written them. In his diary Delacroix speculated on how people like Gautier managed to stay afloat in the desperate *fuite en avant* of their chaotic public and private lives.[54] In Gautier's case it was by writing large amounts very quickly, a tall order even for someone of his facility. Ending a letter to Ernesta Grisi in August 1849 in order to 'me mettre à mon feuilleton', he complained that 'cinq cents lignes de pensum, c'est dur' (*Corr.*, IV, 46).[55] His *feuilletons* for *La Presse* were, on average, three thousand words in length, and in 1848 he published 69 of them (26 on fine art, 43 on theatre), an average of four thousand words every week of the year (and these did not include his music and dance criticism or his creative writing of fiction, poetry, and theatre or his work for other journals). Each article presupposed time-consuming social and professional engagements: in the case of the art journalism, visits to the Salon and to the artists' studio, for example.[56] Not surprisingly, he developed a range of short cuts to cope with the relentless pressure created for him by this need for productivity and we shall see examples of their impact.

It is true that in the autumn of 1848 Gautier began writing the poetry that would be collected into *Émaux et camées* of 1852, including its famous liminary sonnet which acquired subsequently the status that we know.[57] This alleged withdrawal into the pleasures of *l'art pour l'art* notwithstanding, Gautier remained throughout this period and beyond locked onto a journalistic treadmill which occupied most of his waking hours in one form or another.[58] By 1848 he had already been for twelve years a participant in and product of what became known as the industrialization of the French press under the July Monarchy.[59] As we know, it was Gautier's employer, Émile de Girardin, who had been the prime mover of this revolution. Launching *La Presse* on 1 July 1836, Girardin had halved the annual subscription rate for newspapers (from eighty to forty francs) and thereby made it affordable to a wider readership among the middle and lower-middle classes. By opening the newspaper to greater and more diverse sources of income from publicity, he more than offset the potential loss from the lower subscription rate. When other newspaper owners followed suit, the French press was embarked on its journey away from the *journal d'opinion*, in which readership was largely identified with a specific political tendency (the Orleanist consensus in the *Journal des débats*, the legitimist faith in *La Gazette de France*, the moderate republican or liberal opposition in *Le National*, and so on), towards the *journal d'information*. From our point of view it is essential to remember that while preparing his venture, Girardin offered Gautier a place in the new entrepreneurial culture. It was an offer for which Gautier was by then ready and which cannot have been too difficult for him to accept.

In histories of French nineteenth-century literature Gautier's recruitment to *La Presse* in July 1836 has always been overshadowed by the sensation caused by the publication six months earlier of *Mademoiselle de Maupin*, whose preface was canonized in the histories of literary modernism as the manifesto of *l'art pour l'art*.[60] It is true that the preface contains key elements that would be assimilated into art-for-art's-sake aestheticism. It attacked what Gautier saw as the philistinism and utilitarianism of the July Monarchy's dominant bourgeois ideology and, by arguing that the value of a work of art was quite distinct from that of the subject represented, it also attacked the subordination of art's formal means to any external system of ideas, be it moral, social, political, or philosophical, though, as we know, the specific targets for Gautier here were the utopians and humanitarians of social romanticism. Gautier's aggressive defence of the role of form in art became axiomatic for modernism,[61] and with modern literary movements driven by the genealogical and dynastic urge to trace their roots back to founding texts, the preface to *Mademoiselle de Maupin* — separated from, and far more read than, the novel it introduced — was destined for a bright future. Yet the fact remains that in his preface Gautier never used the term *l'art pour l'art* and did not produce anything resembling a 'systematic formulation' of it, with or without reference to painting.[62] Furthermore, he consistently rejected formalism, which he saw as no more than form for form's sake, a reductive manoeuvre whose consequences for art were every bit as negative as content for content's sake. The separation of form and content was in his view the recipe for unsuccessful art.

Despite this, it is clear that by the end of the July Monarchy, opponents of *l'art pour l'art* had firmly positioned Gautier as its leader. In his *Histoire des peintres français au dix-neuvième siècle* of 1845, Charles Blanc, whom Ledru-Rollin appointed Directeur des Beaux-Arts at the beginning of April 1848, had traced the split which had emerged within the younger literary generation in the wake of the revolution of 1830, calling it 'la différence des penseurs aux poëtes' (p. 36). The 'penseurs' wanted, he said, to rehabilitate the art of Jacques-Louis David — 'ils se souvinrent que l'auteur de *Léonidas* [David's *Léonidas aux Thermopyles* of 1814], pour avoir eu l'enthousiasme de l'idée, était devenu le premier peintre de l'Europe' (pp. 37–38) — and to adapt to contemporary social issues the philosophical tradition of the French school which David had in Blanc's view sustained in the late eighteenth century. Blanc referred to these advocates of social romanticism as 'l'école démocratique', naming them and the newspapers they wrote for.[63] The 'poëtes', on the other hand, were 'les matérialistes de l'art' (p. 37). Interested only in form, they had created what he called 'une sorte de franc-maçonnerie à laquelle la masse ne pût être initiée' (pp. 37–38). There were no prizes for identifying the leader of this 'freemasonry':

> Celui qui tenait la plume avec le plus d'éclat, c'était M. Théophile Gautier. Les merveilleux tours de force de Jules Dupré, la solidité des paysages de Cabat, les adresses du pinceau de Flers, la savante maçonnerie de couleurs qui faisait de Decamps un peintre si prodigieux, tout cela servit de texte à des articles où s'étalait le luxe d'une foule d'expressions inconnues au vulgaire, où le jargon de l'atelier amenait son cortège inattendu de mots techniques et de locutions intimes. Le public, étonné, fut introduit dans la cuisine de l'art; il assista à la préparation des couleurs; on lui parla des *dessous*, des *glacis*, des avantages de

l'*empâtement*, et de mille autres choses qui ne l'intéressaient que médiocrement, il faut le dire. Jamais la critique ne s'était prélassée à ce point dans le matérialisme; on eût dit que la forme était le fond même. (pp. 38–39)

Gautier's association with art for art's sake was fixed in the public mind during the July Monarchy through just this type of reductive misrepresentation born of the ambition within the younger generation of social romantics to position themselves at the forefront of the opposition to the Orleanist regime. In the same context of strategic self-positioning, the same label was applied in painting too, with David as the model of the *peintre-penseur* and Ingres the leader of art for art's sake.[64] Not surprisingly, therefore, this group saw the revolution of 1848 as a defeat for *l'art pour l'art* and for Ingres (see below, p. 41). As a corollary, this so-called 'defeat' threatened the position of someone as tarred with the art-for-art's-sake brush and devotion to Ingres as Gautier was. His art journalism in 1848 has as one of its contexts the vulnerability which came from his identification with a temporarily discredited artistic and political label, and we shall see in due course how he dealt with this. But at this stage we need to remember that what drove the preface to *Mademoiselle de Maupin* was Gautier's hatred of censorship, his demand for freedom to write what and as one chooses, in pursuit of human happiness, 'car la jouissance me paraît le but de la vie, et la seule chose utile au monde' (p. 231). What we have there is not the assertion of an autonomous aesthetic sphere but an attack on the campaign for the moralization of literature waged by the ruling elite of the July Monarchy, whose *morale régnante* was subjected in the preface to a stream of provocations.[65]

On 12 April 1834 the massacre in the rue Transnonain drove a sharp wedge through government policy aimed at weaning the lower orders off radical propaganda and political violence.[66] In the ensuing moral and political panic, Adolphe Thiers, Minister of the Interior, banned Alexandre Dumas's play *Antony* from the Comédie-Française; the following month Gautier was himself the object of a virulent attack in *Le Constitutionnel* for the alleged immorality of his article on François Villon, published five months earlier in *La France littéraire*.[67] Gautier and Charles Malo, the editor of *La France littéraire*, decided to sue. After four court hearings, their case was thrown out, the tribunal judging that literary criticism could not provide grounds for defamation. By dating 'Mai 1834' a preface that was almost certainly not written by that date in the form in which it first appeared eighteen months later, Gautier explicitly linked it retrospectively to the court case and to what he saw as the sinister *tartufferie* of politicians, government lawyers, and their accomplices in the literary press. The promulgation of the anti-press laws of September 1835, for which the attempted assassination of Louis-Philippe on 28 July had provided a well-timed pretext, only reinforced the censorship against which the preface spoke so strongly.

In the course of his sarcastic comments on the intolerance of conservative and Saint-Simonian *bien-pensants* under the July Monarchy, Gautier ridiculed the dominant utilitarian ideology: 'Est-on parvenu à boire plus qu'on ne buvait au temps de l'ignorance et de la barbarie (vieux style)? Alexandre, l'équivoque ami du bel Éphestion, ne buvait pas trop mal, quoiqu'il n'y eût pas de son temps de *Journal des connaissances utiles* [...]' (p. 232). Girardin had founded this publication in 1831 in the hope of getting rich by promoting 'l'éducation intellectuelle et politique du citoyen en formant d'abord de bons professionnels'.[68] As its name suggested, it was full of useful information in all sorts of areas and with hindsight we can see how it also provided Girardin with a sort of trial run, professionally and financially, for *La Presse*.[69] For Gautier, attacking utilitarianism in his preface, it was too good a target to miss. We have to assume that the entrepreneur in Girardin, instead of taking offence at Gautier's sarcasm, saw the energy and brilliance of the preface's uncompromising rejection of censorship as just the sort of writing he was looking for to support his latest venture into a new form of daily press. In any event, he was sufficiently keen to secure Gautier's services that he offered him unlimited access to column space there: 'Votre place Monsieur v[ous] est réservée p[ou]r l'article que vous faites, et pour tous ceux que v[ou]s ferez' (*Corr.*, 1, 68–69).[70]

It is essential to remember that Gautier was in on Girardin's venture from the very beginning and that this was no Faustian pact with the devil on Gautier's part, even if there might later be cultural mileage for him in saying that it was. Having let off steam in his preface to *Maupin* at what he saw as the July Monarchy's *moralisme de façade*, the two key issues of his life — his career and the future of French art — remained to be addressed. He could hardly have avoided the harsh reality that his poetry had made little impression beyond Bohemian groups, his short fiction had fared little better, *Mademoiselle de Maupin* had taken over two years to write and not yet made him a penny, and his efforts to promote an alternative, pre-classical canon in his literary criticism had landed him in court. By then even he must have known where the Bohemia of his *Jeunes-France* youth was leading and, unlike his friends Nerval and Borel, he was not going down that road. In accepting Girardin's overtures, he was signing up to his employer's vision of the modern newspaper's cultural mission to inform, educate, and entertain a much broader range of readers than that hitherto catered for by the Parisian press, but then so had Hugo and, faced with his career-changing choice, what better guarantor could Gautier have had?[71] Though the preface to *Maupin* had shown that he remained sceptical about the moralization of the masses, he was quite serious about one educational need which the *Journal des connaissances utiles* had not addressed, that of extending artistic education beyond the July Monarchy's cultural elites to the new public that Girardin proposed to reach through *La Presse*. Nothing proved the urgency of such a programme more in the mid-1830s, as far as Gautier was concerned, than the reputation of Paul Delaroche: 'Certainement l'éducation pittoresque d'un peuple capable de regarder M. Delaroche comme une gloire dont les rayons se confondaient avec l'auréole des grands maîtres, est entièrement à refaire.'[72] If he did have pangs of conscience about compromising with the middle-class market-driven ideology of the Girardin press, the platform that *La Presse* offered from which to spread the word of art to existing and new reading publics evidently eased them. He would provide the artistic education these readers lacked. and he was soon lecturing artists in his newspaper column on their need to do the same.[73]

His first article, published on 26 August, on Delacroix's decoration of the Salle du Trône in the Chambre des Députés, showed how quickly he grasped the requirements and opportunities of Girardin's new press. In it he stated that Delacroix was 'toujours le premier dans toute voie de progrès', France's greatest contemporary exponent of the Italian tradition of fresco art, which was itself a complete education into art's means and collective destination. He urged other artists to abandon the debilitating individualism of academic practices devised for an aristocratic class that had gone for ever and to follow Delacroix's lead in resurrecting the lost forms of public art. He could have republished it verbatim in the spring of 1848. It was polemical but informed, clear with just enough technical language to inspire confidence and pitched at the level required for the new readers aspiring to access to the higher cultural forms. There was praise for the modern as the authentic renewal of tradition, criticism of artists stuck in the rut of a discredited classical tradition, support for a new meritocracy of intelligence. No wonder Girardin was enthusiastic, writing to Gautier on the eve of its publication: 'Je désire de grand cœur que v[ou]s restiez des nôtres' (Corr., I, 74–75), and remain he did.[74]

For historians of French literature the decisive feature of Girardin's commercial strategy in La Presse was the creation of the roman-feuilleton, which made its debut in French literature in Balzac's La Vieille Fille, serialized in twelve instalments in La Presse between 23 October and 4 November 1836 and occupying the feuilleton rubric in the bottom quarter (or rez-de-chaussée) of pages 1 and 2 of the four-page newspaper (the back page of which was reserved for advertising). Girardin never intended, however, the serialized novel to be the only occupant of the rubric.[75] Others included art journalism, theatre reviews, travel writing, reports from the Academies of Science and Medicine, industrial reports, news from the foreign press, and a regular Courrier de Paris feature written by his wife Delphine under the pseudonym of the Vicomte de Launay and which could be on anything of general interest (books, music, fashion, collection) and were designed to attract and retain the widest possible readership.[76] It is difficult to establish to what extent this readership overlapped from one feuilleton rubric to another — whether, for example, those who read La Vieille Fille also read the science reports or Delphine's letters from Paris — but the evidence of the art journalism in La Presse is that painting and the literature of art lent themselves very well to Girardin's marketing strategy and, in particular, to the place of the feuilleton in that strategy, for Gautier included in his art reviews material that could have been written for the Journal des connaissances utiles. Thus, he began his commentary on Daumas's statue Victorina (Salon of 1848) with a brief history lesson on the status of women in ancient Gaul and his analysis of Hébert's painting La Mal'aria (Salon of 1850–51) with a presentation of the epidemiology of malaria. He defended Gérôme against the charge of anachronistic mannerism in his Anacréon, Bacchus et l'Amour (Salon of 1848) with reference to a modern mannerist naturalism apparently also manifested in the education of girls in mid-nineteenth-century France and the behaviour of deer in the forests of the Ardennes. By the end of the century, the emergence of the modernist narrative and of more professionalized, specialized forms of art discourse would discredit the use of such extraneous material in the commentary on art works, but from 1836 this material did not merely enable Gautier to pad out his article, however relevant that consideration was for someone whose income depended on the amount he wrote. It also ensured that the *feuilleton* created intersections between different types and levels of literacy through which readership potential might be maximized.[77] Gautier's acute alertness to these intersections, together with his exceptional literary virtuosity, gave him the means to draw a new public towards his understanding of the direction that French art should take in the modern era. The *feuilleton* encouraged a form of writing which drew more directly on its place of production and encouraged a more flexible response to the social transformations taking place there. It was in fostering and representing a distinctive *parisianisme* of language, manners, and worldview that Gautier, in his art writings and theatre reviews, created the dominant tone of the *feuilleton* of *La Presse*.[78]

As far as writing on the visual arts was concerned, *La Presse* created a far larger demand for copy than the annual Salon review alone could provide, even in the more substantial form it acquired in its new medium.[79] If this increased demand was to be met, the Paris art season had to be extended beyond the three months of the Salon to something closer to that of the theatre. Reports on the decisions of the Salon juries charged with awarding prizes at the end of the exhibition for the best work shown in the different categories were one way of doing this. Reports on the work produced by the winners of the Prix de Rome during their stay at the Villa Médicis in Rome were another. The visit to the artist's studio to give readers a preview of work being produced for the following Salon lent itself particularly to the *feuilleton* rubric. With more than two thousand artists working in Paris during the July Monarchy, the studio visit offered the art journalist a potentially vast supply of material which could be put to use immediately or held in reserve for quieter periods of the year. Combining the inside story on work in progress with society gossip, publicity, and sales news, it quickly became a staple element of art journalism. On 13 October 1836, for example, Gautier's readers learned that Delacroix was working on a battle scene, the *Passage du Pont de Montereau*, Gigoux on an *Antoine et Cléopâtre*, and Louis Boulanger on a portrait of Balzac, all for the Salon of 1837. They were also given 'une nouvelle qui fait sensation dans le monde des arts', the departure of the landscape artist Louis Cabat, 'le plus grand paysagiste de l'école moderne, et cela à vingt ans', to Italy for two years, together with the news that during this period 'nous ne verrons rien de Cabat que deux petits tableaux, vrais perles de sentiment et de couleur qu'il a réservées pour la prochaine exposition'. This article, which though written by Gautier appeared in Delphine de Girardin's *Courrier de Paris* slot, underlined the shifting boundaries between art journalism, the *fait divers*, society gossip, and promotional writing which the *feuilleton* encouraged. As an indication of his increased output, Gautier produced no fewer than seventeen articles between 26 August and 15 December 1836, an average of one a week, not including the six he also wrote during this period for *Le Figaro*.[80] In addition to those already mentioned, subjects ranged from composition in painting to illustrations for Hugo's *Notre-Dame de Paris*, from the applications of the visual arts in everyday life to the Rubens decorations in Antwerp Cathedral. Their number and range of topics indicates the seriousness with which Gautier set about his task of re-educating French tastes in the visual arts, informing, entertaining, and lecturing a readership which included artists, writers, art critics, buyers, and administrators, the educated middle classes, and the more anonymous public of the newly literate, Parisian lower-middle classes. In these articles, he took up where he had left off in the preface to *Mademoiselle de Maupin*.[81] The position he had achieved in art journalism by 1848, and which Pradier's letter acknowledged, testifies to the success with which he had honed his art *feuilleton* to meet the aspirations of his wide readership, making sure, as he moved between registers and tones, that there was something for everyone. On 15 March, the annual Salon opened its doors to the Second Republic and Gautier's own *système des beaux-arts* rose to its first challenge of the new era.

Notes to Chapter 1

1. For the details of Pradier's efforts to secure the sale, see the catalogue of the exhibition, *Statues de chair: sculptures de James Pradier (1790–1852)*, held in Geneva and Paris in 1985–86 (Paris: RMN, 1985), pp. 155 and 366–67. *Nyssia* was no. 4881 in the Salon catalogue, *Explication des ouvrages de peinture, sculpture, architecture, gravure et lithographie des artistes vivants, exposés au Musée national du Louvre le 15 mars 1848* (Paris: Vinchon, 1848), p. 364.

2. The extract quoted narrates the moment at which Candaule, unable to keep to himself any longer the secret of his wife's extraordinary beauty, arranges for an accomplice, Gygès, to hide in her bedroom as she undresses: 'Pour me comprendre, il faut que tu contemples Nyssia dans l'éclat radieux de sa blancheur étincelante, sans ombre importune, sans draperie jalouse, telle que la nature l'a modelée de ses mains dans un moment d'inspiration qui ne reviendra plus. Ce soir, je te cacherai dans un coin de l'appartement nuptial ... tu la verras!' See Théophile Gautier, *Romans, contes et nouvelles* (henceforth *RCN*), dir. by Pierre Laubriet, 2 vols (Paris: Gallimard, Bibliothèque de la Pléiade, 2002), I, 941–89 (p. 965).

3. As President of the National Assembly, Sénard had secured the resignation of the Executive Commission on 23 June 1848 and the transfer of emergency powers to Cavaignac, who, as Minister for War, directed the repression of 23–26 June. Sénard became Minister of the Interior on 25 June, Cavaignac Président du Conseil two days later. As Minister of the Interior, Sénard had jurisdiction over the fine arts (see below, note 12), hence Pradier's letter to him. As Président du Conseil, Cavaignac was charged with the task of forming a new government in the wake of the June Days, but also found the time to have his bust made by Pradier in July. On 4 August Pradier wrote: 'J'espère beaucoup faire prendre ma *Nyssia* au ministre de l'Intérieur pour le musée de Montpellier. Je vais tirer tout ce que je pourrai de service de mon général' (letter quoted by J. de Caso, 'Prix de Rome, sculptures exposées aux Salons et projets pour de grandes statues', in *Statues de chair*, pp. 109–78 (p. 155).

4. On 16 July a 'projet de décret' to release an emergency fund of 200,000 francs for the purchase of art works was announced in *Le Moniteur universel* (p. 1675) and adopted the following day by the National Assembly. Pradier appears to have been one of the first beneficiaries (see *Statues de chair*, p. 155).

5. 'Il est difficile de déterminer si T.G. intervint effectivement en faveur de Pradier. On peut penser cependant que son amitié avec Charles Blanc lui permit d'appuyer la requête du sculpteur' (*Corr.*, III, 364, note 8).

6. The subject of his first piece of art criticism was the bust of Victor Hugo sculpted by Jehan Duseigneur, founder of the 'petit cénacle' which Gautier frequented at the outset of the July Monarchy. See 'Arts: buste de Victor Hugo', *Mercure de France au XIXe siècle*, 35 (October 1831), 95–96.

7. For details see the chapter by G. Garnier, 'La Carrière d'un artiste officiel à Paris', in *Statues de chair*, pp. 77–96.

8. F. de Lagenevais, 'Le Salon de 1848', *Revue des deux mondes* (henceforth *RDM*), 15 April 1848, pp. 283–99; 15 May 1848, pp. 591–606 (p.606). On the collapse of the art market in 1848 see T. J. Clark, *The Absolute Bourgeois* (London: Thames and Hudson, 1973), pp. 49–50, and Chantal Georgel, *1848: la République et l'art vivant* (Paris: Fayard/RMN, 1998), pp. 64–67 and 218–22.

9. 'Beaux-Arts: théâtres', *L'Artiste*, 1 June 1848, pp. 150–52 (p. 152). The following month *L'Artiste* published an anonymous letter to the editor, Arsène Houssaye, entitled 'A propos des inspecteurs des musées de province'. Its author attacked the misleading nature of the contents of the original article, and in particular stated that the 24,000 francs were to be divided between the four inspectors (1 July 1848, p. 190).

10. Anon., 'Revue de la quinzaine: beaux-arts', *L'Artiste*, 15 June 1848, p. 172. It is clear that some destitute artists had enrolled in the national workshops for one franc a day. The sculptor David d'Angers, in the letter he wrote to Charles Blanc in July 1848 urging the government to make major investment in the fine arts, confirmed this. For his letter and Blanc's reply see Marie-Claude Chaudonneret, 'L'Aube d'une République des arts: un programme pédagogique de David d'Angers', in *Les Collections: fables et programmes*, ed. by Jacques Guillerme (Seyssel: Champ Vallon, 1993), pp. 265–74. In *1848: la République et l'art vivant*, Georgel suggests a possible link between the number of artists who enrolled in the workshops and that (113) included on the list of political deportees announced on 1 October 1848 in *Le Moniteur universel* (p. 67).

11. 'Salon de 1848', *La Presse*, 22 April 1848.

12. During the evening of 24 February 1848, Ledru-Rollin, Minister of the Interior in the Provisional Government of the newly proclaimed Second Republic, issued the following decree: 'Tout ce qui concerne la Direction des Beaux-Arts et des Musées, autrefois dans les attributions de la Liste civile, constituera une division du Ministère de l'Intérieur. Le jury chargé de recevoir les tableaux aux Expositions sera nommé par élection. Les artistes seront convoqués à cet effet par un prochain arrêté.' For this decree see Madeleine Rousseau, *La Vie et l'œuvre de Philippe-Auguste Jeanron: peintre, écrivain, directeur des Musées nationaux 1808–1877*, completed and ed. by Marie-Martine Dubreuil (Paris: RMN, 2000), pp. 64–65.

13. On the royal family's patronage of the arts during the July Monarchy, see Michael Marrinan, *Painting Politics for Louis Philippe: Art and Ideology in Orléanist France, 1830–1848* (New Haven and London: Yale University Press, 1988).

14. In his report of 9 October 1848 to the Minister 'sur les arts du dessin et sur leur avenir dans la République', Charles Blanc stated: 'En supprimant la liste civile, on a supprimé du même coup une somme de près de 500,000 fr. qu'elle affectait à l'encouragement des artistes' and urged the minister to reinstate this sum in the Fine Arts budget (*Le Moniteur universel*, 10 October 1848, p. 2763). Eighteen months later the painter Boissard de Boisdenier repeated that the loss of the Civil List amounted to 'une réduction annuelle de quelques centaines de mille francs dans la somme consacrée à la peinture de grande dimension' ('De la condition des artistes et des moyens de l'améliorer, I', *L'Artiste*, 1 February 1850, pp. 100–02 (p. 101)). For Pradier the demise of the Civil List evidently hit sculpture disproportionally hard.

15. By the mid-1840s, Pradier too was dissatisfied with the Orleanist regime, but mainly because it was not buying enough of his work for his liking. His hopes were invested not in the restoration of the republic but in that of the Bourbon monarchy. See Garnier, 'La carrière d'un artiste officiel à Paris', in *Statues de chair*, p. 93.

16. For further information on this strategy see *Statues de chair*, pp. 96 and 141. In the case of the hoped-for *Nyssia* sale, he had contacted, among others, the mayor of Montpellier and the prefect of the Gard region (see D. Siler, 'Documentation', also in *Statues de chair*, p. 366).

17. 'C'est que, depuis longtemps, la sculpture n'avait produit une œuvre si originale. — L'antique n'est pour rien dans cette figure étincelante d'une beauté toute moderne; aucune Vénus, aucune Flore, n'ont à réclamer de bras ou de jambes à cette statue, ou plutôt à cette femme; car elle n'est pas en marbre, elle est en chair; elle n'est pas sculptée, elle vit, elle se tord! Et n'est-ce pas une illusion? elle a remué! Il semble que si l'on posait sa main sur ce corps blanc et souple, au lieu du froid de la pierre, on trouverait la tiédeur de l'existence!' ('Salon de 1847, XI: La Sculpture', *La Presse*, 10 April 1847).

18. A. H. Delaunay, editor of the conservative *Journal des artistes*, who had no time for what he saw as Pradier's adaptation of the classical nude for commercial purposes, was blunt. Referring to Clésinger in the third of his 'Lettres sur le Salon de 1847', he wrote: 'M. Pradier a trouvé son maître, et un maître d'autant plus redoutable, que chez M. Clésinger, il y a l'étoffe du penseur, unie à la main la plus expérimentée, tandis que chez M. Pradier, il n'y a qu'un très habile ouvrier, dépourvu du feu sacré' (28 March 1847, pp. 121–25 (p. 121)).

19. 'Sa *Bacchante*, pour l'œil comme pour l'esprit, est bien la sœur de sa *Femme piquée*, sœur reconnaissable, mais différente, comme doivent l'être les œuvres des natures originales. Dans l'une, c'est l'ivresse, ou, si vous le préférez, la douleur de la volupté; dans l'autre, c'est le pur délire orgiaque, la Ménade échevelée qui se roule aux pieds de Bacchus, le père de liberté et de joie' ('Salon de 1848, 2e article', *La Presse*, 23 April 1848). We can be sure that the satisfaction Pradier felt at the success achieved by his *Nyssia* in the Salon that year, and for which he was awarded a bowl in Sèvres porcelain (the republic's equivalent of the traditional first-class medal), will not have been enhanced by the same award to Clésinger. Years later, Maxime Du Camp still recalled the distaste with which Pradier had responded to Clésinger's success. See *Statues de chair*, p. 87.

20. See Albert Boime, *Hollow Icons: The Politics of Sculpture in Nineteenth-Century France* (Kent, OH, and London: Kent State University Press, 1987), p. 4.

21. See Pierre Vaisse, *La Troisième Republique et les peintres*, p. 33, and 'Considérations sur la Seconde République et les beaux-arts', *Bulletin de la Société d'histoire de la révolution de 1848 et des révolutions du XIXe siècle* (1985), 59–85 (pp. 62–63).

22. The Maison du Roi was itself the successor to the Maison de l'Empereur, for it was Napoleon who in 1804 had removed the museums from the jurisdiction of the Ministry of the Interior. See Vaisse, 'Considérations sur la Seconde République', p. 62.

23. Vaisse commented on the decision relating to the fine arts as follows: 'Leur maintien à l'Intérieur, au lendemain de la révolution de février, tient peut-être à l'intérêt personnel que leur portait Ledru-Rollin, puis, lors de la formation d'un nouveau ministère [on 10 May 1848] à la pesanteur d'un état de fait — à moins qu'on ne pense à l'attention que la police, pendant tout le siècle, a vouée aux théâtres' (ibid., p. 63). On 1 January 1849, *L'Artiste* published Auguste Vacquerie's open letter to Louis-Napoleon urging the creation of a Ministère des Arts et des Lettres. See Lord Pilgrim, 'Mouvement des arts', *L'Artiste,* 1 January 1849, pp. 146–48 (p. 146).

24. Philippe de Chennevières published the petition in *Le Corsaire* of 24 May 1848 and again in 1886, in *Souvenirs d'un Directeur des Beaux-Arts* (Paris: Arthena, 1979), III, 63–65. See Vaisse, 'Considérations sur la Seconde République', p. 63.

25. *L'Artiste* published the petition on 15 July 1848, p. 208.

26. Gautier responded to Pradier's letter by suggesting that they discuss its contents on the way to a hashish evening to which he invited the sculptor (*Corr.*, III, 363–64). Whether Pradier took up the offer of the discussion and the hashish party is unknown. What also remains a mystery is whether its gloomy contents had anything to do with a letter Gautier wrote on 6 August, but did not send, to the Minister for War, in which he expressed his desire to 'se fixer comme colon en Algérie' (*Corr*, III, 364–65). Perhaps the drafting of the letter was sufficient to convince him that this was an implausible career move for someone as Parisian as himself (and rarely more so than when he was away from Paris). Another possible explanation for not having sent his letter is that the same day, the government lifted the ban on *La Presse*, closed down since 25 June by order of Cavaignac, thereby re-establishing his principal source of income, which the ban had interrupted. It is possible that Pradier's letter, coming at a time when Gautier was becoming seriously worried about the impact of the closure of *La Presse* on his financial position (*Corr.*, III, 367–68) may have helped to trigger his request to the minister.

27. 'Salon de 1848', 23 April. In *L'Artiste*, Pierre Malitourne agreed: 'Nous ne pouvons renoncer [...] de joindre notre humble parole aux voix plus puissantes qui appellent avec un intérêt inquiet la sollicitude du pouvoir sur un art qui ne peut vivre que par sa large influence' ('La Sculpture en 1848', 1 June 1848, pp. 141–45 (p. 141)).

28. 'Salon de 1848', 23 April. The republican art critic Théophile Thoré made the same point: 'Un groupe de plâtre, une statue de marbre, où l'exposer, et à qui la vendre? Il n'y a pas à Paris six existences de sculpteurs indépendantes de la publicité des Salons et de la protection de l'État' (*Salons de 1844, 1845, 1846, 1847, 1848* (Paris: Librairie internationale, 1868), quoted in *Statues de chair*, p. 88).

29. The Salon catalogue for 1848 listed three items by Pradier: 'n° 4881 — Nyssia; statue en marbre grec pentélique; n° 4882 — Sapho; statue demi-grandeur en bronze; n° 4883 — M. de Belleyme; statuette en marbre' (p. 364).

30. Baudelaire, on the other hand, had no time for Pradier's work, which he dismissed as a tarting up of antique forms: 'Ce qui prouve l'état pitoyable de la sculpture c'est que M. Pradier en est le roi. [...] Il a passé sa vie à engraisser quelques torses antiques, et à ajuster sur leurs cous des coiffures de filles entretenues' (*Œuvres complètes*, ii, 489).

31. 'Dans une civilisation avancée comme la nôtre, la statuaire a le mérite de conserver la tradition de la beauté, de maintenir les droits imprescriptibles du corps humain, sur qui d'austères doctrines voudraient jeter à tout jamais leur suaire aux plis droits; elle continue ce poëme de la forme, à laquelle les Grecs ont tailleé de si belles odes dans le Paros et le Pentélique; elle est l'anneau qui rattache le monde ancien au monde moderne, car l'esprit divin du paganisme respire encore en elle' ('Salon de 1847, XI: La Sculpture').

32. Reviewing the sculpture on show in the Salon of 1848, Prosper Haussard, art critic for the republican newspaper *Le National*, wrote: 'Gardons, du moins en sculpture, le culte pur de la forme, qui est son essence; sauvons le nu, qui est le type immuable du beau. [...] Le nu antique, c'est d'abord une grande école, une magnifique tradition' ('Salon de 1848', 14 April 1848).

33. Toussaint-Bernard Émeric-David, *Recherches sur l'art statuaire, considéré chez les anciens et les modernes* (Paris: Vve Nyon aîné, an XIII-1805). De Mercey began his review of the sculpture in 1848 by retracing the history of what he considered to be Émeric-David's negative influence on French neoclassicism.

34. As Snell rightly states, Pradier was for Gautier 'sculpture's Ingres', his 'beloved pagan' (*Théophile Gautier: A Romantic Critic*, p. 118). See also Marie-Hélène Girard, 'Gautier et les sculpteurs romantiques', *48/14: la revue du Musée d'Orsay*, 7 (Autumn 1997), 51–57; Cassandra Hamrick, '"L'Art robuste seul a l'éternité": Gautier et la sculpture romantique', *BSTG*, 18 (1996), 439–67, and Francis Moulinat, 'Gautier, Pradier, hellénisme', *BSTG*, 24 (2002), 45–52.

35. A somewhat less canonical predecessor was Boissard de Boisdenier, whose painting *Gygès et Candaule* had been shown in the Salon of 1841. Of this painting by an artist with whom he would be more closely associated by the later stages of the decade, Gautier was as positive as he could be, given that he evidently felt that, in focusing his skills on the accessories rather than the nude's body, Boissard had missed the whole point of the narrative: 'Le corps de la femme est étudié soigneusement, mais les damas, les oreillers, les coussins, sont peints avec une telle perfection que l'accessoire détourne un peu du principal' ('Salon de 1841', *Revue de Paris*, 25 April 1841, pp. 255–70 (p. 256)).

36. The complexity of the triangular relationship in *Le Roi Candaule*, in which Candaule, Nyssia, and Gygès are each in turn seer and seen, has given rise to very interesting studies, notably those of Constance Gosselin Schick, 'Le Donner à voir de Gautier ou pour un Candaule', in *Relire Théophile Gautier: le plaisir du texte*, ed. by Freeman G. Henry (Amsterdam and Atlanta, GA: Rodopi, 1998), pp. 243–63; Stéphane Guégan, 'Le Regard de Gygès', in *Théophile Gautier: la critique en liberté* (Paris: RMN, 1997), pp. 17–37; Wolfgang Drost, 'Der Blick der Frau auf den Voyeur: zu Gautiers Roi Candaule', in *Die Ästhetik des Voyeur/L'Esthétique du voyeur*, ed. by Lydia Hartl and others (Heidelberg: Winter, 2003), pp. 135–45, and Peter Cogman, 'Le Triangle de la mort: du *Roi Candaule* à *Jettatura*', *BSTG*, 18 (1996), 239–54. See also the excellent introductions and notes to *Le Roi Candaule* in editions of Gautier's work by Paolo Tortonese (*Œuvres* (Paris: Coll. Bouquins, 1995), pp. 1620–24) and Pierre Laubriet (*RCN*, i, 1491–520).

37. 'Souvent il la priait de laisser couler sur ses épaules les flots de ses cheveux, fleuve d'or plus opulent que le Pactole' (*RCN*, i, 959). Banville highlighted the theme: 'De Pradier, nous aurons la femme du roi Candaule, peignant et parfumant sa blonde crinière (on la sent blonde), longue comme un manteau de l'ex-roi'. He took the metaphor from Gautier's text, 'Plus longue qu'un manteau de roi', but added the topical 'ex-' ('Salon de 1848', *La Sylphide*, 10 March 1848, pp. 113–16 (p. 114)). Gautier regretted that in Pradier's statue, Nyssia's hair hid part of her back, a reminder that sculpture may be viewed from many angles as the spectator walks round it. We remember that Baudelaire hated the drapery piled up on the nude's back in Pradier's *Poésie légère*, of which 'vue de dos, l'aspect en est affreux' (*Œuvres complètes*, ii, 489).

38. '[... c'est] une pudeur archaïque, asiatique, participant de l'énormité du monde ancien [...]' (ibid., 122). As de Mercey noted: 'Nyssia est absolument nue, et, comme ses bras sont relevés par-dessus la tête pour rattacher sa longue chevelure, nul obstacle ne vient s'interposer entre ses charmes offerts sans voile à l'œil du spectateur' ('Le Salon de 1848', p. 594).

39. 'Nyssia — était-ce un pressentiment instinctif, ou son épiderme entièrement vierge de regards profanes avait-il une susceptibilité magnétique si vive, qu'il pût sentir le rayon d'un œil passionné, quoique invisible? — Nyssia parut hésiter à dépouiller cette tunique, dernier rempart de sa pudeur' (*RCN*, I, 973).

40. As de Mercey suggested: 'Nous soupçonnerions volontiers M. Pradier de n'avoir baptisé sa Nyssia que long-temps après sa naissance et au moment de la lancer dans le monde' ('Le Salon de 1848', p. 594). In fact, Gautier had seen the unfinished statue, already called *Nyssia*, in Pradier's studio the year before ('Salon de 1847, XI: La Sculpture').

41. 'La *Nyssia*, de Pradier, présente des morceaux exécutés avec l'habileté d'un praticien expérimenté; mais la tête est froide et sans vie' (Anon., 'Le Salon de 1848', *Revue nationale,* 23 March 1848, pp. 345–46 (p. 346)); 'La figure en marbre, *Nyssia*, de M. Pradier, ne porte pas un caractère assez marqué pour qu'elle reste comme un de ces types qui se gravent profondément dans la mémoire' (E.-J. Delécluze, 'Salon de 1848', *Journal des débats*, 31 May 1848).

42. In a letter to Gautier in 1849, the painter Léon Riesener, referring to Charles Blanc, commented: 'Comme vous le rencontrez sans doute souvent ainsi que M. Mercey dans les théâtres et que je dois les inviter à venir à Charenton, un mot de vous sur ce sujet ferait recevoir mon offre avec infiniment plus de considération' (*Corr.*, IV, 89–90). Riesener wanted to invite Blanc and de Mercey to see his decoration of the chapel of the Établissement National de Bienfaisance at Charenton, commissioned in 1843 and completed in 1849. See also *Corr.*, IV, 447–48.

43. 'On se réunit chez moi *jeudi prochain 25 mars*, pour parlementer au sujet du jury, de l'exposition, de l'institut, de tout le bataclan, de toutes les misères contre lesquelles nous nous débattons tous depuis si longtemps en vain' (*Corr.*, III, 176, Boissard's emphasis). He may have known Jeanron since the early 1830s (see *Corr.*, IV, 482–83).

44. See my article 'From Store to Museum: The Reorganisation of the Louvre's Painting Collections in 1848', *Modern Language* Review (henceforth *MLR*), 102 (2007), 60–76.

45. In his landmark study *The Absolute Bourgeois*, T. J. Clark, commenting on Gautier's call for the creation of 'armies of painters' charged with the task of decorating the buildings of the republic, wrote: 'Gautier, as usual in his prose, gave voice to the fashionable hopes of 1848' (p. 31). One recent exception is that of Martine Lavaud, who, in her excellent book *Théophile Gautier militant du romantisme* (Paris: Champion, 2001), presents a more balanced view of Gautier's pro- and anti-republican sentiments, though without referring specifically to his art journalism during the Second Republic (pp. 260–63). I shall return to this issue in Chapter 3.

46. Pierre Laubriet, 'Chronologie', in *RCN*, II, p. ix.

47. As Gautier memorably recalled later: 'Lors des glorieuses de juillet, mon père était très légitimiste, et il a joué à la hausse sur les Ordonnances. Vous pensez comme ça a réussi. Nous avons tout perdu: quinze mille livres de rente. J'étais destiné à entrer dans la vie en homme heureux, en homme de loisir: il a fallu gagner sa vie' (quoted in René Jasinski, *Les Années romantiques de Gautier* (Paris: Vuibert, 1929), p. 64). This persistent nostalgia for a life of luxury is a better clue to the chaotic state of Gautier's personal finances that the political context. As the editor of the *RCN* himself notes in relation to 'été 1843': 'Gautier mène grand train, roule voiture et Carlotta [Grisi] semble apprécier les promenades ainsi faites. Il gardera son phaéton jusqu'en 1848. Il a également deux poneys et un domestique. La liaison avec Mme Damarin se poursuit' (I, p. lxxii).

48. Gérard de Senneville, in *Théophile Gautier* (Paris: Fayard, 2004), states that 'les révolutions [of 1830 and 1848] ne portent pas chance aux Gautier' but his account only confirms the extent that the son was as much the author of his own misfortune as the father had been, in the sense that the political events hurt Gautier mainly because the level of debt that he had incurred before February 1848 had left him so exposed: 'Une révolution, cela veut dire des théâtres qui font relâche, des éditeurs qui diffèrent des contrats, des commandes suspendues, des entreprises en déconfiture, un caissier qui refuse de nouvelles avances, bref une situation redoutable pour qui vit d'à-valoir et doit rembourser des dettes. Hetzel ayant fait faillite, Gautier doit souscrire pour 8000 francs de billets à ordre, substituant ainsi à un ami des créanciers inconnus et beaucoup moins accommodants' (p. 185).

49. In a letter at the end of that month to his mother, Adèle, on the subject of the latest debt with which he was having to juggle, he wrote: 'C'est un petit malheur. Ma nouvelle position de

directeur du feuilleton balance et au delà ce désagrément: je serai à mon aise deux ou trois mois plus tard, voilà tout' (*Corr.*, III, 324). As usual Gautier's optimism that solvency was just round the corner was misplaced.

50. In his article 'Opinions professionnelles: critique d'art et économie de la culture sous la Monarchie de Juillet' (*Romantisme*, 71 (1991), 19–31), Neil McWilliam draws on contemporary sources such as E. Charton (1842) and Hector de Robertval (1848) for his account of art criticism at that time as an insecure form of employment generally occupied by young men starting off on 1200 francs per year and rising to about 3000. By comparison Gautier in 1848 was in his late thirties, earning 13,681 francs (virtually twice the 7000 francs for a university professor at the time) on *La Presse* alone. The salary figures given by Marc Martin in 'Journalistes parisiens et notoriéte (vers 1830–1870): pour une histoire sociale du journalisme', *Revue historique*, no. 539 (July–September 1981), 31–74, confirm (p. 64) how well paid Gautier was. He also enjoyed a security of employment exceptional for a Girardin publication, where the turnover of journalists was high. As Martin states: 'Cette mobilité est maximum à *La Presse*. Il est rare que l'on y séjourne de très nombreuses années. Les passages pour un ou deux ans, voire quelques mois [...] sont au contraire fréquents. C'était pourtant l'une des maisons qui payait le mieux' (pp. 68–69). As we saw earlier, Gautier stayed for nineteen years and left of his own accord and much to Girardin's irritation.

51. Girardin made the remark in *La Presse* on 2 February 1847 in response to an article by Gautier the previous day on the financial plight of writers exploited by unscrupulous businessmen. Judging by the tone of his reply, Girardin had taken Gautier's comments personally. The poet Auguste Desplaces sprang to Gautier's defence: 'M. de Girardin, qui n'a cependant pas besoin de quitter sa maison pour savoir que les beaux vers sont une denrée côtée très bas sur la place, rappelait l'autre jour à son feuilletoniste, avec une convenance contestable, les appointemens assez ronds que lui payait *la Presse*. Pourquoi l'auteur de Fortunio, prenant la balle au bond, n'a-t-il pas dit à son tour à quel prix il jouissait de cette rente et de cette publicité?' (*Galerie des poëtes vivans* (Paris: Didier, 1847), p. 40).

52. When *La Presse* reappeared on 7 August, Girardin, demanding an explanation of the closure, wrote of the offending article: 'Si le régime du sabre y était qualifié du "despotisme", il y était en même temps qualifié de "bienfait"'.

53. Gautier's correspondence is littered with his urgent requests to Claude Rouy for payment, occasionally in advance of submission of articles. When, on 22 August 1851, Rouy agreed to pay him for three articles promised but not yet written on the Universal Exhibition in Crystal Palace, he warned Gautier 'de ne plus tenter de récidive. Car en vérité je me mets en flagrante opposition aux formelles instructions des Propriétaires de La Presse, et comme je l'écris à Mad(ame) de Girardin, il n'a pas fallu moins que sa puissante intervention pour me faire dévier du chemin qui m'est tracé' (*Corr.*, IV, 378).

54. 'Comment tous ces fils d'Adam, héritiers des mêmes ennuis que je supporte, comment ces Halévy, ces Gautier, ces gens couverts de dettes et d'exigences de famille ou de vanité, ont-ils un air souriant et calme, à travers tous les ennuis? Ils ne peuvent être heureux qu'en s'étourdissant et en se cachant les écueils au milieu desquels ils conduisent leur barque, souvent en désespérés, et où ils font naufrage quelque jour' (*Journal 1822–1863*, p. 451 (11 August 1854)).

55. Recollecting Gautier's travels in Egypt, Maxime du Camp recalled: 'Chacune de ses étapes se comptait par les pages de copie qu'il envoyait à son journal: il évaluait les kilomètres par le nombre de lignes qu'ils lui coûtaient' (quoted in Marcel Voisin, 'Gautier et la politique', *BSTG*, 15 (1993), 323–39 (p. 336)).

56. Much later he wrote: 'On se représente difficilement le temps, le soin, l'étude, la pratique des hommes et des choses, le voyage incessant aux ateliers, aux expositions, aux ventes publiques, aux vitrines des marchands, qu'il faut pour connaître le personnel de l'art en France; seulement pour ce qui regarde la sculpture et la peinture, c'est une science qui exige la vie d'un critique ('Ceux qui seront connus', *L'Illustration*, 8 June 1872, quoted in Girard, *Théophile Gautier, Critique d'art*, p. 423).

57. The editor's statement on the revolution's 'ruin' of Gautier (referred to above in note 46) is followed by: 'Pour tenter d'échapper à ses difficultés de tout ordre, il se réfugie dans la poésie. Retiré dans un petit logement au cinquième étage du 14, rue Rougement, il commence

à composer les poèmes du premier recueil d'*Émaux et camées*, le sonnet liminaire faisant l'aveu de cette retraite.' By the mid-nineteenth century withdrawal from the world was a well-tried, serviceable Romantic myth of the poet, one which formed part of the reader's *horizon d'attente* and which Gautier used when it suited him. Though poetry may well have provided brief respite from his 'difficultés de tout ordre', moving to smaller, less expensive accommodation was a more realistic response to his financial predicament. As Senneville put it: 'La mort dans l'âme, Théo doit se résoudre à vendre sa voiture et ses deux jolies ponettes blanche, dont il était si fier. Il doit aussi chercher un logement plus modeste' (*Théophile Gautier*, p. 187).

58. Senneville again: 'Pour le moment [summer of 1848], Gautier doit écrire, écrire le plus possible. *La Presse* ayant reparu, il a retrouvé son principal gagne-pain et doit plus que jamais s'attacher à la meule du feuilleton' (p. 187).

59. See Marie-Eve Thérenty and Alain Vaillant, *1836: l'an I de l'ère médiatique: analyse littéraire et historique de 'La Presse' de Girardin* (Paris: Nouveau monde Éditions, 2001); *Histoire générale de la presse française*, ed. by Claude Bellanger and others, 5 vols (Paris: PUF, 1969), II, 91–146; Martin, 'Journalistes parisiens et notoriété', and Pellissier, *Émile de Girardin, prince de la presse*.

60. The following comments by Pierre Bourdieu are typical in this respect. Writing of Baudelaire's promotion of the idea of the writer as an 'aristocrat indifferent to society's honours', he went on to say: 'Writers elaborate the theory of the totally separate economy of this separate world when, like Théophile Gautier in the preface to *Mademoiselle de Maupin*, or Baudelaire in the *Salon of 1846*, they produce with reference to painting the first systematic formulations of the theory of art for art's sake: this singular way of living through art, whose roots lie in an art of living that rejects the bourgeois lifestyle, notably because it is founded upon the act of refusing any social justification for art or the artist himself.' See Pierre Bourdieu, 'The Link between Literary and Artistic Struggles', in *Artistic Relations: Literature and the Visual Arts in Nineteenth-Century France*, ed. by Peter Collier and Robert Lethbridge (New Haven and London: Yale University Press, 1994), pp. 30–39 (p. 32).

61. See Michael Moriarty's opening statement in his essay 'Structures of Cultural Production in Nineteenth-Century France': 'The modernist axioms that the value of an artistic or literary production is not contingent on the intrinsic interest of the object, if any, represented, and that aesthetic responses and judgements are not contingent on ethical or political ones, presuppose the autonomy of an aesthetic sphere' (in Collier and Lethbridge, *Artistic Relations* (see Bourdieu, above), pp. 15–29 (p. 15).

62. Paolo Tortonese had already pointed this out in 1995 in the introduction to his edition of Gautier's works: 'On aurait dû s'apercevoir depuis longtemps, et certains l'ont fait, que cette formule [l'art pour l'art] au destin ambigu (très célèbre et peu prisée) n'apparaît pas dans ladite préface [de *Mademoiselle de Maupin*] (*Œuvres*, p. xviii). Such is the durability of myths, however, that the point bears repeating.

63. 'MM. Alexandre Decamps dans le *National*, Félix Pyat dans la *Revue britannique*, Cavaignac dans la *Revue républicaine*, Thoré dans l'*Encyclopédie nouvelle*, Schœlcher et Haussard dans le *Temps*, Fortoul dans ses livres, Ricourt et ses amis dans l'*Artiste*, écrivèrent contre les tendances égoistes de l'*art pour l'art*' (p. 37).

64. See Andrew Shelton's excellent analysis of this 'art for art's sake' Ingres in his *Ingres and his Critics* (Cambridge University Press, 2005), pp. 129–32 and 171–76. The inadequacy of the label as an account of Ingres's art ensured that it did not survive in the critical reception of his work; in Gautier's case, though it was no more adequate, the heavily selective reading of his work ensured that it did.

65. For this context see Claudine Lacoste-Veysseyre's presentation of *Mademoiselle de Maupin* in *RCN*, I, 1296–98, in which she also draws attention to the contribution made by the Gautier specialists René Jasinski and Georges Matoré to our knowledge of this history.

66. See Pamela M. Pilbeam, *Republicanism in Nineteenth-Century France, 1814–1871* (Basingstoke and London: Macmillan, 1995), p. 125. In view of the impact of the massacre, one wonders how supporters of the regime might have read Gautier's comments in his preface, when the facetious tone of his reaction to Fourier's Malthusian proposals to reduce childbirth took on a harder edge: 'ce qui est plus raisonnable que de pousser les prolétaires à en faire d'autres, sauf à les

canonner ensuite dans les rues quand ils pullulent trop, et à les envoyer des boulets au lieu de pain' (*RCN*, I, 234).

67. The article on Villon was the first in a series of pre-classical literary portraits which Gautier wrote alongside *Mademoiselle de Maupin* and its preface. The portraits appeared in *La France littéraire* between January 1834 and September 1835 and were brought together in *Les Grotesques*, published in 1844. The author of the attack in *Le Constitutionnel* was anonymous, identified simply as 'P', the single letter being a common form of authorial designation in the press of the early July Monarchy, as Gautier himself pointed out in his preface with his reference to 'MM. Z. K. Y. V. Q. X. ou telle autre lettre de l'alphabet entre A et 'Ω' (p. 241). Gautier, on the other hand, put his full name to his articles for by the mid-1830s he was already well aware of the importance of the name as a brand in literature's changing marketplace.

68. See *Histoire générale de la presse française*, II, 115–16.

69. On Girardin's experience in journalism before *La Presse*, see Thérenty and Vaillant, *1836*, pp. 34–37. On the role of the *Journal des connaissances utiles* in this respect, they state: 'Avec le *Journal des connaissances utiles*, comme avec *Le Musée des familles* [which Girardin launched in 1833], Girardin prend conscience que pour élargir son lectorat, il faut à la fois diminuer le prix de vente des journaux et également trouver des sujets larges, propres à intéresser les publics populaires' (p. 36).

70. By the time of the pre-launch publicity for *La Presse*, Girardin had already lined up Gautier as its reviewer for the fine arts. See the exhibition catalogue *La Presse dans le centre de Paris 1830–1851* (Paris: Délégation à l'Action Artistique de la Ville de Paris et Société d'Histoire du Ier et IIe arrondissement, 1981), p. 17, item 56 (illustrated on the inside rear cover, where it is wrongly referred to as item 50).

71. In the pre-launch prospectus, Girardin had prefaced his article 'Principes du journal' with a statement by Hugo: 'Cette œuvre, ce sera la formation paisible, lente et logique d'un ordre social, où les principes nouveaux, dégagés par la Révolution française, trouveront enfin leur combinaison avec les principes éternels et primordiaux de toute civilisation. Concourons donc ensemble, tous chacun dans sa région et selon notre loi particulière, à la grande substitution des questions sociales aux questions politiques. Tout est là. Tâchons de rallier à l'idée applicable du progrès tous les hommes d'élite et d'extraire un parti supérieur qui veuille la civilisation de tous les partis inférieurs qui ne savent ce qu'ils veulent.' See Thérenty and Vaillant, *1836*, p. 44.

72. 'De la composition en peinture', *La Presse*, 22 November 1836. In the preface to *Mademoiselle de Maupin*, he had written: 'Il y a quelques siècles, on avait Raphaël, on avait Michel-Ange; maintenant on a M. Paul Delaroche, le tout parce que l'on est en progrès' (*RCN*, I, 236).

73. 'Voilà une vérité qu'il faut bien que les artistes se mettent dans la tête', said Gautier ('De l'application de l'art à la vie usuelle', *La Presse*, 13 December 1836), referring to the fact that modern artists, through their misplaced elitism and individualism, had lost contact with the public. It was all very well, he argued, to ridicule the philistinism of the bourgeois — 'nous-mêmes nous ne lui avons guère épargné le sarcasme' — but what had artists done to educate their taste?

74. In *1836* Thérenty and Vaillant described Gautier as the embodiment of the paper's wit: 'le rire sous toutes ses formes — de la satire à la drôlerie la plus fantaisiste — est un des ressorts stylistiques les plus constants d'un journal comme *La Presse*. L'esprit, dont Théophile Gautier figure l'incarnation géniale est [...] une spécialité journalistique' (p. 101). See also Cassandra Hamrick, 'The *feuilleton artistique*: On the Margins of Nineteenth-Century Texts (with Théophile Gautier)', in *On the Margins*, ed. by Freeman G. Henry, French Literature Series, 20 (Amsterdam and Atlanta, GA: Rodopi, 1993), pp. 71–85.

75. The genre soon acquired a downmarket and rather disreputable image. As Nicole Mozet reminds us, *La Vieille Fille* was soon getting Girardin into trouble with some of his readers. See Balzac, *La Comédie humaine*, ed. by Pierre-Georges Castex, 12 vols (Paris: Gallimard, Bibliothèque de la Pléiade, 1976–81), IV (1976), 1472.

76. Delphine de Girardin's articles appeared under the *Courrier de Paris* rubric. See *Lettres parisiennes du vicomte de Launay par Madame de Girardin*, ed. by Anne Martin-Fugier, 2 vols (Paris: Mercure de France, 2004).

77. Certainly by 1848 it was a commonplace to state, as de Mercey did, that Salon painters,

boulevard dramatists, and authors of serialized fiction were producing for the same public: 'Elles [les œuvres de cette année] rappellent trop souvent le théâtre de boulevard et le roman-feuilleton' ('Salon de 1848', p. 284).

78. Three of the four articles Gautier published on art-related topics during the period of the serialization of Balzac's *La Vieille Fille* had Parisian landmarks as their subject. These were: 'Statues du Jardin des Tuileries' (18 October); 'Projets d'embellissements pour les Champs-Élysées et la Place de la Concorde' (25 October); 'Travaux de Notre-Dame de Lorette' (1 November).

79. Gautier reviewed the Salons of 1833 and 1834 with one article on each (1835 was one of the rare Salons he did not review) and in 1836 he wrote nine articles, seven on painting to fill out his own periodical, *Ariel: journal du monde élégant*, and two on sculpture in *Le Cabinet de lecture*, the second periodical made necessary by the financial collapse of the first. For his review of the Salon of 1837, his first for *La Presse*, he wrote sixteen articles published between 1 March and 1 May of that year.

80. In 1835 he had published seven articles of literary criticism in two publications; in 1836, thirty-seven articles of art criticism, thirty articles entitled 'variétés', and eleven pieces of literary criticism in no fewer than eight publications.

81. In order, for example, to remind the artists among his readership of his credentials for lecturing them on the need to reconnect with the public, Gautier alluded directly to his message in the preface to *Maupin*: 'personne ne nous a jamais soupçonnés d'être utilitaires, humanitaires, négrophiles et philantropes [*sic*], Dieu merci! Mais nous voudrions que les artistes comprissent qu'ils ont tort de s'isoler ainsi dans je ne sais quelle abstraction idéale en dehors de toute application possible' ('De l'application de l'art à la vie usuelle'). As in the preface, Paul Delaroche was the proof that under the July Monarchy, as in all periods of decadence, 'les idées littéraires ont envahi les arts', in this case the art of portraiture (6 December 1836). In modern dress 'on délaisse le culte du beau, l'adoration de la forme divine, pour je ne sais quel monstrueux fantôme d'utilité' (ibid.).

CHAPTER 2

The 'Detestable' Salon of 1848

Closing his review of the Salon of 1848 in the *Revue des deux mondes*, F. de Lagenevais, alias Frédéric de Mercey, summarized the initial response to the exhibition that year:

> Il faut clore cette longue revue, et cependant nous n'avons pu mentionner bien des ouvrages qui ne sont pas dépourvus de mérite. D'où vient donc qu'à la première vue l'aspect de cette immense collection est si déplaisant? D'où vient que le premier jour, en sortant du Louvre, chaque amateur désappointé condamnait sommairement le Salon de 1848 comme *détestable*? ('Le Salon de 1848', p. 299)

His displeasure and the alleged disappointment of the 'amateurs' (whether understood in a narrow or a wide sense is not made clear) indicate the manner in which the Salon's first-day visitors set the tone for the public's response to the exhibition in the weeks that followed. In 1848 de Mercey had no doubt that the reason for the negative initial verdict was the size of the Salon that year: 'Ce jugement s'explique par cette abondance même'.[1] On 24 February Ledru-Rollin's annexation of the Civil List had *de facto* abolished the Academy's control of the Salon jury process managed by the List's officers, which explained his accompanying decision that the jury, 'chargé de recevoir les tableaux aux Expositions[,] sera nommé par élection'.[2] Five days later, faced with the impossibility of putting in place an elective jury system in time for the Salon to open as planned on 15 March, he announced that there would be no admissions jury that year and invited artists to elect in a general assembly on 5 March a commission of forty members whose task would be to determine the placement in the exhibition of all the work received.[3] In the absence of a jury, over five thousand works were admitted, more than twice the number of the previous year.[4] As far as de Mercey was concerned, the Salon's first visitors had decided that this exorbitant number of works had discredited the event, that the Salon without a jury was no longer the Salon as they understood it. He himself tellingly called it 'cette assemblée populaire des arts' (p. 299), which was something else altogether. To all but the diehard supporters of the Academy, reform of the jury was a long-overdue victory for justice and progress. Its abolition, on the other hand, was an open door to mediocrity and eccentricity. This was a harsh verdict on a pragmatic decision over which Ledru-Rollin had had very little choice in the circumstances and which had created for Jeanron, his new Directeur des Musées Nationaux, a great deal of extra work for which he received little thanks. Among the art journalists, the dissenting voice in the chorus of demand that the jury be reinstated in 1849, albeit on a different basis, was that of Gautier.

In three weeks between 22 April and 10 May 1848 Gautier published in *La Presse* fourteen articles on the Salon, a total of nearly forty-five thousand words. He retained his familiar format, in which an initial overview article on the general context to the exhibition was followed by a short series of articles on sculpture and a longer series on painting (two and eleven articles respectively that year).[5] When he came to the latter, he again followed a familiar sequence based on the hierarchy of genres established in academic tradition, beginning with history painting, the most noble (four articles), followed, in descending order of status, by genre painting (four articles), and concluding with landscape, the transition between genre and landscape being effected by the *animaliers*.[6] He did not need telling that this format was by then leaking seriously at the seams, not least because, as he himself went on to explain in his fourth article, history painting (at least as the academic tradition understood it) was by then to all intents and purposes defunct.[7] The format nevertheless provided for author and reader alike an appearance of authority and structure for the review of an event whose size in 1848 made notions of authority and structure more elusive than ever.

He began his initial overview article by replying to a question he had apparently been asked in the wake of the events of 22–24 February: 'On nous a demandé si nous ferions cette année notre revue habituelle du Salon? — Oui, certainement. Une dynastie a été renversée et la République proclamée: l'art n'en subsiste pas moins.' It is possible that question and answer were his response to Thoré's apology for writing a much shorter Salon review than usual that year:

> Nous n'arrêterons pas longtemps nos lecteurs sur le Salon de 1848. La politique nous réserve des spectacles plus intéressants. Nous faisons aujourd'hui mieux que de l'art et de la poésie: nous faisons de l'histoire vivante.[8]

Judging by the bibliographies, a number of art critics shared Thoré's priorities, for there were certainly fewer Salon reviews published in 1848.[9] Whether the needs of art really did take second place to those of living history for some art journalists or whether their editors decided that there was not quite the same requirement to review a 'popular assembly of the arts' as there was to review the Salon, Gautier was having none of it. He proposed to occupy the higher ground, reminding his readers that while revolutions came and went, art was eternal, and that service in its cause was, in times of political turmoil, more than ever the critic's duty. In his first and fourth articles, in a series of rhetorical flourishes rich even by his standards, he embraced the Second Republic's ambitions for the visual arts and strove to sustain the mood of optimism these ambitions had initially generated. His powerful statement of *ralliement* to the republican vision, coming before his commentary on the works themselves, seems designed to authenticate in advance the judgements he would make on them, given that the republican sympathies of the artists Gautier considered best suited to direct the course of French art in the modern era were, to put it mildly, unproven and that a consensus on the direction to be taken was far from secure.

Having dealt with the timeless, Gautier turned to the topical, the abolition of the *jury d'admission*. Here at least no one could accuse him of opportunism, for by 1848 he had been attacking the Salon jury for fifteen years as another form of the censorship he had ridiculed in his preface to *Mademoiselle de Maupin*.[10] Protests against the jury's decisions had increased during the course of the July Monarchy but in 1847 they had reached a new level. In *L'Artiste* Clément de Ris devoted two articles of his Salon review that year to an attack on the jury, which the journal accompanied with a petition to the King urging reform.[11] Artists and critics, including Gautier, began meeting to plan their campaign (see above, p. 22). From these gatherings an anonymous brochure emerged entitled *De l'exposition et du jury*, put together by Boissard, Villot, and Clément de Ris and published on 12 February 1848. Émile de Girardin, never one to forgo an opportunity for publicity, offered to make *La Presse* available to orchestrate the growing demands among artists and critics for reform of the Salon.[12] Whereas Girardin and the authors of *De l'exposition et du jury* shared the view that a jury was essential if the Salon were to retain credibility as a showcase for French art, Gautier was for abolition pure and simple and made a bold attempt to present Ledru-Rollin's pragmatic decision to dispense with the jury for 1848 as an expression of the republic's defining values.[13] Abolition was, he said, republican in its commitment to liberty ('Point de jury, sous quelque nom que ce soit! Liberté pleine et entière, liberté à tous, aux jeunes comme aux vieux, aux inconnus comme aux illustres, aux habiles comme aux maladroits, aux sublimes comme aux ridicules!'), in its extension of the franchise ('laissez le peuple juger par lui-même! Un jury, même élu par les artistes, ne vaudrait rien'), and even in its abolition of capital punishment for political crimes ('les bourreaux de l'esprit ne sont-ils pas aussi coupables que les bourreaux des corps, et le meurtre d'une idée n'est-il pas le plus grand des crimes?') Besides, he continued in less euphoric and more disingenuous mode, the Salon of 1848 had merely confirmed that the jury was pointless, since its abolition had made no difference to the exhibition, except to allow access to a handful of paintings too hopeless to worry about.[14] What Gautier did not say was that the definitive abolition of the jury in favour of a sovereign public ('cet arbitre souverain' as had called it a year earlier) would have reinforced the role of the press as *contre-pouvoir* in the cultural sphere, by removing an obstacle to the art journalist's assumption of the rights and privileges that came with being the sole intermediary of authority between artist and public. De Mercey's comment showed, however, that Gautier was fighting a losing battle. It was well known that abolition had been adopted for that year only, pending discussion of alternative arrangements to be put in place for subsequent years. Ledru-Rollin's statement of 24 February had clearly implied as much, and no sooner had the Salon opened its doors than the arguments in favour of reinstating the jury on a new elective basis were being put forward.[15]

With the jury dispatched, even if only temporarily, Gautier urged artists freed from its tyranny to seize the moment. Launching into a eulogy to the heroism of modern life, he reminded them of their duty to be worthy of 'ce siècle colossal et climatérique, de ce grand dix-neuvième siècle, la plus belle époque qu'ait vue le genre humain depuis que la terre amoureuse accomplit sa ronde autour du soleil'. Man was conquering time, space, and the forces of nature. New worlds were opening in North Africa, the Orient, America, and the South Seas. All the ancient symbolism, religious and political, needed to be overhauled for the new age of democracy. The opportunities for artists were enormous. A Republican programme of public works would make possible a second Renaissance in public art, which, unlike the first, would engage a widely enfranchised public. All this was still official Republican policy when Gautier was writing his first article, probably in late March, except for the fact that for republican sympathizers, the programme signalled the defeat of the art-for-art's-sake faction with which Gautier was so firmly identified. For Haussard, for example, the republic would usher in a new period in which a reinvigorated national art, united in a common purpose, would banish art-for-art's-sake egoism and preciosity.[16] Gautier's enthusiastic embrace of the new mood may reflect in part a sense of threat at being targeted by the art-for-art's sake political label, but by the time his article appeared on 22 April, the mood itself had passed.[17] As we saw in the previous chapter, the initial optimism among the artists had dissipated by then and, the following day, the first elections under the new regime confirmed that the country was already no longer in the same republic.[18]

Despite these developments on the political front, Gautier renewed his ringing declaration of republican faith in his fourth article, the first on the painting. Before doing so, he reviewed the sculpture in articles 2 and 3, beginning with the key figures and issues that year (Bonnassieux, Pradier, and Clésinger) in the second, and sweeping up the others in the third. Alert as always to the importance of the conditions in which art work was presented, he began by complimenting the new administration on bringing the sculpture up from the Louvre's dark and freezing basement, where it had been shown in previous Salons, into the relative light and comfort of the former Musée Charles X on the first floor. It was, he thought, a good start, the best that could be achieved in the time available and a welcome sign of the republic's good intentions, but it was still not what sculpture needed. He called on the government to go further the following year and provide a purpose-built, ground floor gallery, properly heated and lit, and free of the clutter of the Louvre's permanent sculpture collections which competed for the Salon visitor's attention. Such investment would send the right signal to the public about the importance the new administration attached to this founding art.

Though Pradier's *Nyssia* was given in 1848 the prominence that we have seen in Gautier's review of the sculpture, it was not the work with which he began. This honour, which Gautier did not distribute lightly, went to Bonnassieux's *Jeanne Hachette*.[19] On the face of it this was an odd choice. Bonnassieux enjoyed a successful career under the July Monarchy but could not be said to figure among Gautier's select group of major modern French sculptors, nor does the fact that the latter's commentary on *Jeanne Hachette* appeared logically at this point in his review (in the sense that it was a work created in response to the sort of state patronage which Gautier had just advocated) fully explain its privileged position. *Jeanne Hachette* had been commissioned in 1844 for the series of statues, *Reines de France et des Femmes illustres*, which were to adorn the gardens of the newly extended and refurbished Palais du Luxembourg. In 1472 the eponymous heroine had led the defence of

Beauvais under siege from Charles (le Téméraire), duc de Bourgogne, and the inclusion of this 'héroïne populaire' in the group of illustrious women of France had been Préault's idea.[20] Count Duchâtel, Minister of the Interior at the time, had had no problem with a token working-class heroine, provided she was entrusted to a safer pair of hands than those of Préault, *bête noire* of the Salon juries since his *Tuerie* of 1834.[21] The commission went to Bonnassieux instead, and Gautier's commentary shows why. The sculptor had, he said, made Jeanne's physical energy spiritual while her form remained feminine, thus avoiding the 'vulgaire écueil' of 'une virago aux allures violentes'. The allusion could hardly have been clearer. *Jeanne Hachette* appeared first in Gautier's review because it had suddenly acquired an unforeseen topicality. The fear of 1793 and of state patronage of the fine arts being waylaid by attempts to reinstate the subjects and iconography of that era runs through Gautier's art writings of 1848.[22] It was something else he shared with the republican authorities that year and his comments on *Jeanne Hachette*, no vengeful *fille du peuple*, suggested that there was little to worry about in Bonnassieux's contribution to that debate.[23]

Only when he had reasserted the continuing and in his view indispensable relevance of Pradier's achievement did he turn to the issue in French sculpture which he knew full well had generated most interest in advance of the exhibition: would Clésinger be able to repeat the sensation he had created in the Salon the previous year with his *Femme piquée par un serpent*?[24] Gautier kept his readers waiting for the answer while he reminded them at length of the impact produced by the earlier statue's 'volupté si violente et si furieuse que ses spasmes ressemblaient à la mort à s'y tromper et en prenaient la chasteté', and of the speculation that had surrounded Clésinger's follow-up exhibit. Finally he announced: 'La Bacchante a résolu victorieusement la question.' She was, he said, a worthy pendant of the *Femme piquée*: 'Dans l'une, c'est l'ivresse, ou, si vous préférez, la douleur de la volupté; dans l'autre c'est le pur délire orgiaque.'[25] In her frenzy of devotion to her God of pleasure, Clésinger had achieved a synthesis of modern naturalism and classical inspiration that made his *Bacchante* 'un des plus beaux morceaux de la sculpture moderne pour l'invention de la pose, la hardiesse des lignes et la chaleureuse vigueur de l'exécution'. Sanctioned by the ancient hymns in honour of Dionysus, the inner fire of her arousal threatened to consume the sculptor's bronze and the critic's prose but without the same scandal as that which had greeted the *Femme piquée* of the previous year.[26] The work ensured that Clésinger, more than Pradier, despite Gautier's efforts on behalf of the older artist, was *the* sculptor of the Salon of 1848. Where Gautier considered both artists to be models for French sculpture in the new era, with Pradier closer to the serenity of ancient art and Clésinger to its passion, the *Bacchante* strengthened Clésinger's reputation at the expense of Pradier's among many commentators, who saw in the former's idealized naturalism a return to a national style rooted in the eighteenth century.[27]

With the lessons of what he considered to be the best modern sculpture firmly established, Gautier turned in his fourth article to the painting, beginning with the results of the deliberations by the *jury de placement*, which, in the absence of the admissions jury, had inherited the responsibility for generating controversy. On 12

March, *L'Artiste*, publishing the results of the election of the jury the previous week, shared the general optimism that this first effort of the artists to govern themselves had resulted in fair representation for all tendencies: 'Cette première élection contient donc une moralité, une garantie, une promesse' (p. 12). The morality was that of republican democratic control, the guarantee was of objectivity, the promise was for the collective strength that artists would derive in the future by working together within a framework of rules devised by themselves. A week later, having seen the results, it was, it concluded, 'le même tohu-bohu qu'il y a un an' (p. 17), the usual factional infighting and favours traded, different personnel but the same outcomes. For the republican Haussard, on the other hand, the jury appeared to have dealt with the placement issue in the most logical and practical way possible in the unprecedented circumstances: they had evidently placed what they thought to be the most important work in the best-known and best-lit galleries.[28] In his article the following month, Gautier dismissed some of the sillier conspiracy theories surrounding the jury's decisions — that it had deliberately placed the poorest works in the best positions to ensure that, overwhelmed by ridicule, they served as a lesson to all artists who thought they could succeed without talent or application; that the *assemblée des artistes*, in true republican spirit, had treated the best and worst equally — in favour of the most obvious explanation, that the whole process had been so rushed that muddle, and purely pragmatic considerations such as dimensions, had presided.

When he came to the works themselves, he began as he often did with a history lesson for the benefit of readers for whom first principles still needed to be provided or consolidated. July 1830 had drawn a line under 'la grande peinture'; history painting, in the form in which it had prospered under the Revolution, Empire, and Restoration, had fallen with the Bourbons:

> Ce que l'on appelait jadis la peinture d'histoire n'existe pour ainsi dire plus, du moins à la manière dont l'entendaient David, Guérin, Girodet, Gros, Meynier et les célébrités de l'Empire et de la Restauration; un sujet noble et grave, traité d'une façon épique dans un style d'apparat et sous de grandes dimensions.[29]

Its demise was, he said, inevitable because a new, broader public wanted art whose subjects were closer to their own experience and aspirations and because the dimensions of history painting made it quite unsuited to the forms of modern habitation ('nul aujourd'hui n'est assez bien logé pour céder vingt pieds de muraille à la mythologie'). Only two broad categories of painting remained: mural, which was public and collective, and easel, private and individual, the first intimately related to the architectural spaces which it was designed to decorate and which implied specific technical procedures and constraints; the second, versatile, of modest dimensions and more adapted to the range of budgets, the size of accommodation, and the more frequent house-moves of modern urban life. It was an opposition that ran through French nineteenth-century art theory.[30] Gautier, however, extended the definition of easel painting in a revealing way: 'A elle, la fantaisie, le caprice, le fini d'exécution, la curiosité du détail, le précieux ou le ragoût de la touche; l'originalité peut s'y déployer librement: c'est de la peinture pour la peinture, de l'art pour l'art'. In this way he sought to broaden the definition of art for art's sake beyond the politically charged context of April 1848, in which it labelled those accused of opposing the idea of socially engaged art, to neutralize it by making it synonymous with the entire range of modern easel practice, in which artists and patrons shared a modern emphasis on the display of the medium as a token of originality and value.

The problem in the modern age of individualism, said Gautier, was that mural art had declined in the shadow of easel painting's spectacular market-driven growth. The July Monarchy had at least begun to address the problem by commissioning the decoration of Parisian churches and public buildings.[31] He urged the republic to rise to the challenge of taking state patronage of public art to another level: 'Il faut que dans cinq ou six ans d'ici tous les monumens de Paris, devenu la métropole de la liberté, aient revêtu une robe éclatante de chefs-d'œuvre'. The studios of Renaissance Italy would provide the model for national workshops of the arts.[32] Groups of young artists would decorate public buildings under the direction and supervision of an established master, instead of wasting their time painting for the Salon thousands of works that no one wanted to buy. The republic would provide the decorative programmes, administrative structures, and budgets. Indeed it had already begun to do so, and this idea, 'neuve il y a huit jours, va, tant les choses marchent vite à présent, passer de l'état de rêve à celui de réalité'. Only days before, Paul Chenavard had received a commission to decorate the Panthéon.[33]

When Gautier turned to the painting itself on show in 1848, he began with France's two greatest living painters: Ingres, as usual absent from the Salon, and Delacroix, as usual present. In 1848 the art of Ingres was more than ever the key issue facing French painting as far as Gautier was concerned. In the context of the jury-free Salon which facilitated the promotion of categories of painting (landscape and genre) to which Ingres himself was unsympathetic, the painter's 'longue bouderie du saint Symphorien' seemed to Gautier to be tantamount to desertion in his country's hour of need.[34] Adopting the indignant rhetoric of the republican *pur et dur*, he found Ingres guilty of treason for forgetting that le Beau was a democratic right and not an aristocratic privilege:

> Nous le déclarons ici coupable du crime de haute trahison envers l'art. Le beau appartient à tous, et nul n'a le droit de l'accaparer pour soi. On devrait forcer le peintre du *Plafond d'Homère* et du *Vœu de Louis XIII* à se présenter tous les ans au Salon. Il doit à son pays la vue de ses tableaux.

This vision of Ingres being hauled before a revolutionary tribunal was not entirely tongue-in-cheek and Gautier returned in the next paragraph to what he saw as the painter's dereliction of duty.[35] The *Apothéose d'Homère*, painted in 1827 for the ceiling of the Salle Clarac in the Louvre's Musée Charles X, and the *Vœu de Louis XIII*, painted in 1824 for the cathedral at Montauban and exhibited to great acclaim in that year's Salon before being installed in the cathedral two years later, were for Gautier two of the defining works of modern French painting, and he had no doubt at all that the art of the republic needed to be guided by their example.

The problem of Ingres's absence was compounded for Gautier by what he implied was the relative weakness of Delacroix's submission that year. Though any exhibition of the painter's work could be relied on to generate a warm response on Gautier's part and 1848 was in broad terms no exception, his comments on individual works fell some way short of a ringing endorsement. To be sure, the dramatic arrangement and range of emotional tone in the *Christ au tombeau* was vintage Delacroix, and for those trying to decide whether, in the case of the painting's most controversial feature, the dissonant red drapery of the kneeling figure in the foreground, 'ce ton si éclatant au milieu d'une scène de désolation', was on the part of this 'coloriste si fin et si poétique, une faute, un oubli ou un calcul', Gautier of course had the answer: it served to make all the other colours look drab and lugubrious, in keeping with the subject.[36] In *La Mort de Valentin* from Goethe's *Faust*, on the other hand, though he found the Marguerite figure 'vraiment sublime', he did little more than tell the story for the reader's benefit and confirm the accuracy of Delacroix's representation of the German streets in which the action is set, a sure sign that the painting as a whole had not inspired him. The five lines of verse into which he transcribed Marguerite's anguished pose merely returned to poetry what was poetry's. He found the composition of *Comédiens ou bouffons arabes* (Figure 2.1) diffuse, and certain tones fell short of his idea of an oriental tonal harmony. The fact that he did not engage at all with the highly topical critical debate, in which the colourist trends which Delacroix represented were thought to be the real beneficiaries of the revolution that year, compounds the sense created by his commentary that, for Gautier, 1848 was not a major Delacroix Salon.[37]

In the following four articles Gautier turned his attention to the artists of the next generation on whom his hopes rested for new forms of history painting through which a new and broader public might learn to appreciate the value of its legacy. It was a bold decision to begin with the 24-year-old Jean-Léon Gérôme, who in 1848 was making only his second Salon appearance. On the other hand, the work he had submitted in 1847, *Jeunes Grecs faisant battre des coqs*, had transformed the painter overnight into the leader of a new group calling itself the *néo-grecs*, largely thanks to Gautier's commentary on it.[38] It had been primarily a work of apprenticeship undertaken in response to Gérôme's failed attempt at the Prix de Rome in 1846 and might have been considered as little more than a promising achievement for a first Salon entry but for the fact that Gautier had homed in on it as the sort of antique genre painting that might interest the public in more elevated subjects than those of realism and modern genre. According to Champfleury, Gautier and *La Presse* were orchestrating a campaign to promote Gérôme as the leader of a neoclassical new wave, and the award of a third-class medal to the painter by the Salon's *jury des récompenses* may have reinforced the idea.[39] This success ensured that, one year on, conservative and progressive elements alike were waiting for Gérôme.

In 1848 the painter, in a sign of his already mature alertness to the market, sent to the Salon not an antique genre follow-up to his *Jeunes Grecs* but one history painting, *Anacréon, Bacchus et l'Amour*, a Madonna, and a portrait.[40] *Anacréon* (Figure 2.2) catered to the serious critical debates surrounding the Neo-Greek group's adaptation of history painting, while the Madonna was targeted at the Catholic constituency of public and private buyers, the safest port in the storm battering the art market that year, and portraiture was a potentially lucrative sideline to the artist's work in more prestigious categories. As history painting, *Anacréon* attracted

FIG. 2.1. Eugène Delacroix, *Comédiens ou bouffons arabes*, 1848,
Tours, Musée des Beaux-Arts.
© The Bridgeman Art Library

more attention than the other two works, much of it negative. It was attacked by conservative supporters of the academic tradition for its flattening of form and use of pale colour, which they saw as another example of Ingres's betrayal of the Davidian legacy, and by progressive opponents of the same academic tradition for its failure to adapt Ingres's teaching to the expression of modern ideas.[41] From both sides it was the same charge of mannerism, not a new one by any means in 1848 as far as Ingres and his pupils were concerned.[42] Recognizing the seriousness of the criticism, Gautier met it head-on: 'On accuse le jeune artiste de maniérisme, de puérilités archaïques d'étude ou même de pastiche des anciens maîtres'; but mannerism, far from being an anachronistic affectation, enjoyed, he said, the highest artistic and cultural credentials of which Michelangelo, no less, was the source.[43] The landscape background in *Anacréon* recalled Titian and the putti would not have been out of place in a Raphael, but Gérôme, being 'naturellement maniéré', did not imitate these early masters any more than he did Ingres. He painted like them because he had their artistic temperament: 'il leur ressemble, non parce qu'il les imite, mais parce qu'il est pareil.' The overall greyish-brown tones of *Anacréon* might appear cold but the sobriety and complex tonal harmony demonstrated outstanding technical skill and were entirely appropriate to the melancholy subject, which Gautier helpfully translated for his readers into the modern and more accessible idiom of the *chansonnier* as Death's presence at the feast, 'thème éternel et douloureusement gai de toutes les chansons à boire'. True, *Anacréon* was less 'agréable d'aspect' than *Jeunes Grecs* but it was, he claimed, intellectually more profound and technically more accomplished. It showed that the brilliant student was extending his range, broadening his skills, and consolidating his position in contemporary painting. Few agreed with this assessment.[44] Six weeks later, however, the State paid Gérôme ten thousand francs for *Anacréon*, which appeared to confirm that he had emerged unscathed from some heavyweight criticism and that Gautier himself had been vindicated for his support of the work.

After Gérôme, Gautier turned to another professional acquaintance and personal friend, Théodore Chassériau, who exhibited in 1848 his huge oriental scene *Le Jour du Sabbat dans le quartier juif de Constantine*.[45] The previous year Gautier had fired off another volley against the Salon jury for rejecting this work, which he described as 'le premier où l'Orient moderne soit représenté avec les proportions et le style de l'histoire'.[46] One year on, the rejection served as a badge of honour as he presented the work as an example of the renewal of history painting that could be achieved if artists embraced the new subjects he had identified in his opening article. Previous orientalists such as Decamps and Marilhat had retained the dimensions of easel painting for their oriental scenes. In their work the human figure was episodic, setting off a street, building, or caravan in their tales of oriental life. In the *Sabbat*, on the other hand, the Orient was depicted 'avec des proportions *historiques*' (Gautier's italics) and with the epic vision that these proportions implied. The epic story it told was one of loss, of the impending demise of a civilization on the point of colonial extinction, victim of that very progress which Gautier had embraced, for just as he espoused the call for new subjects in a new age, so he also indulged the nostalgia for lost innocence which haunted its advocates.[47] The analysis of

Fig. 2.2. Jean-Léon Gérôme, *Anacréon, Bacchus et l'Amour*, 1848, Toulouse, Musée des Augustins. © The Bridgeman Art Library

the painting was the longest Gautier devoted to a single work in his entire review that year, but friendship cannot account entirely for its length and prominent early position. Chassériau was among the brightest hopes of 1848, for he appeared to be the most talented of Ingres's pupils, the most willing to pursue the technical and intellectual issues raised by Delacroix, and the best equipped, therefore, to reconcile the line of the one with the colour of the other. The *Jour du Sabbat*, the most important result of his North African journey in 1846, was, said Gautier, his most ambitious attempt to bring his two masters together.

As seen by Gautier, Chassériau's Orient was a 'beau rêve coloré des feux du soleil d'Afrique' and Constantine's Jewish women, dressed in their Sabbath finery, its purest expression. On their behalf Chassériau had drawn on his classical repertoire and Gautier explained their relationship to its medieval princesses, biblical heroines and goddesses of antiquity. In the blank stare, weary gesture, and indolent attitude thought to characterize those who inhabited hot climates, he identified the resignation of the women faced with the impending disappearance of their culture and identity as their city became just another outpost of Parisian manners and fashion. They were the 'belles créatures que la civilisation n'a pas déformées', and the description of face, body, dress, and jewellery shows us what is about to disappear. Through subject and theme, through the Greek beauty of the figures and the oriental violence of the climate, the statuesque linearity and bold colour, Chassériau appeared to wrestle with the tensions between his classical and Romantic instincts. It was a conflict that Gautier himself knew well. His instinct in painting as in poetry was to look for the ways in which classical training had channelled and disciplined Romantic energy. Despite the great qualities of the *Jour du Sabbat*, Chassériau appeared to him to have allowed its Romantic elements to slip the classical leash. He had indulged 'le plaisir de faire un bouquet de tons comme un simple coloriste', the demands of colour had overwhelmed his normally more careful brushwork, producing in places the unfinished aspect of a sketch. His prodigious facility was becoming dangerous, compromising the 'style', 'pureté', and 'noblesse' necessary for serious art. The warning appears designed both to reassure his readers that friendship had not blinded his judgement and to remind them that the philosophical ambition and formal practices of the classical programme, albeit adapted to new subjects and new tastes, remained central to the future direction of French painting.

The conflicting models of emulation that the work of Ingres and Delacroix offered painters of the next generation were a natural transition in his sixth article to the work of Jules Ziegler. Gautier had supported Ziegler since 1833, when in his first Salon review he had praised his *Giotto dans l'atelier de Cimabue* as 'un des morceaux les plus remarquables du Salon'.[48] Five years later, in his review of the Salon of 1838, he had selected Ziegler and his *Daniel dans la fosse aux lions* as the subject of his first commentary, describing him as the leader of a group of colourists who had emerged in the late 1820s in the first heady days of the Romantic revolution led by Delacroix. They had, he said, submitted their colourist instincts to the rigours of Ingres's cult of line, re-emerging the following decade with these instincts intact but disciplined by Ingres's teaching.[49] In Ziegler's case, the Spanish colourism that Gautier had identified in his work had been nicely timed to coincide with the opening in 1838 of the Musée Espagnol and to place him at the head of what predictably became known as the *école néo-espagnole*.[50] The Légion d'honneur followed, and with his career firmly launched as one of the brightest new stars in the Salon firmament, Ziegler had turned his attention to the decorative arts in which he proposed to carve out a second career in the growing applied arts and crafts market emerging in the mid-1830s and for which his success in the Salon would provide important credentials. In 1839 he set up a factory near Beauvais for the production of relief-decorated, salt-glazed stoneware. This second career, however, seriously disrupted the first, and in the years following his success in the Salon of 1838 he sent nothing to the annual exhibition. By the time he did, in 1844, he had been largely forgotten. In 1847 he had returned with *Le Songe de Jacob* and *Judith aux portes de Béthulie*, the second of which in particular had aroused strong interest but divided the critics.[51] Gautier had been the most prominent of its supporters and had stressed its dark and violent atmosphere, derived in his view from Spanish sources.[52] In 1848 Ziegler sought to build on the impact that he had achieved the year before by reworking the Spanish theme in *Charles Quint à Saint Just*, but he had not reckoned on the abolition of the jury and on the size of the exhibition which resulted. Evidently Gautier was needed again.

On 26 April 1848, Ziegler wrote to him (*Corr.*, III, 337–38):

> Mon cher ami
>   Si vous avez à dire quelques mots de mon Charles quint faites le demain je vous en prie.
>   C'est un symbole de *pouvoir déchu* [Ziegler's emphasis] qui aurait semblé une recherche d'actualité si le tableau n'eut été envoyé avant le 20 février. Les peintres ont droit aussi quelquefois au titre de vates consacré aux poètes. C'est un tableau de petite dimension il est vrai mais c'est de l'histoire sous tous les rapports. Ce matin vous mettez le père Ingres en possession des arcanes de Rome et de Florence, Zurbaran aurait du m'échoir en partage. Je réclame. faites [sic] cela demain; cela ou tout autre chose, mais ne m'oubliez pas.
>   votre bien dévoué dans le passé et dans l'avenir
>   J. Ziegler

As the letter indicates, with only one painting in the Salon, and one of modest dimensions at that, a powerful supportive commentary from Gautier, coming as early as possible in his review, was very important to Ziegler. In his letter he urged him to write it that very day and suggested possible approaches, but adding that if Gautier had a better one, that would be fine too. The one approach he preferred to avoid was the most obvious one, that of the topicality of the subject. The contemporary resonances of a painting which showed the abdicated emperor in his monk's cell, all the trappings of power abandoned, and, in the background, the coffin he would soon occupy, could hardly have been clearer in April 1848. On the other hand, if the Romantic poets had made visionary foresight a decisive asset for an artist in the changing and more speculative modern art economy, vulgar opportunism had no such value. Just in case anyone should think, therefore, that he had rushed the work out to coincide with Louis-Philippe's abdication, Ziegler reminded Gautier that he had sent it off to the Salon jury before 20 February, the deadline for submission of work that year and a few days before the unforeseen events which triggered the collapse of the regime.

One approach which Ziegler did suggest was that of the painting's generic status. *Charles Quint* was, he said, history painting, with the prestige that this still implied *quand même* in the traditional hierarchy of subjects, but history as the Romantic generation, reared on Walter Scott, understood it, unburdened by all that mythology to which the modern art public was less sympathetic than its predecessors.[53] But the key approach, as the remainder of Ziegler's letter made clear, was the Spanish reference already associated with his work. He referred to Gautier's fourth article on the Salon which had appeared that morning. The following extract was what had prompted him to write his letter:

> Jamais la connaissance des procédés, le maniement de la brosse et des couleurs, les façons d'empâter et de glacer, tout le côté matériel de l'art, n'ont été plus loin; Venise a été forcée de livrer ses secrets un à un à des questionneurs pressans. La nuit de Rembrandt a été pénétrée, et l'on en sait autant qu'Anvers sur Rubens. Florence et Rome ont été obligées aussi de faire leurs confessions dans l'oreille du père Ingres, et malgré l'air rébarbatif de ses saints, les plaies sanguinolentes de ses Christs et les frocs livides de ses moines cadavéreux, il a bien fallu que l'Espagne catholique livrât sa sombre et riche palette. Murillo a laissé analyser les lèvres pourpres de ses vierges, et Zurbaran les blessures bleuâtres de ses martyrs.

In the promotion of a modern French painter in the mid-nineteenth century few marketing ploys were quite as effective as associating his name with that of a major European Old or Modern Master. In the late 1830s, thanks in no small part to Gautier, Ziegler had acquired the title of French Zurbaran, and though in the intervening period he had been too busy on his second career to protect this status, in 1848 he wanted to reassert what he said was his rightful claim to the title, and urged Gautier to reaffirm his support for it.

Gautier, loyal to his friends as ever, responded with all the speed that Ziegler had requested. Two days later, his sixth article on the Salon began with a long commentary on *Charles Quint à Saint Just*. Sure enough, he began with its generic affiliation, stating that though the work possessed neither the dimensions nor the cast of characters associated with traditional history painting, the artist's 'serious and austere' treatment of his subject had raised the work above the anecdotal to the higher moral and philosophical ground associated with history painting. There followed a four-paragraph description of the subject which took up two-thirds of the commentary. In the first two paragraphs Gautier did not refer to the painting at all but embroidered at length and with all due pathos on the story of Charles V's rehearsal of his own funeral ceremony at which 'il se joue à lui-même la lugubre comédie de ses funérailles', describing this 'terrible auto-sacremental' as 'tout à fait dans le goût espagnol', in preparation for his description of the painting itself. Ziegler had chosen the moment when the abdicated emperor contemplated a miniature showing him in all his former glory.[54] The reader was invited to share the feelings of regret and uncertainty with which the emperor was said to have been visited at this poignant, truly historical moment. The commentary is vintage Gautier, returning to literature what is literature's, drawing out the intellectual, emotional, and moral resonances of the historical narrative before coming to the means by which the painter had resolved the difficulties of its transposition to his own medium.

For his account of these pictorial means, Gautier carried out Ziegler's instructions to the letter, devoting four paragraphs to his description of him as the modern French exponent of the Spanish school's characteristic strengths:

> M. Ziégler semble avoir surpris le secret de ces maîtres [de la Péninsule] à la fois si mystiques et si positifs, revêtant l'idéal le plus abstrait des formes les plus palpitantes de la réalité, et mettant au service du catholicisme le plus spiritualisé la plus puissante exécution matérielle: son talent se rapproche de celui de Zurbaran que nous venons de citer et d'un autre peintre aussi de l'école andalouse, mais beaucoup moins connu en France, nous voulons parler de Juan Valdès Léal, dont les chefs-d'œuvre sont à l'hôpital de la Charité à Séville.

In September 1837 Gautier had presented the work of Zurbaran in his first article on the collection that would be unveiled a few months later as the Louvre's Musée Espagnol. In November 1841 he had published in the *Revue des deux mondes* the first section of his long poem 'Deux tableaux de Valdes Léal'.[55] He was well qualified, therefore, to provide in 1848 a renewed authentification of Ziegler's Spanish credentials and made a series of general analogies between Ziegler's technique in *Charles Quint à Saint Just* and that of the Spanish artists. Having made them, he switched abruptly from the expert's technical discourse of artistic affiliations and painterly means to that of the dealer's promotional literature aimed at the market. *Charles Quint*, he says, would not be out of place between a Zurbaran and a Valdes Leal on the walls of Philip II's Escorial. Having by then worked on *La Presse* for twelve years, Gautier was at ease with publicity's sublimations of the aesthetic, and in his commentary Ziegler's latest work shared by association the prestige enshrined in Zurbaran's Old Master *valeur sûre*, Valdes Leal's Old Master prospects, and the hallowed location of Philip II's palace museum.[56] A first-class medal at the Paris Salon may not have been an achievement at quite that level but once again Gautier's support almost certainly played a part in it. In any event the jury's decision vindicated his judgement.

Gautier followed his efforts on Ziegler's behalf with a long and uneven piece on another of Ingres's pupils, Henri Lehmann. His religious subject *La Vierge au pied de la croix*, one of three commissioned by the July Monarchy for a chapel of the church of Saint-Louis en l'Île, aroused interest for what appeared to be his attempt to emerge from Ingres's influence by using more dramatic light effects and intense colours, an initiative to which Gautier was more sympathetic than other critics.[57] He had reservations about the painting's pyramidal composition, which he found a little too theatrical for the subject, but none at all about Lehmann's representation of Mary, in whom Gautier saw the suffering of the mother rather than the majesty of the Mother of God.[58] In an abrupt switch from maternal grief to *gauloiserie*, he noted that in *Les Syrènes* the sirens, making 'une consommation de poses plastiques assez provoquantes', were evidently counting more on their bodies than on their voices to attract Ulysses and were arranged in poses owing more to geometry than to natural movement. Of the portraits, the most successful was that of Mme A.H.

(Mme Arsène Houssaye) since its naturalness had survived the painter's mannerisms, but Gautier's praise was dictated more by his friendship with the Houssayes. In all, Gautier's analysis of Lehmann's works was supportive but hardly amounted to a vote of confidence in the painter's capacity to inherit the mantle of Ingres.

In his seventh article, his last on history painting, Gautier reflected on the failure of a series of artists to fulfil the promise of their early careers. Hesse, Guignet, Gallait, Schnetz had all succumbed to the disease of hard, inflexible line and heavy opaque colours. In his *Serment du jeu de paume* Couder had failed to rise to the occasion of this 'magnifique élan qui a donné l'impulsion au monde moderne'. In particular, he had failed to overcome the problems that modern dress created for scenes of apotheosis and had made the revolutionary gathering look like bailiffs in a comic opera. Gautier reflected on what Delacroix, Couture, or Chenavard might have made of the same subject and his description was a catalogue of everything that Couder's work lacked.[59]

Having finished with the works that were 'plus ou moins historiques', Gautier turned to genre painting. He included in this category the 'école réaliste' as it had emerged during the 1840s, and it is no coincidence that he began with Millet, whose painting *Le Vanneur* was the revelation from within that unofficial school in 1848.[60] Gautier suggested that Millet's labouring of paint in the work might have been designed to cause maximum offence to 'les bourgeois *à menton glabre*, comme disait Pétrus Borel' and piled up in mock outrage verbal equivalents of its crude technique.[61] The knowing, self-mocking reference to the anti-bourgeois posturing of his *Jeunes-France* youth already helped to defuse the threat posed by Millet's subversive handling of paint, but Gautier went further in praise of its surprising effects: 'Eh bien! ce mortier, ce gâchis épais à retenir la brosse est d'une localité superbe', the winnower's pose was 'magistrale', and the overall effect so authentic that even colour features as potentially disruptive as the red handkerchief tied around the figure's head and setting off the blue of his torn clothes were successfully integrated.[62] Millet only had to heed Gautier's advice and reduce 'de quelques centimètres l'épaisseur de ses empâtements' to remain, he assured him, 'un coloriste robuste et chaleureux' but gain 'l'agrément d'être compréhensible'. As it was, the decision by the *jury de placement* to exhibit the painting in the Salon Carré was a sign that it already enjoyed powerful support.[63] It seems clear that Gautier recognized, on the evidence of *Le Vanneur*, that Millet was a force to be reckoned with and that he therefore needed to be given advice while he was still young enough to listen. The State's decision in August to pay five hundred francs for the painting, ten times the going rate for Millet's work up to that point, may have struck Gautier as quite an accurate market value to place on his words of approval laced with caution.[64]

Some commentators in 1848 thought that Millet's handling of paint in *Le Vanneur* was derived, like that of many other painters, from Diaz.[65] The Salon that year was notable for a change in direction in Diaz's work, and Gautier suggested that it was at least partly due to his attempt to shake off the growing number of Diaz imitators trying to cash in on his successful formula.[66] During the July Monarchy Diaz had secured a steadily rising number of patrons buying into nostalgia for early-eighteenth-century landscapes and *sujets galants* combined with the modern

Romantic virtues of originality and spontaneity associated with his sketch-like treatment. In the Salon of 1848, his *Départ de Diane* was a much larger work than his usual output, and the critics discussed the success or otherwise of his attempt to integrate the firmer lines of Primaticcio and the first school of Fontainebleau into his usual handling of colour, derived from Corregio and Prud'hon. Gautier applauded Diaz for being prepared to break away from his tried and trusted formula but concluded that the painter did not possess the drawing skills needed for work of larger dimensions and would do better to stick with a system that worked for him: 'son *Départ de Diane* ne vaut pas, à notre avis, ces merveilleux bouquets de couleurs, ces splendides écrins de pierreries [...] ce microcosme soyeux, satiné, pelucheux, pleins de bluettes et de rayons.' In a grand gesture of self-reproach which was at the same time a reminder of Gautier's self-proclaimed right to teach the painter his business, he publicly apologized to Diaz for encouraging him to experiment with the subjects and formal disciplines of *la grande peinture*, thereby contributing to the unsuccessful *Départ de Diane*.[67]

Only at the end of his ninth article did he come to the 'école réaliste', introduced in the preceding article with reference to Millet. The Leleux brothers, Adolphe and Armand, were the leading representatives of this first official realism, sanctioned by the purchase of Adolphe's *Danse paysanne* in 1842 by the duc d'Orléans. In 1846 Gautier had called Adolphe 'le Léopold Robert de la Bretagne et des Pyrénées', which aptly summarized the appeal of his picturesque scenes from Breton and Pyrenean peasant life.[68] In the early stages critics tended to relegate Armand's work as a derivative by-product of that of his older brother, and it was to Gautier that Adolphe turned in 1847 for help in persuading them to consider Armand's work on its own merits (*Corr.*, III, 189–90). Gautier duly obliged in his review of their work in the Salon of 1847 and repeated the point the following year, when each of the brothers, he said, 'marche à présent dans sa route, et la distance qui les sépare devient plus grande de jour en jour'. In 1848 he praised Armand's abandonment of the 'intérieurs sombres et bitumeux' of his scenes of Breton family life in favour of the rustic grace of *La Fenaison*, with its happy peasants and nature in sunlight, which Gautier called 'une églogue sans mensonge', a very Parisian contradiction in terms for French rural life in the mid-nineteenth century. He was, however, disappointed by Adolphe for trying, like Diaz, to be what he was not. In his *Improvisateur arabe* he saw again the worrying signs of facility and lazy imitation of Delacroix that he had already noted the previous year, and though these defects were, he modestly said, 'invisibles probablement pour des yeux moins attentifs que les nôtres', he urged Adolphe to address them and to remember that he was a realist, no more and no less: 'l'imagination, la mémoire n'existent dans son talent qu'à de très faibles doses: faire le mot à mot de la nature, tel est son lot.' The painter's submission to the Salon of 1849 (see below, pp. 106–08) suggests that Gautier's comments had hit home.

In genre painting, however, 1848 was the Meissonier Salon, and Gautier devoted one of his longest individual commentaries to the painter's work exhibited that year. As part of his commercial strategy of making buyers come to him rather than going to them himself, Meissonier had not submitted work to the Salons of 1846 and 1847, with the result that news of his return in 1848 generated more than

enough interest to offset the negative impact of open access.[69] Six years earlier
Gautier had been virtually alone in recognizing that Meissonier's relationship to
tradition went beyond the obvious legacy of the Flemish *petits maîtres* with whom
the painter would be henceforth invariably linked. He was, Gautier said, not merely
the equal of Metzu, Dow, and Mieris, since 'M. Meissonier, à la vérité du dessin,
à la finesse de ton, au précieux du pinceau, joint une qualité que les Hollandais ne
possèdent guère, le style'.[70] The composition of the *Fumeur*, the colour harmonies
of the *Joueur de basse*, both shown in the Salon of 1842, were those of the 'vieux
maîtres', by whom Gautier meant the Italian, not Flemish, masters. He made this
point in order to place Meissonier's art above what he saw as the public's trivial
interest in subject matter (the unnamed but immediately recognizable *repoussoir*
was Delaroche).[71] In 1848 he repeated the assertion that Meissonier's work could
be placed 'à côté, sinon au-dessus des productions les plus achevées des Flamands et
des Hollandais' because of his 'largeur de faire étonnante', a largeness of brushstroke
which had none of the 'pointilleuses mesquineries de la miniature, comme leur
dimension pourrait le faire craindre'.[72] Far from being confined within the *petit
maître* status of Flemish and Dutch genre painting, Meissonier was for Gautier in
1848 a genuine 'grand maître', whose work re-established contact with an authentic
early- to mid-eighteenth-century pre-Davidian national tradition and with modern
landscape painting in which the French had been since 1830 the undisputed masters.
So, in his *Trois amis* Meissonier was, Gautier said, as French as Chardin and the café
Procope; the *Jeu de boules* was pure Louis XV, its garden could have been designed
by one of Le Nôtre's successors, and any French Romantic landscapist would have
been proud to have painted its arbour.[73] The painter's return to the Salon in 1848
was, therefore, well timed to take advantage of the revision of French art history
on which the Second Republic was about to embark, notably in its reorganization
of the national collections (see below, pp. 122–25).

Having dispensed in the second half of his eleventh article with the imitators of
Meissonier and in the first half of the twelfth with those of Watteau, Gautier turned
to the animal painters as transition between genre and landscape. In 1848 their
undisputed leader was Rosa Bonheur, and Gautier played his part in promoting
the Second Republic's favourite female artist, the exception who proved the rule.
He ranked her alongside the Dutch seventeenth-century *animalier* Paulus Potter
— praise indeed, since he was, according to Gautier, 'le Raphaël de l'étable'.
Bonheur's *Taureaux de Cantal*, was, he said, perfectly observed and intelligently and
sincerely reproduced. In its representation of the calm solitude of the countryside,
it combined, he said, an authentic contemporary realism with a classical simplicity
of effects. The State paid three thousand francs for it, which in terms of the art
market that summer was a fortune, but evidently not too high a price for France's
Raphael of the cowshed.

In a less succinct variation on the serial novel's *suite au prochain numéro*, Gautier
closed his twelfth article by announcing the subject of the next, which would
appear two days later:

> Maintenant, laissant de côté cette foule de personnages de tous les temps et de
> tous les pays, dirigeons-nous, après avoir donné une tape amicale sur le col des

étalons et sur le flanc des bœufs, vers les belles campagnes que déroulent devant nous les paysagistes. — Sortons avec eux de la ville triviale, inquiète, affairée et tumultueuse; allons chercher le repos et la fraîcheur au sein de cette nature, peinte il est vrai, mais aussi réelle que l'autre; car la création de l'art vaut la création de Dieu. Le ciel est bien, le soleil luit, l'aubépine jette sa neige et son parfum, allons par les prés, par les bois, par les vallons, par les collines, avec Corot, Flers, Lapierre, Anastasi et tous ces charmans compagnons de route qui nous apportent l'odeur des prés et l'arôme du jeune feuillage.

As we know and as Gautier himself already recognized, the development of French landscape painting in the first half of the nineteenth century was directly related to and coextensive with the growth of the city.[74] If there were so many landscape painters in France by the end of the July Monarchy, it was because the growth of Paris, particularly with the end of the Napoleonic wars, had created an environment in which they could thrive. Gautier's invitation to his readers to accompany the artists and himself on a trip to the countryside indicates the cultural changes driving the development of landscape art. The modern landscape painter was the companion, part tourist guide, part health professional, who led the spectator out of the corrupt, overcrowded, and exhausting capital in search of the restorative natural rhythms and equilibrium of the *belles campagnes*. Landscape was one form of the mass consumption of which Paris was the location, and Gautier's position on *La Presse* gave him a platform from which to mediate the cultural promotion (and, by implication, investment potential) of the art of natural landscape, which the Salon juries of the July Monarchy had worked so hard to frustrate.[75]

Once again it was via the potted history lesson that Gautier set about educating his readers in the stages of landscape's cultural formation. In the cyclical view of history characteristic of the Romantic imagination, landscape emerged only at an advanced stage of civilization, heralding a decline which would itself usher in a new beginning.[76] In the art of antiquity, nature was unknown except as an occasional decorative feature in frescoes; during the Middle Ages it was feared as a 'dangereuse tentatrice'; during the Renaissance it served as no more than a backcloth to the action of heroic figures. Seventeenth-century Dutch and Flemish artists, 'moins instruits en mythologie', were the first to paint the natural landscape for its own sake, which French art reached only two centuries later, having passed through the transitional phase of the 'paysage historique'.[77]

When Gautier turned to the work on show, the hierarchy of official art discourse, coinciding with his own hierarchy whose summit Ingres occupied permanently, again made itself felt. Though he recognized that colour rather than line seemed to be the dominant means through which nature presented itself to the artist, he began with Aligny, his Ingres of landscape, recalling his affection for the artist's severe line and serene colour which he had celebrated in a poem he could no longer quite remember but whose opening lines he (mis)quotes.[78] It immediately becomes clear, however, that in 1848 his evocation of Aligny's qualities was no more than nostalgia for what had been lost, sacrificed, as he saw it, 'par un esprit systématiquement rigoureux et cruel envers lui-même'. In Aligny's work, historical landscape's ancient virtues ('la grandeur, la noblesse, le charme austère et sobre qui naît du sacrifice, le sentiment de l'antique, un parfum de Théocrite et de Virgile, une élégance soutenue') had been reduced to a formulaic system of procedures which suppressed all authentic response to natural landscape. He had contracted a severe case of what Gautier called 'la Grèce aiguë, affection [*sic*] qui exige des doses réitérées de Normandie'. His failure was underlined by Corot's successful negotiation of the same visual and literary models. Where Aligny had surrendered his personal vision of nature to the artificial, Italianate *paysage composé*, in Corot's case classical training and literary imagination had remained the servants of the harmony in his work between temperament and the natural world: 'M. Corot, lui, garde toujours sa précieuse bonhomie, sa fraîcheur argentée, sa candeur d'églogue, et traduit Longus en style d'Amyot', the classical codes reinvigorated in the native soil into which they had been translated.[79]

The same affliction to which Aligny had succumbed and the same remedy required were exemplified by the work of Louis Cabat, whom Gautier considered to be the founder of modern French landscape painting. Following the revelation of Cabat's art in the Salon of 1833, Gautier had placed him at the forefront of his campaign against what historical landscape had become during the Empire and Restoration.[80] In Cabat's case too, however, 'le voyage d'Italie l'a perdu lui comme bien d'autres', struck down like Aligny by 'la maladie du style'. Fortunately in 1848 he had returned to his national roots in his *Mare de Brecquigny* but, in a superb *parisianisme*, Gautier stated that Picardy's landscapes, 'comme une épouse légitime supplantée par une courtisane étrangère', had not yet forgiven Cabat for his Italian infidelities. Gautier urged him to get back to some real nature much closer to home: 'cher paysagiste, vous devriez bien venir vous installer dans un terrain inculte que nous vous indiquerons près de l'avenue Sainte-Marie'. Two landscapes by Hoguet of sites 'très peu poétiques en apparence', Montmartre and the Pont-Neuf, reinforced the advice, confirming that the unidealized landscape now reached the very doorstep of the urban consumer at which the genre was targeted. A series of landscapes by the relatively unknown Émile Lapierre catered for the range of forms this consumption took: an Italian scene of a covered path in Florence's Boboli gardens but in which the familiar pillar bearing its marble vase had shed its historical baggage and instead stood out against the sapphirine sky like 'une joue de jeune fille près du ruban bleu de son chapeau de paille'; a hunting scene in which the hunt had lost the scent and a man on horseback asked directions from a peasant in a deserted landscape whose sunset had 'des rougeurs menaçantes' which did not bode well for the rider's safe return; an illustration of Musset's *A quoi rêvent les jeunes filles*, in which Ninon and Ninette converse beneath a statue of Love, and two works, simply entitled *Printemps* and *Paysage*, whose 'grâce printanière' and 'bouquet parfumé' evoke for Gautier the atmosphere of German lieder.[81] The broad historical account of the development of a French natural landscape art was thus followed by an example of one of the journeymen artists who produced it for the mass market. Between producer and consumer, Gautier's short descriptions provided the *mode d'emploi*.

Faced with a huge number of landscapes, Gautier did not stray for long from those who had emerged by 1848 into positions of leadership in the category of natural landscape, and in his final article he returned to Troyon, who 'se place définitivement parmi les premiers paysagistes', and Huet, who, after a long absence from the Salon, 'reparaît avec une quantité de tableaux de pays différents et d'effets variés qui nous prouvent une absence bien employée'. Both were masters of the atmospheres of the countryside, Troyon of its 'humidités' and 'verdures', Huet of its 'grandes masses', to which he sacrificed detail. Huet's work in particular contained an important lesson relating to the stage of development French natural landscape had reached by the end of the July Monarchy:

> Les artistes s'occupent plus maintenant de la rugosité d'une roche, de l'empâtement d'un tronc ou d'une touffe de feuilles que de la physionomie même de la nature. Les sites ont leur mélancolie et leur sourire, leurs tristesses et leurs joies; leurs heures de gaîté folle et de morne abattement, qu'il faut traduire dans leur sens général, sous peine de ne faire qu'un mot à mot inexact. Ruysdael n'y manquait jamais, M. Paul Huet cherche toujours ce sens général et le trouve souvent.

The advocates of historical landscape had stressed the importance of mastering complex and detailed technical skills — the ability to reproduce in precise detail rock formations, tree shapes, the textures of foliage, and so on under different lights — to enable landscape to achieve the prestige associated with *la grande peinture*. From 1830 natural landscape had dethroned its historical counterpart but had retained the emphasis on technical skills. By the mid-1840s Gautier, far from being an art-for-art's-sake materialist, was leading a backlash against form for its own sake, and landscape was the most obvious category in which formal skills were leading to an increasingly undifferentiated mass production. Here, technical mastery of pictorial idioms was taking precedence over what Gautier called 'l'expression du paysage'. If the unidealized landscape was to achieve the critical stature and commercial success of Ruysdael and the seventeenth-century Dutch realists, modern French artists would, he said, have to pay more attention to nature's 'sens general' than they had to its 'mot à mot', to its meaning more than to its literal transcription. On one level the comment was a message for the growing number of realists; on another it brought Gautier back to the beginning of his review, and to his support for the new regime's plans to invest in public art through which to regenerate the skills of fresco art in the service of new ideas. As he had said in the paragraph which had prompted Ziegler's letter, never had knowledge of art's material processes been so advanced and, as he went on to say after the extract quoted earlier, at last the republic would put these skills to use:

> On sait tout faire, seulement on ne sait que faire. Ces mains si expertes, ces pinceaux si savans n'ont rien à peindre; et l'on voit ces pauvres artistes en peine errer le long des galeries et se répandre en toutes sortes de fantaisies plus voulues qu'inspirées: le thème à broder de ces mille variations qui sont tout l'art manque évidemment. La République le donnera sans doute.

The Republican initiative of the open-access Salon of 1848 would, Gautier knew, not be repeated. Other initiatives that year were potentially more far-reaching, and it is to these that we must now turn.

Notes to Chapter 2

1. Clément de Ris confirmed this view within days: 'L'abondance des œuvres qui en résulte est d'autant plus fâcheuse que le Salon de 1848, restreint dans de justes limites, eût présenté, ce nous semble, un intérêt qui disparaît dans le ridicule qui s'attache justement à beaucoup d'œuvres malencontreuses' ('Salon de 1848, III', *L'Artiste*, 26 March 1848, pp. 35–36 (p. 35)).

2. The republican art critic Théophile Thoré began his review of the Salon by celebrating the demise of the jury: 'La révolution de Février a surpris le jury académique en pleines fonctions. On avait commencé déjà la séparation des élus et des réprouvés [...] Mais, au bruit de l'insurrection contre la royauté, les familiers de la Liste civile n'ont eu que le temps d'ôter leurs perruques, et de se sauver. Pour n'être pas reconnu, M. A*** s'était tatoué le visage avec du bitume, et M. B***, comme Louis-Philippe, son maître, s'était coupé les favoris' ('Salon de 1848', *Le Constitutionnel*, 27 March 1848, in *Salons*, p. 557).

3. 'Le citoyen-Ministre de l'Intérieur charge le Directeur du Musée National du Louvre d'ouvrir l'exposition de 1848 sous délai de 15 jours. Tous les ouvrages envoyés cette année seront reçues sans exception. | Tous les artistes sont convoqués à l'École Nationale des Beaux-Arts le 5 mars 1848 à midi pour nommer une Commisssion de 40 membres [...] chargée du placement des ouvrages à exposer avec le concours de l'administration du Musée National' (quoted in Rousseau, *La Vie et l'œuvre de Philippe-Auguste Jeanron*, p. 91).

4. The official catalogue of the Salon of 1847 listed a total of 2321 works; that of 1848, 5180. The previous highest figure was 3318 in 1833, after which the Academy's more severe juries brought the admissions figures back closer to the 2000 mark reached by the end of the Restoration. See Mainardi, *The End of the Salon*, p. 19.

5. It was not unusual for him to begin his Salon reviews with sculpture, in recognition of that art's historical role as the basis of the Western tradition and of its place in his own system of the fine arts. In 1848 it may have seemed to him more important than usual to retain the format in order to reaffirm the continuing relevance of the values associated with sculpture. Alternatively, his reasons may have been more parochial, such as presenting as early as possible in his review Pradier's sculpture of *Nyssia*, with its debt to Gautier's own short story.

6. Indicators of this loose generic structure to the review are posted at strategic points. In the middle of the eighth article, for example, we read: 'Nous voici à peu près quittes avec les grands tableaux plus ou moins historiques [...] nous pourrons passer à la peinture de genre.'

7. Of Émile Champmartin's *Sainte Geneviève* (no. 806 in the Salon catalogue), for example, he wondered 'si la sainte est le prétexte des moutons, ou si les moutons sont le prétexte de la sainte. Nous avions eu d'abord l'idée de ranger cette toile parmi les tableaux historiques, et puis nous l'avons mise avec les tableaux de genre, mais la place n'y fait rien. Cet embarras se reproduit souvent dans une exposition si nombreuse et dans un temps où toutes les limites s'effacent' (*La Presse*, 5 May 1848).

8. 'Salon de 1848', p. 565.

9. A crude statistical analysis of the figures given in Neil McWilliam, *A Bibliography of Salon Criticism in Paris from the July Monarchy to the Second Republic, 1831–1851* (Cambridge University Press, 1991), indicates a 25% drop in the number of Salon reviews published in 1848 compared with previous years (77 as opposed to the average of just over 100 for the majority of the Salons of the 1840s). This lower figure remains the norm throughout the Second Republic. Only in 1857 does it return to its pre-1848 level, a result, presumably, of the interest generated by the Paris Universal Exposition of 1855.

10. See the attack on the jury in his closing remarks on the Salon of 1834 in *La France industrielle* (April 1834), 17–22 (p. 22).

11. 'Salon de 1847: le jury', *L'Artiste*, 14 March 1847, pp. 17–18, and 'Les Refus du jury', *L'Artiste*, 27 June 1847, pp. 218–21.

12. 'Invited' by Gautier to express his views in his own newspaper, Girardin proposed that the existing jury arrangements be retained but that artists be given the right of appeal against rejection of their work. Under his scheme, the Salon would close after forty days and reopen ten days later for a ten-day exhibition of the work submitted by appeal. The jury this time would

be the public: 'Le public jugerait en dernier ressort; d'une part il réformerait des jugements arbitraires et erronnés; d'autre part, il condamnerait les prétentions illégitimes et souvent ridicules' (*Corr.*, III, 184). It was in effect the first proposal for a Salon des Refusés. Gautier began his Salon of 1847 by quoting Girardin's letter and applauding the new role it would provide for the public, 'cet arbitre souverain' ('Salon de 1847', *La Presse*, 30 March 1847).

13. Gautier would certainly have known of the pro-Republican David d'Angers's proposal for the abolition of the Salon jury which had been published in *L'Artiste* on 11 April 1847. Gautier did not pick up, however, the sculptor's argument for abolition as a preliminary to the creation of a dual Salon system, involving a permanent exhibition, whose exhibits would be renewed every six months, and a quinquennial exhibition in which only the most outstanding work shown at the permanent exhibition during the previous five years would be shown. In 1850 Boissard de Boisdenier took up and reformulated David's dual exhibition idea but retained the role of the jury to ensure the minimum standards (or 'connaissance suffisante') necessary to prevent democracy descending into the anarchy of open access, as had been the case in his view in the Salon of 1848. See his two articles entitled 'De la condition des artistes et des moyens de l'améliorer', published in *L'Artiste* on 1 February (pp. 100–02) and 1 March 1850 (pp. 136–39).

14. 'Cette année, l'on a tout reçu et tout exposé. Le Salon offre-t-il beaucoup de différence avec les Salons des années précédentes qui avaient subi l'épuration préalable? Nullement. L'aspect général en est le même, à part quelques toiles barbares ou risibles dont le nombre ne dépasse pas une douzaine.'

15. Bayle Saint-John, an English friend of Jeanron, confirmed the temporary nature of the jury's demise: 'It was at his [Jeanron's] suggestion that it was resolved, for that one year, whilst new regulations were being decided on, all the works of art presented should be exhibited' (see Bayle Saint-John, *The Louvre, or Biography of a Museum* (London: Chapman Hall, 1855), p. 110. From early March 1848, discussion was already taking place on the form the jury would take from 1849. Houssaye, for example, initially believed that the election of the *jury de placement* by the artists themselves augured well for the future: 'Ce résultat fait songer à ce que sera le jury de l'an prochain, si, comme on doit le supposer, on a recours à la voie de l'élection pour le constituer' (*L'Artiste*, 12 March 1848, p. 12). Even Thoré felt that some 'comité intelligent' was needed to keep out the 'images excentriques' and the 'ordures inqualifiables' ('Salon de 1848', pp. 559–60). Despite the view of Clément de Ris that 'la nécessité d'un jury sérieux demeure suffisamment démontrée aujourd'hui à quelques esprits qui admettaient en principe la mesure expéditive que la nécessité a forcé de prendre cette année' ('Salon de 1848, III', pp. 35–36), Gautier persisted: 'Déjà nous avons vu avec chagrin des esprits bien intentionnés, mais timides, alarmés de quelques extravagances, redemander, sinon l'ancien jury, du moins une institution équivalente avec des garanties électives. Nous ne voulons pas que la porte soit fermée pour personne: aujourd'hui, l'exclusion pourrait être juste; demain, elle serait inique [...] L'admission de mille croûtes nous chagrinerait moins que le renvoi d'un seul tableau de mérite.'

16. 'Alors nous pourrons voir au Salon notre école régénérée unir dans un but commun tout le génie qu'elle éparpille aujourd'hui, et poursuivre de concert, non plus l'art pour l'art, pour ses finesses précieuses, pour ses habiles reflets des vieux maîtres, mais l'art pour le beau, pour le grand, pour le bon, l'art qui se vivifie dans l'esprit national et tire sa poésie de l'humanité' ('Salon de 1848', *Le National*, 23 March 1848).

17. Given the length of Gautier's Salon reviews, his usual practice was to begin writing soon after the Salon's opening and to complete a number of articles before the first appeared, so that the whole sequence could be published over a relatively short period of time and before the Salon closed (see *Corr.*, IV, 288–89).

18. As republicans in Paris feared, in the elections to the Constituent Assembly the provinces voted for a National Assembly which was moderate republican or conservative. See Maurice Agulhon, *1848 ou l'apprentissage de la république* (Paris: Éditions du Seuil, 1973), pp. 54–59, and Sylvie Aprile, *La IIe République et le Second Empire, 1848–1870* (Paris: Pygmalion, 2000), pp. 79–85.

19. *Jeanne Hachette*, marble statue, no. 4623. Beauvais, Hôtel de Ville. In 1848 Bonnassieux also exhibited a marble statue of *La Vierge mère* (no. 4624), commissioned for the church at Feurs (Loire). On Bonnassieux see Léo Armagnac, *Bonnassieux, statuaire, membre de l'Institut, 1810–1892* (Paris: Picard, 1897).

20. See the catalogue of the exhibition *Auguste Préault, sculpteur romantique, 1809–1879* (Paris: Gallimard/RMN, 1997), p. 158.

21. See Isabelle Leroy-Jay Lemaistre, ' "Ses œuvres sont les strophes en pierre, en marbre, en bronze, en bois, du poème de la douleur humaine" ', ibid., pp. 79–80.

22. In his first article on the Salon, he had already urged the Second Republic to create its own iconography: 'Les formules qu'employait la République de l'ancien régime ne peuvent en aucune manière convenir à la nouvelle, et s'en servir serait méconnaître ou fausser les tendances modernes.'

23. In the Orleanist *Revue des deux mondes*, de Mercey argued that Bonnassieux's academic training had prevented him from representing Jeanne with historical authenticity: 'Le talent pur et gracieux de M. Bonnassieux convenait mal à l'énergique représentation de l'héroïne populaire de Beauvais; l'attitude de la combattante est naturelle, mais elle n'indique pas suffisamment l'action. [...] Elle n'est ni assez femme ni assez soldat et n'est pas surtout assez fille du peuple' ('Le Salon de 1848', pp. 597–98). In the republican *Le National*, on the other hand, Haussard was very positive: 'Sa *Jeanne Hachette* est tout à la fois une figure ingénue et une statue idéale, la femme du peuple et l'héroïne. Il n'a touché et à la coiffe et à la robe portée par Jeanne qu'autant qu'il le fallait pour la noblesse de l'ajustement, et il n'a donné à la jeune héroïne que l'air de force et de grandeur qui convient à la simplicité populaire' ('Salon de 1848', 14 April 1848). As we shall see in the next chapter, Gautier believed that grace and distinction should be republican virtues too.

24. In 1848 Clésinger exhibited his marble statue *Bacchante* (no. 4667), and three marble busts, of Mme S. C... (no. 4668), Mme de L... (no. 4669) and Mme D... (no. 4670). Mme S.C. was Solange Clésinger, George Sand's daughter, who had married Clésinger in 1847, Mme D. was Sand herself (Mme Dudevant), Mme de L... was Elisa de Lucenay, a friend of Apollonie Sabatier, Baudelaire's future muse, 'La Présidente' (see below, note 26).

25. Even so, Gautier prefaced his commentary on the work itself with a volley of fireside maxims with which to justify Clésinger's decision to produce in 1848 a pendant to the *Femme piquée* of the previous year: 'Tout homme d'ailleurs a un type intérieur qu'il reproduit sans cesse. Chacun frappe sa monnaie à son coin [...]; il ne sort des choses que ce qu'elles contiennent. Il ne jaillit pas de vin d'une barrique d'eau et les pommiers ont toujours produit de fort mauvaises oranges', and so on. Gautier evidently believed that within his readership there was a constituency which could be encouraged to adhere to his choice of artists via these homilies to contemporary Parisian common sense.

26. It was alleged that Madame Sabatier had posed for the work at the instigation of her lover.

27. Again de Mercey's comments are revealing: 'l'art a rarement atteint à une réalité si saisissante, et cela sans rien sacrifier d'un certain idéal sans lequel l'art n'existe pas [...] c'est la souplesse et le jet hardi des sculpteurs du dernier siècle, combinés avec la grace académique de Canova, avec le naturalisme de M. Pradier [...] on doit lui savoir un gré infini [...] surtout de ce qu'il n'est ni Grec, ni Italien, de ce qu'il est lui-même' ('Le Salon de 1848', pp. 596–97). Haussard agreed with this assessment but saw it more in terms of promise than achievement. Having criticized Pradier for facility and repetition and praised the exuberance of Clésinger's strengths and weaknesses, he argued that 'la république va changer heureusement les tendances de M. Clésinger, agrandir et épurer sa pensée et sa main' ('Salon de 1848', 14 April 1848). The fact that within days of the revolution he had donated a bust of Liberty to the State was for Haussard an encouraging sign of this more positive direction his art would take.

28. 'Il ne faut pas reculer d'abord devant ce nombre effrayant de 5,180 ouvrages, reçues sans examen, et qui se déploient, à perte de vue, dans les longues enfilades des musées du Louvre. Pour la peinture, l'intérêt principal, la valeur sérieuse de l'exposition se concentre presque entièrement dans la partie la mieux éclairée du musée des tableaux: le salon carré et deux travées d'honneur, la première et la troisième de la grande galerie' ('Salon de 1848', 23 March 1848). On 15 June he closed his final article with a tribute to the 'nouvelle direction du Louvre, qui s'est piquée de justice et de sympathie pour chacun et pour tous, dans la distribution des places et de la lumière'.

29. Many commentators made the same point. By way of example, Clément de Ris: 'la peinture dite historique s'en va lentement, et, au point où elle était arrivée, nous n'avons pas la force de

lui adresser un regret. La plupart du temps elle était une manifestation de l'impuissance et de la faiblesse. MM. Blondel, Garnier, Picot, Abel de Pujol, etc., lui ont porté un coup qui l'a tuée.' ('Salon de 1848, III', p. 36); de Mercey: 'l'école historique, en retraite depuis bien des années, semble aujourd'hui s'être retirée de la lice et avoir laissé le champ libre à la peinture anecdotique' ('Le Salon de 1848', p. 284).

30. As Marc J. Gotlieb has shown in relation to Meissonier. See *The Plight of Emulation: Ernest Meissonier and French Salon Painting* (Princeton University Press, 1996), pp. 19–20.

31. In 1836 Gautier had sought to alert public opinion to this issue by attacking modern painters, sculptors, and architects for the misplaced individualism which had led each group to see its art as being distinct from, and superior to, that of the other two: 'Si l'architecte, le sculpteur et le peintre, cette trinité inséparable, voulaient se rejoindre, ils auraient bientôt fait rentrer dans leur ancien rang secondaire le maçon, le mouleur et le faiseur d'images' ('De l'application de l'art à la vie usuelle').

32. The importance of the example set in monumental art by the Italian Renaissance masters was another commonplace in mid-nineteenth-century art theory. See Gotlieb, *The Plight of Emulation*, p. 21. Gautier would almost certainly have known of the 1846 article by Gustave Planche in the *Revue des deux mondes* to which Gotlieb refers.

33. Marie-Claude Chaudonneret, 'Le Décor inachevé pour le Panthéon', in *Paul Chenavard: le peintre et le prophète* (Paris: RMN, 2000), pp. 67–79. On the July Monarchy's public art, see Marrinan, *Painting Politics for Louis-Philippe*; idem, 'Historical Writing and the Writing of History at Louis-Philippe's Versailles', in *The Popularization of Images: Visual Culture under the July Monarchy*, ed. by Petra ten-Doesschate Chu and Gabriel P. Weisberg (Princeton University Press, 1994), pp. 113–43; Georges Brunel, 'Peintures commandées pour les églises de Paris', in *Les Années romantiques: la peinture française de 1815 à 1850* (Paris: RMN, 1995), pp. 61–75, and, in the same volume, Claire Constans, 'Versailles: les grandes commandes', pp. 86–97.

34. On the attacks to which Ingres's *Martyre de saint Symphorien* had been subjected in the Salon of 1834 and his decision never again to submit his work to the Salon, see *Ingres 1780–1867* (Paris: Gallimard/Musée du Louvre Éditions, 2006), pp. 239–44 and 253–59); Shelton, 'Le Martyre de Saint Symphorien at the 1834 Salon', Chapter 1 of his *Ingres and his Critics*; Georges Vigne, *Ingres* (Paris: Citadelles & Mazenod, 1995), pp. 196–200.

35. Of Delacroix, Gautier said: 'il apporte à chaque Salon son tribut et se soumet, avec le plus complet abandon, à l'appréciation publique. Il ne fait pas le mystérieux et n'invite pas ses dévôts à venir l'admirer dans des chapelles particulières. Discuté violemment, exalté par les uns, dénigré par les autres, il ne s'est jamais piqué d'amour-propre, et loué ou blâmé, il continue son œuvre avec courage.' The 'chapelles particulières' and 'amour-propre' were unmistakeable references to Ingres.

36. 'Cette tache écarlate, plaquée au premier plan, donne une tristesse immense à la localité générale du tableau; elle rend terreux, malades, livides et verdâtres tous les autres tons. Grace à cette rude dissonance, rien n'est plus lugubre que ce ciel lourd, épais, grisâtre, où rempent [sic] des nuages éventrés.'

37. In *L'Artiste* of 9 April, Houssaye, referring to the opposition between the *dessinateurs* (Ingres and neoclassicism), and the *coloristes* (Delacroix and Romanticism), which, by the end of the July Monarchy (and for long after), served as the standard account of modern French painting, stated that the revolution of 1848 was a victory for the colourists: 'aujourd'hui [...] en art comme en politique la victoire a donné raison aux exubérants et aux coloristes' (p. 75). A week earlier in the same periodical, Clément de Ris had made the same point, having included the Davidians and the *juste milieu* painters as two further elements of the equation: 'Après avoir rejeté les formules étroites de l'ancienne académie, après avoir fait justice des principes inféconds de M. Delaroche, après s'être arrêté avec M. Ingres à aller chercher à travers trois siècles des tons effacés sur la palette du Perrugin ou de Raphaël, on arrive enfin à reconnaître que dans la sphère artistique aussi les idées ont progressé [...] et qu'enfin l'avenir appartient à ceux qui demandent la liberté dans l'art. Celui qui de nos jours personnifie le mieux ce symbole est M. Delacroix' ('Salon de 1848, IV', 2 April 1848, pp. 58–60 (p. 58)). In the republican daily *Le National*, however, Haussard expressed reservations about *Le Christ au tombeau*, *Bouffons arabes*, and the *Mort de Lara* ('Salon de 1848', 23 March 1848). On the Delacroix work shown in 1848 see Lee Johnson,

The Paintings of Eugène Delacroix, 6 vols (Oxford: Clarendon Press, 1981–89), III (1986), 12–14, 114–16, 190–91, 221–23.

38. The Neo-Greeks were a group of painters who emerged from the studio of Charles Gleyre, who had taken over the pupils of Paul Delaroche when he had closed his studio in 1843 to leave for Italy. Of the *Jeunes Grecs*, Gautier wrote: 'Il faut beaucoup de talent et de ressources pour élever une scène épisodique au rang d'une composition noble, et que ne désavouerait aucun maître' ('Exposition de 1847', *La Presse*, 31 March 1847).

39. In August 1848 Champfleury wrote that 'l'école Gérôme a été semée, plantée et arrosée dans les plates-bandes du jardin *La Presse* par cet illustre horticulteur aux longs cheveux qu'on appelle Théophile Gautier' (in Champfleury, *Œuvres posthumes: Salons 1846–1851* (Paris: Alphonse Lemerre, 1894), pp. 93–95). Irrespective of the light-hearted tone of the comment, the suggestion that Gautier was the spokesman for a 'stable' of young Neo-Greek painters backed by the Girardins (Émile's political friends and the influential habitués of Delphine's Salons) undoubtedly played on public perceptions of how the art market was now operating. Champfleury also recounted a conversation with 'Théophile [Gautier] qui s'extasiait beaucoup devant le *Combat de coqs*' but on which Champfleury had poured scorn, arguing that the work was 'moitié *distingué*, moitié *canaille*', that its figures were a product of Gleyre's classical training, that its fighting cocks were derived from eighteenth-century realist animal scenes, and that the classical and realist parts of the painting had remained distinct (ibid., pp. 103–05).

40. *Anacréon, Bacchus et l'Amour* (no. 1932), *La Vierge, l'Enfant Jésus et saint Jean* (no. 1933), and *Portrait* [of Armand Gérôme] (no. 1934). See Gerald M. Ackerman, *Jean-Léon Gérôme* (Paris: ACCR Édition, 1986), pp. 186–88.

41. Clément de Ris, congratulating himself for not having gone overboard twelve months earlier about the *Combat de coqs*, went on to say: 'Il est bon d'étudier l'antique, et les figures des vases étrusques ont une majesté de lignes que personne ne peut songer à contester; mais, tout en se livrant à cette étude, il faut en approprier les résultats aux idées modernes et faire la part du progrès [...] Malheureux abus du talent et du parti pris, que celui qui fait ainsi violemment reculer un art qui a besoin de toutes ses forces vives pour marcher à la découverte de terres nouvelles' ('Salon de 1848, IV', p. 60).

42. See Neil McWilliam, *Dreams of Happiness: Social Art and the French Left 1830–1850* (Princeton University Press, 1993), pp. 224–25.

43. 'La forte école florentine regorge de sublimes maniérés, en tête desquels il faut inscrire Michel-Ange.'

44. De Mercey thought that with Gérôme's ability, 'toute cette puérile affectation d'archaïsme [in *Anacréon*], toutes ces imperfections calculées ne sont que plus condamnables' ('Le Salon de 1848', p. 289). Of the same painting, Delécluze said that 'l'imitation de quelques maîtres de la fin du quinzième siècle, et d'Andrea Mantegna entre autres, y est flagrante [...] Sous la protection de quelque grand maître ou d'école célèbre que l'on veuille faire passer le pastiche, je le poursuis, je le condamne toujours' ('Salon de 1848', *Journal des débats*, 5 April 1848). Clément de Ris said that 'Anacréon est conçu dans des idées d'excentricités fâcheuses qui fausseront tout à fait le talent de ce peintre, s'il s'obstine à les poursuivre' ('Salon de 1848, IV', pp. 59–60). Even in relation to Gérôme, however, there was no simple convergence between aesthetic and political standpoints. The republican Haussard, for example, was very complimentary. Noting in *Anacréon* the borrowings from a range of Renaissance sources, he stated that 'l'ensemble sévère et doux de cette œuvre n'en est pas moins tout à l'honneur de M. Gérôme, et le jeune artiste a le droit d'être fier de la belle précocité d'étude et du noble esprit déjà mûr qu'il apporte à ses premiers essais' ('Salon de 1848', 20 May 1848).

45. The painting was subsequently destroyed. See the catalogue of the exhibition, *Chassériau: un autre romantisme*, ed by Stéphane Guégan, Vincent Pomarède, and Louis-Antoine Prat (Paris: RMN, 2002), p. 194, and Christine Peltre, *Théodore Chassériau* (Paris: Gallimard, 2001), pp. 130–34.

46. 'N'est-ce pas une honte et une infamie que quelques membres de l'Institut, dont les noms sont inconnus et les œuvres risibles, aient eu l'outrecuidance de rejeter un tableau de cette importance, qui, outre le mérite qu'il renferme, est le premier où l'Orient moderne soit représenté avec les proportions et le style de l'histoire?' His commentary on the rejected painting is a good example

of his practice of undoing the jury's decision by presenting the work in his review on the same basis as those accepted.

47. 'Dans cette rue fantastique aux maisons qui surplombent portées par des escaliers renversés, aux toits peuplés de cigognes, aux fenêtres grillées de treillages de cèdre et que traversent au galop les cavaliers du désert, vont bientôt passer des patrouilles de gardes nationaux absolument pareils à ceux de la rue Saint-Denis.'

48. 'Salon de 1833', *La France littéraire*, no. 6 (March 1833), 139–66 (p. 157).

49. 'Ardent fauteur de l'émeute coloriste, il [Ziegler] passa chez M. Ingres, où il fit pénitence de ses excès, puis repris de l'amour de la lumière, il fut étudier les Vénitiens et les grandes écoles d'Italie; et de toutes ces diverses études, se dégagea une large et franche originalité. Le Giotto regardant des manuscrits enluminés dans l'atelier de Cimabué répond à la phase sobre et modérée. C'est une figure élégante et fine jusqu'à la maigreur: des petits bras d'enfant, minces et frêles, mais d'un dessin charmant, un profil délicat, un contour serré, renfermant une teinte locale d'une simplicité excessive, voilà les symptômes où se reconnaît l'influence presque tyrannique de M. Ingres; cependant le coloris, quoique étouffé, est déjà séditieux et se rapproche de l'ardeur sombre des tableaux espagnols' ('Salon de 1838', *La Presse*, 16 March 1838).

50. See Baudelaire, *Salon de 1846*, p. 5. On the Musée Espagnol, see Jeannine Baticle and Cristina Marinas, *La Galerie espagnole de Louis-Philippe au Louvre 1838–1848* (Paris: RMN, 1981). On Ziegler see Marguerite Coffinier, *Jean-Claude Ziegler, 1804–1856: sa vie, son œuvre* (Beauvais: GRECB, 1978).

51. On the critical reception of Ziegler's work in the Salon of 1847, see Stéphane Guégan, 'Ziegler dans l'œil des critiques', *Bulletin des musées et monuments lyonnais*, 4 (1990), 12–21.

52. 'Ce tableau, d'un aspect ferme et décidé, rappelle pour la netteté des contours, la localité rembrunie des chairs et des étoffes, le caractère violent et sombre de la composition, certains maîtres de l'école espagnole, Alonzo Cano ou Juan Valdez Leal' (*La Presse*, 2 April 1847).

53. In the same fourth article on the Salon of 1848, a few paragraphs before the one to which Ziegler was responding, Gautier had written: 'Maintenant on est un peu revenu de la peinture historique et l'on pense qu'Andromaque a bien assez pleuré Hector, que Didon doit avoir fini de conter ses aventures, qu'Oreste s'est bien assez débattu contre les furies, et qu'il a eu le temps d'aller s'asseoir sur la pierre Cappautas pour se débarrasser de leurs obsessions.' Ziegler was thus returning to Gautier his own argument in favour of a recycled form of history painting adapted to modern needs.

54. This detail was important because, as Delécluze had pointed out in his commentary on the painting on 10 April, 'L'inconvénient de ce sujet résulte de ce que le portrait que tient l'empéreur est fort petit, présenté de profil, en sorte que le spectateur, ne pouvant voir ce qu'il représente, l'une des conditions indispensables pour l'explication de ce sujet fait complètement défaut. L'opposition entre Charles Quint ayant renoncé au monde et voyant tout à coup son image couronnée n'existe réellement que quand on a lu la notice. Le sujet n'est donc pas assez *pittoresquement* écrit' ('Salon de 1848', 16 April 1848, Delécluze's emphasis). Gautier's description also corresponds, therefore, to an embellished catalogue 'notice'.

55. 'Collection de tableaux espagnols', *La Presse*, 23 September 1837. For the poem on Valdes Leal, see Gautier, *Voyage en Espagne suivi de Espana*, ed. by Patrick Berthier, pp. 492–97.

56. Other commentators not bound by Gautier's duty of friendship were less complimentary about *Charles Quint*. De Mercey felt that its dimensions had prevented it achieving the status of history painting on which Ziegler was counting and though he confirmed the connection with Zurbaran, it was as pupil, not equal: 'Il ne faut voir dans cette composition qu'une étude sévère dans le goût de Zurbaran' ('Le Salon de 1848', p. 291). 'Dans le goût de' no doubt fell short of what Ziegler wanted to read.

57. For Clément de Ris, he was 'une des plus regrettables victimes des préceptes de M. Ingres' on account of the 'grâce pénible et maniérée' of his modelling ('Salon de 1848, IV', p. 60).

58. 'Ah! pauvre mère, ce n'est pas seulement dans le front de ton fils que cette couronne a enfoncé ses pointes sanglantes [...] toi aussi a été crucifiée!' With reference to Bruno Foucart's study of French religious painting in the nineteenth century, Georges Brunel saw in *La Vierge au pied de la croix* 'une inflexion du sentiment religieux qui devait être caractéristique de la seconde moitié du xixe siècle: l'émotion humaine l'emporte décidément sur le sentiment de la majesté divine' (*Les*

Années romantiques, p. 415). See Foucart, *Le Renouveau de la peinture religieuse en France (1800–1860)*, Paris: Arthena, 1987).

59. Clément de Ris made the same point: 'M. Couder, en prenant pour sujet de son tableau *le Serment du Jeu de Paume*, a entrepris une œuvre de beaucoup au-dessus de ses forces', adding: 'Un homme seul jusqu'ici a un talent assez fort pour entreprendre de rendre sans trop d'infériorité la fièvre qui agitait les masses à cette époque: cet homme, c'est M. Delacroix' ('Salon de 1848, III', p. 36).

60. *Le Vanneur*, long believed to have been destroyed, was rediscovered in an American attic in 1972. On the history of the work, see *Jean-François Millet*, catalogue of the exhibition in Paris in 1975–76 (Paris: Éditions des Musées Nationaux, 1975), pp. 73–75.

61. Millet 'truelle sur de la toile à torchons, sans huile ni essence, des maçonneries de couleurs qu'aucun vernis ne pourrait désaltérer. Il est impossible de voir quelque chose de plus rugueux, de plus farouche, de plus hérissé, de plus inculte.'

62. Given the significance of the 'bonnet rouge' in Delacroix's *La Liberté guidant le peuple* and the instructions to painters taking part in the competition for a figure of the Republic that the Phrygian bonnet had to be included (see below, p. 70), it is reasonable to assume that visitors to the Salon would have interpreted the red headgear as symbolic rather than naturalistic colour.

63. 'Il est très probable que le jury, en plaçant le tableau dans la grande salle de l'exposition, voulait souligner l'actualité du sujet' (*Jean-François Millet*, pp. 73–74). De Mercey noted its placement ('Le Salon de 1848', p. 287), and Clément de Ris, commenting that Hédouin's *Moulin arabe*, another genre painting from the realist group, 'tient parfaitement sa place dans le salon carré' ('Salon de 1848, V', p. 68), confirmed that the assumption that placement of a painting in the Salon Carré was *prima facie* evidence of official status still operated in the open-access Salon of 1848.

64. See *Jean-François Millet*, p. 74.

65. De Mercey, for example, commented: 'Cette année, les imitateurs de M. Diaz se sont singulièrement multipliés [...]. M. Millet (Jean-François) est celui des imitateurs de M. Diaz qui serre le maître de plus près. Il prodigue comme lui l'empâtement dans les ombres comme dans les clairs, mais sans le même art, et trop souvent il arrive à donner à sa peinture un aspect rebutant' ('Le Salon de 1848', p. 287).

66. Diaz has 'essayé de dérouter ses imitateurs, qui lui marchent déjà sur les talons' (*La Presse*, 3 May 1848).

67. 'N'avons-nous pas dit que Diaz se laissait trop mener par sa brosse, que sa peinture s'effrangeait et s'effilait en bavochures [...]. C'est ainsi que de braves peintres sont poussés au style par d'honnêtes feuilletonistes qui pensent agir pour le mieux et perfectionner les talents qu'ils aiment. Que Diaz se moque donc des sages conseils que nous avons pu lui donner [...] Nous lui en parlerons plus de la ligne et du modelé, mais, pour Dieu, qu'il se garde du style.'

68. 'Salon de 1846', *La Presse*, 3 April 1846.

69. As Clément de Ris put it: 'Depuis quelques années il s'était tenu en dehors du Salon, et, retiré dans son atelier, laissait la vogue attendre à sa porte' ('Salon de 1848, V', p. 68). On Meissonier see *Ernest Meissonier: rétrospective* and Gotlieb, *The Plight of Emulation*.

70. 'Salon de 1842', *Cabinet de l'amateur et de l'antiquaire* (1842), 119–28 (p. 122). In his discussion of the differences between Meissonier's pictorial aesthetic and that of the Flemish painters, Gotlieb points out that Second Empire critics had noted them, including Gautier in his 1862 essay on Meissonier (*The Plight of Emulation*, pp. 102–06). It is clear, however, from his comments in 1842 on Meissonier's first Salon work, that Gautier was already alert to them twenty years earlier.

71. '*Le Fumeur* est un exemple bien fort contre les gens [...] qui s'attachent au sujet en peinture et qui n'admirent un tableau que d'après le plus ou moins d'intérêt de la scène qu'il représente. La peinture n'est pas un drame, et les toiles anecdotiques qui plaisent tant aux bourgeois par les idées qu'elles réveillent dans leur tête sont le plus souvent d'abominables croûtes' (ibid.).

72. It is revealing in this respect to note the warmth of the commentary on Meissonier by Delécluze, the guardian of the Davidian faith: 'Je mettrai en première ligne les compositions de M. Meissonier. Dans ses *Joueurs de boule*, entre autres, cet artiste est arrivé à un point de perfection rare; car le naturel de l'ensemble de la composition, ainsi que celui de l'attitude et de l'expression

des personnages, sont en accord parfait avec la vérité du coloris, et présentent une exécution pittoresque complètement exempte de manière. M. Meissonier est du très petit nombre des peintres de talent de nos jours qui *peignent* et ne *touchent* pas' ('Salon de 1848', 5 April 1848, Delécluze's emphasis).

73. 'Chardin n'a rien fait de plus sincèrement bourgeois du dix-huitième siècle, lui qui en était [...] On dirait vraiment que M. Meissonier, par un miracle d'intuition rétrospective, passe ses soirées à voir jouer aux dominos et aux échecs des habitués du café Procope du temps de Diderot, du neveu de Rameau, de Piron et de Voltaire.' We remember too that Meissonier's work had first come to Gautier's attention in 1837 when he had admired his 'délicieuses illustrations de la Chaumière Indienne de Bernardin de Saint-Pierre'. See 'Illustrations de *Paul et Virginie*', *La Charte de 1830*, 11 December 1837 (repr. in *Fusains et eaux-fortes* (Paris: Charpentier, 1880), pp. 197–205).

74. See Nicholas Green, *The Spectacle of Nature: Landscape and Bourgeois Culture in Nineteenth-Century France* (Manchester University Press, 1990). Or, as Gautier put it: 'l'homme est un être social, et il faut qu'il soit bien dégoûté de ses semblables pour s'éprendre des arbres' ('Le Salon de 1848', 9 May 1848).

75. The clearest example was of course their systematic refusal of the work of Théodore Rousseau.

76. So, 'par une bizarrerie de l'intelligence humaine, qui va toujours du compliqué au simple, le paysage n'a été cultivé que dans ces derniers siècles [...] L'amour de la nature ne vient qu'aux civilisations avancées, aux époques de décadence et de corruption.' As we shall see, the theory reappears in his analyses of Chenavard's decorative scheme for the Panthéon and Villot's reorganization of the Louvre collections.

77. The key figure in the 'paysage historique' at the end of the eighteenth century, as both practitioner and theoretician, was Pierre-Henri de Valenciennes, whose manual of perspective and landscape, *Elémens de perspective pratique à l'usage des artistes* (1799) 'provided the basis for nineteenth-century landscape painting' (Albert Boime, *The Academy and French Painting in the Nineteenth Century* (London: Phaidon, 1971), pp. 136–42; see also Green, *The Spectacle of Nature*, pp. 112–13). In an obituary article on the landscape painter Prosper Marilhat, which he wrote a few weeks after completing his Salon review, Gautier, recalling the impact that Marilhat's *La Place de l'Esbekieh au Caire* had made on him in the Salon of 1834, had the following courtesies for the historical landscape: 'Ce superbe goût, qui règne encore sur les papiers de salle à manger des auberges de province, était cultivé avec succès par beaucoup de membres de l'Institut. Un arbre dans un coin, une montagne dans le fond, une fabrique à fronton triangulaire sur le bord d'une nappe d'eau formant cascade, un Ulysse, une Io ou un Narcisse pour animer la chose, tel était le programme' ('Marilhat', *RDM*, 1 July 1848, pp. 56–75 (p. 59), repr. in *L'Art moderne* (Paris: Michel Lévy, 1856), pp. 95–128).

78. 'La nature, soit vivante, soit inanimée, se présente sous un double aspect à l'artiste, la forme et la couleur: la couleur semble appartenir plus particulièrement au paysage, puisque l'anatomie des arbres n'a pas la précision rigoureuse de l'anatomie du corps humain, et que la ligne d'un horizon peut s'infléchir à droite ou à gauche sans grands inconvéniens' (*La Presse*, 9 May 1848). In 1839, Gautier had dedicated his poem 'A trois paysagistes' to Bertin, Aligny, and Corot in response to their work in the Salon that year (see *Poésies complètes* (henceforth *PC*), ed. by René Jasinski, 3 vols (Paris: Nizet, 1970), II, 225–29). The six-line extract on Aligny begins: 'Aligny qui, le crayon en main, | Comme Ingres le ferait pour un profil humain'.

79. Jacques Amyot (1513–93) published in 1559 his translation of *Les Amours pastorales de Daphnis et de Chloé* by Longus.

80. 'Comme les Bertin, les Rémond, les Rénier, les Watelet et toute cette école décrépite semble fausse, maniérée, froide, laide et hideuse auprès des paysages de Cabat!' ('Salon de 1834', *La France industrielle* (April 1834), 17–22 (p. 21)).

81. In fact, the *Paysage* was accompanied in the Salon livret by a quatrain from Gautier's own poem, 'Villanelle rythmique' of 1837 (*PC*, II, 208): 'Sous les pieds égrenant les perles | Que l'on voit au matin trembler, | Nous irons écouter les merles | Siffler' (ll. 5–8). It is one example of landscape painting in the 1840s drawing on the themes of pastoral poetry, the revival of whose early forms Gautier had himself been instrumental in stimulating.

CHAPTER 3

Competitions, Commissions, and the Return of Ingres

In the previous chapter we saw Gautier's response to Ledru-Rollin's decision to abolish the *jury d'admission* for the Salon of 1848. During the same initial phase of the Second Republic, the Provisional Government took two other important decisions which were also designed to give a new republican direction to government policy for the fine arts and to secure public support for it. The first, announced to coincide with the opening of the Salon, was to hold a competition for a figure of the Republic; the second was to commission the decoration of the Panthéon, awarded in mid-April to Paul Chenavard.[1] As far as the figure of the Republic was concerned, Gautier was opposed in principle to the idea of an open competition as a means of achieving an official symbol of the republican idea. Far better in his view for the government to commission figures of the Republic from a painter and sculptor elected by their peers. In the case of the Panthéon decoration, he not only supported the principle of the commission but also the government's choice of artist, and he was virtually alone in supporting both. In addition, he did not share the view, widely held in pro-Republican circles, that in the conventional polarization in modern French painting between the *dessinateurs* and the *coloristes*, of whom Ingres and Delacroix respectively were the figureheads, the revolution of 1848 had signified the triumph of the colourist tendency. When, in the immediate aftermath of the June Days, Ingres finally completed his *Vénus anadyomène*, begun forty years earlier, Gautier reaffirmed his faith in the relevance of Ingres's work to the future direction of French art.[2] If it is true, therefore, that in his support for Republican art policy, 'Gautier in his prose gave voice to the fashionable hopes of 1848',[3] it is also true that he had the courage of some unfashionable ones. By following in this chapter Gautier's engagement with the three issues identified in its title, we shall have a better sense of the originality of his position in the French art field of the mid-nineteenth century and of the tenacity with which he defended it.

Gautier did not wait for the announcement of the competition for a figure of the Republic to call for a new republican iconography. He had already done so in his theatre review of 6 March, his first article to appear after the collapse of the July Monarchy:

> Que notre révolution soit originale; qu'elle invente ses costumes, ses chants,
> sa terminologie, ses emblèmes, ses armoiries; qu'elle ait son art particulier et

reconnaissable à tout jamais; que, dans trois mille ans, en faisant des fouilles sur l'ancien emplacement de Paris, on retrouve entières ou mutilées, mais toujours admirables, des statues qui fassent dire: 'C'est du beau temps de l'art français, de l'époque de la seconde république!'[4]

On 29 February the Théâtre de l'Opéra, renamed for the purpose the Théâtre de la Nation, had reopened with Auber's most famous and very topical opera, *La Muette de Portici*, a celebration of the Neapolitan revolutionary Tommaso Aniello's revolt two centuries earlier against the Spanish authorities. It had first been staged twenty years before to the day, on 29 February 1828, and a performance of the opera in Brussels in 1830 was credited with having been the signal for the Belgian uprising against the Dutch.[5] This latest Parisian performance contained for Gautier disturbing signs of a lack of originality as far as the future of republican iconography was concerned. At a key moment Aniello's followers, decked out in rosettes and tricolour flags, pressed around their leader as he burst forth with an entirely anachronistic rendition of the Marseillaise. Gautier reminded his readers that in the brave new world of the Second Republic, art should not be placed at the service of a political idea, however worthy: 'Que le beau soit le vêtement du bon. Les nobles pensées se traduisent aisément en nobles formes: point de dédain farouche pour l'art amoureux de sa propre perfection. L'art existe par lui-même et moralise par sa seule beauté.'

Only six months earlier, in a review of Töpffer's *Réflexions et menus propos d'un peintre genevois*, Gautier had restated his views on the beautiful in art.[6] Unlike life, art, he said, was not subject to time; unlike science, it was not subject to progress. Its purpose was to express the Beautiful, an objective, absolute ideal, which the true artist carried within and which was made manifest through the transformation, not imitation, of the forms of the material world. Art for art's sake was, he said, form for Beauty's sake. Form existed for the purpose of Beauty as Beauty for the purpose of form. The sculpture of antiquity, polytheistic, anthropomorphic, had achieved the fullest surviving realization of art for art's sake's means and ends. In painting, line, colour, and relief formed the trinity of expressive means, each with its laws and procedures, but available for all manner of association, according to time, place, and temperament, for like God's house, the Beautiful had many rooms. No artist, legitimist, Orleanist, Bonapartist, or republican, was excluded *d'office*, provided that Plato's law — 'le beau est la splendeur du vrai' — was observed. This Platonic formula was the basis of Gautier's 'apoliticism'.[7] He had no difficulty with the idea that art might represent contemporary social or political history. Delacroix's *La Liberté guidant le peuple* of 1831 had demonstrated that such subjects were entirely compatible with the highest achievements in art and, as we shall see, the awful events of June 1848 would only bring further confirmation of this, as far as Gautier was concerned. Art for art's sake was not, therefore, in his view political detachment or aesthetic materialism, but the moral force of beautiful forms, a lesson as relevant to a modern republic as to any other regime.[8] If art was to prosper in the new era, artists, critics, and administrators had to resist the temptation to subject its forms to what Gautier called the 'ferocious disdain' of Jacobin fundamentalism. They had to recognize that only by encouraging a proper respect for art's formal means would the Second Republic be able to avoid the sterile imitation of the art of its predecessor and to create its own iconography from engagement with the modern world.

Outmoded iconography was not, however, the only threat that art faced in the wake of the revolution of 1848. Lack of investment was another. Of *La Muette de Portici* Gautier said that 'nous eussions voulu un peu moins d'hymnes et un peu plus de spectateurs. La salle était presque entièrement vide, et l'on y comptait à peine cinq ou six femmes.' Though by 29 February the streets were calm, a week later theatregoers were still not venturing out, at least not to the Opéra, which, despite its new name, presumably still retained connotations of frivolity and indulgence with which it was thought wise in the circumstances not to be associated. Gautier was convinced, however, that if the upper and middle classes stayed at home, the downturn in commercial activity would become as great a danger to the Second Republic as war had been to the first. They needed to realize, he said, that spending on luxury items such as the arts was a republican act and a patriotic duty. By providing work for those who practised the range of skills and crafts on which artistic creation depended, they would be reducing the risk of more radical temptations:

> Il faut retourner à l'Opéra, aller au bal, dépenser; la prodigalité, à présent, voilà l'économie. Le luxe est saint: sans la honte de l'aumône, sans l'injustice de la spoliation, le luxe accomplit la division des fortunes et fait participer les pauvres aux biens des riches; tel caprice coûteux d'une coquette sauve la vertu d'une honnête ouvrière [...] Ainsi, changez bien souvent de robes et de chapeaux; que les vitres des hôtels flamboient splendidement la nuit. Ne faisons pas à cette révolution, qui s'est montrée si grande et si probe, l'injure de fermer notre tiroir quand elle passe: que ce chiffre sinistre de 93 s'efface des mémoires.

The idea that expenditure by the rich was socially beneficial in that it provided work for the poor had a long history by 1848, but Gautier's point that patronage of the arts was wealth redistribution without any of the unpleasant side effects had a precise and urgent relevance that year. State commissions for the decoration of existing and new buildings, and private investment in the art market would provide work for thousands of artists and artisans but if further encouragement were needed, the 'chiffre sinistre de 93' said it all.[9]

There was much talk in 1848 of Athens, Sparta, and America, but models closer to home and of more recent origin were pressing stronger claims to republican legitimacy during the period leading up to the revolution that year.[10] The new republic's first official ceremony, held to honour the dead of 24 February, had unintentionally underlined the urgent need for new forms with which to rally support for the republic. The crowd had of course honoured the fallen and applauded the values of democracy and the right to work for which they had died, but the allegorical float drawn by eight white horses and bearing a great jumble of symbolic items (tricolour flags, plough, hand of justice threatening the sky, lances, and olive branches) 'n'était pas de nature à faire aimer la république'.[11] The news was out that the government was planning a competition for painters and sculptors to devise new symbols of the republic, and if the allegorical float was anything to go by, it could not come soon enough. As Gautier had warned in his first Salon article that year: 'Les formules qu'employait la République de l'ancien régime ne peuvent en aucune manière convenir à la nouvelle, et s'en servir serait méconnaître ou fausser les tendances modernes.'

The invitation to painters and sculptors to take part in a competition to produce a figure of the Republic was widely welcomed, but the problem that had plagued the Salon that year from the moment it opened its doors also fatally undermined the competition. The failure to control the number of entrants was again blamed for ensuring the triumph of mediocrity. As one anonymous critic said: 'Le succès d'hilarité obtenu par le Salon de 1848 a été dépassé! C'est tout dire.'[12] It is true that it would have been difficult to create more unfavourable conditions for success. Many of the best-known artists did not take part, either because they had been elected by their peers to serve on the competition jury, alongside the ministers and *hommes de lettres* nominated by Ledru-Rollin, and were therefore barred, or because they were unwilling to expose their reputation to the risk of rejection in an open competition in which a sketch by a major rival (or even a pupil) might be preferred to their own. In addition, the timescale of only three weeks between the announcement of the competition and the deadline for the submission of the preliminary sketches (of which the best three would be selected and their artists invited to work them up into a finished painting) was very tight, reflecting the sense of urgency within government circles for new republican symbols (national elections were only weeks away) but allowing little time for ideas to be worked through. Furthermore, many of these artists did not think of themselves as committed republicans in any real sense, had not expected only three weeks earlier to find themselves in a republic so soon, and had no clear idea of what sort of republic the government wanted them to be in. In this respect they were not helped much by the competition's guidelines, which succeeded in being both vague and prescriptive at the same time. The official proclamation indicated only that the sketch was to contain a single figure but that 'le choix de l'attitude, des accessoires et des attributs est laissé au goût de chaque concurrent'.[13] Further details came subsequently in the form of a letter apparently sent from Ledru-Rollin's office to a unnamed sculptor and widely circulated in the press. In the version published in *L'Artiste* they were introduced by the cautionary comment that if they were from Ledru-Rollin, 'il faudra avouer que lui seul a compris la figure symbolique de la République française.'[14] According to the letter, the sketch was still to be of a single figure (female evidently went without saying) representing the republican trinity of liberty, equality, and fraternity, but now it was stated that she was to be seated to create the idea of stability and draped in the colours of the tricolour unless 'l'art s'y oppose', in which case the artist should 'faire dominer les couleurs nationales dans l'ensemble du tableau' in ways unspecified. The Phrygian bonnet, on the other hand, was compulsory but the figure was not to appear too warlike, for her strength was 'morale avant tout' and the republic was strong enough to have no need of helmets and pikes. If the fasces was included, the axe should be removed or at least its blade broken.[15] If all this information was insufficient, the addressee only had to call in to discuss it further since, 'comme il n'y a pas de précédents pour cette figure, tout est à faire'. It is not known whether the offer was taken up but it is little wonder that artists were confused, that they resolved in their different ways what was unclear or ignored what was clear when it suited them to do so. In any event they had the difficult task of reconciling at short notice their private view of the republic with what they took to be the idea of itself that it wished to present and, for help in achieving it, they turned, not surprisingly, to the well-thumbed manuals of iconography.[16]

Despite these difficulties, over five hundred sketches arrived by the deadline. When they went on show, the critics had a field day. The following examples illustrate the tone of the response to what an anonymous author of a venomous piece in *L'Artiste* called 'une bien triste réalisation de l'égalité dans la médiocrité':[17]

> Sur quatre cents esquisses peintes, il n'y en a pas vingt, en effet, qui aient été produites par des gens à peu près peintres [...] Le reste est le produit d'une réunion fantastique de portiers en goguette, de marmitons sans ouvrage, d'enfans au-dessous de sept ans ...

> Que l'on ferme au plus tôt l'exposition, triste produit de ce concours. Le public rit, nos artistes rougissent, notre école est calomniée. Les quatre ou cinq cents esquisses peintes [...] dépassent tout ce qu'on peut imaginer de turpitudes grotesques.

> Notre école en était-elle réduite à cet état d'abaissement honteux, de stupide dévergondage, de conceptions ridicules, d'exécution déplorable? Ou bien — au nom de la liberté nouvelle — voulait-on protester ainsi contre la tyrannie odieuse du dessin, et dire aussi son fait au despotisme de la couleur?[18]

By the time Gautier intervened publicly on 21 May, the exhibition of sketches was over, the whole project reduced to farce. Undeterred, he began in non-judgemental, pedagogical mode, stating that since antiquity had not created a specifically republican iconography, the majority of artists, pressed for time, had chosen the simple option of conflating Republic and Liberty. He therefore guided readers through the symbolism of appearance, dress, and attributes in Tiberius Gracchus's temple to Liberty on the Aventine hill in Rome. The problem with the conflation of republic and liberty was that it left equality and fraternity out of the picture, despite the insistence in the letter published in the press that the republican trinity was the 'caractère principal du sujet' and that, as a result, 'les signes des trois puissances' had to be visible. From this point of view Gautier thought that the single-figure requirement was an unnecessary complication. Why not three figures instead? That would at least have allowed artists the more flexible option of exploiting the symbolism of the Three Graces. The lack of flexibility had made it inevitable that they would turn to representations of the first French Republic (and its 'all too significant axe') when the last thing the Second Republic needed was the iconography of civil war and the Terror. Far from being the new, this was the all too familiar:

> C'est sous cette physionomie un peu farouche et menaçante que la République s'est manifestée à la France: objet d'idolâtrie pour les uns, et de terreur pour les autres, son type s'est gravé dans les mémoires d'une manière ineffaçable, et cette difficulté n'est pas une des moindres que nos artistes aient à vaincre; s'ils le rappellent, ils effraient; s'ils s'en écartent, ils ne sont plus intelligibles;

> pourtant la République de 93 n'est pas la République de 1848; il faut l'espérer du moins.

And what was the reward for those artists who overcame these multiple difficulties and managed to sketch the difference between the first and second French republics in three weeks? The few whose work was judged sufficiently worthy to be developed into a finished painting would receive the princely sum of five hundred francs, which would hardly cover the cost of materials. It was, said Gautier, 'de la plus mesquine insuffisance'.

When he turned to the exhibits themselves, Gautier's response was as much one of dismay as one of anger. This 'épanouissement de vanités en délire' was 'décourageant, honteux, fait pour navrer l'âme'. The figures of the Republic were for the most part revolutionary furies, wielding every attribute under the sun, except the printing press, despite the fact that the printer's workshop was, he said, adapting a central theme of his preface to *Mademoiselle de Maupin*, 'le vrai temple de la liberté républicaine'. The three colours produced 'des effets d'arc-en-ciel et de glaces panachées des plus hasardeux'. How was it possible, he asked, that so many talented artists could fail to rise to such a solemn occasion? What was one to make of 'ce déplorable fatras, parmi ces formes qui grimacent et ces couleurs qui hurlent', which appeared to be designed 'à faire aimer l'absolutisme'? Then again, what could you expect of a procedure flawed in principle and mismanaged in practice? There were of course some exceptions, the usual ones as far as Gautier was concerned — Chassériau, Ziegler, Flandrin, Gérôme, Muller, Landelle, Diaz, and the Neo-Greek newcomer Henri-Pierre Picou, who had confirmed that his success in the Salon that year was no fluke[19] — but, oddly, no mention at this stage of the Daumier (Figure 3.1), to which he would return in December (see below, p. 87). The overall result, however, was deplorable and so unnecessary. If only the government had invited artists to elect in secret ballot those of their number best suited in their view to represent the ideal of the modern republic, everyone knew that Ingres and Delacroix would have won hands down. 'Le peintre de *l'Iliade armée* et celui de la *Liberté* de juillet' would have guaranteed a successful outcome, and for those who found either Ingres's line or Delacroix's colour unpalatable there was, he said, always Delaroche, who in any poll of artists would obviously have finished third, the safe pair of hands between these two towering, antagonistic figures.

Gautier's wishful thinking about the election of the three most likely artists of the republican idea led him to muse over an analogy between them and the national colours:

> Sans vouloir assigner aucune nuance politique à ces trois maîtres, l'on peut dire, en suivant l'ordre des couleurs du drapeau national, que M. Ingres eût fait la république bleue, M. Delaroche la république blanche, M. Delacroix la république rouge. La première eût été belle et sereine, la seconde tranquille et décente, la troisième forte et passionnée.

His readers would have needed little prompting to make the analogy for themselves: Ingres in conservative blue, Delacroix in radical red, and Delaroche in safe bourgeois *juste milieu* white, it was such an obvious one to make.[20] In the case of Ingres, Gautier's reference to the *Iliade armée* was presumably to the female figure

Fig. 3.1. Honoré Daumier, *Esquisse de 'La République'*, 1848, Paris, Musée d'Orsay. © Patrice Schmidt, Musée d'Orsay

dressed in red and seated below Homer in the artist's 1827 *Apothéose d'Homère*, forming with her companion, *Odyssée*, dressed in green, the lower left corner of the triangle of which the head of the enthroned Homer forms the apex.[21] With her authority clear in her direct gaze, sword, and strong red robe, but also in repose — for she is seated, her hands enfolding her crossed knees, her sword resting by her side against the plinth (and not held despite Gautier's loose use of 'tenant') — she possesses some of the key attributes outlined in the ministerial guidelines. Even so, the intransigent neoclassical Ingres would have seemed a strange choice in 1848 for authorship of the figure of a modern republic. When hopes in the republican competition were all but ended and the idea emerged, in part perhaps thanks to Gautier, that Ingres was the one to salvage something from the wreckage, the painter himself was determined to have nothing to do with it.[22]

Delacroix, on the other hand, was the obvious choice for the post of official artist to the Second Republic. The revolution of 1848 appeared to have settled the matter of the long-standing rivalry between *les dessinateurs* and *les coloristes* for supremacy within the academic system, with victory going to the colourists. In *L'Artiste* of 9 April, Houssaye stated (pp. 75–76) that 'aujourd'hui [...] en art comme en politique la victoire a donné raison aux exubérants et aux coloristes'. He was only repeating what his own art critic, Clément de Ris, had stated the previous week, that French art had seen off Davidian orthodoxy, Ingres's anachronisms, and Delaroche's *juste milieu* compromises and that it was therefore time for Delacroix to assume his rightful place (see above, p. 62, n. 37). As de Ris was expressing these views, Delacroix's *La Liberté guidant le peuple* was being restored to the Luxembourg museum in Paris, on Jeanron's recommendation and Ledru-Rollin's instruction, sixteen years after it had first been hung there.[23] It had been acquired by the State after the Salon of 1831, only to be removed the following year when its representation of the Parisian people's victory on the barricades no longer seemed to the Orleanist regime to be an appropriate reference to its origins. Delacroix was elected on 4 March 1848 President of the Société Nationale des Artistes, and *La Liberté* was such an obvious point of reference for the new republic that, in the immediate aftermath of the February revolution, it was rumoured that he was already working on a follow-up. As we know, Théophile Thoré even had a title for it, *L'Égalité sur les barricades de février,* and hoped to see it soon hanging alongside its sister, *La Liberté,* behind the President's chair in the National Assembly.[24] Unfortunately there is no evidence that Delacroix was doing any such thing. As far as we know, he never painted *L'Égalité guidant le peuple,* but had he done so, it would very likely have joined *La Liberté,* not in the National Assembly, but safely out of sight in some republican vault.[25] In the meantime, the leader of the *coloristes* had as little sympathy for the Second Republic as did the leader of the *dessinateurs,* a rare occasion on which the two had something in common.[26]

As for Delaroche, his correspondence for 1848 reveals the extent of his pessimism about the future for his own art and for art in general as a result of the upheavals of that year. The interruption in state patronage and the collapse of the market had undermined still further a temperament assailed by personal tragedy and physical ailments. On 9 June, in a letter to his friend Henri Delaborde, he poured out his despair:

Mes ressources s'épuiseront vite. Tout ce que je possède est en rentes chemin de fer et une somme de 40000 francs hypothéquée dont on ne me paye pas les intérêts. D'un autre côté, l'art est perdu pour longtemps en France, et, admettant que le gouvernement, ce dont je doute, m'offre des travaux, je suis dans une position à les refuser par sympathie pour les misères de mes camarades. Je ne puis donc songer à gagner de l'argent en France.[27]

In August, convinced that 'la lutte sociale est loin d'être terminée' and that 'nos ennemis sont toujours là, et ce ne sera qu'à force de batailles qu'on pourra les réduire à un long silence', he was still finding it impossible to work. 'Depuis le mois de février, ce n'est qu'avec des efforts inouïs que j'ai terminé mon Napoléon', the first version of *Le Général Bonaparte franchissant les Alpes*, commissioned by an English aristocrat, the third Earl of Onslow.[28] The significance for Delaroche of the series of portraits of Napoleon he produced from 1838 through to the mid-1850s, of the Davidian references some of this work contained (notably David's *Napoléon traversant les Alpes* of 1801 in the case of the 1848 painting), and of the rise to political power of Bonaparte's nephew, determined to use the Napoleonic myth for his own ends, only distanced the artist still further from authorship of a figure of the Republic 'tranquille et décente'.

When the exhibition of sketches closed its doors, there was some talk of holding the competition again.[29] The June Days removed what little enthusiasm there might have been for that. Six months later Gautier found himself in agreement with the judges, who concluded that none of the paintings worked up from the sketches selected in May should be declared winner of the competition. In the meantime, the closure of *La Presse* forced him to seek other outlets for his art journalism. Within the space of ten days, between 28 July and 8 August, Gautier published three items, 'La République de l'avenir', 'L'Atelier de M. Ingres en 1848', and 'Plastique de la civilisation: du beau antique et du beau moderne'.[30] Though their convergence appears to have resulted from a haphazard series of circumstances related to Gautier's financial straits, they are linked in multiple ways. In the first he enlarged on themes already expressed in his review of *La Muette de Portici*, but his vision of the republic of the future was also related to that of Ingres and, given that Gautier visited the artist in his studio in order to write the second of the three articles, it is not unreasonable to assume that this shared vision figured in the discussions between artist and critic.[31] The third article picked up elements of the first two and linked in turn to the major piece of art journalism that Gautier published in early September, the seven articles on Chenavard's Panthéon commission. Indeed the relationship between the two suggests that he may already have been in possession of Chenavard's notes when he wrote 'Plastique de la civilisation'.

In 'La République de l'avenir' he returned to the Fourierist perspectives of the Second Republic's initial phase. The events of June made it easier to write about the republic of the future than that of the present, but he repeated his view that the republic was the system of government best suited to deliver the fundamental human aspiration to happiness by removing the constraints on freedom which opposed it.[32] He explained the etymology ('la chose publique, la chose de tout le monde, le gouvernement de tous par tous'), the means ('ce gouvernement se réalise au moyen du suffrage universel'), and the outcome ('l'égalité des droits et des devoirs'). Compared to this authentic republic, 1793, with its Committee of Public Safety, guillotine, 'et autres moyens terroristes', was a travesty, a product of a half-baked, ill-digested classical education, in which impoverished 'maîtres de pension' had force-fed generations of pupils a diet of 'le brouet noir de Lacédemone et les légumes de Cincinnatus' (p. 230), Spartan austerity, and Roman asceticism. This pseudo-republic, 'farouche, pauvre et mal nourrie', sustained only an ill-tempered egalitarianism of the mediocre and the envious. For Gautier, as for Fourier, social equality was impossible, on the basis of the usual analogy with nature. 'La société, en bonne mère, ne doit avoir de préférence pour aucun de ses enfants, mais elle ne peut pas faire qu'ils soient pareils' (p. 232). True equality was the removal for all citizens of the obstacles to the fulfilment of human potential. Emancipation was the law of human history, technology would free the proletariat from the modern forms of serfdom.[33] In the republic of the future all would enjoy the benefits of a society which was 'opulente, splendide, spirituelle et polie'. Against the odds, the Fourierist utopia held on tenaciously in Gautier's writing and would soon reappear in his articles on the Pantheon project.

For Gautier these debates on the ideal republic were suddenly displaced by what was for him the single most important art event of this turbulent period. Around the end of June, Ingres had put the finishing touches to his *Vénus anadyomène* (Figure 3.2), begun forty years before.[34] In early August, he opened his studio and invited the public to view this latest work and his portrait of the *Baronne James de Rothschild*, also completed that year.[35] Gautier was evidently one of a more select group of artists, critics and potential buyers invited to see the two paintings in advance, and in Gautier's case to prepare an article on them.[36] It was published in *L'Événement* on 2 August, presumably to coincide with the opening, and if so, to good effect according to Champfleury, who stated that 'Théophile Gautier a envoyé avec un feuilleton plus de trois mille personnes dans l'atelier de M. Ingres'.[37] Even allowing for exaggeration, the figure demonstrated again how effectively Ingres had orchestrated public interest in his work. The simultaneous presentation of both new works, each in its own room, appeared designed to demonstrate his unique mastery of art's classical and modern idioms, ideal beauty and nature, line and colour, definitive archetypal nude and the portrait of the modern patron in sumptuous dress and exclusive accessories. As L.G. pointed out in the *Revue des deux mondes*, it was the same lesson as that demonstrated by Ingres's work two years earlier in the first Bazar Bonne-Nouvelle exhibition.[38] It also combined perfectly the artistic and social event, with, very broadly, the *Vénus* targeted at the artists, connoisseurs, and aesthetes and the Rothschild portrait at the social elites.[39] For Gautier, this was France's greatest living painter reasserting his authority over French art. Unlike others, he did not make the connection between this reassertion of authority in art and the *retour à l'ordre* achieved a month earlier in the streets of Paris.[40]

For Gautier the *Vénus* confirmed and vindicated the lesson with which he had begun his review of the Salon of 1848: political upheaval was transitory, art eternal.[41] 'Malgré les émeutes et les révolutions' and in the midst of arguments about the art

FIG. 3.2. Jean-Auguste-Dominique Ingres, *Vénus anadyomène*, 1808–48,
Chantilly, Musée Condé.
© The Bridgeman Art Library

of the future, Ingres had returned to the sources of the Western tradition and to its archetypal subject, the female nude:

> Il ne nous est rien resté des merveilleux peintres grecs; mais, à coup sûr, si quelque chose peut donner une idée de la peinture antique telle qu'on la conçoit d'après les statues de Phidias et les poèmes d'Homère, c'est ce tableau de M. Ingres; la *Vénus Anadyomène* d'Apelle est retrouvée. Que les arts ne pleurent plus sa perte. (p. 246)[42]

Only five months earlier, Gautier had celebrated in the Venus of another painter the same recovery of this lost original, perfect model. Referring to Chassériau's *Vénus Aphrogénée*, on show in the third exhibition organized by the Association des Artistes in the Bazar Bonne-Nouvelle, he had commented:

> On dirait un dessin que Praxitèle aurait tracé sur le coin d'un bloc de Pentélique, pour se rendre compte d'une idée de statue. Il ne reste rien de la peinture des Grecs — les fresques de Pompeï et d'Herculanum ne sont que des travaux de décoration — mais elle devait ne pas beaucoup différer de celle de M. Théodore Chassériau'.[43]

As this example shows, the expression of regret for the definitive loss of the classical tradition's Greek sources could on occasion be little more than another item in Gautier's extensive repertoire of rhetorical flourishes, for use on occasions when a stronger form of praise than usual was required, socially or professionally. Its use in the case of Ingres's work was a different matter, however, for here no amount of hyperbole could do justice as far as Gautier was concerned to Ingres's achievements, and he of all people knew better than to take liberties with the painter's sense of his own place in the classical tradition. The definitive loss of the Greek sources represented for Ingres the opportunity to take on in the modern era the role and status of founder of this tradition and Gautier's much more emphatic and specific praise of the *Vénus anadyomène* compared to that of the version by Chassériau confirms that he was well aware of Ingres's ambitions in this regard.[44] Indeed it seems not impossible that Ingres returned to his own *Vénus* painting when he did because he had seen Chassériau's work in the Bonne-Nouvelle exhibition, and/or read Gautier's comments on it. The annual Bonne-Nouvelle event had, after all, fond memories for Ingres since it was at the first exhibition of the Association des Artistes there two years earlier that he had triumphed in the first public exhibition of his work for twelve years, following the hostile reception of his *Martyr de saint Symphorien* at the Salon of 1834.[45] Given the importance that Ingres attached to his status in relation to the classical tradition, he was unlikely to be indifferent to the implication that one of his own pupils had displaced him as the source of a key archetype within this tradition. In *L'Artiste*, where for two years Paul Mantz and Clément de Ris had been waging a campaign against Ingres, an editorial quoted Gautier's claim: '"La Vénus Anadyomène d'Apelles est retrouvée, s'écrie un critique enthousiaste. Que les arts ne pleurent plus sa perte"' but responded: 'Non: La Vénus d'Apelles est à jamais perdu et nul, parmi nous, n'en retouvera le type idéal.[46] For the advocates of new forms and subjects in 1848, the position that Ingres had assumed in contemporary art and Gautier's support for the painter's claim to be the authority of the classical tradition could not go unchallenged.[47]

Gautier's reiteration of the role of the avatar in human history (in this case the birth of Venus derived by Apelles from Hesiod's *Theogony* and recreated by Botticelli, Titian, and Ingres) comes just over halfway through the article.[48] It concludes the long opening sequence, in which the artist's place in this exceptional lineage is presented and the reader is prepared for its latest revelation, and introduces the analysis of the work itself. In advance of his commentary on the work, Gautier piles on the elements of a psycho-biographical myth of Ingres: the contrast between his modest studio and the riches it contains, his exemplary career of heroic resistance to adversity, the *Vénus anadyomène* as the site of a struggle between the young artist and the old, and of the melancholy passage of time which has destroyed the pure forms and chaste nudity of the thirteen-year-old model who had posed for the original 1808 version, but which is in turn defeated in the victory over time represented by the eternal youth of Ingres's art. In Gautier's potted biography Venus's perfect equilibrium between the innocence of youth and the knowledge of experience embodies the artist's own victorious resolution of the dramatic struggle between the young and old master triggered by his belated return to a work begun so many years before: 'Fraîcheur, naïveté, timidité adolescente, tout s'y retrouve; c'est la candeur adorable du génie, mais sans l'inexpérience et les erreurs. C'est l'étude d'un élève peinte par son maître' (p. 246).

This equilibrium is the subject of Gautier's description of the *Vénus*. It consists of a series of short paragraphs, each pointing to a salient feature of the myth. Gautier begins with the key element of Venus's age, 'de treize à quatorze ans', displayed, as he sees it, in the contrast between her face and body, in the tension between her divine innocence and her emerging physical beauty.[49] Her blue eyes are 'doucement étonnés' and her smile is 'plus frais qu'un cœur de rose', for at this moment when Venus, 'vierge encore', emerges from her mother the sea, she is still 'presque enfant', but the swelling of her breasts and the curves of her hips show that nature's work has begun:

> Vénus est précoce: la gorge se gonfle, soulevée par un premier soupir; la hanche se dessine, et les contours s'enrichissent des rondeurs de la femme. Rien n'est plus fin, plus pur, plus divin que ce corps de Vénus vierge. (p. 247)

Stimulated by her precocious forms to imagine her first sigh lifting her breasts, Gautier leaves the reader to wonder whether it is one of regret for innocence soon to be lost or of pleasure soon to be savoured, or indeed both at once. Displayed at this privileged moment of transition between child and young woman, the 'rondeurs de la femme' vie with her divine virginity. In this way she has been 'mise en état de lutter avec Marie, la Vénus chrétienne', a perfect fusion of Christian spirituality and pagan sensuality. That this moment will be fleeting is clear from the *putto* who holds out a mirror through which Venus will at any moment accede to 'la conscience de sa beauté'.[50]

Gautier's description of the portrait of Baroness Rothschild is much shorter than that of the *Vénus*, reflecting no doubt the relative weighting, as far as he was concerned, of the archetypal classical nude and the modern portrait. Here, the authentic Greek models which Ingres commanded in the *Vénus* are put, from Gautier's point of view, to less exalted use in such accessories as the lady's black velvet toque reflecting contemporary Parisian taste for the Greek look.[51] The incipient sexual tension of the *Vénus* is replaced by elegance, coquetry, and the high society 'conversation spirituelle, commencée dans la salle de bal ou au souper' which Gautier can almost hear as he views the portrait, such is the power of Ingres's realism. In a few short paragraphs he pays homage to the diplomacy with which the painter 'a su être opulent sans être fastueux' (i.e. had avoided the danger of creating an over-ostentatious display of her enormous wealth which might have been thought to be in poor taste at a time of economic difficulties) and to the power of his colour, as manifested in her sumptuous dress, 'que n'attendraient que difficilement les coloristes les plus vivaces de notre école'. The *Baronne James de Rothschild* was a reminder that even on his opponents' natural territory of contemporary portraiture, realism, and colour, it was Ingres who set the standards.

Gautier's article 'Du beau antique et du beau moderne' was intended to be the first of a series to appear under the title 'Plastique de la civilisation' but was instead the only one to appear. On the long-running debate on whether modern forms of beauty were inferior to those of antiquity, it contained nothing that Gautier had not already said repeatedly between his preface to *Mademoiselle de Maupin* and his 1847 review of Töpffer's *Réflexions et menus propos d'un peintre genevois*. The divine beauty of human form expressed in antiquity's anthropormorphic polytheism, persecuted by Christianity's Jewish and Essenian doctrines, had been restored by the pagan Catholicism of the Renaissance, only to be overturned again by the Reformation. The history of the world was that of this struggle between affirmation and denial of the original antique model of the Beautiful. In the modern world the negative Protestant spirit had prevailed, witness its 'grand mot — l'utile' (p. 202). There was no question, however, of not accepting civilization 'telle qu'elle est, avec ses chemins de fer, ses bateaux à vapeur, ses machines [...] et tout son outillage cru jusqu'à présent rebelle au pittoresque'. What was required in 1848, as it already had been in 1836, was for artists, conscious of the tradition of beauty, to take back from 'des vaudevillistes, des maçons, des mouleurs et des fabricants de vernis' (p. 203) responsibility for the creation of beautiful forms from the materials of the modern world. In his next article Gautier would show them how to go about it, another case of 'la suite au prochain numéro'.

It is not known why Gautier's first article on the *Plastique de la civilisation* was also the last. It may simply be that by the following month another major series of articles, devoted this time to Chenavard's Panthéon commission, was requiring more urgent attention.[52] In this new context Gautier pursued the issues raised in 'Du beau antique et du beau moderne'. Whether these new articles were written on his own initiative, or in response to a request from the artist himself or from those in the Republican administration associated with it, in particular Charles Blanc, the project was by the summer of 1848 in need of support.[53] For those who had initially welcomed the competition for a figure of the Republic for appearing to confirm that state commissions would henceforth be distributed on the basis of equal opportunity for all rather than the abuse of privilege in favour of a chosen few, Ledru-Rollin's choice of Chenavard for the commission had been a brutal disappointment. A storm of protest greeted the news that 'un inconnu' had, without consultation and in violation of basic republican principles, been awarded the first major commission of the new regime and for the decoration of a monument sacred to republican memory.[54] On the face of it Chenavard should have been an odd choice for Gautier too, who might have been expected to harbour serious reservations about a painter believed to subordinate pictorial form to the expression of ideas and whose work was subsequently described by Baudelaire as 'une réaction contre l'école de l'art pour l'art'.[55] Yet Gautier's response was one of unreserved support, presenting Chenavard in his Salon review in April as 'un des plus grands artistes de ce temps-ci, et le seul qui puisse porter, sans être écrasé, la gigantesque coupole qu'on vient de lui mettre sur le dos'. The burden of the Panthéon was not just that of the sheer scale of the decoration needed, and which made it an impossible task for a single artist. It also posed the problem of knowing what sort of monument it was and what sort of pictorial idiom was best suited to its decoration. In his first article for *La Presse* in 1836, on Delacroix's decoration of the Chambre des Députés, Gautier had stated that Gros, commissioned to decorate the Panthéon's cupola, had executed an easel painting instead of a mural — 'la coupole du baron Gros était plutôt un tableau d'histoire circulaire, avec un plafond par-dessus, que tout autre chose' — and Delacroix himself, in an article published only days before Gautier's first on the Chenavard project, made the same point that Gros had been crushed by what Gotlieb called 'the massive emulative challenge' represented by the Panthéon's cupola.[56] Yet, in full knowledge of how strong a claim he was making, Gautier asserted that the Panthéon was just the sort of challenge Chenavard needed to express the full range of his talents and that he was the painter best equipped to rise to it. As we know, the hopes of both painter and critic were not to be realized. By the Spring of 1851 both were feeling the full force of the Catholic reaction and the project, planned to take eight years, was already stillborn by the time Louis Napoleon's coup d'état on 2 December 1851 sealed its fate. Four days later, in a move designed to reinforce Catholic support for the coup, the Panthéon became a church again. The inscription 'Aux grands hommes la patrie reconnaissante' was removed from its entablature, marking the defeat of republican commemoration and celebrating the monument's return to the Catholic fold. Within a few months the Archbishop of Paris had put the project out of its misery.

Gautier had not waited until the advent of the republic to make powerful public statements in support of Chenavard.[57] By April 1848 he had known him for nearly two decades (since the premiere of *Hernani* in February 1830) and was fully aware of the seriousness with which he had studied oriental and mythological symbolism, Hegel's philosophy of history, and Ballanche's theory of palingenesis. But, as he explained in his Salon article, this pupil of Ingres and Delacroix had accompanied his immersion in these philosophical traditions with a profound study *in situ* of the practice of mural painting by the Italian Renaissance masters and the modern German Nazarenes.[58] There was therefore no danger of him repeating Gros's mistake of treating an architectural surface as though it were an easel.[59] Chenavard's grasp of the large historical and philosophical issues would enable him to set this latest phase of republican development in the wider narrative of human history and progress. The decoration of the Panthéon would provide the model for that of all the churches, monuments, and public buildings of the republic. Pre-republican architecture, be it Catholic, Bourbon, or Bonapartist, would be given a facelift embodying the new ideas. New buildings would proclaim the renaissance of French public art: a National Assembly to dwarf London's new Parliament buildings, a Palais de l'Industrie to proclaim French confidence in its science and technology, and all the other places for politics and pleasure needed by a more open and democratic society. Quite predictably the railway stations were singled out for special mention as the new cathedrals of the republican faith in liberty and progress.[60] By September this ambitious programme had been obliged to face up to some harsh financial realities, and the 'utopie fraternelle et universelle, humaniste et réconciliatrice du quarante-huitard', which had underpinned Chenavard's own vision, to the even harsher realities of the June Days.[61] There is good reason to believe that, for Gautier's articles, Chenavard provided the material for him to write up in his own way.[62] In doing so, Gautier took a courageous stand in support of the artist, who was a personal friend, and Charles Blanc, who had invested his own reputation so heavily in the choice of the artist for the project.[63]

Gautier began his sequence of articles by reminding readers of Chenavard's ambition to represent the 'histoire synthétique de ce grand être collectif [...] composé de tous les hommes et de tous les temps, dont l'âme générale est Dieu' (p. 5). He closed them by setting out the protocols which would operate between Chenavard, Papéty (his chief collaborator), and the 'vingt-cinq ou trente peintres amis, disciples ou simples travailleurs' (p. 91) who would work to Chenavard's instructions. He did not need to be told that for a modern public the idea of a collective art form ran counter to the individualist culture of easel painting, in which brushstroke displayed the flourish of the artist's signature, nor that the idea of workshops had been a particular casualty in June.[64] Such issues would also soon prove problematic for Chenavard's collaborators, who found it increasingly difficult to come to terms with the idea of subordinating their own personalities to his vision and be paid a mere ten francs a day for the privilege.[65] But in September 1848 Gautier would not be discouraged. Chenavard at the Panthéon was a modern Briareus, 'un cerveau et mille bras!' (p. 91), who would succeed: 'Les dessins que nous avons vus nous permettent, dès aujourd'hui, d'affirmer que le problème est résolu victorieusement' (p. 5).

Spared by Chenavard's extensive notes from having to bone up on all the religious and philosophical history, Gautier would have been quickly at ease with the project's broader narrative. Its synthesis of history, knowledge, and faith sat comfortably with Gautier's own belief in an absolute Beauty which transcended provisional regimes and periods. Chenavard's purpose was not that of celebrating the Panthéon's myth of collective national memory or reconciliation between republican faith and the Catholicism of the monument's patron saint, Geneviève.[66] Gautier applauded Chenavard's respect for its pagan roots and structure, and his courage in rising above its specifically republican pedagogy.[67] His decorative scheme would recount not the lives of the saints, whether religious or secular, but the apotheosis of reason and historical truth. His mural technique, freed from the debased forms of nineteenth-century neoclassicism and empowered by his return to the authentic sources and highest achievements of the decorative medium in his study of Michelangelo's decorations for the Sistine chapel, would realize this triumphant universality in formal terms.[68]

Gautier's first two articles led the reader in the artist's footsteps to each of the four points of the cross in turn, describing the paintings which would present on the walls the artist's 'gigantesque illustration de l'Histoire universelle de Bossuet' (p. 32). The first chapter took the narrative from the Flood to the end of the ancient world, the second from the coming of Christ, birth of the modern world, to the discovery of America and emergence of Napoleon. The curved arch at the far end of the building opposite the entrance (the tip of its Greek cross shape) showed 'le fait capital qui a changé la forme de la civilisation' (p. 16), the coming of Christ. In Chenavard's illustration of the Sermon on the Mount we were shown not the 'Christ dogmatique et théocratique tel que le catholicisme l'a arrangé pour ses besoins' (p. 17) but the 'blond rêveur qui se fût volontiers promené sous les ombrages de l'Académie entre Platon et Socrate' (ibid.). His audience was not that of the apostles, fathers of the Church, doctors of theology, or saints of the calendar but 'tous ceux qui ont aimé le Christ pour lui-même et l'ont cherché avidement, fût-ce en dehors du dogme, fût-ce à travers l'hérésie' (ibid.). All those who had sought universal happiness were God's children, whether the Church had embraced or persecuted them.

Following the two chapters dealing with Chenavard's representations of human history, Gautier described the four enormous triangular pillars which support the dome and which would present the four ages of human intelligence (religion, poetry, philosophy, and science), each with its corresponding metallic emblem (gold, silver, bronze, iron) and accompanied at its base by a statue of its exemplary historical figure (Moses, Homer, Aristotle, and Galileo). On each side of each pillar a painting would reinforce the appropriate theme. To the historical exposition contained in the first two chapters, the pillars added the intellectual synthesis to complete the human dimension of Chenavard's project. From there, the presentation moved to the birth and genealogy of the Gods, whose successive incarnations, presented in a frieze unfolding above the historical pictures, were seen as following the progress of the universe in perfect parallel, 'car la théogonie est soumise aux mêmes lois que la cosmogonie' (p. 40):

> La marche de cette procession théogonique se règle sur les tableaux historiques placés au-dessous d'elle. Chaque religion correspond à une période de l'humanité; peu à peu le ciel se civilise comme la terre. Les dieux descendent avec des hommes des hauts plateaux de l'Himalaya, pour se répandre dans la Perse, la Chaldée et l'Égypte. Ils suivent la grande migration des peuples, et à chaque pas ils se dépouillent de quelque forme étrange, de quelque symbolisme monstrueux, pour se rapprocher de la forme humaine. (p. 44)

Emerging as vague and shadowy forms from primeval chaos, proceeding through their Indian and Egyptian manifestations to their anthropomorphic Greek forms, 'types de la beauté la plus parfaite' (p. 40), and culminating in Jesus 'qui met une âme céleste dans le corps de l'Apollon pythien et réunit toutes les perfections' (ibid.), each manifestation brought them closer in appearance to man, made in the likeness of God. The fourth article took the description of the frieze from the Greek gods to the age of the artist's contemporaries, completing the immense procession 'de l'ombre du passé à l'ombre de l'avenir' and culminating in a mystery, 'comme toute chose humaine' (p. 58).

The remaining chapters dealt with with Chenavard's scheme for the decoration of the floor of the building, for which he planned five circular mosaics arranged in the form of a cross, and of which the largest would be the central mosaic, itself set in the centre of the building beneath the dome. Where the walls and vaulted arch would illustrate humanity's historical and theogonic development, the mosaic floor would represent its metaphysical foundations; after the narrative of the different phases of the 'grand être collectif', the philosophical theory that underpinned it. At the summit of the central circle, the Word was the supreme deity. In the beginning was the Word and light was its form: 'La lumière est la forme du Verbe. Le premier mot prononcé sur le néant produisit le jour! Cette parole: Que la lumière soit! fit éclater dans le vide des milliards d'étoiles et de soleils!' (p. 60). The circle would show the fusion of all religions:

> Par ce monument fait avec les symboles de tous les cultes fondus ensemble, Chenavard a voulu marquer que toutes les religions n'étaient que des formes diverses de la même idée, et que, vues d'une certaine hauteur, ces formes devaient êtres indifférentes: c'est le Verbe, le grand Pan que l'humanité adore sous une multitude de pseudonymes: tous les noms de divinités sont les épithèthes de la litanie de ce Dieu unique, général, éternel. (pp. 62–63)

The mosaic circles illustrated the divinity's multiple forms, its old and new testaments, ancient and modern worlds, its fables and codes, its ever-increasing transmissions and exchanges. In its latest incarnation the age of steam and American democracy had begun:

> Napoléon, que l'on aperçoit debout, la face tournée vers le spectateur, vêtu du manteau impérial, couronné de laurier comme un César romain, est le dernier homme de l'ère antique, comme Washington est le premier homme de l'ère moderne; l'un enterre le vieux monde, l'autre inaugure le nouveau; le Corse ferme une civilisation, l'Américain en ouvre une autre. (pp. 69–70)

Washington stood on the last step of the present. The staircase led down to the bowels of the earth, each step taking humanity back to the primeval chaos to complete the circle of creation and destruction. At the bottom of the composition, a purifying fire from which a phoenix emerged was the means by which the circular process would begin again. In a final synthesis of pagan and Christian worlds, the four mosaics attached to it in the form of a cross would represent the punishments and rewards of the afterlife, hell in the circle forming the left branch of the cross, purgatory the base (nearest the entrance), the Elysian fields the tip, and paradise the right branch. Each location has its own emblematic virtue or vice: envy, doubt, understanding, love. Together they provided revelation of human finality:

> L'envieux a les supplices, l'indifférent les limbes, le philosophe le banquet de Platon, l'amoureux l'objet de son désir, Marie ou Psyché, l'âme seule ou l'âme avec le corps, suivant son vœu. L'homme se juge lui-même et le tribunal

suprême n'est qu'un symbole. Mortels, ne vous tourmentez pas quand vous sortirez de la vie. Vous portez en vous-même votre enfer et votre paradis; vous aurez tout ce que vous aurez voulu. (p. 83)

As far as Gautier was concerned, Chenavard's project represented the most ambitious decorative programme ever attempted.[69] Never before had the human mind, renouncing the joys of paradise in favour of the knowledge of good and evil and the burdens of free will, been celebrated in such a supreme effort of art. For intellectual scope and technical mastery, only the work of Michelangelo would bear comparison. Despite an immediate context that was optimistic only for the advocates of order by force, it retained, Gautier said, a message of hope for the future, which was destined in the short term to be American and driven by steam, but in the longer term to complete the cycle of creation and destruction, from which humanity 'jaillira plus jeune, plus brillante' (p. 72) with new gods, heroes, and poets for its dreams. The optimism was more Gautier than Chenavard, who was gloom personified.[70] The artist's pessimistic views on the exhaustion of modern civilization were known, but even in the aftermath of the June Days, Gautier was still prepared to defend publicly the *quarante-huitard* faith in the future. The tragic end of history was one romantic myth that he could not embrace.

In the absence of most of the notes that Chenavard provided for Gautier, the nature and extent of the variations between Chenavard's iconographic programme and Gautier's commentary will remain impossible to determine. What is important for our purposes, however, is the fact that for Catholic opponents of the project, the distinction was immaterial. It is well known that by the spring of 1851, a resurgent Catholic revival had the Panthéon project firmly in its sights. Less well known is the fact that it was Gautier's commentary, rather than the preparatory drawings themselves, that fuelled Catholic anger. In a meeting of the Société pour la Conservation des Monuments Français, held at the end of February 1851 under the aegis of a Catholic organization calling itself the Congrès des Diverses Académies de France, a painter by the name of Pernot denounced, 'au nom du bon goût et des convenances de l'art', not Chenavard's work on the project, which he gave no evidence of ever having seen, but Gautier's account of it:

Ce peintre, suivant un de ses amis, M. Théophile Gauthier [*sic*], a peint sur ses cartons 'tous les paradis, tous les Walhalla, sans compter les cosmogonies orientales, les jugements derniers, les fêtes, les orgies, les *Conciles*, les triomphes, les grandes scènes de la Convention, etc.

'Chacun, ajoute-t-il, pourra faire sa prière dans *cette Église universelle*, ce sera le *Temple de la Raison*. Historien des religions anciennes, Chenavard est le prophète de la religion nouvelle, etc.'.[71]

Pernot ended his 'quotation' (in fact an amalgam of words and phrases thrown together in the guise of a quotation) by helpfully identifying the source: 'Extraits des feuilletons de la *Presse* du commencement de septembre 1848'. The Society, reluctant to give credence to the fact that 'un plan aussi monstrueux pût être encore en voie d'exécution' (ibid.), instructed Pernot and three fellow society members to investigate further and report back. Having received confirmation that the artist was indeed still engaged on his 'monstrous' project, the Society decided 'qu'il soit

pris en ce jour une résolution réparatrice, une résolution vengeresse d'une violation
flagrante des lois de la civilisation chrétienne, de la morale publique et du bon
goût dans les arts', citing again in evidence the project 'tel qu'il est connu d'après
des articles de journaux écrits by des amis de l'artiste' (the 'friends' being Gautier,
whose articles in *La Presse* were again referred to in a footnote). The motion itself
cannot have made pleasant reading for Gautier:

> Au nom de la civilisation chrétienne, au nom de la morale et du bon goût,
> elle [La sociéte française pour la conservation des monuments] déclare qu'elle
> regarderait comme un scandale et comme une profanation la réalisation d'un
> projet qui aurait pour base l'idée panthéistique de Rome païenne, et qui
> placerait à côté du vrai Dieu les faux Dieux du passé et les faux prophètes de
> l'avenir. (p. 532)

In response to the motion, carried unanimously, the Catholic writer and
politician Charles de Montalembert promised the Society that, as a member of the
Commission du Budget in the National Assembly, he would oppose any further
allocation of public funds to the Chenavard project. For Gautier this must all have
seemed like the return of the Church militant in its most unpleasant form and an
unwelcome reminder of his legal skirmishes with the conservative Right during
the mid-1830s.

In a letter that Chenavard sent to various newspapers and in which he defended
his project against this charge of atheistic plot against the one true Church, he sought
to extricate Gautier from the trouble that loyalty to his friend's artistic programme
had caused for him.[72] In *Le National* the republican Prosper Haussard, a supporter of
Chenavard's project, noted that the Catholic campaign waged against it was based
less on the iconographic programme itself than on the 'enthousiasme indiscret de
quelques critiques, et notamment sur les extraits des feuilletons de notre brillant
confrère de la *Presse*'. Claiming to be astonished that anyone could possibly confuse
the two, he managed both to support the artist and to put down the critic:

> Ainsi, le compte-rendu d'une œuvre fait par l'esprit artiste et poète, que nous
> connaissons tous, imagination luxuriante de formes, enivrée de couleurs, se
> jouant à tous les tours de force de la métaphore et de l'antithèse, emportée à tous
> les vents, à tous les vols de la fantaisie et de l'improvisation, critique passionnée,
> admirative, et grossissante, ce compte-rendu pourrait être pris rigoureusement
> et textuellement, esprit et lettre, pour l'œuvre qu'il paraphrase: un tel compte-
> rendu sera l'œuvre elle-même!'[73]

How much Haussard knew of the collaboration between Chenavard and Gautier
during the summer of 1848 cannot be determined. He may genuinely have
considered Gautier's support of the project to be more of a hindrance than a help or
decided that the mistrust of the 'génie du paradoxe' Gautier was as well established
in Catholic opinion as it was in certain republican circles and might therefore be
used to deflect conservative attacks from Chenavard. Be that as it may, the artist no
doubt appreciated his intervention more than the critic did.

Ten months later, in response to the decision to return the Panthéon to the
Church, thereby ensuring that Chenavard's work would never decorate it, the
distinguished conservative critic Gustave Planche published a powerful article

in support of the preparatory sketches in terms which entirely vindicated the claims that Gautier had made in April 1848 about Chenavard's suitability for the commission.[74] Planche went as far as to express the hope that the quality of the work that he had seen would persuade the administration to 'les placer dans une des salles du Louvre, en attendant qu'ils reçoivent une destination définitive' (p. 377). Even this intervention, however, failed to prevent its cancellation. Chenavard himself never recovered from the blow and, in denial, continued to work on his project throughout the rest of his life. Gautier moved on, as he was bound to professionally. Writing on the Universal Exposition in 1855, where eighteen of Chenavard's monochrome paintings (*grisailles*) for the Panthéon went on show alongside the work of the Germans Cornelius and Kaulbach, to which they were intellectually and technically most closely related, he saw the major decorative projects currently under way in Paris as a powerful force for the renewal of history painting in the grand manner, a legacy of sorts for Chenavard's failed project.[75]

In the autumn of 1848 there remained the unfinished business of the competition for the figure of the Republic. The paintings completed from the sketches selected by the jury in May went on show in the École des Beaux-Arts in conditions that seemed somehow appropriate for the whole sorry episode.[76] Such had been the confusion created by the guidelines for the initial stage of the competition that for this second stage artists were given as much latitude as they needed to rework their sketches, but the results were little better. Daumier and Hippolyte Flandrin, whose sketches had generated the greatest interest in May, failed to produce a final version and their absence removed what little hope there was of salvaging something from the competition's wreckage. Gautier attributed Daumier's non-appearance to 'soit lassitude, soit inexpérience' and Flandrin's to his own dissatisfaction with the quality of his initial sketch (which had been placed first in May).[77] These were more comfortable explanations than those which a deeper analysis of the relationship of both artists to the republic might have yielded.[78] Given his very public commitment to the *néo-grecs*, Gautier was disappointed to see that neither Gérôme nor Picou had succeeded in making the successful transition from sketch to finished painting and not surprised that Diaz was evidently uncomfortable with large-scale allegorical projects. He thought that with just a little more of what he called 'caractère' and 'vigueur', Landelle's version would have been a worthy winner and, here again, at least on the basis of those which have come down to us, Gautier's judgement seems sound.

Gautier's last piece of art criticism in 1848 was written just as Louis Napoleon swept to power in the first (and last) presidential elections of the Second Republic, and though it was devoted to a decorative work commissioned by the July Monarchy four years earlier, it picked up in important respects some of the artistic aspirations of the first phase of the Republican government.[79] It presented Chassériau's decoration of the *escalier d'honneur* of the Cour des Comptes in the Palais d'Orsay, and, like the articles on the Chenavard commission, it was almost certainly written in association with the artist himself.[80] Unlike the Panthéon programme, Chassériau's commission enabled Gautier to give his readers a guided tour of the completed project, taking them from the bottom of the grand staircase to the top and drawing attention at each stage to the formal and technical issues involved in a large-scale decorative scheme.[81] When in the 'bloody week' of May 1871 the retreating communards set fire to the Cour des Comptes and Conseil d'État, Gautier's description became the most complete surviving record of Chassériau's work.

Taken together with Gautier's description, the surviving fragments of the work, transferred to canvas and preserved in the Louvre, indicate that Chassériau set out to demonstrate his mastery of a classical decorative idiom based on antithetical allegorical schemes, while incorporating references to contemporary progressive or republican ideas.[82] Gautier points out the work's representation of central, traditional oppositions Force and Order, War and Peace, but also draws attention to its more contemporary references to colonial war as a means to bring enlightenment to benighted civilizations still locked into barbarism and to commerce as a force for mutual understanding between peoples.[83] The female figure which personnifies Force possesses the attributes required by the symbolic figure of the Republic whose force is moral rather than physical.[84]

The election of Louis Napoleon as first President of the Second Republic on 10 December 1848, and his first cabinet appointed ten days later, signalled clearly enough that the republic founded in February had been consigned to history. In the fine arts, the republican competition and the Panthéon project effectively went with it, two ambitious initiatives that had gone badly wrong. For Gautier, the consolation that Ingres had overcome the obstacles to completion of the *Vénus anadyomène* was briefly offset by the artist's intervention in an area of more immediate significance for the future of the French fine arts than the republican competition or even the decoration of the Panthéon. By the autumn of 1848, rumours were spreading that there might be no Salon in 1849 and that Ingres himself was advocating abolition of the institution altogether.[85] Though the painter may have been in a minority of one, the discredited Salon of 1848 was casting a long shadow. Gautier would call that of 1849 'la prémière exposition de la République car celle de l'année passée avait été préparée sous la monarchie'.[86] Given all that had intervened since March 1848, the 'first Salon of the Second Republic' assumed even more importance than usual.

Notes to Chapter 3

1. See Marie-Claude Chaudonneret, *La Figure de la République: le concours de 1848* (Paris: RMN, 1987); *Paul Chenavard: le peintre et le prophète*, dir. by Marie-Claude Chaudonneret (Paris: RMN, 2000); Marc Gotlieb, 'Chenavard's Lesson', in *The Plight of Emulation*, pp. 53–95; Georgel, *1848: la République et l'art vivant*.
2. See 'L'Atelier de M. Ingres en 1848', *L'Événement*, 2 August 1848 (repr. in *Fusains et eaux-fortes*, pp. 239–50).
3. Clark, *The Absolute Bourgeois*, p. 31.
4. 'Feuilleton dramatique', *La Presse*, 6 March 1848 (repr. in *Histoire de l'art dramatique en France depuis vingt-cinq ans*, 6 vols (Paris: Hetzel, 1858–59), v (1859), 240–41).
5. In his entry on Auber in his *Dictionnaire universel des contemporains*, Gustave Vapereau stated: 'M. Auber eut bientôt sur la scène du grand opéra [...] son plus beau triomphe. Le 29 février 1828, *La Muette de Portici*, en cinq actes, paroles de M. Scribe et Germ. Delavigne, prit au répertoire de notre premier théâtre une place qu'elle a gardée, à côté des plus belles œuvres de Rossini et de Meyerbeer. Une foule de morceaux, l'ouverture, des mélodies, des chœurs, firent aussitôt le tour de l'Europe; un duo surtout, *Amour sacré de la patrie*, devint comme une seconde Marseillaise,

et, deux ans plus tard, chanté par Nourrit, fut le signal, à Bruxelles, de la révolution du 25 août 1830', 4th edn (Paris: Hachette, 1870), pp. 66–67 (p. 66).

6. 'Du beau dans l'art: *Réflexions et menus propos d'un peintre genevois*, ouvrage posthume de M. Töpffer', *RDM*, 1 September 1847 (repr. in *L'Art moderne*, pp. 129–66). See in this respect Wolfgang Drost, 'Rodolphe Töpffer et Charles Baudelaire esthéticiens — affinités et influences — et le rôle de Théophile Gautier', in *Propos töpfferiens*, ed. by Danielle Buyssens and others (Geneva: Société d'études töpfferiennes, 1998), pp. 173–88. On the idea's sources in German aesthetic theory and its penetration in France via Constant, Madame de Staël, and Cousin, see Albert Cassagne, *La Théorie de l'art pour l'art en France* (Paris: Lucien Dorban, 1959); Stephen Bann, 'Entre philosophie et critique: Victor Cousin, Théophile Gautier et l'art pour l'art', in *L'Invention de la critique d'art*, ed. by Pierre-Henry Frangne et Jean-Marc Poinsot (Presses Universitaires de Rennes, 2002), pp. 137–44; Stéphane Guégan, 'Gautier et l'art pour l'art 1830–1848', *48/14: la revue du Musée d'Orsay*, 5 (1993), 63–68; Franck Ruby, 'Théophile Gautier et la question de l'art pour l'Art', *BSTG*, 20 (1998), 3–13; Lavaud, *Théophile Gautier militant du romantisme*, pp. 398–408.

7. On the issue of Gautier's politics, the following articles will provide a concise but wide-ranging history of the question: René Jasinski, 'Théophile Gautier et la politique', in *Actes du quatrième congrès international d'histoire littéraire moderne* (Paris: Boivin, 1948), pp. 119–33 (repr. in Jasinski, *A travers le XIXe siècle* (Paris: Minard, 1975), pp. 229–48); Andrew Rossiter, 'Gautier et le "Livre du peuple" de Lamennais', *Histoire politique et histoire des idées (XVIIIe–XIXe siècles)* (Paris: Les Belles Lettres, 1976), pp. 181–207); Voisin, 'Gautier et la politique'; Peter Whyte, 'Théophile Gautier, poète-courtisan', in *Art and Literature of the Second Empire/Les Arts et la littérature sous le Second Empire*, ed. by David Baguley (University of Durham, 2003), pp. 129–47.

8. For the wider debates surrounding the opposition between didactic art and art for-art's sake in 1848 see Neil McWilliam, 'Art, Labour and Mass Democracy: Debates on the Status of the Artist in France around 1848', *Art History*, 11 (1988), 64–87.

9. This message reiterated Gautier's long-standing conviction (already seen in his 1836 articles in *La Presse*) of the need for the state to stimulate public consumption of the arts, but it also coincided in the cultural sphere with his newspaper's very recently discovered republican sympathies. On 25 February, the day after urging Louis-Philippe to abdicate in favour of the regency, Émile de Girardin rallied to the Republic in his editorial entitled 'Confiance! Confiance!', in which he urged the financial and commercial sectors to rally to the new regime: 'Que toutes les boutiques s'ouvrent! Que les transactions ne s'interrompent pas! Que les caisses du commerce et de la banque ne se ferment point! Que la Bourse reprenne ses opérations! C'est le moment d'acheter de la rente, non d'en vendre; pour l'honneur de notre pays, il faut soutenir nos cours.' See Pellissier, *Émile de Girardin*, pp. 190–92.

10. As Gautier put it: 'Ce n'est pas la république de Lacédémone, c'est celle d'Athènes qu'il nous faut.' In his opening article on the Salon of 1848, Gautier said that the Salon jury had been 'emporté par ce vent acerbe et purificateur qui a soufflé quinze jours avec tant de violence, et qui venait d'Amérique'. As we shall see, he returned to the idea of American democracy as the birth of the modern age in his articles on Chenavard's decorations for the Panthéon. Like everyone else, however, he knew that the historiography of the first French Republic had been transformed by Louis Blanc's *Histoire de la Révolution française*, Esquiros's *Histoire des Montagnards*, Lamartine's *Histoire des Girondins*, and the first volume of Michelet's *Histoire de la Révolution*, all published in Paris in 1847.

11. 'Mais hélas! Le style de ce véhicule, sans forme et sans grandeur, n'était pas de nature à faire aimer la république. Ce n'était ni un char, ni une table, ni une caisse, mais quelque chose de vague et d'inconnu que la langue humaine n'a pas encore nommé' (Paul Mantz, 'Les Cérémonies de la République', *L'Artiste*, 12 March 1848, pp. 7–9 (p. 8)).

12. *Le Canard* (14–21 May), quoted in Chaudonneret, *La Figure de la République*, p. 173.

13. The proclamation is reproduced in Georgel, *1848: la République et l'art vivant*, p. 29.

14. *L'Artiste*, 30 April 1848, p. 112.

15. The axe in particular was a delicate matter. As Gautier noted: 'Pendant la Révolution française, elle [la figure de la République] se coiffe elle-même du bonnet de l'affranchie, tient d'une main le niveau et de l'autre s'appuie sur un faisceau de baguettes d'où sort une hache beaucoup trop significative' ('Concours pour la figure de la République', *La Presse*, 21 May 1848).

16. In his article on the 'Concours pour la figure' Gautier referred to Cesare Ripa, Gravelot, and Cochin. Cesare Ripa's *Iconologia* of 1602 had been published in French in 1637 as *Iconologie, ou Explication nouvelle de plusieurs images, emblèmes et autres figures hyérogliphiques des vertus, des vices, des arts, des sciences* ...; Gravelot (Hubert François Bourguignon, *dit*) and Charles-Nicolas Cochin had provided the drawings for Charles-Étienne Gaucher's four-volume *Iconologie, ou Traité de la science des allégories*, published in Paris in the mid-eighteenth century.

17. Anon., 'Concours: figure symbolique de la République', *L'Artiste*, 30 April 1848, pp. 108–09.

18. The first is from the unsigned article in *Le Canard* (see above, note 8), the second by Haussard in *Le National* (1 May), the third by Laurent Jan in *Le Siècle* (27 November). In *La Figure de la République* (pp. 133–74), Chaudonneret gives the full text of eighteen of the most important articles published on the exhibition, including the extracts quoted here.

19. Picou, along with Jean-Louis Hamon, shared a studio with Gérôme, which for Champfleury made him a member of what he called 'l'école de Gérôme' (see above, p. 45). Gautier had implicitly agreed with this description, for immediately after his warm support for Gérôme in the Salon of 1848, he had welcomed Picou's debut Salon appearance by stating that his *Cléopâtre et Antoine sur le Cydnus* (Aix-en-Provence, Musée des Beaux-Arts) 'se classe parmi les sept ou huit toiles les plus importantes du Salon'.

20. Reconciliation represented by the association of the tricolour's three colours had a history going back to the first Fête de la Fédération, on 14 July 1790. See Raoul Girodet, 'Les Trois Couleurs', in *Les Lieux de mémoire*, ed. by Pierre Nora, 3 vols (Paris: Gallimard, 1984–92), I: *La République*, pp. 5–35 (pp. 10–13).

21. In his 1855 description of the painting on show that year in the Universal Exposition, Gautier described her as 'altière, regardant de face, vêtue de rouge et tenant l'épée de bronze d'Achille', forming with *L'Odyssée* the couple of Homer's 'deux immortelles filles', through whom 'l'action et le voyage' contrast (*Les Beaux-Arts en Europe*, 2 vols (Paris: Michel Lévy, 1865), I, 145–46). It seems that Gautier cannot be referring to *L'Iliade*, the oil painting reproduced in Vigne (*Ingres*, p. 273) and dated by him (p. 271) as being 'au début des années 1850' (though against the reproduction on p. 273, he inserts 'vers 1855'), and by Clark as 'some time in 1850 or thereabouts' (*The Absolute Bourgeois*, p. 68). The first list of his work made by Ingres himself, the *Cahier IX* reproduced in facsimile in Vigne (p. 325), who dates it from 'peu avant l'année 1851', contains the artist's reference to 'l'iliade et l'odissée' (*sic*), which implies that Ingres may have begun working on separate paintings of each female figure for some unspecified period before that date and that, in his reference to the *Iliade armée*, Gautier may be indicating an early version of *L'Iliade* seen in Ingres's studio, rather than to the *Apothéose d'Homère*. For *L'Iliade*, Ingres turned the step 90°, seating the figure on the end visible to the spectator. Her attribute, the sheathed dagger, which in the 1827 painting directed the spectator's eye upwards towards Homer, now rests against the step, bisecting the female figure's red dress.

22. 'On assure qu'on veut assouvir sur moi le mauvais concours de la République en me chargeant de la faire, moi seul. Que Dieu détourne de moi ce fléau d'intentions ministérielles auxquelles je suis, d'ailleurs, très décidé de refuser net' (letter of 3 November 1848 from Ingres to Marcotte, quoted in Vigne, *Ingres*, p. 264).

23. 'Sa *Liberté aux barricades de Juillet* vient d'être installée au Luxembourg, à côté de ses *Grecs de Scio* [*Les Massacres de Scio*]: deux beaux épisodes de l'histoire contemporaine' (Thoré, 'Salon de 1848', in *Salons*, p. 561).

24. 'On dit qu'il a entrepris *L'Égalité sur les barricades de Février*; car notre révolution est la glorieuse sœur de la révolution nationale, glorifiée il y a dix-huit ans [...] Que Delacroix se hâte, et nous verrons ses deux pendants au-dessus de la tête du président de l'Assemblée nationale' (ibid., pp. 561–62). See Clark, *The Absolute Bourgeois*, p. 126.

25. On the history of *La Liberté* see Johnson, *The Paintings of Eugène Delacroix*, I, 151; Hélène Toussaint, '*La Liberté guidant le peuple*' de Delacroix (Paris: RMN, 1982); Arlette Sérullaz and Vincent Pomarède, *Eugène Delacroix, 'La Liberté guidant le peuple'* (Paris: RMN, 2004). See also Delacroix's recently published letter of 17 March 1848 to Garaud, Directeur des Beaux-Arts for five weeks until 1 April 1848, in *Eugène Delacroix: nouvelles lettres*, ed. by Lee Johnson and Michèle Hannoosh (Bordeaux: William Blake, 2000), pp. 60–61.

26. For Delacroix's involvement in the politics of 1848, see Clark, *The Absolute Bourgeois*, pp. 126–29. For Ingres's views on the Second Republic and his support for Cavaignac's repression in June, see *Ingres 1780–1867*, p. 323.

27. Quoted in *Paul Delaroche: un peintre dans l'histoire* (Paris: RMN, 1999), p. 270.

28. See Stephen Bann, *Paul Delaroche: History Painted* (London: Reaktion Books, 1997), pp. 245–56.

29. Houssaye floated the idea in *L'Artiste*, saying that the public, having had a good laugh at the results of the first competition, now wanted to see some serious work, while the artists wanted to redeem themselves for the initial failure of the competition. In the meantime, he republished Gautier's brief history of the iconography of Liberty from his review of the exhibition of sketches ('École Nationale des Beaux-Arts: symbolisme de la République', *L'Artiste*, 15 June 1848, pp. 160–61).

30. 'La République de l'avenir', *Le Journal*, 28 July 1848 (repr. in *Fusains et eaux-fortes*, pp. 227–38); 'L'Atelier de M. Ingres en 1848', *L'Événement*, 2 August 1848 (repr. in *Fusains et eaux-fortes*, pp. 239–50); 'Plastique de la civilisation: du beau antique et du beau moderne', *L'Événement*, 8 August 1848 (repr. in *Souvenirs de théâtre, d'art et de critique* (Paris: Charpentier, 1883), pp. 197–204). His overdue obituary article on Marilhat was certainly submitted before the closure of *La Presse*. Beginning with a nostalgic account of the rue du Doyenné Bohemia in 1833, when he had made Marilhat's acquaintance, it consisted mainly of extracts from the artist's letters to his own sister, written during his oriental travels of 1831. On Gautier and Marilhat see Frans Amelinckx, 'Théophile Gautier et Marilhat: peintures, textes et contextes', in *Théophile Gautier: l'art et l'artiste* (= *BSTG*, 4.1–2 (1983)), I, 1–9.

31. Compare for example Gautier's final paragraph in 'La République de l'avenir' — 'Nous la voulons fermement cette belle république athénienne, pleine de lumière et de bourdonnements joyeux, chantée par le poète, sculptée par le statuaire, colorée par le peintre' — with Ingres's comment in a letter to Gilibert in May 1848 on 'la république que tout le monde veut, mais que tant d'anges infernaux veulent rouge, quand nous la voudrions sur la ressemblance d'Astrée, belle et noble vierge, noble et pure!', in *Lettres d'Ingres à Gilibert*, ed. by Marie-Jeanne and Daniel Ternois (Paris: Champion, 2005), pp. 365–66.

32. 'Quel est l'instinct le plus vif de l'homme? Celui de la liberté. Pourquoi désire-t-il être libre? Pour chercher le bonheur. Qu'est-ce le bonheur? C'est le bien-être intellectuel et physique acquis sans faire tort à personne' (p. 231). On Gautier's contacts with Fourier's ideas and terminology, see P. S. Hambly, 'Théophile Gautier et le fouriérisme', *Australian Journal of French Studies*, 11 (1974), 210–36.

33. 'Aux esclaves ont succédé les serfs, aux serfs les ouvriers ou les prolétaires, comme on les appelle aujourd'hui. L'amélioration est sensible, mais bientôt l'ouvrier sera affranchi lui-même. [...] Les machines feront désormais toutes les besognes pénibles, ennuyeuses et répugnantes' (p. 237).

34. In a letter of 9 June Ingres wrote: 'Mais comme ce tableau est extrêmement délicat, et quoique j'aie beccoup [*sic*] travaillé, ce n'est cependant que d'hier que je l'ai terminé. Phisiquement [*sic*], à présent je vais lui donner la dernière main, et elle est tout pour l'œuvre! Cela me tiendra bien encore 8 ou 10 jours de travail.' By 29 June, 'La Vénus' was 'presque terminée, elle le serait sans les tristes événemens [of the June Days]'. See *Lettres d'Ingres à Marcotte d'Argenteuil*, ed. by Daniel Ternois (Nogent-le-Roi: Librairie Jacques Laget, 1999), pp. 130–33. On the painting see *Ingres 1780–1867*, pp. 48–50 and 323–24, and Vigne, *Ingres*, pp. 265–66.

35. *Baronne James de Rothschild*, 1844–48, private collection. See *Portraits by Ingres: Image of an Epoch*, ed. by Gary Tinterow and Philip Conisbee (New York: Metropolitan Museum of Art, 1999), pp. 414–25; Carol Ockman, *Ingres's Eroticized Bodies: Retracing the Serpentine Line* (New Haven and London: Yale University Press, 1995), pp. 67–83; Shelton, *Ingres and his Critics*, pp. 189–92; *Ingres, 1780–1867*, pp. 322–23.

36. He cannot have been the only critic invited to perform this function, because on 1 August a certain L.G. published in the *Revue des deux mondes* an article entitled 'Vénus anadyomène: portrait de Mme de Rothschild, par M. Ingres' (pp. 441–49). In the bibliography of the *Revue des deux mondes*, the author of the article is identified as L. de Geofroy. In *Ingres and his Critics*, Shelton retains this identification of L.G. (but in the variant form of L. de Geffroy) but concedes that, on the subject of this critic, 'the biographical dictionaries are silent' (p. 184).

Silent, I believe, with good reason, for in the same *Revue des deux mondes* bibliography, Louis de Geofroy is also credited as being the author of the review of the Salon of 1849 (15 August 1849, pp. 559–93), whose author in the journal itself is named as the same F. de Lagenevais who had published in the *Revue des deux mondes* a major article on Ingres on 1 August 1846 (pp. 514–41) and, as we have seen, reviewed the Salon of 1848. Louis de Geofroy is therefore, I believe, a pseudonym of a pseudonym, the L and G being the common feature of all three identities (L.G., L. de Geofroy and F. de Lagenevais) assumed by Frédéric de Mercey, an important Ingres ally in the upper echelons of the fine arts administration (as chef de bureau in Charles Blanc's office) and, as such, a very suitable choice to complement Gautier in the public presentation of his two latest works.

37. *Œuvres posthumes: Salons 1846–1851*, p. 112). Gautier's article was republished in *Fusains et eaux-fortes*, pp. 239–50). All subsequent references to the article are taken from this edition.

38. 'Il y avait là [in the Bazar Bonne-Nouvelle] comme deux catégories distinctes, presque deux manières, dans lesquelles l'art du peintre aux prises, tantôt avec le modèle et la nature, tantôt avec l'idéal et la tradition, se maintenait toujours à une égale hauteur. On trouve précisément, dans les deux tableaux que M. Ingres vient d'exposer, une expression complète de ce contraste' (p. 442).

39. In the gushing commentary in *L'Illustration*, we learn that 'les riches et les heureux de ce monde [...] accourent en foule', that the courtyard of the Institute is filled with 'ces voitures blasonnées, ces chevaux qui piaffent, ces cochers en perruque à marteau et ces valets de pieds en conciliabule', and that 'il s'agit pour eux du portrait de madame de Rothschild'. The *Vénus* does not get a mention.

40. Shelton shows very well the willingness of many commentators to make this connection (*Ingres and his Critics*, pp. 184–85). As it happens, his examples do not include the short article in *L'Illustration* referred to in the previous note and which opens tellingly with the statement: 'Tous les arts semblent heureusement rendus à leur ancienne activité' (where 'ancienne' implies unmistakeably pre-February/June 1848) and depicts an aristocratic class celebrating together the elevation of one of their own to artistic immortality.

41. This was evidently a more significant lesson in August 1848 than in February. Shelton rightly notes that virtually every critic pointed out that Ingres had worked on the *Vénus* during the bloodiest phase of the June Days and that this information 'could only have come from the artist himself' (p. 185). As we saw above, Ingres stated in his letter to Marcotte that the events had in fact delayed his work, but no doubt he was happy in public to allow the rather different history of its completion to prevail.

42. Visiting Ingres's study the previous year, Gautier had closed his short description of the unfinished work with a first draft of this analogy: 'On dirait un Corrège, ou mieux encore quelque tableau d'Apelle retrouvé sous les décombres d'une ruine d'Athènes, car c'est ainsi que l'on imagine la peinture grecque' ('Une visite à M. Ingres', *La Presse*, 27 June 1847). One year later reference to the intercessor between Ingres and the source of the tradition has gone.

43. 'Troisième exposition de l'Association des artistes', *La Presse*, 13 February 1848.

44. Ingres's ambition in relation to the classical tradition is analysed by Norman Bryson in his *Tradition and Desire: From David to Delacroix* (Cambridge University Press, 1984). See also Shelton's comments on Bryson's analysis in 'Ingres et la critique moderne' (in *Ingres 1780–1867*, pp. 21–31).

45. Art historians do not appear to have linked Ingres's resumption of work on his *Vénus anadyomène* to the reappearance of Chassériau's painting, initially shown at the Salon of 1839, in the Bonne-Nouvelle exhibition of 1848, but it seems to me possible that Gautier's comments on the relationship between Chassériau's Venus and the lost original Greek sources may have touched a raw nerve in Ingres. On the reception of Ingres's work at the 1846 Bonne-Nouvelle exhibition and on that of his *Vénus anadyomène*, see *Ingres and his Critics*, pp. 146–92.

46. Anon., *L'Artiste*, 15 August 1848, p. 239.

47. Clément de Ris, for example, reviewing the third exhibition of the Association des Artistes stated, against all the evidence, that the first, 'celle de 1846 [...] a été si funeste à M. Ingres' ('Troisième exposition de l'Association des artistes', *L'Artiste*, 23 January 1848, pp. 177–80 (p. 178)).

48. The following month, in his articles on Chenavard, Gautier repeated the avatar theme. Referring to the representation of Napoleon seated in a boat and surrounded by Cyrus, Alexander, Caesar, and Charlemagne, he explained that 'l'artiste laisse entendre que dans sa pensée une âme unique par des *avatars* successifs est apparue à des époques diverses sous ces cinq noms illustres' (*L'Art moderne*, p. 31). After these 'conquérants unitaires', we are shown 'la série des *Avatars* ou incarnations de la divinité sous des formes diverses' (pp. 40–41) (Gautier's italics).

49. This tension is absent from his description of the unfinished version one year earlier. Here, the Venus has 'l'âge éternel des déesses — quinze ans' ('Une visite à M. Ingres'). It is instructive in this respect to compare Gautier's description of the final version with that of L.G., who retained the academic model of the description of paintings, moving from background to middle distance to foreground and from periphery to centre: 'L'aube se lève [...] Dans le fond [...] La brise [...] apparaît la déesse' ('Vénus anadyomène', p. 444). This is in part because he is writing for a different readership, one more likely to be familiar with the traditional rhetorical procedures associated with the description of paintings, but also because the academic description is central to his effort to describe what he saw as Ingres's achievement and which Shelton calls its 'complete desensualisation of the all-too-carnal motif of the female nude' (*Ingres and his Critics*, p. 188). L.G.'s description of the image erases the conflict between sensuality and innocence which had become central to Gautier's description of the finished work.

50. In his commentary on the painting in 1855, Gautier made this detail more explicit: 'de petits Amours, dansant sur le bout des flots, présentent à la déesse nouvelle un miroir de métal poli; après s'être regardée, elle sera femme tout à fait; elle aura conscience de sa beauté' (*Les Beaux-Arts en Europe*, I, 152).

51. 'Cet Athénien de la rue Mazarine [Ingres at the Institute] a eu la coquetterie de mettre son grand goût au service du journal des modes, et ce béret, que signerait Mme Baudrand, est, malgré son exactitude, du plus beau style grec' (p. 249).

52. Published on 5–11 September 1848, they were republished in *L'Art moderne*, pp. 1–94. All subsequent references to these articles will be to this edition. For an extensive series of illustrations of Chenavard's work on the project see Chaudonneret, *Paul Chenavard: le peintre et le prophète*.

53. When Charles Blanc brought Chenavard and his project to Ledru-Rollin in mid-April, the minister was apparently so impressed that he decided there and then to award Chenavard the Panthéon commission (see Chaudonneret, 'Le Décor inachevé', p. 67). His exclusion from the government formed in the wake of the June Days deprived Chenavard of key support, and Gautier's articles may be a response on his or Chenavard's or Blanc's part to this change in the political context.

54. A. H. Delaunay, editor of the *Journal des artistes*, stated: 'Ce premier acte officiel du nouveau directeur [des beaux-arts, Charles Blanc] est un début des plus malheureux. C'est une violation flagrante du principe républicain' (21 April 1848, p. 93). On 30 April Houssaye published in *L'Artiste* (pp. 106–07) a letter from an artist writing under the pseudonym of Euphanor and claiming to speak for the vast majority of artists, expressing outrage that '*un inconnu*' had been awarded a commission of that importance without regard to the democratic principle of the '*concours* jugé par un jury *élu*'' (p. 107, Euphanor's italics). Having welcomed Chenavard's commission in the previous issue of *L'Artiste* on 16 April in terms identical with those of Gautier's fourth article on the Salon of 1848, Houssaye dissociated himself from the contents of Euphanor's letter. On the Panthéon see *Le Panthéon: symbole des révolutions: de l'Église de la Nation au Temple des grands hommes* (Paris: Caisse national des monuments historiques, 1989); Mona Ozouf, 'Le Panthéon', in *Les Lieux de mémoire*, ed. by Pierre Nora, 3 vols (Paris: Gallimard, 1984–92), I: *La République*, pp. 139–66.

55. See 'L'Art philosophique', of 1855 (in *Œuvres complètes*, II, 601).

56. See Gotlieb, *The Plight of Emulation*, p. 53. The challenge Gros faced was that of emulating Jacques-Louis David. Six months after his Chenavard articles, Gautier repeated his view that in the Panthéon commission (1811–24) Gros had attempted a historical subject which did not suit him in a medium which he did not understand. See 'La Galerie française, I', *La Presse*, 13 February 1849 (repr. in *Tableaux à la plume*, pp. 30–46 (p. 39)).

57. Two years earlier he had warmly praised Chenavard's painting *La Palingénésie sociale*, and added:

'Nous avons insisté longuement sur ce nom d'une notoriété restreinte, car Chenavard, sans avoir beaucoup occupé les clairons de la publicité, a cependant eu sur l'art de ce temps-ci une influence occulte mais véritable' ('Salon de 1846', *La Presse*, 2 April 1846).

58. According to Gautier, Chenavard 's'est livré à une étude consciencieuse et philosophique de la peinture; il a vu toutes les galeries de l'Europe, analysé, copié et commenté toutes les fresques monumentales, et, par une fréquentation assidue, pénétré dans l'intimité secrète de Michel-Ange, de Raphaël, des dieux et des demi-dieux de l'art; à force d'écouter les discours muets de leurs chefs-d'œuvres, il a recueilli des phrases mystérieuses qu'ils ne disent point à d'autres' (p. 3).

59. 'Esprit vaste, tête encyclopédique pour ainsi dire, élevé sur les genoux de Michel-Ange, Chenavard a trouvé, comme le robuste Florentin, que la peinture à l'huile était bonne pour les femmelettes, et il n'a pas fait trois tableaux dans sa vie' ('Salon de 1848', *La Presse*, 26 April 1848).

60. His homage to railway stations — 'lieux imposans et sacrés, d'où partent les veines artérielles qui portent la pensée et la richesse au monde' — could have come from a mid-nineteenth-century investment prospectus. Gautier had clearly come a long way since his article a decade earlier in which he had dismissed this Anglo-Saxon invention as a financial non-starter ('Le Chemin de fer', *La Charte de 1830*, 15 October 1837 (repr. in *Fusains et eaux-fortes*, pp. 185–95)).

61. The phrase is Chaudonneret's ('Le Décor inachevé', p. 67). At the end of his fourth article on the Chenavard project, Gautier summarized his account of the narrative contained in the mural paintings and frieze by describing the subject represented in the impost: 'Il est emprunté à la célèbre chanson de Béranger: Peuples, formez une sainte alliance, | Et donnez-vous la main. Toutes les nations du monde ingénieusement personnifiées y célèbrent l'agape de la fraternité universelle' (p. 58).

62. In *Une collaboration inconnue: la description du Panthéon de Paul Chenavard par Gautier et Nerval*, Archives des lettres modernes, 48 (Paris: Minard, 1963), Jean Richer stated, on the basis of an anonymous three-page manuscript contained in the Lovenjoul Gautier archive (Mélanges littéraires Gérard de Nerval, D.741, fols 100, 101, 131), that Gautier's text had been written in collaboration with Nerval. Recently, however, Pierre-Olivier Douphis has convincingly shown that the manuscript, almost certainly a fragment of a much longer text, was written by Chenavard ('Le Poète et l'artiste-philosophe: une collaboration retrouvée entre Gautier et Chenavard en 1848', *BSTG*, 23 (2001), 21–36).

63. 'Il n'eût pas fallu une grande hardiesse d'initiative pour prendre MM. Ingres, Delaroche et autres, qui ont fait leurs preuves: on pouvait ainsi prévoir d'avance les résultats; mais une originalité nouvelle ne se fût pas produite, et un splendide horizon de l'art serait resté voilé à tout jamais' (pp. 1–2). He even paid Ledru-Rollin, by then removed from the government, the (admittedly back-handed) compliment that the appointment of Chenavard 'sera peut-être le seul acte de son ministère dont la postérité lui saura gré' (p. 93).

64. In easel painting, 'la touche du maître en fait la plus grande valeur et l'idée d'une vaste composition rendue par des mains étrangères choque nos préjugés d'individualisme' (p. 2).

65. Gautier argued — but to no avail — that if the arrangement was good enough for Rubens, it should have been good enough for Chenavard's assistants and pupils: 'Pierre-Paul Rubens [...] demandait un florin par heure et ne se croyait nullement déshonoré pour cela' (p. 93).

66. See Chaudonneret, 'Le Décor inachevé', p. 67. See also her article 'L'Aube d'une République des arts', in which she points out that 'David [d'Angers] voulait également placer des "grands hommes" devant le Panthéon, conformément à la destination de ce temple de la patrie. Le décor du Panthéon en est alors conçu comme celui d'un musée historique et patriotique' (p. 270). Gautier supported Chenavard's wider ambition: 'A part le talent que le peintre y peut mettre, n'y a-t-il pas autant de poésie, de haute moralité, de beauté véritable enfin, dans la représentation des grandes actions et des hommes illustres, l'honneur de la famille humaine, sans distinction de lieu, de temps et de secte, que dans celle de miracles et de martyres où l'art n'est pas plus respecté que la vérité historique?' (p. 5).

67. Of the building itself, Gautier noted: 'Le Panthéon est un temple et non pas une église, sa forme essentiellement païenne se refuse aux exigences de la religion catholique [... Il] a la forme d'une croix grecque, c'est-à-dire dont les branches sont d'égale longueur, contrairement à la croix

latine où les bras sont plus courts que le pied' (pp. 4–5); of Christ: 'Sans refuser au Nazaréen sa qualité divine, Chenavard ne l'a pas cependant présenté sous son côté surnaturel et fantastique, pour ainsi dire. Il a plutôt vu en lui le philosophe, le moraliste imbu des doctrines esséniennes, l'initié des mystères égyptiens, le dépositaire de l'antique sagesse de Moïse, et surtout l'ange de la bonne nouvelle, le verbe de l'esprit moderne' (p. 16); of art flattering political regimes: 'Certes rien n'était plus facile que de couvrir ces vastes surfaces de flatteries peintes à l'adresse du jour [...]. L'occasion était belle pour Chenavard de mettre là des tambours, des canons, des troupiers de Sambre-et-Meuse, des grognards de l'empire, mais l'artiste dégage toujours l'idée des faits' (pp. 89–90).

68. For Gautier the gain was evident in the first work on the left on entering the building, Chenavard's representation of the Flood was 'non pas pris comme ceux de Poussin ou de Girodet, dans le sens épisodique d'une douzaine d'hommes qui se noient d'une façon plus ou moins théâtrale, mais entendu comme le cataclysme destructeur du monde primitif et des races antédiluviennes' (p. 7). In the planned circular mosaic depicting hell and forming the left arm of the cross-shaped decoration on the monument's floor, Chenavard displayed 'cette prodigieuse science du corps humain, cette invention d'attitudes violentes et de raccourcis strapassés que nul n'a possédée au même degré depuis Michel-Ange' (p. 74).

69. 'Nul édifice antique ou moderne n'a vu se déployer sur ses murailles un plus vaste poème pittoresque' (p. 84).

70. On Chenavard's pessimism, see Gotlieb, 'Chenavard's Lesson', pp. 60–62.

71. The meeting was organized by the association Institut des Provinces, founded by the archaeologist Arcisse de Caumont, who was also a prominent figure in the activities of the Société pour la Conservation des Monuments Français. See 'Congrès des diverses Académies de France', *L'Ami de la religion* (4 March 1851), pp. 528–32, which includes (pp. 530–32) the text of the report by Albert Du Boys, 'fait au nom de la commission d'enquête nommée par la Société française pour la conservation des monuments', in the wake of Pernot's denunciation of Chenavard's project.

72. *L'Ami de la religion* published the letter on 15 March (pp. 603–05). In it Chenavard referred to 'd'anciens articles de journal qui, quels qu'ils soient, ne sauraient être en cause' (p. 604).

73. 'Les Peintures murales de M. P. Chenavard, au Panthéon', *Le National*, 9 March 1851. On Chenavard's response to the attack see Chaudonneret, 'Le Décor inachevé', p. 70.

74. 'Quelle que soit la destination donnée à ce travail [...], il est certain qu'il suffira pour établir sa renommée. Ce n'est pas seulement le travail d'un penseur habitué à méditer sur la marche de l'esprit humain, c'est aussi la révélation d'un peintre familiarisé depuis long-temps avec la langue de son art'. ('Les cartons de M. P. Chenavard', *RDM*, 15 January 1852, pp. 362–77 (p. 363)).

75. On the Chenavard work on show in 1855, see Chaudonneret, 'Le Décor inachevé', p. 72, and my article 'Gautier et la peinture allemande à L'Exposition Universelle de 1855', pp. 233–34. In his comments on Chassériau's decorations for the Chapelle des Fonts Baptismaux in Saint-Roch, Gautier stated: 'Loin que la grande peinture soit abandonnée, elle est, au contraire, plus cultivée que jamais et dans les meilleures conditions de l'art. Les tableaux d'histoire et de sainteté ne se font plus sur toile, mais sur les murs de monuments et des églises' (*Les Beaux-Arts en Europe*, II, 241).

76. The exhibition and that of the work submitted by the students of the French Academy in Rome had, Gautier said, 'passé presque inaperçus' in the run-up to the presidential elections. The figures of the Republic went on show in a room which was so poorly lit on one side that hanging arrangements had to alternate to ensure that all could be seen, and in which reproductions of Michaelangelo's *Last Judgment* provided a powerful distraction: three forms of relegation that seemed to sum up the competition's fate ('École Nationale des Beaux-Arts: exposition des figures du concours pour la République', *La Presse*, 5 December 1848).

77. Gautier said that in May Daumier's sketch had been 'jugée par tous une des plus remarquables' but he himself had not commented on it at the time. Champfleury was the most fervent champion of Daumier's figure of the Republic, noting that 'il a fallu cette sérieuse et forte esquisse du caricaturiste, pour prouver aux incrédules que Daumier peut marcher à la suite de Delacroix, d'Ingres et de Corot, les trois seules maîtres de l'école française actuelle' (*Œuvres posthumes. Salons 1846–1851*, p. 97).

78. See in this respect Henri Loyrette in *Daumier 1808–1879* (Paris: RMN, 1999), p. 248; Clark,

The Absolute Bourgeois, p. 107; Chaudonneret, *La Figure de la République*, pp. 59–66, and Georgel, *1848: la République et l'art vivant*, pp. 49–60.

79. 'Palais du Quai d'Orsay: peintures murales de M. Théodore Chassériau', *La Presse*, 12 December 1848.

80. See Peltre, *Théodore Chassériau*, p. 158.

81. Thus he explains, in relation to the first work encountered on entering, 'espèce de carton moitié tableau, moitié bas-relief, en grisaille', entitled *Guerrier et chevaux*: 'Le peintre a pris avec raison le parti incolore pour cette partie de l'édifice éclairée par des jours de reflet et où ne tombe jamais la lumière franche, car la valeur des tons n'est pas appréciable à cette lueur crépusculaire. Ces compositions modelées avec du noir et du blanc, presque de la même nuance que la pierre, sont harmonieuses et douces, et préparent bien l'œil aux peintures qui vont suivre. C'est pour emprunter à la musique un de ses termes, une introduction en mode mineur à l'éclatante symphonie pittoresque développée dans les hauteurs de l'escalier.'

82. Peltre points out the relationship between Chassériau's allegorical design and those adopted by Delacroix for the hemicycle of the Palais Bourbon and by Ingres for his unfinished decorative project for the chateau at Dampierre (p. 158). See also, in the catalogue of the 2002 exhibition *Chassériau: un autre romantisme*, Vincent Pomarède's commentary on *La Force et l'Ordre*, the surviving fragment of the central mural, flanked by *L'Ordre pourvoit aux besoins de la Guerre* on one side and *La Paix protectrice des Arts*, on the other (pp. 221–22).

83. As Gautier put it: 'Certes, c'est une mauvaise chaire pour professer qu'un champ de bataille, mais c'est de là seulement qu'on peut se faire entendre des populations incultes ou abruties; du peuple civilisé à peuple barbare, une victoire est une leçon [...] reliés par le commerce qui fleurit dans la paix, les différents peuples se visitent et apprennent à se connaître.'

84. 'C'est surtout par la majesté de l'attitude, le commandement du geste et l'autorité irrésistible du regard qu'il a caractérisé son emblème et fait comprendre qu'il s'agissait ici encore bien plus de la force morale que de la force physique.'

85. In his review of the paintings of the figure of the Republic, he expressed the hope that Daumier would submit to the Salon of 1849 the painting which he had failed to complete in time for the exhibition in November 1848 but added: 'si nous avons un salon de 1849 — doute pénible!'. On the rumour surrounding Ingres's views on the Salon, see below, p. 98.

86. 'Salon de 1849', *La Presse*, 26 July 1849. In *Le National* Haussard had also described the Salon of 1848 as 'l'arriéré de l'ancienne direction, le dernier legs de l'ex-liste civile' ('Salon de 1848', 23 March 1848).

CHAPTER 4

The Salon of 1849:
'La première exposition de la République'

On 15 June 1848, an editorial in *L'Artiste* bade a not very fond farewell to that year's Salon and the competition for a figure of the Republic:

> L'exposition est close. Les peintres et les sculpteurs reprennent tristement leurs œuvres et se croisent les bras, à part les vingt hommes de génie qui ont concouru deux fois pour la figure de la République. Nous ne regretterons pas bien vivement le Salon de 1848, à part quelques tableaux et statues hors ligne. [...] Espérons en l'avenir, mais, au train dont on va, il n'y a pas d'avenir pour l'art. Nous commençons à croire qu'il n'y aura pas de salon en 1849. (p. 172)

On 1 August the same review carried an extract of the report by David d'Angers to the 'comité de l'Intérieur sur la situation des artistes' (p. 224). It painted a bleak picture of a professional class made destitute by the collapse of the art market and urged the minister to provide with immediate effect the levels of state patronage needed to trigger a recovery.[1] In response to the report, Charles Blanc, Directeur des Beaux-Arts, informed David d'Angers that the state of public finances made it impossible for him to obtain from the government the sort of investment he was proposing and which went far beyond the two hundred thousand francs of emergency funds just voted by the Constituent Assembly for the purchase and commission of art works.[2] This sum, however modest, ensured some relief in the short term but left larger issues unresolved, as Clément de Ris pointed out in his note on the ceremony held on 20 August for the prizewinners of the Salon of 1848 and presided over by the Minister of the Interior, Antoine Sénard:

> Nous ne pouvons achever ces lignes sans exprimer le regret que M. le ministre n'ait pas précisé un peu plus les intentions du gouvernement républicain en faveur des artistes, et ne les ait pas entretenus de choses qui les intéressent spécialement; telles que la nouvelle organisation à apporter aux musées nationaux, les modifications que devra subir nécessairement le jury de peinture et l'institut dont l'aveugle tyrannie a été si funeste aux arts pendant dix-huit ans, les mesures à prendre pour qu'à l'avenir l'exposition des tableaux modernes ne se fasse pas au détriment des anciens, et tant d'autres questions qui eussent certainement intéressé l'auditoire devant lequel il s'adressait.[3]

As far as the first of these items of special interest was concerned, there would soon be progress to report. Seven days after the awards ceremony, the first stage of the administration's reorganization of the Louvre collections went on show to the public (see the following chapter). On the other items, reform of the Salon jury, the future of the Institute (by which Clément de Ris meant reform of the Académie des Beaux-Arts and the École des Beaux-Arts), and the proposed change of location for the Salon of 1849, information was slower to emerge. The commission set up in late March by the Second Republic's first, short-lived Directeur des Beaux-Arts, the sculptor Joseph Garraud, to make proposals for reform of the Académie and École des Beaux-Arts quickly agreed to disagree about the need for reform in general and for reform of the Salon jury in particular.[4] As for the Salon's proposed relocation, it was only in late October that it was announced that a decision in principle had been taken to move it from the Louvre to the Tuileries.[5] There was, however, one important condition attached: 'Cette décision ne pourra, du reste, avoir son effet qu'autant que des considérations de sûreté publique n'empêcheraient pas les ministres de la guerre et des travaux publics de donner leur adhesion à ce projet.' With a right of veto entrusted to the ministers responsible for the management of public order and safety and with no date given for the opening of the first Salon in the new location, the announcement did little to alleviate anxieties about the Salon's immediate future.

On 1 December, L'Artiste returned to the uncertainty: 'On ignore encore s'il y aura un Salon de 1849. Ce qui est certain, c'est que ce serait un Salon curieux. L'exposition aurait lieu aux Tuileries. Mais aura-t-on à exposer autre chose que des premiers-Paris?' (p. 116). Four days later, Gautier relayed the doubts to his wider audience in La Presse (see above, p. 96 n. 85). When official confirmation finally did come the following week that the Salon would take place in 1849 in a new location, L'Artiste welcomed it in terms which reflected the growing exasperation within the art community.[6] New anxieties were fuelled when it was rumoured 'de source certaine' that in one of the first meetings of the new Permanent Commission for Fine Arts, 'l'un de ses membres les plus influents, un académicien de la section de peinture', had advocated abolition of the Salon altogether.[7] Though the author was naming no names, it was an open secret that the academician in question was Ingres (he and Delaroche were in any event the only two members of the commission drawn from the painting section of the Academy).[8] 'Heureusement', this 'déplorable proposition' had been rejected and the commission had proceeded to discuss the composition of the jury, whereupon a new danger had emerged: 'On parle malheureusement d'y adjoindre cinq ou six *amateurs* qui seraient choisis par le ministre', a recipe for trouble as far as the editorialist was concerned.[9]

The turn of the year brought more uncertainties. The Salon's proposed location changed again, no longer the Tuileries but the Palais National, as the Palais-Royal was by then known. A commission established by the Ministers of the Interior, Finance, and War had agreed to bring the Palais National within the jurisdiction of the Ministry of the Interior and to allocate it in particular to the Salon. The Finance Committee of the National Assembly had approved the project and the Minister for Public Works had been invited to submit a bid for the funding of the necessary renovation and restoration work. The Salon was due to open in March but, as L'Artiste asked, 'y aura-t-il des tableaux? Les Diogènes de la critique y perdront leurs lanternes.'[10] It repeated the question later that month when it was confirmed that the Salon would not open before May.[11] On 15 February, there was good news at last. The Permanent Commission for Fine Arts had agreed on reform of the Salon jury's composition and regulatory framework. The new arrangements were those outlined in the brochure *De l'exposition et du jury*, published anonymously on 12 February 1848 by Boissard, Villot, and Clément de Ris. In *L'Artiste*, in which a substantial extract had appeared only a week after its publication,[12] news of the reform was celebrated, except for the role allocated to amateurs, which it continued to deplore. In addition, though it acknowledged that certain artists were entitled to be exempted from the obligation to submit their work to the jury, it feared that the effects of the abuse of this right during the final stages of the July Monarchy would continue to make themselves felt for some time to come.[13] These reservations notwithstanding, the editorialist was briefly carried away with optimism:

> Malgré l'admission forcée de quelques médaillistes injustement récompensés sous l'ancien régime, malgré les difficultés matérielles qu'on rencontre dans la disposition des galeries du Palais-National, le Salon promet d'être brillant et chacun s'y prépare en silence. C'est beaucoup pour les artistes de travailler avec sécurité et de ne plus se sentir menacés par l'odieux jury qui si longtemps les opprima. Pour être admis au Salon, le talent ne nuira plus. Décidément, la République est la bienvenue puisqu'elle nous affranchit et puisqu'elle nous organise. (p. 190)[14]

The optimism faded as the following month passed with still no final decision on the time or place for the Salon.[15] Only in mid-April were the uncertainties removed with the announcement that the Salon would open in the Palais des Tuileries on 15 June. This date, three months later than usual, created new problems. Who, it was asked, would be at the Salon in the middle of June? Certainly not the buyers, nor perhaps even the artists themselves, given the delay in making the announcement, coupled with its tight deadline of mid-May for the submission of work to the jury.[16]

The political situation that summer added to the concerns. The elections to the Legislative Assembly on 13 May 1849 had reinforced Louis-Napoleon's victory five months earlier by triggering the collapse of the moderate republican consensus in place in the Constituent Assembly since 23 April 1848. The result was a sharp increase in political polarization.[17] The opening of the Salon had coincided with the declaration of the state of siege which had followed the demonstration organized on 13 June against the Italian expedition.[18] In Paris, Nerval knew that on hearing this news Gautier, on his way back to Paris from a visit to London and Amsterdam, would be worrying about *La Presse* being shut down again, and/or the opening of the Salon being delayed. As far as *La Presse* was concerned, Nerval was able to reassure him.[19] As for the Salon, his news that 'on n'a pas ouvert le Musée aujourd'hui 15' turned out quickly to be a false alarm, as he confirmed in a second letter the following day.[20] This was important information for Gautier, given the difficulties that the political situation and a new cholera outbreak were creating for Parisian theatres that summer, threatening his principal source of income.[21]

On his return to Paris in the third week of June, Gautier discovered the full impact of the uncertainties that had surrounded the preparations for the Salon that year. In the wake of what he called 'tant d'inquiétudes, de misères, de désastres et de calamités de toutes sortes', many of the best-known artists had, as the editorialist in *L'Artiste* had feared, not submitted their work. Gautier was 'douloureusement frappé de l'absence de presque tous les noms illustres ou fameux' and responded by naming and shaming no fewer than fifty-seven painters and six sculptors who in his view had deserted France in her hour of need: 'dans la situation où nous sommes, aujourd'hui qu'il y a péril dans la demeure, il nous semble que l'absence ressemble à la désertion et la paresse à la peur.'[22] The greater (or more famous) the artist, the greater the responsibility to lead by example in times of trouble, but once again Ingres and Delaroche had failed to show:

> Ni M. Ingres, ni M. Delaroche n'ont exposé. Ils sont coutumiers du fait. C'était l'occasion ou jamais de ne plus faire chapelle à part [...]. C'est un crime, dans ces temps de nuit intellectuelle, de tenir la lumière sous le boisseau.

This new lecture to artists on their patriotic duty had a more serious edge than that of the year before, when Gautier had threatened Ingres with a Committee of Public Safety (see above, p. 44). It expressed in more sombre tones his real sense of the Salon's importance, not just as a shop window through which to help rebuild the shattered art market, nor even as a showcase for values which transcended political and social upheavals, though these factors were already important enough for him, but as a testimony to the human spirit fighting for its very survival. Who, if not artists, asked Gautier, 'représentera le génie humain entre la barbarie rouge et la barbarie blanche?'. Everyone knew what was meant by 'barbarie rouge', especially as the first anniversary of the June Days approached, but 'barbarie blanche' was in the circumstances provocative, an echo perhaps of Nerval's reference to the 'férocité des gens paisibles' in his letter of 16 June.[23]

Glad to be able to dispense at last with the outburst against the jury with which he had begun so many of his previous Salon reviews since 1833, Gautier again began his commentary on the works themselves with the sculpture.[24] Here, three issues dominated: the return of Préault after an absence of over a decade, the continued efforts of Pradier to retain a dominant position, and the emergence of Cavelier.[25] Like the majority of critics, Gautier began his review with Préault, devoting an entire article, the first of his three on sculpture, to a celebration of the artist's triumph over the Salon juries that had excluded him for most of the July Monarchy.[26] For Gautier the sculptor had finally achieved his rightful place in the Romantic pantheon alongside Hugo, Delacroix, and Berlioz; it was one that Gautier had himself attributed to Préault for fifteen years. In reality, however, there was still strong resistance to Préault in 1849. His most important work that year, *Christ*, representing Christ's agony on the cross, was initially rejected by even this first republican jury and admitted only during the 'séance de révision' three weeks before the Salon opened.[27] In the republic as in the monarchy, the representation of the Son of God was a serious matter. The realism with which Préault had depicted Christ's suffering was considered incompatible with His divinity, especially that summer when orthodox Catholicism had been reinvigorated by the electoral success of the Party of Order.[28] Gautier poured scorn on the official representations of Christ's agony on the cross, what he called the 'Christs doucereux et bénins [...]

et qui semblent plutôt suspendus par des rosettes à un mètre d'acajou que cloués par des pointes de fer à un arbre de douleurs':

> Les partisans de ces fades effigies, toujours dominés par leurs souvenirs classiques, prétendent que l'expression de la souffrance n'est pas convenable, et que le Christ étant Dieu ne doit pas se tordre dans le supplice comme un simple criminel. Oui le Christ est Dieu, mais il est homme aussi, et ce n'est pas un fantôme insensible qu'il laisse attacher à la croix pour nous racheter: il pâtit dans sa chair comme les deux voleurs ses compagnons.

With reference to this new emphasis on Christ's humanity rather than divinity, we saw earlier that Lehmann had encountered a similar problem the previous year with his *Vierge au pied de la croix*, but where Lehmann's painting had met with only a certain reticence and unease, Préault's *Christ* generated more explicit hostility.[29] Gautier dismissed the attacks in his inimitable way by reminding his readers that Spanish artists, who took no lessons in Catholicism from anyone, had always represented Christ's physical suffering on the cross with brutal realism:

> Les Christs de Montanez, de Roldan, de Berruguete, de Cornejo Duque et de cette admirable école de sculpteurs en bois, pour ainsi dire inconnus du reste de l'Europe [Gautier excepted, of course], ont toujours sur leur corps les stigmates du supplice imités avec une affreuse vérité.

By 1849 Gautier had been defending for almost a decade Préault's depiction of Christ's agony by linking it to those by Spanish artists, but he was evidently still struggling to impose this particular Spanish ancestry on the critical reception of Préault's work.[30]

For Pradier, the return to the Salon of the sculptor whose career he had, as a member of the jury during the July Monarchy, helped to obstruct presented a new threat, one which overshadowed the pleasure he would have taken from the absence of Clésinger that year.[31] Once again, however, Gautier was equal to the circumstances. After Préault and the artist-martyr's triumph over adversity, he presented Pradier and the artist-hero's fidelity to his ideal above the clamour of events.[32] In his commentary on *Chloris caressée par Zéphir* he rebutted criticisms of the alleged naturalistic shortcomings in the young woman's body and Pradier's use of polychromy.[33] The main attack, however, focused on the sensuality of the nude's response to Zephyr's whispered caresses. Where de Mercey, for example, in ill-concealed distaste had resorted to the clichés of the *roman-feuilleton* to describe her pose, Gautier deflected the criticism with an analogy between the springtime setting and Chloris's pose, what he called 'la puberté de l'année et de l'âge'.[34] The tension in her body was that of April's delicate balance between winter's last chills and summer's first heat — 'quelque chose de frileux dans sa pose montre que malgré le soleil brillant, le zéphyr qui caresse son épaule nue a trempé son aile dans la neige' — and between the first penetrating scents of the flowers and the awakening in her of 'le trouble amoureux du printemps'. De Mercey was evidently not convinced by this more elegant interpretation, and his comments were a sign that some powerful opinion-makers in the French art world were losing patience with what they saw as Pradier's increasing vulgarization of the classical nude.[35]

With Cavelier, a new rival had appeared in Pradier territory. His *Pénélope* had been the revelation of the exhibition of the *envois de Rome* held in the École des Beaux-Arts the previous autumn. Gautier had been fulsome in his praise of its reconciliation of naturalism and style: 'l'accent de nature et de vérité que M. Cavelier a rencontré n'a rien ôté au style à la fois élégant et noble de cette belle statue.'[36] Associating the topos of the living statue with the voyeuristic impulse that we saw above in relation to Pradier's adaptation of *Le Roi Candaule* (and that Gautier's male readers in *La Presse* will have recognized), he gazed fondly at Penelope's breasts which, 'doucement soulevés par une respiration paisible, palpitent sous les plis d'une légère tunique' and urged her to remain sleeping so as not to put an end to 'de si charmantes indiscrétions'. Though in his Salon review he toned down the erotic reverie before the sleeping woman, he reiterated his belief in her synthesis of the real and the classical female form, in the enduring power of the traditional classical model into which a refined modern sensuality breathed new life: 'Sa figure est d'abord une femme qui dort, ensuite c'est une Grecque, et enfin c'est Pénélope.' De Mercey stated even more emphatically that this work enacted the classical nude perfectly for modern sculpture:

> Depuis le retour aux traditions de l'antique, la sculpture moderne n'a rien produit d'un goût plus pur que cette composition [...] à coup sûr, par la noblesse de la pensée, par l'ordonnance et la chaste beauté de la composition, il l'emporte dès aujourd'hui sur plus d'une renommée acquise [...] l'avenir et la gloire [...] sont pour celui qui conserve religieusement la dignité de son art, qui dédaigne de vulgaires suffrages et ne se fait pas le pourvoyeur des instincts grossiers et dépravés. (pp. 589–90)

Pradier and Clésinger were certainly the principal targets of de Mercey's comments on 'plus d'une renommée acquise'.[37] With support like that Cavelier duly won the first-class medal for sculpture in the Salon of 1849, with Pradier and Préault taking only second-class medals. Perhaps as much in hope as in expectation, Pradier predicted that Cavelier would be no more than a one-hit wonder.[38]

For the painting, Gautier retained his familiar sequence (three articles on history painting, followed by one each on travel subjects, contemporary realism, animal painting, and landscape painting, with one article, the tenth, used to sweep up works when this 'ordre bien distinct' broke down). With so many of the most prominent painters absent, some of the second rank were thrust into the limelight.[39] Among the history painters, Muller's first-class medal in 1848 ensured advance publicity for his submission and the *jury de placement* had helped by giving his *Lady Macbeth* one of the best locations in the exhibition.[40] Though these factors helped to generate public interest, they did not secure a critical success for Muller.[41] De Mercey was particularly harsh, accusing him of reducing Shakespeare to boulevard melodrama and Lady Macbeth to a 'grisette exaspérée', making Muller sound like Delaroche without the talent. Gautier, supporting the public's taste against that of his fellow critics, was the exception that proved the rule. He complimented Muller's technique and the intelligence of his interpretation (of the opening scene of Act V). His mild reservations about the artist's infidelity to details of the original text were offset by praise for the work's 'certain air anglais et romanesque', with its vague echoes of Fuseli, Lawrence, and 'even' Angelica Kauffmann, artists as yet little known to the wider French public, which was thereby invited to take confidence from Gautier's expertise in the matter.

Like many of his *confrères*, Gautier coupled his comments on Muller with those on Duveau's *La Peste d'Elliant*. The painting, showing a mother pulling a cart carrying the bodies of her nine dead children and screaming out to heaven in pain and anger, while the father, driven mad with grief, is dancing, had acquired a lugubrious topicality as a result of the cholera outbreak in Paris that summer. For many critics the work was visual melodrama, but Gautier raised its credibility through relevant Spanish analogies in the work of Valdes Leal and Zurbaran.[42] He then turned to Delacroix, despite the fact that the painter's main submission that year was a pair of flower paintings which formed an odd sequel to Muller and Duveau in an article devoted to history painting.[43] To justify Delacroix's inclusion at this point rather than relegate his flower painting to a later article dealing with still life, Gautier resorted to formulaic praise of the 'style imprimé aux fleurs [...] 'traitées avec une largeur de touche, une puissance à effet et une facilité tout historiques'. Of their role in the wake of the painter's withdrawal from the events in Paris a year earlier, he said nothing, explaining his choice of subject merely as 'un caprice bien compréhensible chez un coloriste'.[44] There can be no doubt that he knew of Delacroix's intention to 'sortir un peu de l'espèce de poncif qui semble condamner tous les peintres de fleurs à faire le même vase avec les mêmes colonnes ou les mêmes draperies fantastiques qui leur servent de fond et de repoussoir',[45] for in his commentary he praised the two works for their break with the tradition in which flowers were 'traitées ordinairement d'une façon toute botanique' and in which the overall visual effect was sacrificed to the emphasis on naturalist detail. Unlike Delacroix himself, Gautier had no reservations and — the Spanish reference again — compared his flowers to those of Velasquez. The critical success of the flower paintings helped to offset the lack of enthusiasm generally felt for the other work Delacroix submitted that year. *Othello et Desdemona* was widely criticized, notably for Desdemona's pose, which Gautier defended as that of a 'sommeil agité de sombres pressentiments'.[46] He also praised its economy of means ('art admirable du peintre, qui dit tant avec des moyens si simples, et traduit tout l'effroi de Shakespeare en quelques coups de pinceau') but again few agreed with him. As for the smaller version of the *Femmes d'Alger*, Gautier spent more time comparing present and past practice of the art repetition in general than on Delacroix's example, on which a single short sentence on his preference for the 1834 original said it all. As in 1848, it is clear from what Gautier does not say as much as from what he does that for him Delacroix had again failed to deliver a Salon performance commensurate with the needs of the moment.

With Gérôme among the absentees in 1849, the Salon that year exposed the Neo-Greek school's lack of depth. Gautier rebaptized it 'l'école des délicats', which gave a loose thematic coherence to his sixth article, in which he grouped lesser-known artists with little else in common. The return of Gérôme's teacher, Gleyre, to the Salon after a four-year absence aroused considerable interest, and de Mercey considered his *Danse de bacchantes* the only history painting worthy of the name in the Salon that year. Gautier, on the other hand, considered the subject unsuited to Gleyre's temperament. For Gérôme's friends and acolytes, Picou and Hamon, Gautier had only lukewarm praise. Picou's submission was disappointing after his success the previous year both at the Salon and in the republican competition, while Gautier's comments on Hamon's work were no more than *passe-partout* ('espèces d'Alexandrins de la peinture très spirituels, très subtils, très fins, très adroits et très littéraires').

Landelle's association with Gérôme and Hamon made his work a logical transition to Gautier's seventh article. He had commented positively on Landelle's work in every Salon since 1846, and the painter had accompanied him to London in June 1849 and drawn at least two portraits of him (*Corr.*, IV, 487) on that occasion. His very supportive comments in December 1848 on Landelle's *République* (see above, p. 87) had clearly strengthened the relationship between them. Gautier began his article with two substantial paragraphs on the painting, which formed part of Landelle's submission to the Salon of 1849. Omitting the reservation he had expressed earlier about the figure's need for a little more 'caractère et vigueur', he now described her as just the sort of image of the Republic that was required for the times, 'le génie de la France, si vous voulez, plutôt que la farouche Euménide que nos pères ont adorée ou détestée' — *la force tranquille*, in other words, a term which, as it happens, he very nearly used. His comment was a discreet appeal for calm in the feverish atmosphere of the early summer of 1849.[47]

Gautier followed Landelle with a celebration of the return to the Salon of another friend, Léon Riesener, a cousin of Delacroix, with whom Riesener occasionally collaborated, and another victim of the Salon juries of the July Monarchy. Loyal to his friends as always, Gautier did his best on behalf of work for which his enthusiasm was not unreserved. In addition to associating him with much better-known victims of the previous juries, Préault, Barye, and Rousseau, he drew on his repertoire of valorizing analogies: 'Riesener [...] est à Delacroix ce que Jordaens est à Rubens'; with his talent for painting children he could 'tenir sa place parmi les Amours de Corrège', while his portrait of his wife 'est un des bons qui se soient faits dans ce genre depuis Latour'. He also used his review to praise Riesener's decoration of the Établissement National de Bienfaisance in Charenton, which the painter had invited him to visit with Delacroix and Préault (*Corr.*, IV, 41–42) and in whose Virgin Mary surrounded by angels and faithful he found, as he had in Lehmann, a less sullen form of religious painting, 'un certain air de fête que nous préférons aux peintures grognonnes et renfrognés sous prétexte d'orthodoxie catholique'.

This sequence of commentaries linked loosely under the category of history painting closed with Gautier's response to two works by Antigna which served as a transition to the genre work and realism that dominate the second half of the review. He was not instinctively drawn to what he thought of as Antigna's prosaic subjects and crude technique, so that his willingness to overcome these reservations is significant.[48] The female figures in *Après le bain* were certainly no goddesses or princesses but 'tout bonnement de grandes filles un peu communes', yet their firm modelling and natural flesh-tones made up to some extent for their lack of grace. It was a scene of 'une vie triviale, mais forte' in a luxurious landscape under an excellent sky, realism but with just enough value added to compensate for the subject's lack of ideal. *La Veuve* showed the hardship of a poor family kneeling around the straw-filled mattress on which lay the husband and father, 'mort de misère, de fatigue ou de manque de travail'. Gautier was sufficiently moved by Antigna's response to and treatment of the subject to extend the category of the *genre historique* to include the artist's contemporary social themes:

> Cette scène, qui convient au talent de M. Antigna, est peinte avec un pathétique sentiment de la réalité et une grande force de pinceau: c'est le genre élevé aux proportions de l'histoire, le drame remplaçant la tragédie dans la peinture comme dans la littérature, mouvement rationnel et qui doit se propager dans toutes les branches des arts: car pourquoi la douleur d'une pauvre femme d'ouvrier, ayant perdu son mari, ne serait-elle pas représentée de grandeur naturelle comme celle d'Andromaque ayant perdu Hector? Le fait n'est-il pas tout aussi intéressant pour nous? N'a-t-il pas de quoi nous prendre aux entrailles, et ne mérite-t-il pas autant d'arrêter nos regards attendris?

The article ends with this series of rhetorical questions which show Gautier, having said only days before that the true artist worked in the realm of ideas rather than facts, recognizing the force of Antigna's demonstration that the realm of facts mattered and that the artist had an obligation of human sympathy for the victims of contemporary society. It would be possible to see Gautier merely catering here to a section of the readership of *La Presse* whose tastes for modern or social subjects had not yet been addressed in his review but for the fact that in his ninth article, published four days later, he returned to the issue of contemporary realism in the context of the altogether more unsettling and irrefutable work of Adolphe Leleux and Meissonier.

In the meantime, the travel painters enabled him to continue his theme of modern life. Here he renewed the hopes that he had celebrated with *quarante-huitard* universalist fervour in his Salon of fifteen months earlier and in which colonial adventures, allied with the new possibilities in transport, were making possible the transfusion of art by new subject matter.[49] In his account, Decamps, Delacroix, and Marilhat had blazed the trail and Adolphe Leleux had brought his own brand of official July Monarchy realism to North African subjects. In 1849 art's 'confrérie voyageuse' had a new recruit who owed nothing to these predecessors and for whom Gautier predicted greatness. That year Fromentin exhibited five works which placed him overnight 'au premier rang des paysagistes exotiques'. Unprecedented in the authenticity of its representation of North African light, colour, and movement, his art was one of the small number of revelations in the Salon of 1849.[50] Unlike other *salonniers*, Gautier reinforced Fromentin's achievement by adding a favourable paragraph on each of the two works submitted by Auguste Salzmann, who had accompanied the painter on his North African journey of 1847–48 and whose technique clearly owed much to his.[51]

Adolphe Leleux's travel paintings provided the transition to Gautier's ninth article for, like Meissonier, he had, in a complete break with precedent, briefly put aside the subjects on which his reputation had hitherto been based, subjects which, whether in time or place, had been far removed from those of contemporary

Paris, in order to represent a scene from the revolution of 1848. Not the February revolution and certainly not the competition for a figure of the Republic, but the June insurrection, with its awful legacy of civil war. Of the two, only Leleux's *Le Mot d'ordre* (Figure 4.1) was shown in the Salon. Meissonier's *Souvenir de guerre civile* (Figure 4.2) had not been finished in time. At least that was the official reason, one which Gautier duly reported, but the 'delay' may also have been the result of advice from Meissonier's colleagues on the Salon jury that the memory of the events was still too raw for a work in which the artist, in Gautier's words, 'est arrivé d'un seul coup au comble de la terreur'.[52] Be that as it may, Gautier had seen the work at the *ébauche* stage in Meissonier's studio and had been so astounded by what he called 'un événement pour l'art' that he presented it in his Salon review alongside Leleux's *Le Mot d'ordre* as the two masterpieces of the June Days.[53]

In *Le Mot d'ordre* Leleux had put aside his Breton, Spanish, and Arab peasants in order to portray what Gautier called 'les sauvages des villes'. In the mythology of 'Paris, ville malade', no description of the Parisian poor was by that time more commonplace, and Gautier enlarged it with the equally familiar reference to these 'natures incultes et rudes que la civilisation n'a touchées que pour les corrompre'. Nor can he have been the only one to make the joke that the painting's title should really have been *Le Mot de désordre*. In this respect, Leleux's three figures presented three very recognizable Parisian stereotypes. The one on the right of the painting was, said Gautier, 'une nature de chasseur, de contrebandier, de guerillero' (in Parisian mythology they amounted to much the same thing), an ex-soldier perhaps but without the discipline. The character on the left was, he was sure, always in trouble with the police and no doubt the prison of Rochefort or Toulon had his description. Ravaged by misery and vice, he was 'le type de la dégradation et de l'abrutissement'. As for the adolescent between them, he was obviously the 'voyou de 1848', son of the 'voyou de 1830', of whom no description was needed since Auguste Barbier had already provided it in his poem 'La Cuve' of October 1831, of twelve lines of which Leleux's painting was, Gautier said, 'une exacte traduction'.[54]

If the iconography of *Le Mot d'ordre* was clear, its moral lesson raised the same moral and social issues as Antigna's victim of hunger, exhaustion, or unemployment:

> Et maintenant, quel est l'effet moral qui résulte du tableau? Est-ce la pitié ou l'horreur? Est-ce un jugement ou une protestation qu'a voulu faire l'artiste? Ni l'un ni l'autre; il a vu et il a peint, comme c'était son droit; la peinture a l'impartialité muette de la nature. Malheureux et coupables, telle est l'idée que suscitent ces trois hommes armés au pied de cette barricade échangeant le mot de désordre.[55]

Despite the negative associations of Leleux's three Parisian types, the painting refused to choose between sympathy and condemnation.[56] Gautier would not have been surprised by this refusal because in the Salon of 1848 he had specifically advised Leleux not to seek to interpret the reality he observed, but to restrict himself to the observation that played to his strengths as an artist: 'il faut qu'il copie tout d'après nature [...] l'imagination, la mémoire n'existent dans son talent qu'à de très faibles doses; faire le mot à mot de la nature, tel est son lot; ce qu'il entreprendrait hors de là ne lui réussirait pas.'[57] Gautier felt that a neutral approach to subject matter

FIG. 4.1. Adolphe Leleux, *Le Mot d'ordre*, 1849, Versailles, Musée National du Château.
© The Bridgeman Art Library

suited Leleux's more limited artistic talents but his account of this neutrality was itself hardly neutral, as de Mercey's comments show. In the context of the summer of 1849, to describe the insurgents in *Le Mot d'ordre* as 'malheureux et coupables' instead of simply 'coupables' was not innocent.

The same impartiality, however, worked to even more disturbing effect in Meissonier's *Souvenir de guerre civile*.[58] Though Gautier was presumably not the only critic to have seen the *ébauche* in the artist's studio, he alone went public with his astonishment that Meissonier, the painter of all that eighteenth-century 'petit monde qui semble aller de la taverne de Brawer au café Procope, propre, lustré, poudré' could possibly have produced a work 'tout à fait imprévu dans le talent de l'artiste'. His surprise increased at each stage of his detailed study of its composition: the sombre street, with its closed-off perspective, bullet holes, and blank windows; the demolished barricade with its layer of bodies lying in the apparently random positions in which they had fallen; their horizontality and foreshortening, which initially prevented the spectator finding a stable, secure point of view from which to strike out across the image, and forced the eye to dwell on each detail in order to disentangle the piled-up jumble of bodies; the single boot in the lower left-hand corner, 'tombé sans doute d'une jambe emportée par un boulet'; the figure in the foreground whose blue shirt, off-white body, and red trousers gave him 'l'air du drapeau renversé de l'émeute'; the figures in the foreground drawn not from life but from the model, and in whom invention, arrangement, and pose had generated 'toute l'affreuse beauté que comporte un pareil sujet'. The reference to the fallen flag of revolt was an obvious one for Gautier to make in view of his comments on the tricolour during the republican competition the previous year (cf. above, p. 72) and it must have been difficult for him to see the painting as anything other than a negation of Delacroix's *La Liberté guidant le peuple* and its triumphant central flag. But he also recognized how the horizontality emphasized the tricolour's left-to-right sequence of *bleu, blanc, rouge* in the dead man's clothes, how the torso's off-white tones reinforced the drained, jaded tones of the blue and red garments and blended into those of the paving-stones, matter returning to matter. If, as seems possible, the painting's absence from the Salon was due to a form of self-censorship that Meissonier had assumed (or been persuaded to assume) in the interests of public order, Gautier circumvented this decision in the same way as he had undone the censorship of the July Monarchy's Salon juries. He used his review to reinstate the painting, to make it one of the events of the Salon that year.

Following on from his commentary on Meissonier and brief comments on several pupils of Adolphe Leleux (Chaplin, Hédouin), Gautier finally began in print his long and fractious relationship with the work of Courbet.[59] With hindsight it is not difficult to see that the Salons of the Second Republic were, in part at least, the Courbet Salons, that the forward momentum of his career during this period was a key element in what was going on. In 1848, the painter had, like everyone else, been taken by surprise by the abolition of the jury, and the collection of exhibits he had hastily put together was more or less lost in the vast number of works on show. If Gautier had seen any of the ten works Courbet had submitted, he had not mentioned them in his review.[60] But in 1849 he would have had little excuse for

FIG. 4.2. Ernest Meissonier, *Souvenir de guerre civile*, 1849, Paris, Louvre.
© The Bridgeman Art Library

overlooking the huge *Une après-dînée à Ornans* (Figure 4.3) and the widely noticed *L'Homme qui regarde des estampes*.[61] His comments were positive but they were general and superficial and did not engage seriously with Courbet's treatment of his subjects. He ignored even the most obvious point, that of the size of *Une après-dînée à Ornans*, which exercised other critics, for whom such dimensions belonged to history painting, not genre.[62] He adopted an evasive, patronizing tone, saying that the painting, 'forte et vivace, a le charme des choses simples, et ne manque pas d'une certaine poésie', though he did not say which sort. Instead he chose to lace his commentary with facile Parisianisms about 'cette manière de passer le temps' in a backwater like Ornans and about provincial ladies 'qui aiment le genre troubadour et les crevés à l'espagnole' but who would probably be put off by these rustic types whose clothes had obviously not come from 'chez Chevreul et Buisson'. In 1849 Gautier could not avoid Courbet since no one else did, but the signs are that he did not want to discuss him. On the other hand, there is no mistaking the company that Courbet keeps in Gautier's review. In the ninth article, he is one of only four artists discussed and the other three are major figures that year. In the twelfth, devoted to landscape, he follows Corot, who for many critics was the star of the Salon of 1849. Gautier's comments on Courbet were noticeably less warm than those on these other artists and this may have been intended to put Courbet in his place, but the painter's presence in such company nevertheless marked an impressive entry into Gautier's field of vision and he did recommend Courbet for a second-class medal, which was duly awarded. Perhaps he was trying to draw Courbet's anger, to suggest to him that there were rewards to be had in confining himself to the more limited and sympathetic Antigna model of realism. Perhaps in 1849 Courbet's work did not yet suggest to Gautier that this more respectable form of realism was about to be shoved aside by the painter's major realist works. Gautier would fully recognize that only in 1850–51, when he would devote the longest article he wrote that year on a single artist to his new sense of the threat that Courbet's art posed.

Gautier closed his ninth article by welcoming Daumier's arrival in the Salon with greater enthusiasm than he had that of Courbet. His view that Daumier's figure of the Republic had been one of the most positive outcomes of the competition (see above, p. 87) was reinforced by this latest evidence that it had also encouraged him to devote more time to his painting. *Le Meunier, son fils et l'âne*, based on La Fontaine's fable, confirmed that he was far more than a 'simple caricaturiste' or 'grotesque travestisseur de la forme humaine'.[63] Alone among the *salonniers* Gautier went straight to the connection with Rubens and Flemish line.[64] He urged Daumier to have more confidence in his brushstroke and colour, assuring him that if he did, his reputation as a painter would soon equal that as a caricaturist.

The tenth article is one of the catch-all pieces that every Gautier Salon review contains. They act as a sort of safety net for the system of categorization that the review has implemented up to this point, sweeping up works which he wishes to include but which for whatever reason have not found a place within the main categories established from the outset of the review. In such articles Gautier races through the exhibition 'prenant le bon partout où il se trouve'. On this occasion they include a Verdier portrait, a *Triomphe de la Vérité* by Mussini showing the

FIG. 4.3. Gustave Courbet, *Une après-dînée à Ornans*, 1848
Lille, Musée des Beaux-Arts
© The Bridgeman Art Library

impact of Chenavard's philosophical painting, Nègre's figure of the Republic (most unusually, male), Penguilly-L'Haridon's *Don Quichotte* and *Cabaret breton*, 'ces deux bijoux', and the mandatory burst of Spanish local colour, generated this time by Giraud's *Danse de Bohémiens aux environs de Grenade*, before which Gautier once more regales his Parisian readers with the *gitana*, *muchachos*, and *sombrero de calana* of their imaginary tourist Spain. Unfortunately for the harassed *salonnier*, the 'bon partout où il se trouve' category, inherently borderless and unkempt, was also one of the fastest growing in contemporary art and Gautier was obliged to spill over into the first third of his penultimate article in his efforts to cater for 'tout ce qui dénote du talent, du travail, un effort soutenu, une aspiration intelligente vers le beau'.

This interlude over, Gautier returned to the two remaining subject categories, those of the *animaliers* and landscape painters. The role of animal painting in the familiar hierarchy of subjects was, we are told, that of 'une transition entre la vie ayant conscience d'elle-même et la vie silencieuse et confuse du paysage'. Here, at least, things became more straightforward, such was the consensus during the Second Republic surrounding Rosa Bonheur's supremacy in this category. In 1849 it was reinforced by her *Attelage nivernais* (Figure 4.4). For Gautier, as for many commentators, the comparison with George Sand's *La Mare au diable* proved irresistible; like them he was seduced by Bonheur's prettified rustic scene, with its cows 'à l'œil grave et doux, au fanon majestueux' pulling the plough in the immemorial re-enactment of the art of Ceres.[65] For the less classically minded, Gautier had a more telling form of authentification. Having just returned from Holland where 'nous avons examiné avec la plus bienveillante attention les plus beaux Paul Potter qui soient au monde', he could vouch without fear of contradiction for the fact that when it came to representing the beasts of the field, not even Potter's animals, 'payés des prix si fabuleux', could compare with *Attelage nivernais*. With comparisons like that, the three thousand francs that Charles Blanc paid for it must have seemed like a wise use of public money.[66]

The remainder of the article continued on the same theme of the promotion of non-heroic subjects to equal status with those consecrated by tradition. Jadin's dogs were 'le livre d'or de la chiennerie' and worthy of Landseer. This was 'de la grande peinture, dans l'acception rigoureuse du mot', warranting even a reference to Titian and Velasquez. Following the example of such illustrious predecessors as Sneyders and Desportes, the farmyard scenes of Théodore Rousseau showed chickens 'de grandeur naturelle', which, as Gautier helpfully explained, was an 'honneur que la volaille reçoit rarement, la grandeur naturelle étant réservée au héros'. Exceeding even these examples, however, was that of Bonvin, whose three small paintings achieved the major Second Republic accolade of the analogy with Chardin, 'le plus vrai des peintres de cette époque maniérée' of the early eighteenth century.[67] It only remained in the final paragraph to compose the *suite au prochain numéro*, to announce that the twelfth and final article would be devoted to a celebration of landscape, for which many of his readers had perhaps been waiting all along.

The review of landscape opened as it did the previous year and many before that with a brief historical overview. Nature, unknown to the ancients, feared by Christianity, was discovered by Jean-Jacques Rousseau, with the landscapes of

FIG. 4.4. Rosa Bonheur, *Attelage nivernais*, 1849, Paris, Musée d'Orsay.
© Patrice Schmidt, Musée d'Orsay

Ruysdaël the exception which proved the rule. Cabat was the Messiah of this new religion and Flers the Precursor who first made the break with historical landscape: 'il [Cabat] a cru qu'une belle forêt pouvait se passer de Céphale et Procris, et qu'un Ulysse tout nu n'était pas indispensable dans les roseaux.' The event of the Salon of 1849 was Théodore Rousseau's consecration after fifteen years of rejection by the juries of the July Monarchy. The pre-eminence which Gautier gave Rousseau over Corot was a significant reversal of official attitudes during the Second Republic. 'Les honneurs du Salon sont incontestablement pour M. Corot', said de Mercey ('Le Salon de 1849', p. 580), who based his sense of Corot's superiority on a telling distinction:

> Les paysages de M. Corot parlent à l'âme et font rêver; ceux de M. Rousseau ne parlent qu'aux yeux [...] M. Rousseau, le réaliste par excellence, se trouve, lui, infiniment plus éloigné de la nature que M. Corot, toujours candide et vrai dans son interprétation. (p. 582)

The jury had placed Corot's *Vue prise en Limousin* and Rousseau's *Lisière de forêt, soleil couchant* side by side presumably to encourage this sort of discussion. There is no doubt that most commentators shared de Mercey's sense of priorities nor that 1849 represented Corot's breakthrough to critical acclaim.[68] Gautier's emphasis on Rousseau's work that year made him the beneficiary of the comparison but it was Corot's *Christ aux Oliviers* with which most critics began. For de Mercey the painter had succeeded in creating in this work a form of historical landscape suited to the modern era ('c'est un tableau d'histoire, le seul vraiment original qu'on puisse concevoir aujourd'hui et qui réponde exactement au sentiment de notre époque'), but Gautier's commentary severed the link with historical landscape, saying that, despite the religious subject, Corot had given precedence to inanimate nature over humans ('il a donné, comme c'était son droit de paysagiste, la prédominance aux végétaux sur les êtres animés'). By discussing Corot only after Rousseau, he had subordinated his achievement in the natural landscape to Rousseau's.[69] De Mercey's analysis followed a familiar strand in the reception of Corot's work since the Salon of 1835, in which he had shown *Agar dans le désert*.[70] Gautier had praised the painting in the same terms in his own Salon review the following year (he did not review that of 1835), in which he referred, as de Mercey did in 1849, to Corot's succession to Poussin and to his Virgilian eclogues. His less enthusiastic comments in 1849 are perhaps to some extent due to his sense of the familiarity of Corot's work but seem mainly to be the result of the deeper and more powerful questions that Rousseau's landscapes appeared to him to be posing.

The qualities that Gautier found in Rousseau's landscapes were, as de Mercey's comments suggest, ones with which many commentators were uneasy, now that he was no longer the martyr of the July Monarchy juries. Rousseau, he said, had gone further in his representation of nature 'pour elle-même, sans idéal, sans composition, et sans drame introduit'. Rousseau did not tidy up nature, his mysterious, impenetrable landscapes gave little scope for reassuring pantheism. Gautier typically recognized the extent to which, in this 'paysagiste un peu sauvage', this was down to the technique he had evolved to represent effects in nature which were barely representable:

> Les *Terrains d'automne* représentent un de ces aspects très fréquens dans la nature, mais que l'art semble inhabile à rendre; ces mousses desséchées, ces feuilles rougies qui s'entassent, ou que le vent d'octobre promène, ces herbes flétries qui penchent, tout ce détritus de la brillante végétation de l'été qui va former une couche de plus à la croûte terrestre, ne peuvent guère fournir le sujet d'un tableau. La nature alors revêt des formes si étranges et transpose si bizarrement les couleurs qu'elle semble mensongère reproduite par les moyens de l'art.

What remained to be seen was how Rousseau's highly personal, eccentric treatment of nature would evolve now that, with the demise of the old jury, the artist had access to the wider public of the Salon, 'dont l'admiration ou le blâme lui donneront ce sentiment de proportion que l'artiste n'acquiert jamais sans cela'. Having settled definitively in Barbizon within his own artistic community, Rousseau could now embark on the long-overdue engagement with the wider public. The result, Gautier sensed, would no doubt have important consequences for the future of landscape, but in which precise direction he could in 1849 only guess.

The balance of his commentary suggests that the 'first Salon of the Republic' was a disappointment for Gautier, an essentially transitional event that had left unresolved the implications of the change of regime that the open Salon of the previous year had arrived too soon to address. There had been highlights to savour of course: Préault's and Rousseau's revenge against the Salon juries of the July Monarchy, Fromentin's emergence, Corot's success, and Meissonier's extraordinary representation of the June insurrection. But even these could not compensate for the absence of Ingres and of so many of his chief lieutenants past or present (such as Lehmann, Paul and Hippolyte Flandrin, Ziegler, Chassériau, Aligny, Gérôme), or for the somewhat diminished presence of Delacroix, whose exhibits that year appear to have reinforced in Gautier the sense that the painter was no longer the force he had been. Brave foot soldiers were all very well, but the absence of the generals had left the field open to the new generation of artists, whose relationship to the legacy of their two great predecessors, locked in a rivalry which had appeared to define French painting for two decades, was unclear. If Gautier had hoped that the first Salon of the Republic would bring revelation of powerful new work through which to take this legacy forward into the republican phase, his review of the event appears to imply that it had not lived up to his expectations. Nor would he have been reassured by Champfleury's confidence that the Salon of 1849 had seen the emergence of 'trois nouveaux maîtres: Daumier, Courbet, François Bonvin, c'est-à-dire une jeune peinture sérieuse et déroutante pour toute la génération des peintres qui se sont suicidés par l'abus du *procédé*'.[71] The previous year Gautier had already made the same diagnosis of an overemphasis on technique for its own sake (see above, p. 58), but he could scarcely have wished to see the cure located solely in realist initiatives whose forms remained to be seen. At the institutional level too, the future was unclear. The success or otherwise of the Salon's change of location and season was under discussion and the implications of the departure from the Louvre would need to be established. In more ways than one, the next Salon, at the century's midpoint, would be an appropriate time for clarification. But the Salon was not the only major arena in which the future of French art was to be engaged. The museum was another, and here too Gautier would play a significant role.

Notes to Chapter 4

1. Artists, it said, 'ne peuvent prendre part aux travaux manuels de terrassement, et pourtant beaucoup d'entre eux (des élèves de l'École de Rome même) se sont vus poussés par la misère à s'embrigader dans les ateliers nationaux. Cette triste ressource leur manque aujourd'hui' (ibid.).

2. For David d'Angers's proposal and Charles Blanc's reply, see Chaudonneret, 'L'Aube d'une République des arts'.

3. C.R., 'Distribution de prix aux artistes: Salon de 1848', L'Artiste, 1 September 1848, p. 15. A summary of the Minister's speech, published in Le Moniteur universel of 21 August, indicates why Clément de Ris might have felt that it was somewhat short on detail: 'Le Ministre de la République n'a répudié aucune des gloires de l'art passé, aucune des conquêtes que nous a léguées la monarchie, et séparant le Gouvernement nouveau de ceux qui avaient méconnu les grands principes de l'égalité et de la fraternité, il a su rattacher l'art de nos jours, et l'avenir qui l'attend, aux grandes traditions des républiques de l'Antiquité. Paris, a-t-il dit, se souviendra de Sparte pour ses mâles vertus, et d'Athènes pour l'éclat dont elle fit rayonner les arts' (p. 2087).

4. Garraud occupied the post of Directeur des Beaux-Arts for five weeks, from 24 February to 1 April 1848, at which point he was replaced by Charles Blanc. On Garraud's commission, of which the painter Horace Vernet was president, see Pierre Vaisse, 'Considérations sur la Seconde République et les beaux-arts', Bulletin de la Société d'histoire de la révolution de 1848 et des révolutions du XIXe siècle (1985), 59–85 (pp. 68–72).

5. L'Artiste, 1 November 1848, p. 83.

6. 'La commission permanente des beaux-arts daigne enfin prendre la parole et rassurer nos inquiétudes. Il y aura une exposition en 1849, elle le déclare aujourd'hui au Moniteur, et cette exposition n'aura pas lieu au Louvre' (Lord Pilgrim, 'Mouvement des arts', L'Artiste, 15 December 1848, pp. 125–27 (p. 126)). On 29 October, the new Minister of the Interior, Jules Dufaure, had created a Permanent Commission for Fine Arts to advise on all matters of state patronage, including the Salon. Meeting for the first time on 24 November, its membership included Ingres, Delacroix, Delaroche, and Jeanron. See Vaisse, 'Considérations sur la Seconde République et les beaux-arts', p. 67.

7. 'Lord Pilgrim' went on to say: 'Il n'en faillait pas davantage pour inquiéter à un haut degré tous les artistes qui trouvent chaque printemps au Salon un peu de publicité pour leur œuvre, et pour leur nom un peu de bruit' (p. 126).

8. Jean-Louis Fouché, in 'L'Opinion d'Ingres sur le Salon: procès-verbaux de la Commission permanente des beaux-arts (1848–1849)', La Chronique des arts et de la curiosité, 14 March 1908, pp. 98–99, and 4 April 1908, pp. 129–30, gives the full membership of the Commission and reports Ingres's call for the Salon's abolition.

9. 'Les amateurs, en admettant que ce mot ait une signification quelconque, apporteront toujours dans les questions de cette nature une passion ou une ignorance qui ne pourront que mettre en péril les véritables intérêts des artistes' (Lord Pilgrim, p. 126).

10. Lord Pilgrim, 'Mouvement des arts', 1 January 1849, p. 147.

11. 'Les artistes sont tous heureux de ce retard, qui permettra d'achever plus d'une œuvre sérieuse. Y aurait-il beaucoup d'exposants?' (P.M., 'Assemblée générale des peintres à l'Institut', L'Artiste, 15 January 1849, pp. 163–64 (p. 164)). The anonymous author did not answer his own question, providing instead the latest news from the artists' studios.

12. M..., 'Histoire de l'oppression dans les arts', L'Artiste, 20 February 1848, pp. 243–48.

13. 'Seront reçues sans examen les œuvres présentées par les membres de l'Institut, par les grands prix de Rome, par les artistes décorés pour leurs œuvres et par ceux auxquels auront été décernées des médailles ou récompenses de première et de deuxième classes' (Lord Pilgrim, 'Mouvement des arts', L'Artiste, 15 February 1849, pp. 188–91 (p. 189)).

14. Gautier, who, as we saw in Chapter 3, had argued against the reinstatement of the jury, no doubt recognized the strength of support for a jury elected by the artists themselves. Champfleury on the other hand was in no sense reconciled: 'Quant au jury, il est honteux que la République rétablisse cette triste invention: sous aucune forme le jury n'est possible' (quoted by Lord

Pilgrim, 'Mouvement des arts', *L'Artiste*, 1 May 1849, pp. 33–36 (p. 36)). As for many things he disapproved of, he assumed Ingres was to blame ('sans doute l'aura voulu ainsi M. Ingres' (ibid., p. 35) but Ingres, having failed to secure abolition of the Salon itself, had in fact argued before the commission that the jury should not be reinstated, for the same reason that Gautier had given: that the public was the only jury needed.

15. Lord Pilgrim again: 'Rien n'est décide encore ni pour le jour ni pour le palais. Pourquoi pas les Tuileries? Qui donc aujourd'hui oserait habiter les Tuileries, si ce n'est les arts?' ('Mouvement des arts', *L'Artiste*, 1 April 1849, pp. 14–15 (p. 15)).

16. 'Qui donc sera à Paris le 15 juin? Peut-être à l'ouverture du Salon y verra-t-on la foule encore, mais huit jours après les galeries seront désertes; on n'y rencontrera guère que les travailleurs sans travail. L'ancien public du Samedi — le public qui après tout achète des tableaux, — sera à Spa, à Londres, aux Pyrénées, partout, hormis à Paris' (Lord Pilgrim, 'Mouvement des arts', *L'Artiste*, 15 April 1849, pp. 26–27 (p. 26)).

17. The collapse of support for moderate Republicanism to only 11% of the poll left its supporters with only 100 seats in the new Assembly, while the 'parti de l'ordre' (which grouped Orleanists, legitimists, and Bonapartists) took 50% of the poll and 500 seats. It was, however, the surprisingly strong performance of a left-wing alliance of socialists, democrats, and radicals which, with nearly 40% and 200 seats (and still referred to in the political discourse of the time as the 'Montagne'), reinforced the impression of a country divided between red and white camps. See Agulhon, *1848 ou l'apprentissage de la république*, pp. 88–96, and Roger Magraw, *France 1815–1914: The Bourgeois Century* (London: Fontana, 1983), pp. 133–40.

18. On 11 May in the National Assembly, Ledru-Rollin denounced Louis Napoleon's Italian expedition as a violation of Article V of the preamble of the Constitution and urged that the ministers responsible be prosecuted. When his proposal was defeated, the leaders of the left-wing group in the Assembly called for a demonstration on 13 June. It was easily repressed, with a number of leaders, notably Ledru-Rollin, being forced into exile, and a state of siege was declared two days later in Paris and Lyons.

19. On 15 June he wrote: 'Je suis allé le jour même à *La Presse* où Neftzer [the newspaper's administrator] n'était pas trop rassuré cependant il paraît sûr qu'on n'entravera pas le journal, lequel du reste n'est pas du tout dans la même situation qu'à l'époque de Cavaignac [in June 1848]' (*Corr.*, IV, 31). Nefftzer was right: *La Presse* remained open. Only the left-wing press was targeted.

20. 'Le Musée est ouvert malgré ce qu'on avait dit, malgré l'aspect de la cour [of the Palais des Tuileries] remplie de chevaux et de dragons que j'ai vus hier, il paraît qu'on entre par le jardin' (*Corr.*, IV, 32).

21. On 23 July *La Presse* spoke of the 'état de pénurie', 'marasme', and 'situation désastreuse' in the theatres (*Corr.*, IV, 36). That day, Louis de Cormenin suggested to Gautier that since they were still in a period of 'disette théâtrale où le critique n'a que quelques maigres vaudevilles à pâturer', they might do a series of articles on actors and their techniques (ibid., pp. 34–35).

22. 'Salon de 1849, premier article', *La Presse*, 26 July 1849.

23. Reassuring Gautier that Paris was calm again after the events of 13 June, Nerval had said: 'La pauvre montagne [Ledru-Rollin and his followers] est rasée, les principaux sont arrêtées et ils ont été peu brillants on n'a plus rien à craindre que la férocité des gens paisibles, lesquels ne tarderont pas à nous ramener d'autres dangers' (*Corr.*, IV, 32). It is difficult in this respect not to be reminded of Flaubert's representation of political reaction in June 1848 in *L'Éducation sentimentale*.

24. Of the jury he noted: 'La manière dont on a formé le jury, — bien que nous eussions préféré pas de jury du tout, — nous semble la plus rationnelle, et il est difficile aux jugés de décliner la compétence des juges, puisque ce sont eux-mêmes qui se les choisissent' ('Salon de 1849, premier article'). The new jury was more tolerant and more representative than its predecessors, and had also brought the exhibition back to a more manageable size (2500 exhibits instead of the 5000 in 1848).

25. Pouring scorn on the fear in certain quarters that the jury's acceptance of Préault's work would signal the end of civilization, Gautier commented: 'Mon Dieu non! Tout s'est passé le plus paisiblement du monde: la foule, après s'être arrêtée aux marbres de MM. Pradier et Cavelier,

regarde curieusement les bronzes de M. Préault, et ces trois noms sont les premiers que chacun cite en parlant de la sculpture.'

26. The exceptions were the Salons of 1834, where his *Tuerie* had caused a sensation, and 1837, in which he had shown a *médaillon en plâtre*.

27. See *Auguste Préault, sculpteur romantique*, p. 172.

28. Most notably, Falloux, Ministre de l'Instruction Publique et des Cultes since 20 December 1848, was preparing his law which would re-establish Catholic influence over primary education.

29. De Mercey scolded Préault for forgetting the lesson of the ancients, that 'le calme des attitudes' was the 'condition indispensable du beau' (F. de Lagenevais, 'Le Salon de 1849', *RDM*, 15 August 1849, pp. 559–93 (p. 589). In *L'Artiste*, the author of 'Critique de la critique' (15 September 1849) said that in the *Christ*, 'les qualités mêmes de M. Préault, poussées à l'excès, deviennent un défaut: ce Christ est tellement un homme que ce n'est plus un Dieu' (p. 179) and Pierre Malitourne, unable to make up his mind, simply reported that 'on a pu reprocher à cette figure de ne pas avoir allié à la puissante expression de la douleur humaine l'accent de la noblesse divine' ('La Sculpture en 1849, II', 15 October 1849, pp. 209–11 (p. 210)).

30. Gautier had first praised an earlier Préault *Christ* (also known as the *Christ de Saint-Gervais*, after the church in which it was placed in 1847) in *La Presse* of 3 April 1840. He returned to it in 1841 (*Revue universelle*, May 1841, p. 389), when he first compared it to the work of the Spanish artists he had seen during his travels in Spain. Presenting the *Christ* shown in 1849, Isabelle Leroy-Jay Lemaistre notes: 'Comparé au *Christ* de Saint-Gervais, c'est le calme et l'assagissement des formes qui frappent. Ce n'est plus le Christ révolté décrit par Marc, mais le Christ résigné décrit par l'Évangile de Jean. Les jambes sont simplement juxtaposés et la tête retombe lourdement sur l'épaule. On peut imaginer qu'à la suite de l'évocation des *Christ* espagnols par Théophile Gautier à son retour d'Espagne, Préault avait été entraîné dans cette voie. La position de la tête comme l'exagération de la barbe et de la chevelure où s'enfonce la couronne d'épines, font effectivement référence aux *Christ* de Montañès avec une expression de sauvagerie exacerbée par l'aspect inachevé de certains fragments' (*Auguste Préault, sculpteur romantique*, p. 172). Gautier's comment in 1849 — 'La douleur est si effroyable que malgré l'âme divine qui habite son enveloppe humaine, il pousse vers son père un cri d'appel et de désespoir en lui demandant pourquoi il l'a abandonné' — argues against the distinction between the two Christs to which Leroy-Jay Lemaistre refers.

31. De Mercey was evidently only repeating common knowledge in his pointed comment: 'M. Pradier, jaloux apparemment du succès que M. Clésinger avait moissonné dans son domaine' ('Le Salon de 1849', p. 590).

32. 'Ainsi nous aimons Pradier ne se détournant pas une minute de son cher rêve grec et saluant la révolution de février par une Chloris en marbre de Paros. Pendant que tout le monde s'occupait de réformes, d'élections, de Plaine et de Montagne, lui [...] se choisissait un modèle et cherchait pour le réaliser une colonne tombée de quelque temple de Vénus.'

33. As Gautier put it: 'On a dit que les bras étaient un peu grêles pour les jambes, ou les jambes un peu fortes pour les bras', a charge he rejected on the grounds that Pradier had represented naturalistically the real, uneven development of the female body in the early stages of puberty. On polychrome sculpture, de Mercey was dismissive: 'Je ne parle pas des fantaisies polychromes que M. Pradier affectionne; il y a long-temps que le bon goût en a fait justice' ('Le Salon de 1849', p. 590) but Gautier defended Pradier again on the grounds of authenticity, arguing that polychromy was a familiar practice in antique sculpture.

34. De Mercey: 'Quel abandon, quelle langueur, quel *tremolo* dans ce corps qui se courbe pour aspirer le souffle désiré! Comme cette gorge s'enfle, comme cette bouche se pâme, comme ses yeux se meurent! Voilà une belle représentation, monsieur Pradier, et l'on ne saurait trop louer le scrupule pudique avec lequel vous avez jeté sur le tout un titre mythologique, passeport bien plus décent que la fameuse couleuvre en plomb inventée par M. Clésinger [in his *Femme piquée par un serpent*, shown in 1847]' (ibid.).

35. 'On ne retrouve vraiment plus ici cette perfection exquise du ciseau qui ferait de M. Pradier le plus grand des sculpteurs, s'il la mettait jamais au service d'une noble pensée. Il semble que M. Pradier, en abaissant davantage ses conceptions, soit condamné à perdre une partie de ses moyens' (ibid., pp. 590–91).

36. 'École Nationale des Beaux-Arts: exposition des figures du concours pour la République'. In many reviews the widespread praise of Cavelier's statue was made in the context of discussions on the future of the École de Rome itself. Gautier had first attacked the institution in 1832 in his article 'Examen critique des écoles de Rome et de Paris en 1832' (*La France littéraire*, 4 (October 1832), 74–86). In 1848 he had begun his review of the Rome work with a scathing attack on the Villa Médicis: 'Tout arbre, produisant de mauvais fruits, a dit l'Évangile, sera coupé et jeté au feu. Si l'on appliquait ce précepte du divin maître à l'école de Rome, elle sentirait un peu le fagot à l'heure qu'il est.' In *L'Artiste,* however, Pierre Malitourne saw *Pénélope* as proof of the enduring viability of the institution ('La Sculpture en 1849', 1 October 1849, pp. 193–95 (p. 194)).

37. De Mercey's very next words, following the 'instincts grossiers et dépravés' were: 'M. Pradier, jaloux apparamment du succès que M. Clésinger avait moissonné dans son domaine'.

38. See G. Garnier's comment in 'La Carrière d'un artiste officiel', p. 95.

39. As he put it, the foot soldiers had replaced the captains: 'Les soldats ont remplacé les capitaines et la bataille n'a pas été perdu pour cela. Comme toujours les pauvres ont été généreux et les riches avares; ce sont ceux qui n'avaient rien qui ont donné, et si la première exposition de la République, car celle de l'année passée avait été préparée sous la monarchie, n'a pas étalé aux yeux des murailles nues, c'est à eux qu'il faut en rendre grace.'

40. De Mercey confirmed the advance publicity: 'Il était bruit par avance de ce tableau, qui promettait, disait-on, un grand peintre d'histoire de plus' ('Le Salon de 1849', p. 567). Gautier confirmed the privileged placement: 'La *Lady Macbeth* occupe la plus belle place dans une pièce qui ne contient que trois tableaux, et peut être regardée comme le Salon carré de la nouvelle exposition.' That it had retained this privileged position after mid-July, when the jury had considered appeals by the painters against its initial placements, confirmed in Gautier's view the success of *Lady Macbeth*: 'Quelle que soit l'école à laquelle il appartienne, personne ne songe à mettre une autre toile à cette place: c'est le plus bel éloge que nous en puissions faire.'

41. The main exception was the Davidian Delécluze, who described *Lady Macbeth* as 'l'ouvrage capital de l'Exposition' ('Exposition des ouvrages d'art aux Tuileries en 1849: premier article', *Journal des débats*, 25 June 1849).

42. 'Il faudrait aller jusqu'aux Espagnols pour trouver l'équivalent de cette funèbre peinture. Ribera, Zurbaran qui pourtant sont passablement sinistres et féroces, n'ont rien de plus terrible et de plus glaçant: Juan Valdès Leal, le peintre des têtes coupées, pourrait entrer en lutte avec son effroyable tableau de l'*Hôpital de la Charité à Séville*, où l'on voit, dans un caveau ouvert, une suite de cadavres passant par tous les degrés de la putréfaction, depuis la mort récente, jusqu'à l'état de squelette' (*La Presse*, 1 August 1849).

43. In the autumn of 1848 Delacroix had begun a series of five flower pieces. Those shown in the Salon of 1849 were *Fleurs et fruits* and *Fleurs*, nos 501 and 502 in Johnson, *The Paintings of Eugène Delacroix*, III (1986), 261–63.

44. In *The Absolute Bourgeois*, Clark described them as a 'response to the events of revolution — a deliberate grand withdrawal to a world of private sensation, a world of traditional painterly problems' (p. 131).

45. Letter of 13 November 1848 to Mme de Forget, quoted in Johnson, *The Paintings of Eugène Delacroix*, III, 261.

46. See Johnson, ibid., p. 117.

47. 'La République nouvelle doit se représenter sous les apparences de la force calme et souriante, avec la force de sévérité aimable et de grace austère.'

48. 'M. Antigna, nature un peu épaisse, talent un peu lourd, creuse son sillon avec énergie et persévérance. Il appartient à la race de ces bœufs de la peinture dont Dominiquin faisait partie, et qui finissent par laisser leur trace sur le champ de l'art.'

49. 'Aux écoles italienne, flamande, espagnole et française doit succéder une seule école, l'école universelle, où seront représentés les types de l'humanité entière, et les aspects multiformes de la planète que nous habitons' (*La Presse*, 7 August 1849).

50. De Mercey, for example, wrote: 'Il serait long de faire la liste de nos arabisans. [...] Leur maître à tous, un artiste d'un vrai talent, et dont je ne sache pas qu'il eût encore rien paru, c'est M. Fromentin' ('Le Salon de 1849', p. 575).

51. 'Avec plus de correction dans le détail et plus d'élégance de lignes, M. Auguste Salzmann nous paraît avoir compris l'Afrique dans le même sens clair, azuré et pulvérulent.'

52. Clark, in *The Absolute Bourgeois*, noted that Meissonier had withdrawn the painting from the Salon of 1849 at the last minute (p. 28) and Hungerford, in *Ernest Meissonier: rétrospective*, is surely right in suggesting that Meissonier is unlikely to have submitted an unfinished painting and then withdrawn it (p. 166). His colleagues on the jury could not reject the work since his medals from previous Salons gave him automatic right of entry, but they certainly could have urged him not to show it, particularly as the Salon was due to open on the eve of the first anniversary of the events depicted. Instead he included the work in his submission to the Salon of 1850–51.

53. 'Ces terribles et désastreuses journées de juin auront produit deux chefs-d'œuvre: le *Mot d'ordre*, de Leleux, et *la Rue* de Meissonier' (*La Presse*, 8 August 1849).

54. The twelve lines were the ten of stanza 6 and the first two of stanza 7 of the nine-stanza poem. In view of Gautier's commentary on the painting, it does not seem to be a coincidence (or simply a wish to fill up a few extra lines in his review) that after stanza 6, which describes the boy's many vices, the first four lines of stanza 7 speak of his courage, love of liberty, and 'beautiful' death, and that Gautier included the first two lines in his quoted extract. See Auguste Barbier, *Iambes et poèmes*, 5th edn (Paris: Masgana, 1845), pp. 65–70.

55. De Mercey was baffled by Leleux's choice of subject. Why on earth choose Paris in winter, revolutionaries in rags, and a Paris urchin? At least warmed by the Spanish or oriental sun, he added, poverty could achieve a degree of 'poétisation' ('Le Salon de 1849', p. 575). De Mercey assumed it was a painting of February, not June, 1848, a revealing error, as Clark pointed out in *The Absolute Bourgeois* (p. 24).

56. 'Salon de 1848', *La Presse*, 3 May 1848. Clark argued that Gautier was right in his assessment of Leleux's impartiality but that 'he was wrong if he thought impartiality here was natural. On the contrary, the "fact" of revolution is prised apart from its value; we are given, on purpose, pictures without meaning, where meaning is what we look for' (*The Absolute Bourgeois*, p. 28). This seems to me to be a misreading of Gautier's use of 'natural' here. One year after the June Days and with Paris once more in a state of siege, Gautier, like Nerval, feared conservative reaction as much as revolution. His reference to nature is to its lack of factionalism, not its lack of meaning. The rebels in *Le Mot d'ordre* were both innocent and guilty, just as nature was both bountiful and destructive.

57. 'Salon de 1848', 3 May 1848.

58. Meissonier initially submitted it for the Salon of 1849 under the title *Juin*. In his commentary Gautier called it *La Rue* and *Rue après les journées de juin*. It acquired its definitive title, *Souvenir de guerre civile*, for the Salon of 1850–51.

59. See Francis Moulinat, 'Théophile Gautier et Gustave Courbet', *Les Amis de Gustave Courbet*, 83 (1990) [unpaginated], pp. [5–31]; Jean-Pierre Leduc-Adine, 'Théophile Gautier et le réalisme: Courbet, Millet, Manet', in *Théophile Gautier: l'art et l'artiste* (= *BSTG*, 4.1–2 (1983)), I, 21–33, and *Théophile Gautier: Courbet, le Watteau du laid*, ed. by Christine Sagnier (Paris: Séguier, 2000).

60. Champfleury could not resist a dig at Gautier for that: 'Celui-là, l'inconnu [Courbet], qui a peint cette *Nuit* [*classique du Walpurgis*] sera un grand peintre. Théophile Gautier, qui aime à découvrir les jeunes talents, et qui les cherche, l'a oublié' (Bixiou [pseudonym of Champfleury], *Le Pamphlet*, 28–30 September 1848). Gautier may not have been looking for Courbet in 1848, and with over 5000 works on show it had been hard enough finding the work he was looking for, but it is possible, as Girard suggests (in *Théophile Gautier, Critique d'art*, p. 292), that he had been put off by the directness with which Courbet had sought from him two years earlier a mention in his review of the Salon of 1846 (see *Corr.*, III, 36). In 1849 Champfleury claimed to have been the only critic to notice Courbet's work the previous year — 'Seul, l'an passé, j'avais dit son nom et ses qualités' (*La Silhouette*, 22 July 1849) — but Haussard, in *Le National* of 15 June 1848, was another: 'Courbet fait apparition de peintre.' Gautier may have noted that comment more than the work which prompted it. See also T. J. Clark, *Image of the People* (Thames and Hudson, 1973), p. 50.

61. See in this respect *Gustave Courbet (1819–1877)* (Paris: Éditions des Musées Nationaux, 1977), pp. 26–27, and Clark, *Image of the People*, pp. 50–51.

62. De Mercey commented: 'On s'explique difficilement pourquoi M. Courbet a fait un tableau de genre sur une toile de cinq pieds. [...] Pour que nous nous intéressions à ces dîners rustiques sous le manteau de la cheminée et à tous ces détails prosaïques de marmite, de crémaillère, de table et de siège de bois, il faudrait nous les montrer, comme font les Flamands, par le petit bout d'une lunette qui les poétise en les éloignant' ('Le Salon de 1849', p. 578). To prove his point he used Meissonier's *Le Fumeur* of 1842 as a stick with which to beat Courbet.

63. On the painting see *Daumier 1808–1879*, pp. 249–50.

64. 'Le geste des joyeuses commères qui gouaillent le meunier est hardi [...] et montre une certaine puissance à la Rubens, un flamboiement de lignes à la flamande tout à fait remarquable.'

65. In the *Journal des débats* of 25 June 1849 Delécluze provided the most authoritative voice in support of the work's encouragement for those of a religious sensibility: 'Ainsi, cette composition de *genre*, ce tableau d'*animaux*, comme les faiseurs de classifications pourraient le désigner, présente par le fait un sujet biblique des plus élevés, et traité avec une supériorité remarquable' (Delécluze's italics).

66. Gautier's comparison with Potter must have raised the financial stakes as far as Bonheur's work was concerned. Given de Mercey's strategic role in state patronage during this period, it is therefore interesting to see how little he was taken in by Bonheur's rustic idyll: 'Ses bœufs [...] se groupent bien, tirent avec ensemble et vigoureusement. On pourrait bien leur reprocher un soin trop exquis de leur personne, mais ce sont peut-être des bœufs de ferme-modèle, mieux étrillés que des bœufs du commun [...] Les prairies du fond sont si bien tenues, les arbres si bien taillés! il n'est pas jusqu'aux mottes de terres qui n'aient un aspect correct et élégant. [...] Décidément la poésie fait tort à la peinture.' He nevertheless went on to say that 'cet *Attelage nivernais* n'en est pas moins un excellent tableau, et les bœufs de Mlle Bonheur n'ont pas leurs pareils à l'exposition'.

67. In 1849, Bonvin exhibited *La Cuisinière*, *les Buveurs*, and *le Piano*. Champfleury made implicitly the same reference to Chardin: 'François Bonvin, peintre de la famille, mérite un Diderot enthousiaste. Pour lui, un pot, une cruche, un vase, une tasse, sont des *sujets* aussi compliqués et aussi mystérieux qu'un homme, aussi aimables, aussi étranges qu'une femme' (*Œuvres posthumes*, p. 163, his emphasis).

68. See Théophile Gautier, *Bonjour Monsieur Corot*, ed. by Marie-Hélène Girard (Paris: Séguier, 1996), p. 15. Champfleury took issue with what he saw as an organized mystification of Corot in the Salon of 1849, preferring to see him as an artist experimenting with the range of landscape types: 'Corot-Théocrite n'a aucune signification [...] N'a-t-il pas fait des paysages religieux, des paysages historiques, des paysages antiques, des paysages modernes? Ce titre de *Théocrite* a dû plus d'une fois troubler la tête du bonhomme sorti à l'âge de trente ans d'une boutique de marchand drapier' (*Œuvres posthumes*, p. 160). On Corot see Peter Galassi, *Corot in Italy: Open-Air Painting and the Classical-Landscape Tradition* (New Haven and London: Yale University Press, 1991); *Corot, 1796–1875* (Paris: RMN, 1996); *In the Light of Italy: Corot and Open-Air Painting* (New Haven and London: Yale University Press, 1996).

69. Another important art critic of the time who did the same was Prosper Haussard in *Le National*, and it is instructive to compare his comments with those of Gautier. For Haussard, for whom 'la marque supérieure d'une œuvre d'art, c'est de provoquer à la pensée et à la poésie, d'émouvoir et d'enivrer tout notre être', Rousseau's art was a Shakespearean love affair with nature: 'Pour le paysagiste qui séduit et dérobe la nature, comme Othello sa Desdemone, la magie, c'est de l'aimer et d'en être aimé. Ce sentiment profond, cette communication sympathique, voilà la magie de M. Rousseau, sa force de paysagiste, inscrit désormais au premier rang de notre école' ('Salon de 1849, II', 10 July 1849). Gautier, on the other hand, went further in his effort to understand the way in which Rousseau's technical performance went beyond this pantheist magic.

70. See Susan Greenberg, 'Reforming *Paysage historique*: Corot and the Generation of 1830', *Art History*, 27 (2004), 412–30 (p. 414).

71. *Œuvres posthumes*, p. 165 (his emphasis).

❖

CHAPTER 5

'N'oubliez pas le guide':
The 'Études sur les musées' of 1849–1850

We have seen that within hours of the proclamation of the Second Republic on 24 February, Ledru-Rollin annexed the Civil List's attributions in the Direction des Beaux-Arts et des Musées and put an end to the Academy's right, managed under the List's aegis, to select the jury of the annual Fine Art Salon. In that context we saw the part played by what I called the Boissard group in the attacks in 1847 on the Salon jury as it had functioned under the July Monarchy. By the end of 1847, with *De l'exposition et du jury* despatched to the printers, Clément de Ris had turned his attention to another issue which had certainly figured among 'tout le bataclan' that Boissard had mentioned to Gautier. For Clément de Ris reform of the national museums was every bit as urgent as that of the Salon jury and directly related to it in the sense that, as far as he was concerned, the Institute's influence over the fine arts in France was the factor common to both issues. Between 20 February 1848 and 15 January 1849 he published five articles for *L'Artiste* on the subject of reform in the Louvre, and a sixth on the Luxembourg museum, which was considered to be to an extension of the Louvre specializing in contemporary French art, as indicated in its title of Musée des Artistes Vivants.[1] Between 17 December 1847 and 1 December 1849 he also published seven articles on French provincial museums.[2] The first four pieces on the Louvre and the Luxembourg appeared either side of the events of 22–24 February themselves and outlined the reforms he wished to see introduced in the two museums. The fifth and sixth appeared in December 1848 and January 1849 respectively and assessed the reforms which Jeanron and Villot had implemented up to that point. Between 10 February 1849 and 7 September 1850, Gautier also published nine articles on the Louvre, Luxembourg, and provincial museums.[3] This chapter will deal with the reform of French museology undertaken during the Second Republic and the ways in which Gautier extended the discussion of issues that Clément de Ris and others had placed so firmly on the agenda.

In discussions of the reforms advocated by critics of the July Monarchy's management of the national museums, the Louvre was, of course, the focal point. Though the order of priorities might vary from one critic to another, the list of grievances set out by Clément de Ris would have provided a large measure of common ground between them. This museological *cahier de doléances* would have included the following: the Civil List, responsible for providing a legal and administrative framework believed to have placed the national collections at the disposal of the King;[4] the sacrifice of these collections to what critics considered to be the July Monarchy's self-serving prestige projects, the creation of the Musée Historique at Versailles from 1833 and the Musée Espagnol, opened in 1838 and supplemented by the Standish bequest three years later;[5] the neglect of the national school in favour of the Italian, German, and Flemish Old Master collections;[6] the failure to use the architectural divisions of the Louvre's Grande Galerie to promote a rational and coherent distribution of the exhibition space between the three major European schools, the Italian (which included the Italianate Spanish), the German (including Flemish and Dutch), and the French;[7] the lack of catalogues for the majority of the collections and the inadequacy of the few catalogues that did exist;[8] the abandonment in attics and storerooms of hundreds of works which had never been catalogued or exhibited;[9] the annual disruption to the museum's business caused by the Salon, which for almost half the year denied public and artists alike access to the permanent collections hidden behind the temporary galleries;[10] the unprofessional standards of restoration.[11] As if all this were not bad enough, some of the galleries were in a state of serious disrepair and the area surrounding the museum was little more than a slum.[12]

No sooner had Clément de Ris begun to publish his denunciation of the July Monarchy's mismanagement of the Louvre than the regime was swept from power and the museum's new Director, Jeanron, and Curator of Paintings, Villot, set to work on the reforms for which Clément de Ris had become the spokesman. As far as the national collections were concerned, the first fruits of their reorganization went on show to the public on 27 August 1848, when the Louvre reopened after the period of closure that always followed the end of the Salon and during which the temporary galleries erected for the purpose in the Salon Carré and the Grande Galerie were dismantled and the exhibits removed.[13] At this point the public not only discovered significantly larger Old Master collections than those previously exhibited, thanks primarily to Villot's audit of the contents of the Louvre's storerooms and attics. It also found them arranged in a new way, with the Salon Carré now functioning as a gallery of masterpieces (itself based on the model of Florence's Palazzo degli Uffizi) which in turn opened onto the Grande Galerie's sequence of nine *travées*, in which were presented in chronological order the history of the Italian, German, and French schools, each occupying three *travées*. On 21 November the Modern French Masters, defined for the purpose as post-1715, were presented in the same arrangement, with the Salon des Sept Cheminées containing the gallery of masterpieces and the Galeries du Bord de l'Eau providing the historical overview of developments in painting between the death of Louis XIV and the early July Monarchy.[14]

Though Clément de Ris himself, in his article of 1 December (CdR5), had reservations about some of the modern French work chosen to occupy the gallery of masterpieces in the Salon des Sept Cheminées,[15] there is no doubt that the reorganization implemented by Jeanron and Villot met with a level of approval within the artistic community and wider public unmatched by the other major initiatives on the part of the fine arts administration of the Second Republic, such as the competition for the figure of the Republic, the Panthéon commission, or the abolition of the jury for the Salon of 1848. In response to the report presented on 7 December 1848 by Ferdinand de Lasteyrie, secretary to the commission set up to examine the question of the renovation of the Louvre, the National Assembly voted to allocate two million francs to the renovation of the Salon Carré, the Grande Galerie, and the Galerie d'Apollon, a sure sign of its recognition of the cultural and economic implications of a strategy designed in its view to restore the Louvre's position as the world's greatest site of Old and Modern Master painting collections.[16] This apparent vote of confidence in the Directeur des Musées Nationaux and his Curator of Paintings in the Louvre had, however, the unexpected side effect of triggering an angry outburst from Clément de Ris in a postscript to his article of 15 January 1849 (CdR6):

> P.S. — Au moment où s'impriment ces lignes, une partie de l'œuvre de M. Jeanron, la décoration du Salon carré, est détruite. Tous les tableaux sont enlevés, et il ne reste que les quatre murs. La commission nommée par l'Assemblée nationale pour surveiller l'emploi des deux millions en a décidé ainsi. On parle de projets d'embellissement absurdes, de tentures de velours rouge, de moulages dorés, d'encastrements en bois sculpté où les tableaux seraient fixés à demeure, d'espacer les cadres de façon à laisser apercevoir au public émerveillé le beau velours rouge qui couvrira la muraille, d'une foule d'élégances féeriques [...]. Le tout coûterait plus de cinq cent mille francs. En vérité, nous ne comprenons pas cette rage de gaspiller l'argent dont on est saisi en France sous la République comme sous la Monarchie. (p. 152)

At the beginning of January 1849 the Salon Carré had been emptied and the refurbishment work had begun. As Paul Mantz later stated, others shared the anxieties of Clément de Ris in relation to the rumours circulating in early January 1849 about the forms that the decoration of the Salon Carré might take.[17] Jeanron, on the other hand, far from considering his presentation of the reorganized Salon Carré of 27 August as having been 'destroyed' by this new closure, as Clément de Ris claimed, was anxious for the refurbishment to be expedited as quickly as possible.[18] It is difficult to believe that Clément de Ris, with his access to Jeanron and Villot, was unaware of this. Paradoxically, however, Jeanron's desire to press ahead so as not to lose the political momentum behind the Louvre's renovation and De Ris's outburst against the forms that this renovation might take may have had a common thread, in the sense that the election of Louis Napoleon on 10 December had created an immediate and serious threat to Jeanron's position. The princess Mathilde Bonaparte, Louis Napoleon's cousin, and mistress of the comte de Nieuwerkerke, had succeeded in having her lover appointed, by personal decree of the new president, to Jeanron's post of Directeur des Musées Nationaux. The new Interior Minister, Leon Faucher, appears to have been one of the influential figures whose support helped Jeanron to hang on to his job until the end of 1849.[19] It would not have been surprising, however, if Charles Blanc too had sensed that his own position had been weakened in the wake of Jeanron's; and sure enough, three months after Jeanron's departure, Blanc was gone too, replaced by a nonentity, Sylvain Guizard. In January 1849, Clément de Ris may well have feared that the gains that Jeanron and Villot had made in the Louvre following the fall of the July Monarchy were under threat from the new leadership of the Second Republic.

It may not, therefore, be a coincidence that Gautier intervened in the Louvre debates at this point with his three articles on the 1848 reorganization of the museum's painting collections, as these had been revealed to the public in the late summer and autumn of 1848. He began with what was in the circumstances a pointed declaration of support for Jeanron and Villot:

> Le Musée [du Louvre] a pris un aspect tout nouveau, grâce à MM Jeanron et Villot, et semble, depuis le remaniement opéré dans les peintures, dix fois plus riche qu'auparavant; car s'il est important pour les mots d'être à leur place, il l'est bien davantage pour les tableaux. (*TP*, p. 3)

He outlined the redistribution of the work of the Old (Italian, German, and French) and Modern (French) Masters between the galleries of masterpieces (in the Salon Carré and Salon des Sept Cheminées) and the galleries (the Grande Galerie and Galeries du Bord de l'Eau), stressing what he saw as the crucial innovation of the chronological presentation of the national schools in the work exhibited in the galleries. This arrangement had, he said, made visible on the walls of the Louvre what for him was the law of art's historical development from idealism to naturalism, a law confirmed by the evolution of genres (from religious art to landscape) and of forms (line evolving from straight to curved, colour from gold backgrounds to blue to the colours of landscape). It also demonstrated that in the modern age France was now 'le seul pays où l'on fasse réellement et sérieusement de la peinture' (*TP*, p. 62), for whereas the other great national schools had one by one fallen into decline, in France, even in the 'époques les plus déplorables' (ibid.), by which he meant the Davidian domination of the painting of the first Republic, Empire, and early Restoration, great artists had emerged (Prud'hon, Géricault, Sigalon) to generate renewal. However reductive its idealist account of art's fundamental laws of development and decline, no other commentary on the reorganization of the national collections in 1848 presented so forcefully the scale of Jeanron's and Villot's achievement in transforming within the space of a few months the Louvre's fortunes and prestige in the national and international art arena. Once again, from his position in *La Presse*, Gautier articulated the Second Republic's aspirations in a crucial area of its fine-art policy, presenting a quasi-official narrative of republican museology and of the Louvre's pivotal role within its institutions.

It is possible to suggest, therefore, that the Louvre articles represented the high point of Gautier's relationship with the Second Republic's two most important managers of the fine arts administration during the first half of the regime's short life. During the July Monarchy, Blanc and Jeanron had represented distinct strands of opposition to the regime, with Blanc the more moderate reformist and Jeanron the radical republican, but both were opposed to the art for art's sake of which Gautier was believed to be the key figure. The latter's strong support in September 1848 for Chenavard's Panthéon programme and in February 1849 for the Jeanron and Villot reforms in the Louvre, together with the changed circumstances in which the two administrators found themselves following Louis Napoleon's election, evidently reduced this earlier distance between the three for on 13

October 1849 the *Bibliographie de la France* announced as forthcoming the *Histoire des peintres de toutes les écoles, depuis la Renaissance jusqu'à nos jours,* to be published by Blanc, Gautier, and Jeanron. The history would appear only from 1861, under Blanc's direction and with no involvement that we know of on the part of either Gautier or Jeanron.[20] Yet the public association of the three in October 1849 on a new history of European art spoke for itself in terms of Gautier's association with the new republican era of French art.[21]

The interest generated by the ongoing transformation of the Louvre opened up for Gautier a new source of material for his art column in *La Presse* which he exploited in earnest the following summer, when he needed to service his debts and finance his trip to Italy (between 3 August and 19 November 1850). He began with the Musée des Antiques, inaugurated in November 1800 by Napoleon and taking in the ground-floor Salle de Diane (beneath the Salon Carré) and the Salle des Cariatides. It provided the opportunity for another of his celebrations of the golden age represented by antique sculpture's anthropomorphic polytheism. With the painting lost for ever (notwithstanding his 1848 comment that Ingres had resurrected the Venus of Apelles in his *Vénus anadyomène*) and no art criticism of the period to provide detailed description of it, there remained only fragments of sculpture through which to contemplate the miraculous development of ancient art. After reflecting on the issues of authenticity and restoration involved in the transmission of ancient art to the present day, he began with the collection's most famous piece, the *Vénus de Milo*. With firm historical information in short supply, he was free to speculate on the merits of the different hypotheses concerning the direction of Venus's missing arms. Did they originally draw a god or human lord towards her perfect bosom 'où la perfection idéale de la déesse se mêle au charme le plus féminin?' (*TP*, p. 72). Opinion was divided. Had the artist represented the moment at which she received from Pâris the prize for her beauty, with her expression signalling the joy of triumph, for what else other than the pleasure of defeating her rivals could make a woman 'si superbe et si rayonnante'? Gautier thought that this was too modern an explanation, though presumably not too Parisian male. Did etymology contain the answer since Melos, the original name for the isle of Milo, was Greek for 'apple'? In his view the direction of the little of the arm that remained suggested otherwise. Was she holding a shield presented to her by Mars? He thought it unlikely that the Greeks would have wanted to hide part of a perfect body. A detailed examination of the statue, taking into account the fact that her left side appeared to be less finished than the right, which suggested that the sculptor was hindered by the presence of a second figure close to her, led Gautier to propose that this second figure was Mars returning from war, 'ce qui explique l'expression victorieuse et souriante de la Vénus' (p. 73). This in turn explained the direction of the arms 'le plus naturellement du monde', with the left arm resting on the god's left shoulder while the right 's'appuyait sur la mâle poitrine de l'amoureux guerrier'. Having solved for his readers the mystery of the missing limbs in a manner worthy of Vidocq or *Les Mystères du peuple*, Gautier then dismissed this detective work as immaterial, since all that mattered was its radiant beauty, a perfect expression of the pagan ideal.

Gautier followed his presentation of the *Vénus* with brief comments on *Le Tibre* placed nearby. It was, he said, a definitive expression of 'la force tranquille, la sécurité puissante' (*TP*, p. 75) but one which for modern visitors carried a sombre lesson of the decline and fall of empire. *Le Gladiateur*, an improper title in Gautier's view 'car elle [la figure] n'a aucun des accessoires qui spécifient les gladiateurs' (p. 76) and, unusually for antique sculpture, bearing the signature of the artist, expressed not the brutal physical force of Hercules but 'le courage de l'âme'. Here too Gautier's notes from an art history lesson are accompanied by the same philosophical hindsight as in the case of the *Vénus*. *Le Gladiateur* also bore, he said, the signs of 'la décadence prochaine', inscribed in 'nous ne savons quelle fièvre d'exécution', through which the artist had striven for effects of movement and emotional expression beyond the means of sculpture and which showed that 'les données naturelles vont s'épuiser et ont besoin d'être rajeunies' (p. 77). Other works are summarized in the sort of *passe-partout* comment ('d'un caprice si vigoureux', 'd'une beauté si mâle') useful for the reader's own engagement in the social conversation of art before Gautier closes, appropriately enough, with the *Repos éternel*, the pagan vision of death, far superior in his view to the 'hideux squelette qui symbolise la mort dans les idées chrétiennes' (p. 79). Christianity, he said again, 'n'a pas fait fleurir la sculpture' and, in another example of the skill with which the *feuilletoniste* managed the *suite au prochain numéro*, he announced the subject of the next article in his series: 'il faut attendre la Renaissance pour continuer le siècle de Périclès, et Michel-Ange pour reprendre le ciseau des mains de Phidias' (ibid.).

For the same reasons as those that drove the reorganization of the painting collections, Jeanron had been determined from a early stage of his directorship to reorganize and promote the Louvre's Musée Français de la Renaissance.[22] Gautier began his inventory of the museum's riches by explaining why: 'Ces salles [...] sont infiniment nationales, puisqu'à l'exception de Michel-Ange, tous les artistes dont les œuvres s'y trouvent sont des maîtres de France' (*TP*, p. 81). He outlined briefly the history of French sculpture, from its early role prior to François I as an auxiliary to architecture, from which it derived the benefits of association with the distinguished architects of the thirteenth and fourteenth centuries. While pre-Renaissance French sculpture therefore had to be studied *in situ*, sculpture's emancipation from architecture came in the sixteenth century via the study of the ancient sculptors, and Gautier devoted half his article to the two Michelangelo pieces, *Esclave mourant* and *Esclave rebelle*, to which he referred with the museum catalogue's more general title of *Deux captifs*. He began with their history, also lifted from the catalogue, from arrival in France as a gift from Roberto Strozzi to Henri II to their entry into the Louvre (in 1754) and Leloir's rescue of the two works on the point of being sold off during the revolutionary upheavals.[23] Having done so, Gautier explained how the spectator's initial enthusiasm for the sheer beauty of the figures gradually gave way to the 'rêverie involontaire' triggered by the oppositions between them. Here Michelangelo's power as both artist and thinker took the spectator into the deepest levels of feeling, his unfinished areas (in this case the feet 'restés captifs dans le marbre') and baffling accessories ('l'ébauche d'une tête de singe' in the marble support of the *Esclave mourant*), preventing resolution of his exploration of the mysteries of human experience:

> Maintenant, ces morceaux laissés imparfaits par Michel-Ange à presque toutes ses statues, ces accessoires intelligibles, tout ce qui, chez cet homme colossal, surprend et confond notre imagination, était-ce le résultat d'un calcul qui nous échappe ou d'une bizarrerie réelle, comme il semblerait à notre vue un peu trop faible pour pénétrer dans les profondeurs d'un pareil génie? (pp. 86–87)

He was, he said, as powerless to answer such questions as had been Vasari, Michelangelo's contemporary and friend, confirming the sculptor's status as the Romantic archetype of the unfathomability of genius.

In the wake of Michelangelo, a Florentine colony established itself in Fontainebleau, and from this 'Italie improvisée à soixante kilomètres de Paris' a group of French sculptors derived that 'air de famille' from which the national sculpture drew its initial impetus. In a few short paragraphs Gautier presented the best-known works of Goujon, Pilon, Puget, Houdon, and Canova through a sequence of masterpieces that form the key stages of French sculpture's development from the sixteenth century to the nineteenth. Of Goujon 'le Louvre est le vrai monument', on the inside with *Diane* and the four female figures, the *cariatides de la tribune des musiciens*, from which the Salle des Cariatides took its name, on the outside in the bas-relief figures on the ground-floor east façade of the Cour Carrée. The *Trois Grâces* was the purest example of Pilon's work but Gautier defined it only in its generality, 'moins savante' than Goujon but his equal 'comme charme et comme fantaisie' (*TP*, p. 88). Puget was the towering figure, 'le plus grand statuaire de son époque, et peut-être l'artiste le plus franchement français dont nous puissions nous glorifier', the first to give marble 'le vrai aspect de la chair' (p. 89). His *Milon de Crotone* was 'peut-être la plus furieuse chose que la sculpture ait produite' (ibid.) but no mention is made of the distance between its baroque sensibility and the dominant classicism of the period as Gautier draws analogies instead with Flemish realism and the 'naturalisme sauvage' of Spanish art (p. 90). Houdon's *Diane chasseresse* represents the eighteenth century but only on this occasion from the anecdotal point of view, that of the French kings' taste for dressing (and in Houdon's case undressing) their mistresses in the guise of the goddess of hunting. Finally, Gautier's admiration for Canova would have been much greater had he not inspired 'toute une école fade et ratissée' (p. 91) from which Pradier was, he said, endeavouring to extricate contemporary French sculpture. He ended by paying tribute to Villot, the success of whose chronological arrangement of the sculptures was, he said, a worthy accompaniment to that achieved by his reorganization of the painting collections, but Gautier's rapid and superficial presentation of modern French sculpture could hardly be said to have made best use of the narrative possibilities which Villot's efforts had made available.

The two-part article on the Musée Espagnol was not, as its title might have suggested, a presentation of the debates taking place at the time on the issues surrounding the exiled King's claims to the collections that it housed. It is more likely that Gautier included the Musée Espagnol while there was still time to do so, before a final decision was taken on the future of the collection which might be lost to the nation. In August 1850 the legal debates triggered by the *comité de liquidation*, set up by the Provisional Government to oversee the dissolution of the Civil List, were continuing within the Conseil d'État. Only four months later did it decide that, in the words of Haussard in *Le National*, 'le musée Standish étant un legs fait à la personne de Louis-Philippe et le musée Espagnol une acquisition provenant des deniers du domaine privé, l'État n'avait rien à y réclamer'.[24] The Republican government had sought to reach agreement with Louis-Philippe on a price for the two collections but could not meet his financial demands (of 1.2 million francs) for the work in the Musée Espagnol proper, excluding the Standish bequest, a figure which Haussard described as 'une prétension exorbitante'. Like Clément de Ris, Haussard believed that though 'quelques morceaux s'y distinguaient par leur valeur d'art ou leur curiosité réelle [...] l'ensemble, le bloc, encombrait et déshonorait le Louvre'. Gautier referred to these issues only to the extent of agreeing that 'quand la galerie fut déballée [in 1837], éprouva-t-on une certaine surprise, la part d'admiration faite aux huit ou dix chefs-d'œuvres qu'elle contient [among nearly 450 works], à voir ces toiles enfumées, noires, peintes comme des enseignes de bière, et qu'on aurait pu prendre pour le rebut de la pacotille des Indes' (*TP*, pp. 95–96).

For a new generation of readers of *La Presse*, Gautier retraced the history of the collection. Before the Romantic movement, Spain, isolated geographically and riven by internal political strife, was unknown in France:

> L'Espagne est le pays romantique par excellence; aucune autre nation n'a moins emprunté à l'antiquité. Baignée par la Méditerranée et l'Océan, séparée de l'Europe par une haute chaîne de montagnes, la Péninsule n'a subi aucune influence classique, et les Maures, s'en emparant après les Vandales et les Goths, ont rompu le fil de la tradition romaine. (*TP*, p. 102)

Legal obstacles restricted the export of Spanish art objects, but the Regency's suppression of the religious orders and closure of monasteries had released a substantial number of art works of varying quality, many of which one way or another found their way onto Taylor's boats. Gautier's own subsequent journey to Spain had convinced him that Taylor had done as well as he could, given that the royal collections and Madrid's museum already contained the best work of Velasquez and Murillo. The French government's major mistake had come, he claimed, a decade earlier, when it had failed to buy up the collection of Spanish art formed during the Empire by Marshal Soult. Had it done so, Taylor would not have needed to spend the money he did on acquiring a lot of dross. The ten or so masterpieces he did bring back, added to the Soult collection, would have provided the Louvre with 'une tribune espagnole dans le goût du salon Carré et de la salle dite des Sept-Cheminées' (*TP*, p. 98), that is, combining the gallery of masterpieces with the chronological presentation of the history of the national school, which, as Villot's reorganization of the Louvre's collections two years earlier had already shown, was now the canonical mode of presentation for French museum collections.

When the Musée Espagnol had opened its doors, the work was not presented in chronological order. Of the five rooms allocated to it, one each had been reserved for the work of Velasquez, Murillo, Ribera, and Zurbaran, with the fifth being used to sweep up everyone else. This arrangement had coincided with and reinforced French perceptions that Spanish art consisted of four painters, whose work taken together covered the range of cultural stereotypes of Spain at that time. As Gautier put it:

> Velasquez représente le côté aristocratique et chevaleresque; Murillo, la dévotion amoureuse et tendre, l'ascétisme voluptueux, les Vierges roses et blanches; Ribera, le côté sanguinaire et farouche, le côté de l'inquisition, des combats de taureaux et des bandits; Zurbaran, les mortifications du cloître, l'aspect cadavéreux et monacal, le stoïcisme effroyable des martyrs. Que Velasquez vous peigne une infante, Murillo une Vierge, Ribera un bourreau, Zurbaran un moine, et vous avez toute l'Espagne d'alors, moins les pauvres, dont tous les quatre excellent à rendre les haillons et la vermine. (*TP*, pp. 98–99)[25]

This last point, on the representation of the poor (whose domain was, it went without saying, coextensive with the ugly), had important implications for French debates in 1850, when the emergence of realism was placing it firmly on the agenda for contemporary French artists and their critics. Gautier was at pains to ensure that his readers understood where this feature of Spanish art was coming from: 'Cet amour de guenilles picaresques, commun à presque tous les maîtres espagnols [...] s'explique cependant par l'absence de toute imitation antique, la passion du réalisme et l'idée catholique' (p. 99). With no classical tradition to come between them and their twin aspiration to the expression of realism and faith, Spanish artists rehabilitated everything that the classical *beau idéal* had outlawed. Ribera, for example, 'proteste, au nom du réalisme, contre les abstractions de l'idéalisme grec et fait entrer dans les régions de l'art toutes les laideurs jadis repoussées' (p. 101). What, however, made this an important issue in current French critical debates was the fact 'par le cachet puissant qu'il leur imprime, il les élève au style et leur donne des lettres de noblesse' (ibid.). The brutal realism with which Spanish art represented *le laid* and which set it apart in European art history could be assimilated by exponents of other art traditions, founded on classical principles, through the elevation of the artist's sentiments when faced with the ugly and the power of his technique to express these sentiments. For Gautier, it was essential that the French realists assimilated this Spanish lesson. For the Spanish artist, beggars and bandits were 'laids, pauvres, dégoûtants, mais non abjects, car chez eux la misère n'a pas tué le courage'. Four months later Courbet's submission to the Salon of 1850–51 would polarize French art debate around this issue and, in particular, create for Gautier the most serious challenge to his aesthetic system that he had yet faced.

For the second part of his article, Gautier applied to the chronological development of the Spanish school the same division into four which Alphonse de Cailleux, Directeur Général des Musées for much of the July Monarchy, had adopted for the Musée Espagnol, but where Cailleux had used the fourfold division to allocate rooms within the museum to individual artists, Gautier presented Spanish art in terms of four regional schools, those of Toledo, Valencia, Seville, and Madrid. Where Villot's revised Louvre catalogues had retained early Spanish art as a subcategory of the Italian school (Gautier had referred to this larger grouping of Italian and Spanish art as the 'école du Midi'), Gautier presented Spain's four regional schools as embodying the same historical paradigm of rise and fall that had characterized its Italian, Flemish, and German counterparts in his commentary on the Villot–Jeanron reorganization eighteen months earlier. Spanish art began began with the school of Toledo and its 'sauvagerie presque byzantine', 'couleurs éclatantes plaquées sur fonds d'or', and 'formes raides' (*TP*, p. 106), of which El Greco was the outstanding figure. Faced with the difficulties which the French encountered in interpreting work so far outside their canons of taste, Gautier created the portrait of an artist whose exceptional technical skills and effects resembled those of Titian, of whom he was thought to be a pupil, to such an extent that El Greco's efforts to free himself from this disabling authority had driven him mad: 'C'est le délire, mais c'est le délire du génie, et à travers toutes ces formes incohérentes, tracées par la main tremblante du cauchemar, étincelle çà et là une tête admirable et se cambre un corps de la plus fière tournure' (p. 108). In the gallery of artistic parallels between painters and writers, Gautier attached him firmly to the alienated and isolated Romantic poet. In the school of Valencia, Joanes had added an austere Catholicism to his deep assimilation of the lessons of Raphael while the Ribaltas, father and son, served as the transition to Ribera. His attachment to the Neapolitans for much of his life had made him better known in France than others of his compatriots, but Spanish domination of Naples had, for Gautier, reinforced his Spanish roots in Valencia, his birthplace, which explained French surprise in 1837 at the discovery of a painter whom they thought they knew but whose *espagnolisme* was a revelation. After the two Espinosas, young and old, the school of Valencia had died out, supplanted by that of Seville, which Gautier called the Venice of Spain on account of its great colourists, of which he presented a long list, whose essential figures were Murillo, Velasquez, and Zurbaran. The Madrid school marked the decline of the development of which Seville was the summit. Coello was to Madrid what Tiepolo was to Venice and Maratta to Rome, the last representative of the line, 'l'art dans sa décadence, avec ses recherches, ses maniérismes et ses facilités désastreuses, mais [...] encore de l'art' (p. 113). In a brief final paragraph, Gautier hinted that in the modern period Goya, while still being 'le dernier descendant de Velasquez' (p. 114) that he had been in the initial French response to his work in 1838,[26] had recovered something of the 'originalité espagnole' (ibid.); but the lack of any analysis of this feature suggests that at this stage and despite the eight Goyas of the Musée Espagnol, Gautier was no nearer to grasping how Goya had done so. His 1850 article on the Musée Espagnol integrated the one national tradition absent from the broad historical narrative of the decline and fall of the European Old Master tradition which he had presented eighteen months earlier in his commentary on the Salon Carré and the Grande Galerie, and of which France was, in the age of history, the exception that proved the rule.

In his series of articles on museums the next piece, devoted to the Luxembourg museum, stands apart, for here Gautier set out to 'régler nos comptes avec celui [musée] du Luxembourg' (*TP*, p. 116), which since 1818 had been allocated to contemporary art works commissioned by the state or purchased following their exhibition in the Salon, with a view to their possible transfer to the Louvre and immortality on the artist's death.[27] He began with its history, indissolubly associated with that of Marie de Médicis, represented in the cycle of paintings (1622–25) commissioned from Rubens for the west wing of the palace but removed to the Louvre in 1818 to help fill the spaces left there by the return to their country of origin of the art works looted by Napoleon's armies. Gautier regretted their removal and urged the government to restore them to the palace for which they had been created. Having done so, he proceeded to settle his scores with the Luxembourg's existing collection, beginning as he intended to continue:

> Elle [cette galerie] semble se ressentir de l'ancien voisinage de la Chambre des pairs. Si elle n'était émaillée çà et là de quelques œuvres de Delacroix, Ingres, Couture, Scheffer, Devéria, fleurs vivaces implantées dans le tuf de ce terrain ingrat, on y bâillerait comme en plein Institut et on serait tenté d'inscrire au frontispice de la salle: 'Hôtel national des invalides de la peinture'.
> (pp. 116–17)

In 1850 the last bastion of the Davidian resistance, 'le musée du Luxembourg, semblable à l'Institut dont il pourrait bien être une succursale, une dépendance, a conservé son culte fidèle pour les vieux oripeaux qui n'ont plus d'autre asile que sa voûte hospitalière' (p. 118). Deprived of its right to determine the Salon jury and evicted from the Salon Carré, the Davidian school was left with this one retreat, abandoned by the public and ignored by the art students, who on study days planted their easels in front of Couture's *Orgie romaine* and Delacroix's *Femmes d'Alger* instead (p. 118). Gautier was willing to make the odd exception among these 'vieilleries' but, claiming again to be more comfortable distributing praise than sarcasm, he moved on to the Romantic painters and took another opportunity to recount the insurrection triggered by Delacroix from 1822, when the artist had shown *Dante et Virgile* at the Salon, and remembered by Gautier with increasing fondness as it retreated further into history. The homage to the four works on show in the Luxembourg in 1850 (*Dante et Virgile*, *Massacre de Scio*, *Noce juive*, *Femmes d'Alger*) was followed by the no less ritual attack on Delaroche as the Casimir Delavigne of painting, enlarged on this occasion by the use of another familiar disparaging reference in the Delaroche literature of the time, that of John Opie.[28] This reductive opposition between the positive and negative representatives of Romantic painting was followed by brief accounts of the failure of Scheffer and Devéria to fulfil the hopes they had raised in the Salon of 1827. As always, however, in Gautier's history of nineteenth-century French art, it is Ingres, the 'fanatique exclusif de Raphaël et de l'antiquité', who dominates. Whatever the subject or genre, his work was for Gautier the decisive authority for the continuing relevance of the *grand style* in the modern age. The work in the Luxembourg collection — *Saint Pierre* (*La Chapelle Sixtine*) (1820), *Roger délivrant Angélique* (1819), and *Luigi Cherubini et la muse de la poésie lyrique* (1842) — was a master class in the lessons that only he provided.

Gautier's conclusion that, apart from about twenty works, 'le reste est au-dessous de la critique' and that the collection was hopelessly unrepresentative of the work of living French artists was a common enough refrain during the Second Republic. In April 1848, Clément de Ris had expressed the hope that the museum, which had hitherto offered only 'une majorité imposante de tableaux absurdes ou ridicules' (CdR4, p. 73), would now be able to achieve for contemporary painting the same model of museological excellence as that for which once again 'la Tribune à Florence' (ibid.) was the point of reference. Freed from the chaotic mismanagement by whim and intrigue which had for him characterized the previous administration and as a result of which 'les enfants efflanqués de David y régnaient en souverains, s'y étaient cantonnés et personne, grâce à une déplorable mais haute influence, ne pouvait les en débusquer' (ibid.), the Luxembourg might at last become a truly representative display of contemporary French art.[29] Gautier's commentary suggested, however, that two years on little had changed, despite the efforts of Jeanron to extend the range of exhibits to include the realists and landscapists whom the Second Republic was actively promoting.[30] Gautier would have been aware of these efforts and he alluded to, but declined to comment on, one aspect of them — 'Ce n'est pas ici le lieu de proposer un autre mode d'organisation pour l'exposition permanente des ouvrages applaudis aux Salons et achetés pour le compte de l'État'(*TP*, p. 129)[31] — but the fact that the Luxembourg did not include a single work by Meissonier, Decamps, Rousseau, Dupré, Chassériau, Roqueplan, Louis Boulanger, Isabey, 'ni enfin vingt autres talents chers au public et connus de l'Europe entière' required what he called urgent and radical reform (ibid.). The following month, it appeared that Gautier's demand had been heard by the administration, for in a meeting of the Conservatoire des Musées Nationaux on 28 October 1850, Jeanron's successor, Nieuwerkerke, stated that he intended to 'ôter une grande quantité des tableaux qui sont au Luxembourg' since he wished that 'l'école française soit enfin représentée dans les galeries du Luxembourg'.[32] Jeanron's successor evidently found as Jeanron had that things moved more slowly in the Luxembourg than in the Louvre for, nine months later, Clément de Ris returned to the subject to protest that the progress achieved in the Louvre only made the lack of it in the Luxembourg even more anomalous and that no one in the press '— sauf M. Théophile Gautier — n'a fait remarquer et n'a flétri cette anomalie'.[33]

Both in content and in tone this latest article by Clément de Ris was very close to that of Gautier. There was the same sarcasm directed at the list of minor artists of the Restoration whose work was still being exhibited over thirty years later ('tous appartenant plus ou moins directement à la triste école de David, qui a failli un instant étrangler l'art français');[34] the same indignation at the list of those not represented and who should have been (almost identical with that of Gautier); the same use of rhetorical questions raised and answered in feigned astonishment and genuine outrage, such as what idea of contemporary French art could a foreign visitor possibly take from a visit to the Luxembourg? 'Une bizarre idée', replied Gautier (*TP*, p. 129), 'une idée déplorable et grotesque', said Clément de Ris (p. 161). But where Gautier had allotted half his article to the works in the collection which recounted the post-Davidian history of Ingres's rebellion and Delacroix's revolution, Clément de Ris focused on the fact that control of the most important institution devoted to contemporary art still appeared to be exercised by what he thought of as the relics of the Davidian past. How was it possible that the 'école de la Restauration' still dominated the collection to the extent that it did and in violation of the museum's explicit role to be, as its title proclaimed, an *Exposition des artistes vivants*?

> Beaucoup de ces artistes qui, à en croire le titre, devraient être vivants, sont morts depuis de longues années; et, ce qu'il y a de piquant, c'est que c'est le livret lui-même qui donne la date de leur mort et condamne ainsi le rédacteur du livret et le conservateur du Musée [in 1847] [...] Parmi ces cent dix-huit artistes *vivants* dont le Musée possédait les œuvres en 1847, vingt-trois étaient

morts, et quelques-uns en 1810, c'est-à-dire depuis trente-sept ans. Pourquoi donc laisserait-on leurs tableaux ou leurs statues exposés? Était-ce inattention, était-ce malveillance? Et, dans tous les cas, que doit-on penser d'un Musée ainsi dirigé et où l'arbitraire pouvait s'ébattre aussi à l'aise? (p. 162)

For an explanation of the fact that the managers of the Luxembourg had failed in their duty to see that their own rules about the removal of works from the collection on the death of their authors were respected, Clément de Ris appeared to hesitate between incompetence and conspiracy but his instincts were usually to see the dead hand of the Institute at work.[35] He was opposed to a complete cull of the work representing the surviving contemporary practitioners of 'l'art de 1815–1825', for that would constitute an act of revenge unworthy of the new era and would deprive artists and public of the didactic value that came from having before it all 'les pièces du procès' that a truly representative collection of contemporary art would create for the work of the Neo-Davidians. Like Gautier, Clément de Ris wanted to eradicate the remaining remnants of their tyranny but without making martyrs of them.

The one major subject on which Clément de Ris intervened in his article and Gautier did not was that of the extension of the Luxembourg's collection beyond painting and sculpture, whose hitherto exclusive right to representation in the national museum devoted to the work of living artists was in his view a throwback to an earlier vision of the hierarchy of the arts. Here Clément de Ris advocated the creation within the Luxembourg of a museum of lithography and of the different branches of engraving. He emphasized the national history and character of these forms and, significantly, their superiority over their English counterparts.[36] More explicitly than for Gautier, the economic stakes involved in the European competition for museum supremacy were never far away for Clément de Ris, but neither was his view that the museum should as far as possible demonstrate the range of artistic activity available to the artist at any given phase of historical development. The more complete the range of the museum's collections, the more powerful was the sense of relationship between the individual work of art and the historical paradigm from which it derived its meaning, 'la loi historique, si féconde pour l'interprétation des œuvres'.[37] He was proposing that the state embark on a new stage in the formation of the Luxembourg museum on the assumption that it would reinforce the dominant epistemological model of historicism. Gautier's article, directed at a less specialized readership than that of L'Artiste and one for whom the existing collection was almost certainly less well known, settled for the less ambitious target of presenting the existing collection as a further demonstration of a simplified history of French painting during the first half of the nineteenth century.

In his final article in the series which became the 'Études sur les musées', Gautier turned to another major aspect of French museology of the nineteenth century, that of the development of the provincial museums, in this case the museum at Tours. From the early 1840s criticism of the state of neglect into which these museums had allegedly been allowed to fall frequently accompanied that relating to the Louvre. Théophile Thoré, for example, in the Bulletin des arts of 1842, had deplored the absence of catalogues, neglect of art works, and incompetence of curators and urged the Paris administration to integrate them within a centralized museum policy.[38] As with the Louvre, the Second Republic saw it as its duty to realize the ambitions of the first, which had founded the provincial museums under the Directory, so that as soon as Jeanron was appointed Directeur des Musées Nationaux, he asked Ledru-Rollin to include 'la direction et la surveillance des Musées départementaux' within his responsibilities.[39] In a report submitted to Jeanron in March 1848 Philippe de Chennevières stated that 'il était clair qu'il entrait dans la pensée de la [première] République de former de tous ces musées des départements un système de rayonnement des arts dans les divers points du territoire français, système admettant évidemment unité d'impulsion, centre actif et fécondant' but that this ambition had been thwarted by a range of factors, the most important of which was the failure of successive regimes to exert control over the provincial museum director, 'omnipotent pour le bien, mais surtout pour le mal de sa collection'.[40] Outside the government it was once again Clément de Ris in *L'Artiste* who led the campaign for reform, with seven articles over a period of two years, supported in his efforts by a further four articles from other more or less regular contributors to the journal.[41]

In September 1850 Gautier was therefore a relative latecomer to this debate during the Second Republic, but before the change of regime, he had occasionally laced his travelogues with comments on the local museum. A case in point was his visit in 1840 to that in Bordeaux, recounted in his *Voyage en Espagne*. Here he discovered 'une belle collection de plâtres et un grand nombre de tableaux remarquables' but which 'il est impossible d'accrocher avec moins de goût et de discernement; les meilleures places sont occupés par d'énormes croûtes de l'école moderne du temps de Guérin et de Lethière'.[42] It was not unusual in Parisian criticisms of the provincial museums to find these combined failings of incompetent curatorship and reactionary artistic taste, as Thoré and Chennevières confirmed, and Gautier began his commentary on the museum in Tours with regrets that the Parisian dominance in French art had reduced the provinces to a 'stérilité déplorable; nulle part une école [de beaux-arts]; nulle part, même pour l'artiste sérieux, les moyens matériels d'exercer son talent et d'enfanter son œuvre' (*TP*, pp. 132–33). He therefore suggested that one means of watering this cultural desert would be for the state to commission the decoration of public buildings, which would oblige artists to take up residence for extended periods in the provinces and leave behind an artistic legacy which would in turn encourage vocations in the fine arts. Not surprisingly after such an unpromising *entrée en matière*, Gautier entered the museum 'presque à notre corps défendant' and only in the hope of seeing Delacroix's *Improvisateur marocain*, purchased by the State following the Salon of 1849, but found to his surprise that the museum's holdings 'sont loin d'être à dédaigner' (p. 135), with two works by Rubens, one Tintoretto, two Lesueurs, one Caravaggio, and a few Mantegnas. In Tours as in Bordeaux the mediocre occupied the most favourable positions (in this case 'deux immenses toiles du comte de Forbin, désastreusement craquelées') while the best work 'se morfondent sous un jour beaucoup moins favorable' (pp. 135–36), but Gautier was now minded to be more philosophical about this, given that it had required the overthrow of the monarchy to bring about change to a similar state of affairs in the Louvre.

After a brief presentation of the history of the collection, of which the starting-point had been the work salvaged from the revolutionary confiscations of local castles and religious institutions, Gautier turned his attention to the work itself, presenting in rapid sequence by means of brief descriptions of the subject the two Rubens works, the *ex-voto de la famille Plantin* and *Mars couronné par Vénus*, Tintoretto's *Judith présentée à Holopherne*, Fréminet's *Jugement dernier*, Poussin's *Bacchanale*, two Lesueurs, *Saint Louis lavant les pieds des pauvres* and *Saint Sébastien secouru par les saintes femmes*, two Mantegnas, *Le Christ au jardin des Oliviers* and *Résurrection du Sauveur* (evidently part of a series of Stations of the Cross of which the Louvre possessed others), three Bouchers, not identified by Gautier but leading him to feel that the painter's rehabilitation, following the unjust oblivion to which, thanks to David, he had been consigned, had gone quite far enough: 'Un ou deux Boucher amusent; trop de Boucher produisent l'effet écœurant d'une indigestion de sucreries' (*TP*, p. 141). From the same era two agreeable works by Restout, *Saint Benoît en extase* and *Sainte Scolastique*, were weakened by a facility which 'dégenère un peu trop en *pratique*, comme on disait, en *chic*, comme on dirait aujourd'hui' (ibid.), since Gautier liked to remind his readers that he was teaching them not only how to see paintings but also how to talk about them in society. His one genuine discovery was that of a local landscape artist named Houïlle, whose four paintings of the banks of the Loire and the Seine occupied 'un heureux milieu entre la sévère perfection des Hollandais et les allures peut-être un peu trop tourmentées des paysagistes de nos jours' (p. 141), but if he did find Delacroix's *Improvisateur marocain*, he either forgot to mention it, or ran out of space, or decided that his description of it in his review of the Salon of 1849 enabled him to dispense with another on this occasion.

From communion with absolute beauty in the Louvre's Salon Carré to an hour or two spent in a provincial museum which, all things considered, had turned out to be a more pleasant experience than he had expected, Gautier's texts on French museums in the mid-nineteenth century are a further illustration of the range of material on which he brought his erudition, versatility, and facility to bear. In his support for the museum policy of Jeanron and Villot, there are times when he appears to form a sort of unofficial double act with Clément de Ris, the one addressing the more specialized readership of *L'Artiste* while the other educated and entertained the broader-based readership of *La Presse*. From a quasi-religious awe in the face of the transcendent masterpieces of the European tradition to the enthusiastic embrace of the historical paradigm for the interpretation of art works and from there to patronizing Parisianisms on benighted provincials cut off from the artistic life of the capital, Gautier had a tone for every occasion. He concluded his article on the museum in Tours by promising that it would be the first of many. What had been achieved in the Louvre should, he said, be extended to every museum in France until the nation, assuming to the full its exemplary role as the sole surviving guardian of the great tradition, achieved, as Renaissance Italy had done before, 'à chaque halte, dans des cités même peu importantes, d'admirables écoles [d'art] ayant chacune leur accent, leur saveur particulière, leur goût de terroir' (*TP*, p. 132). As far as Gautier was concerned, 'nous sommes bien résolu à ne jamais nous lasser d'en parler, tant qu'il nous restera une voix et une plume'.

This new promise of the 'suite au prochain numéro' was not kept and there was no sequel in the proposed series on 'Les Musées de province'. A little over two weeks later, on 24 September, *La Presse* began publishing Gautier's articles on his Italian travels. They included museum visits, but with the reorganization of the art of the past well under way, it was time in the autumn of 1850 to return to the art of the present.

Notes to Chapter 5

1. 'Remarques sur le Musée du Louvre', 20 February 1848, pp. 248–50; 'Le Musée du Louvre', 19 March, pp. 29–30; 'L'École française au Louvre', 26 March, pp. 39–40; 'Le Musée du Luxembourg', 9 April, pp. 72–74; 'Nouvelle Galerie française du Musée du Louvre', 1 December, pp. 110–12; 'Musée du Louvre: Grande galerie', 15 January 1849, pp. 149–52. For convenience these articles will be referred to in the text through the abbreviation CdR, followed by the number of the article in the sequence. On the Luxembourg museum see Geneviève Lacambre, 'Les Achats de l'État aux artistes vivants: le musée du Luxembourg', in *La Jeunesse des musées* (Paris: RMN, 1994), pp. 267–77; the same author's introduction to the exhibition catalogue, *Le Musée du Luxembourg en 1874* (Paris: Éditions des Musées Nationaux, 1974), pp. 7–11; Chantal Georgel, 'Le Musée du Luxembourg sous la Seconde République', in *1848: la République et l'art vivant*, pp. 148–63. In her 1994 article Lacambre states: 'En 1818 [when the Museum opened], considéré comme une extension spécialisée du Louvre, le Luxembourg est d'abord réservé aux artistes de l'"'école moderne de France" et aux techniques les plus nobles, la peinture et la sculpture' (p. 270).
2. 'Le Musée de Tours', 17 December 1847, pp. 103–06; 'Le Musée de Rouen', 15 June 1849, pp. 90–94; 'Le Musée de Rennes', 15 August 1849, pp. 150–53; 'Le Musée de Nantes', 15 September 1849, pp. 180–85; 'Des Musées de province, I', 1 November 1849, pp. 6–8; II, 15 November 1849, pp. 22–25; III, 1 December 1849, pp. 38–41. See also his book *Les Musées de province*, published in two volumes in 1859.
3. 'Le Musée ancien', *La Presse*, 10 February 1849; 'La Galerie française', 13 and 17 February 1849; 'Le Musée des Antiques', 27 July 1850; 'Le Musée français de la Renaissance', 24 August 1850; 'Le Musée espagnol', 27 and 28 August 1850; 'La Galerie du Luxembourg', 2 September 1850, and 'Le Musée de Tours', 7 September 1850. These articles were subsequently published under the collective title of 'Études sur les musées' in *Tableaux à la plume*, pp. 1–143. All references to these articles will be to this edition and preceded where appropriate by the abbreviation *TP*.
4. 'La loi qui plaçait les musées dans les attributions de la liste civile en était en premier lieu la cause [of the neglect of the Louvre]. La personne royale, aux termes de la loi, disposait comme elle l'entendait des richesses du musée du Louvre' (CdR6, p. 149).
5. On the Musée Historique, see Marrinan, *Painting Politics for Louis-Philippe*; Marie-Claire Chaudonneret. 'Historicism and "Heritage" in the Louvre, 1820–1840: From the Musée Charles X to the Galerie d'Apollon', *Art History*, 14 (1991), 488–520; eadem, *L'État et les artistes: de la Restauration à la Monarchie de Juillet (1815–1833)* (Paris: Flammarion, 1999); Pierre Sesmat, 'Le Musée historique de Versailles: la gloire, l'histoire et les arts', in *La Jeunesse des musées* (Paris: RMN, 1994), pp. 115–21. In 1835 the July Monarchy sent Isidore Taylor to Spain to buy Spanish art. The Musée Espagnol was created in three rooms of the Louvre's Galerie de la Colonnade to house the 446 works which Taylor brought back. Frank Hall Standish was an English author, patron, and collector, resident in Seville, who amassed nearly 500 paintings and drawings. See Baticle and Marinas, *La Galerie espagnole de Louis-Philippe*.
6. 'Les tableaux de l'école française, celle que nous connaissons le moins, sont odieusement mal placés. Personne n'a jamais regardé les Lahire, les Patel, les Vouet, les Claude Lefevre, les Dufresnoy, les Sébastien Bourdon, les Jouvenet, par la bonne raison qu'on ne peut les voir' (CdR1, p. 250).
7. 'La galerie du Louvre se compose [...] de trois grandes travées séparées par des entre-colonnements formant eux-mêmes des espèces de petites salles. La division méthodique et rationnelle se trouvait donc parfaitement en rapport avec la division architecturale' (CdR6,

p. 150). But under the previous regime 'on ne se faisait aucun scrupule de la rompre par l'adjonction de tableaux étrangers à l'école dans laquelle ils figuraient; les compositions d'une même époque et d'un même maître se trouvaient désunies' (ibid., p. 149).

8. 'Le Louvre contient quinze différentes collections [...] Eh bien! Sauf les dessins et les tableaux de la grande galerie, aucun des objets contenues dans ces collections n'est catalogué [...] Les deux seuls livrets que l'on puisse se procurer aujourd'hui [...] sont si fautifs qu'il vaudrait presque autant qu'il n'en existât pas' (CdR1, p. 249).

9. 'Il existe au Louvre des greniers remplis jusqu'aux genoux de toiles qui ne sont jamais visitées, et qui, à plus forte raison, n'ont jamais été cataloguées' (CdR1, p. 250).

10. 'Sous la monarchie de Juillet, le Salon prenait six mois par an, ou peu s'en faut; c'étaient six mois de perdus pour ses travaux et c'est peut-être là une des causes de l'incroyable désordre qui a régné pendant dix-huit ans dans cette magnifique collection' (Clément de Ris, 'Le Salon de 1851', L'Artiste, 1 January 1851, pp. 225–26 (p. 225).

11. 'Pour ne citer qu'un seul fait qui sera le dernier, nous dirons que l'arbitraire seul, et le plus souvent, hélas! la plus complète ignorance décidait des tableaux à restaurer que l'on confiait à des barbouilleurs, Dieu sait lesquels!' (CdR2, pp. 29–30).

12. For further details see Rousseau, La Vie et l'œuvre de Philippe-Auguste Jeanron, pp. 74–76.

13. On the new arrangements, see my article 'From Store to Museum'.

14. For a map of the first floor of the Louvre in 1848–49 showing the galleries referred to here, see Rousseau, p. 177.

15. See 'From Store to Museum', pp. 68–70.

16. For the composition of the commission and the text of de Lasteyrie's report see Le Moniteur universel of 11 December 1848, p. 3531.

17. When the refurbished galleries, inaugurated by Louis Napoleon on 5 June 1851, were opened to the public, Paul Mantz recalled some of the same initial fears relating to the decoration as those referred to by Clément de Ris: 'Mais on parlait en même temps [in January 1849] de décorer le grand salon [Salon carré], et, pour ceux qui connaissent le goût de nos architectes, cette promesse était une menace. Jamais entreprise, en effet, ne contint plus de dangers' ('Les Salles du Louvre', L'Artiste, 15 June 1851, pp. 145–48 (p. 145)).

18. 'Dès le premier janvier [1849], on commence les travaux, car Jeanron espère, après ce premier succès [the loi du 12 décembre which allocated the budget of two million francs], poursuivre sa campagne et obtenir, par tranches successives, les crédits nécessaires à l'aménagement complet du musée' (Rousseau, La Vie et l'œuvre de Philippe-Auguste Jeanron, p. 77).

19. See Le comte de Nieuwerkerke: art et pouvoir sous Napoléon III (Paris: RMN, 2000), p. 14; Chennevières, Souvenirs d'un Directeur des Beaux-Arts, I, 63.

20. Histoire des peintres de toutes les écoles, 14 vols (Paris: Vve J. Renouard and H. Loones, 1861–76).

21. Another element that should be mentioned in this context is the article entitled 'Manufactures nationales de Beauvais et des Gobelins' which Gautier published in La Presse on 10 September 1849. Quite apart from his long-standing interest in the technical issues involved in the practice of the decorative arts and in art's applications in everyday life, his article again supports the Republican government's initiatives in the reorganization of these institutions. He followed this up with an article the following year on the 'Exposition des manufactures nationales de porcelaine, vitraux et émaux de Sèvres, de tapis et de tapisseries des Gobelins et de Beauvais, faite au Palais-National' (La Presse, 1 June 1850). See also Pierre Vaisse, 'Le Conseil supérieur de perfectionnement des manufactures nationales sous la deuxième république', Bulletin de la Société de l'Histoire de l'Art français (1974), 153–71.

22. Rousseau described the situation which Jeanron was determined to remedy: 'Les sculptures de la Renaissance et des Temps Modernes sont groupées depuis 1824 dans la galerie d'Angoulême [named after Charles X's son, the duc d'Angoulême, a fact of which oddly Gautier claimed to be unaware (TP, p. 80)], qui comprend cinq salles dans lesquelles les monuments sont exposés sans ordre. Rarement ouvert au public, ce musée est à peu près ignoré' (p. 199). The first three rooms were opened to the public in January 1850, immediately after Jeanron's departure from his post of Director, and were hailed by L'Artiste as further proof of his enlightened management (Anon., 'Mouvement des arts', L'Artiste, 1 February 1850, p. 108). The fourth and fifth, which housed work by Puget and Canova respectively, opened four months later.

23. On Alexandre Lenoir's salvage of French antiquities during the revolutionary period, see Stephen Bann, *The Clothing of Cleo: A Study of the Representation of History in Nineteenth-Century Britain and France* (Cambridge University Press, 1984), pp. 77–92.

24. 'Revue des beaux-arts', *Le National*, 26 November 1850. Haussard's article was republished in *L'Artiste* of 15 December (pp. 222–23).

25. In 'La Portée de la Galerie espagnole: fortune critique', Cristina Marinas placed the four artists in descending order of their popularity in 1838: Murillo, Velasquez, Ribera, and Zurbaran (*La Galerie espagnole de Louis-Philippe*, pp. 21–23).

26. See Marinas, p. 24.

27. For this reason the museum was known as 'l'antichambre du Louvre'. On the significance of the decision in 1816 to convert the Luxembourg palace into a national museum for the work of contemporary artists (opened on 24 April 1818 on the anniversary of the king's return to France), see Lacambre, 'Les Achats de l'État aux artistes vivants'.

28. *Les Enfants d'Édouard* of 1830 was a 'digne illustration pour la tragédie de Casimir Delavigne', while his *Mort d'Élizabeth* of 1828 was a 'grand tableau de genre, d'un ton lourd et violacé et d'une composition un peu trop empruntée à celle d'une vignette du peintre anglais Opie' (*TP*, pp. 126–27). On the analogy between Delaroche and Delavigne repeatedly made by Gautier and Dumas, see Bann, *Paul Delaroche*, p. 28, and on Delaroche's alleged borrowings from Opie, ibid., pp. 91 and 126.

29. 'Au point de vue administratif c'était un désordre réjouissant, si l'on pouvait se réjouir du désordre. [...] Le directeur de ce musée dépendait de l'administration de la Liste Civile; mais les galeries appartenaient à la Chambre des Pairs, qui y plaçait des hommes de service qui alors n'avaient aucun ordre à recevoir du directeur du musée. [...] Enfin, certains tableaux appartenaient à la Liste civile, d'autres au ministère du Commerce ou de l'Intérieur, d'autres enfin à la Chambre des Pairs. Je laisse à penser l'ensemble qui devait résulter de cette agréable organisation' (CdR 4, p. 73).

30. See in this respect, Rousseau, *La Vie et l'œuvre de Philippe-Auguste Jeanron*, pp. 204–05, and Georgel, 'Le Musée de Luxembourg', pp. 148–52.

31. In September 1849, Jeanron had proposed the creation of a space in the Luxembourg for temporary exhibitions of all the items bought by the State before they were despatched to their various provincial destinations. See Rousseau, p. 205.

32. Quoted by Georgel, p. 152. Jeanron had created the Conservatoire des Musées Nationaux in 1848. It consisted of the heads of the different departments within the Louvre and was chaired by the Director.

33. 'Musée du Luxembourg', *L'Artiste*, 1 July 1851, pp. 161–63 (p. 161).

34. Ibid.

35. As, for example, when he explained the absence of the work of those more recent artists who he felt should be represented: 'Ne suit-on pas dans chaque exclusion l'influence de l'Institut, qui a toujours, par système, barré le passage au talent.' The museum's statutes required that work exhibited in the Luxembourg be removed on the artist's death and be sent either to the Louvre, if judged to be of sufficient merit, or to another (usually provincial) museum or placed in storage.

36. 'Peu de personnes se rendent compte de l'état, des progrès, des transformations de cet art [la gravure] qui jadis, en France [...] jeta un éclat si vif et si national [...] Bien peu de personnes connaissent les progrès de notre gravure en bois, pour laquelle nous étions jadis tributaires des Anglais. Enfin j'ai signalé au dernier Salon une branche de la gravure à laquelle les reproductions du Musée des dessins ont donné une énorme impulsion, c'est la gravure *de fac-simile*. Sous ce rapport, les artistes anglais, si adroits en ce genre, sont dépassés par les nôtres' (p. 162). Stephen Bann notes that by the Restoration period the Paris-trained artists formed the leading school of engraving in continental Europe and that their 'main challenge seems to have come [...] from the upstart printmakers of Great Britain'; see his *Parallel Lines: Printmakers, Painters and Photographers in Nineteenth-Century France* (New Haven and London: Yale University Press, 2001).

37. Mantz, 'Les Salles du Louvre', p. 147.

38. See Rousseau, *La Vie et l'œuvre de Philippe-Auguste Jeanron*, pp. 206–08.

39. Ibid., p. 206.

40. See Chennevières, *Souvenirs d'un Directeur des Beaux-Arts*, IV, 68–69. Chennevières was not best pleased when his report appeared in *Le Moniteur* of 10 April 1848 under Jeanron's name. See Rousseau, p. 207. One of the consequences of the report was the creation of the four posts of inspector of provincial museums whose salary, wrongly quoted, was one of the subjects of complaint in the petition published in *L'Artiste* of 1 June 1848 (see above, p. 16).

41. Chennevières, 'Musée de Cherbourg', 26 December 1847, pp. 115–18; 'Le Musée d'Amiens', 15 December 1849, pp. 55–57; Arsène Houssaye, 'Les Musées de province', 16 April 1848, pp. 89–90, and Paul Mantz, 'Le Musée de Toulouse', 15 August 1848, pp. 225–29.

42. *Voyage en Espagne*, ed. by Berthier, p. 38. The editor refers to Gilberte Guillaumie-Reicher's thesis, *Théophile Gautier et l'Espagne* (Paris: Hachette, 1935), in support of his statement that Gautier's description of the Bordeaux collection was 'très inexacte' (p. 553).

CHAPTER 6

Breaking Ranks at the
Salon of 1850–1851

The Salon of 1850–51 was a significant moment in French art of the nineteenth century. This is not simply the wisdom of hindsight. Commentators at the time had a firm sense of it, even if on ideological grounds they disagreed about the reasons and implications. The arrival at the century's halfway point encouraged commentators to look back over developments in French art since 1789 and, in the light of them, to view with renewed hope or anxiety the first Salon of the second half of the century. Nearly three years after the overthrow of the monarchy, certain things seemed already clear. The Second Republic had as yet achieved nothing like the symbiosis between art and politics that David's neoclassicism appeared to have offered under the First. The hopes invested in a golden age of republican art had been forced to face some harsh political and economic realities and no radical reform of state patronage of the arts was visible on even a distant horizon. Museology apart, the one area in which genuine change had been achieved was the Salon. The government's decision to hand over responsibility for the election of the Salon jury to the artists themselves had given the event the republican credentials of an extended franchise. It was taken for granted that this democratic control would change the nature of the institution, though whether for the better or the worse remained to be seen.

The implications of the changed environment in which the Salon now operated were potentially far-reaching. A more democratic, less sectarian jury was likely to admit the work of a larger number and wider range of artists than its predecessors under the July Monarchy had done. This would in turn impact on the balance between the different categories of subject on show and their relationship to what were thought of as conservative or progressive trends in contemporary art. It was quickly common ground that the essential painters in the Salon of 1850–51 were Muller, Courbet, and Corot (though not necessarily in that order) and that their work offered, in the categories with which they were associated (history painting, realism, and landscape respectively), approaches whose effect was to define that year's Salon as modern, or democratic or republican, even socialist (these terms were broadly interchangeable for many commentators). But the admission of a larger number and wider range of artists went further than the issue of the nature of the work on show. In 1833, Louis-Philippe had, albeit unwittingly, inaugurated the process of democratization of the Salon when he had accepted the artists' request that it become an annual event. By the end of the Orleanist regime, annualization was taken for granted as a 'droit acquis'. In 1848 the Republican government's decision to extend this process by ending the Institute's control of the jury had reinforced the idea that admission to the Salon was an artist's democratic right (albeit one requiring assurance of minimum standards of competence, for it was widely agreed that no one stood to gain by a repetition of the open Salon of 1848), not a privilege reserved for an elite. It was also a professional and economic necessity, for the contact with the public which it provided was the condition of the artist's livelihood. This combination of professional entitlement and economic necessity made the concept of periodicity, even annual, less tenable, notably among those who had campaigned most vigorously on behalf of an end to the Institute's control of the jury process. There thus emerged proposals for a dual system involving a permanent exhibition and a quinquennial Salon, presenting the most important work shown in the permanent exhibition during the preceding five years, with an elected jury making the selection.[1] As an indication of this connection between the artists' new control of the jury process and the periodicity of the Salon, we have only to remember that for the Salon of 1852, the first following Louis-Napoleon's coup d'état of December 1851, the right of artists to elect the jury was effectively abolished (with half the jury, including the Chair, nominated by the Minister) and that from 1853 and for over a decade, the Salon became biennial.[2]

The Salon of 1850–51 opened its doors on 30 December 1850, the first Salon to be held in the winter months since that of 1827–28. The break with the tradition of the spring exhibition established by the July Monarchy was inevitable once the authorities, having consulted the Commission des Beaux-Arts, had agreed that the Tuileries Palace had proved in 1849 to be an unsuitable venue.[3] In 1848 the Finance Minister had created a commission to make recommendations on the uses that might be made of the royal palaces which under the July Monarchy had been dependencies of the Civil List but which had been annexed by the Republic. The commission had expressed the view that the Palais National (Palais-Royal) might be allocated to the fine arts and, in particular, to the annual Salon, albeit on a provisional basis, since, in accordance with the law of 4 October 1849, studies were under way to determine whether the second floor of the Louvre might be renovated and refurbished with a view to providing a permanent home for the annual exhibition. On 17 January 1850 *Le Moniteur universel* published the *projet de loi* relating to the Salon that year and in which it was announced that a request for the funds needed to hold it in the Palais National had been submitted to the Commission du Budget. The Commission had responded favourably in mid-April but it was only on 9 October that the Assemblée Nationale approved the decree setting out the arrangements. The change of location was generally well received but the same could not be said about the change of dates.[4]

Gautier's travels in Italy during the summer and autumn of 1850 took him away from the discussions taking place in Paris on the future of the Salon. Instead he reimmersed himself in the art of the Italian masters, which would figure prominently in his travel writing published in *La Presse* that autumn. On his return he quickly resumed the studio visits which always occupied the weeks leading up to the opening of the Salon.[5] In the final week of January 1851, three weeks after the opening, he began writing his review, the first article of which would appear on 5 February.[6] There would be twenty-three in all, by some distance the longest Salon review he wrote for *La Presse* and almost twice that of 1849.[7] For three months he averaged two 3000-word articles a week, a tall order even for someone of his facility. Because of, or despite, the length of his review, he sought to retain the traditional sequence of generic categories. The opening article, entitled 'Réflexions préliminaires', was followed by six on history painting and one on realism. These eight articles were followed by three in which the generic thread was all but broken by the diversity of work on show.[8] At the end of the eleventh article, the review's halfway point, Gautier appeared to realize that the reader's attention might be broken too if he did not return to the familiar sequence of categories.[9] There followed two articles on portraits, three on genre painting (the third running over into article 17 to mop up works he had omitted to mention, with the space intended in this article for the *animaliers* and still life reduced as a result), two on landscape (the first on the naturalists, the second on the *paysagistes de style*, until this latest categorization gave way halfway through the second article to the more random selection of memory), and three on sculpture. The twenty-third and final article presented the official ceremony for the prizewinners, along with Gautier's acerbic comments on those who in his view had been unjustly overlooked. Each new category was introduced by his reflections on its place in the history of the fine arts, its key figures among the artists of the past and its interest for a modern public. Thus we learn, for example, that, with the exception of Toussenel, no philosopher or naturalist had come close to the painter's knowledge of animals,[10] that still life's humble subjects had tempted the greatest artists, and that landscape was for societies grown old, when the weariness of civilization encouraged the search for refuge in the bosom of nature. These cultural commonplaces could be assimilated easily by a diverse readership such as that of *La Presse* and helped to shore up generic distinctions which still had their uses for the *salonnier* but which were under increasing pressure from the growing number of artists prepared to mix and match subjects and techniques in response to changing public taste.

Like many commentators, Gautier began his preliminary reflections with approval of the change in the Salon's location. He shared the general view that the temporary galleries erected for the purpose in the courtyard of the Palais-Royal were a great improvement on the Tuileries Palace. The architect had ensured that natural light arrived in the galleries in the same way as in the artist's studio, and the walls had been painted in neutral tones which enhanced rather than detracted from the work on show.[11] Nevertheless, Gautier continued to maintain that the Louvre was the Salon's natural location and that the plan to convert the museum's second floor into a permanent home for the event should be implemented without delay. As for the Salon itself, his initial reaction, again like that of many commentators, was that it was an improvement on those of the previous two years. Surveying the century's enormous achievements to date in so many fields, he expressed satisfaction that art had not been left behind in the great leap forward. The content was similar to that of his opening article in 1848, and though the tone was more sober than euphoric and less explicitly pro-Republican, he was pleased to confirm that in the Salon that year 'les diverses tendances de l'art s'y lisent visiblement, et ces tendances sont bonnes'.

For his preliminary historical survey of the painting itself, he retained the familiar chronological landmarks and language of political change. The Romantic revolution was 'un 93 pittoresque'. Delacroix, Boulanger, Devéria, Scheffer, leaders of the *coloristes*, were its 'montagnards', with Ingres and the *dessinateurs* its 'Girondins'. According to this account, the two groups had shared, in the early stages of their common struggle against the forces of reaction, an affinity for the art of the sixteenth century and for a more faithful study of nature, with the result that while Ingres was roundly rejected by the Davidians of whose food he had partaken, he was embraced by the Romantics and, among whom, by no one more than Gautier himself. As the Romantic emphasis on colour had become more pronounced, however, Ingres's distaste for the new movement had grown and, with it, the public perception of two opposing groups. Within this reductive schema, each group had its genre painters, landscape artists, sculptors, and occasional traitor who changed sides.[12] Initially the hostility between the rival camps had left no room for a third way, as demonstrated by the case of Delaroche, 'trop classique pour les romantiques et trop romantique pour les classiques', as Gautier put it. With the passage of time, however, and 'l'apaisement des anciennes fureurs, l'école de Delaroche commença à se faire jour'. In a changing atmosphere marked by greater tolerance and eclecticism, the new generation 'hésitant à se déclarer *flamboyants* ou *grisâtres*, admettaient de moyens termes'.[13] The new jury established in 1849 was more tolerant than its reactionary predecessors under the July Monarchy, and the abolitionist Gautier noted no doubt with approval 'ce tumulte de tableaux admis presque sans choix'.

In terms of this deliberately simplified account of modern French art, however, the Salon of 1850–51 showed that the period of two decades during which the two opposing groups had emerged and fought each other to a ceasefire was over. The troops had been disbanded or had broken ranks. There were no more generals at the head of battalions, no more battalions. It was every man for himself, picking up whatever ammunition or regimental colours had been left lying around after the skirmishes:

> Les divisions que nous avons indiquées tout à l'heure n'existent plus. Ingres et Delacroix ont licencié leurs troupes; dessinateurs et coloristes se sont réconciliés, ou plutôt chacun cherche fortune sans se soucier de ce que fait l'autre. L'individualisme domine; [...] le talent se démocratise en ce sens qu'il est le partage d'un grand nombre, au lieu de se limiter comme autrefois dans une dizaine de noms.

History painting 'proprement dite' was finished, the number of paintings representing what had once been understood by that term could be counted on the fingers of one hand, 'et de ce côté la tradition est rompue'. Religious paintings, few in number and short on quality, fared no better. 'Le Salon de 1850–51 n'est ni historique, ni religieux, ni mythologique, ni révolutionnaire, ni classique, ni romantique, il est individuel et panthéiste.' There had never been so many talented artists, helping themselves to the lessons of old and new masters for whatever met their immediate needs. Whether this was the democracy of talent or the anarchy of individualism, whether it was exciting or worrying, depended on your point of view, and Gautier moved between optimism and concern from one article to another. There was no shortage of positives — the usual ones, Gérôme, Chassériau, Lehmann, Meissonier, Corot for the painters, Pradier, Clésinger, Préault for the sculptors — but in the climate of individualism that followed in the wake of disbanded armies and broken ranks, one negative feature particularly troubled him. With Ingres missing once again, Gautier had hoped that 1850–51 would see another great Delacroix Salon, that the painter's new work would define the event that year, as it had done before in the heady days of the Romantic revolution. Gautier appears to have believed that a new generation of artists was crying out for the sort of leadership that Delacroix had provided for the previous one but, if so, he was forced to recognize that they would be disappointed again: 'Cinq ou six petits tableaux rayés de l'ongle du lion sans doute, mais peu importants, ne répondent pas à l'attente que fait naître ce grand nom de Delacroix.' He urged him to reassert his authority in 1852:

> Il serait utile à sa gloire d'arriver au Salon prochain avec quelque tableau comme la *Barque de Dante*, le *Sardanapale*, la *Liberté de Juillet*, le *Pont de Taillebourg*, les *Femmes d'Alger*, l'*Entrée de Croisés à Constantinople*, le *Triomphe de Trajan* dont nous parlions tout à l'heure, quelque large toile où, comme dans ses peintures murales, il pût remuer une composition abondante et tumultueuse, étincelante de couleur, fourmillante de vie, antique de sentiment, romantique d'exécution, et montrer à tous qu'il est encore le maître sans rival, le représentant le plus fidèle de l'art dans la première période de ce siècle, dont il a épousé toutes les passions, toutes les inquiétudes et tous les rêves.

This pictorial programme confirmed the enduring value for Gautier of the Romantic legacy with which Delacroix was so closely identified, but its subtext was the challenge posed in 1850–51 by Courbet. Gautier did not have to say that Delacroix's failure to respond to the challenge of leadership that year had allowed Courbet to fill the vacuum. The order in which he presented the painters in his review said it for him. His commentary on Delacroix appeared only at the beginning of the seventh article, which the painter shared with Robert-Fleury and Louis Boulanger, neither of whom could be considered major figures. Courbet had already featured in the fourth and was the only artist that year to have an entire article to himself in Gautier's review.

Commenting in his first article on the general dispersal of the artistic groupings which had characterized the earlier decades of the nineteenth century, Gautier had drawn attention to the emergence of what he called 'une école réaliste démocratique', and though he had not named Courbet, there was already no doubt at this stage that he was the leader of this new 'school' and the source of the threat that it posed:

> A travers cette diffusion générale, on voit poindre une école réaliste démocratique, pour qui les *Paysans*, de Leleux, sont des aristocrates; cette école, ou plutôt ce système, prêche la représentation exacte de la nature dans toute sa trivialité, sans choix ni arrangement, avec la fidélité difforme du daguerréotype. Nous discuterons plus loin ce programme, qui a des chances de rallier bien des fantaisies errantes et des vocations incertaines, par cela même qu'il est absolu.

C'est quelque chose dans une époque troublée et qui ne cherche qu'une théorie nette et carrée.

As with Delaroche in the 1830s, when it had seemed to Gautier that he had to demolish public support for a form of painting which in his view undermined everything that the Romantic revolution stood for, so again in 1850–51 he evidently believed that Courbet threatened art's vital interests. Now 'démocratique' evoked radical excess rather than republican progress. The idea that Courbet could be contained within the Leleux model of realism was no longer tenable. For Gautier he did not represent a school as much as a system, with all that this term implied in intransigence, in the subjection of temperament to the tyranny of the idea, be it moral, political, or philosophical. In the face of nature Courbet had abdicated his responsibility to select and organize in the interests of art's higher purpose. Instead he had chosen to descend to the mechanical reproduction of nature's lowest common denominators. His method was a panacea for the weak-minded, looking for simple solutions 'dans une époque troublée'. Having invalidated the whole project from the outset, Gautier did not keep his readers waiting long for the more detailed attack on Courbet's art that he had promised. After his opening article of preliminary considerations, he produced six articles on history painting (relegating in the process the articles on sculpture to the end of his review), followed by one on realism. But instead of discussing Courbet in the eighth article along with the more established realists such as Leleux and after the representatives of the traditionally more ambitious genre of 'la grande peinture', he gave Courbet an article to himself in the middle of the series on the history painters, which in itself emphasized the fact that, for Gautier, Courbet's threat lay precisely in his claim that his realist subjects were the new history painting. Worse still as far as Gautier was concerned, the claim appeared to have the support of the *jury de placement*, which had placed *Un Enterrement à Ornans* alongside works whose subjects and dimensions placed them unambiguously in the category of history painting, even if it were a category undergoing a process of change.

Gautier devoted the second and third articles of his review to the work of the newer generation of history painters (Muller, Barrias, and Laemlein in the second, Ziegler, Yvon, Duveau, and Verdier in the third). He opened with Muller's *Appel des dernières victimes de la Terreur* (Figure 6.1), whose political subject and huge size had made it one of the most talked-about paintings that year. The public flocked to it but the critics, with the notable exception of Gautier, slated it.[14] In fact, only when compared to their attacks could Gautier's commentary be considered positive. He applauded the painting's intellectual ambition, exemplified in the portrayal of Chénier, who sits in the foreground lost in poetic inspiration, staring out towards the spectator, his back turned to the functionary calling out the names of that day's victims, and composes the 'Ode de la Jeune Captive' which will ensure the posthumous revenge of genius over the 'stupide couteau'. But like Muller's more hostile critics, Gautier too found the impression of terror diluted by the subject's fragmentation into a series of separate episodic vignettes and by the arrangement of the aristocratic victims in the foreground, whose dress, pose, and expression seemed to him to be more those of an aristocratic drawing-room than a republican prison.[15]

Fig. 6.1. Charles-Louis Muller, *Appel des dernières victimes de la Terreur,*
Paris, Louvre
© The Bridgeman Art Library

He too expressed the fear that Muller 'n'en vienne à donner trop d'importance au sujet, à l'anecdote, lui qui peut mieux que tout autre se passer de ce moyen d'attraction'. Typical of this anecdotal interest was the question most asked of the painting that year: was this an accurate portrayal of Chénier?[16] For Gautier this was less important than determining whether the poet's expression conveyed the serenity of inspiration rising above 'la brutalité du fait' but he recognized where the public's interest lay in the scene and that Muller had played to it.

It was Delécluze who once again expressed most clearly conservative opinion about the work.

> Les *Condamnés* de M. Charles Müller, autant par les qualités brillantes qui s'y trouvent que par les défauts qu'ils renferment, résument complètement l'état de l'art à l'exposition de 1851: la transition du style élevé au style vulgaire, ou en d'autres termes l'abandon de la peinture historique et le triomphe de la peinture de genre.[17]

For Delécluze genre painting was purely market-driven ('l'art ravalé au goût des amateurs qui est particulièrement recherché et cultivé aujourd'hui', p. 229). It was the triumph of trade over emulation, of fame over reputation.[18] The dimensions of Muller's huge canvas were designed to trick the public into thinking that among the new generation of painters history painting, as the tradition of the 'école française' presented it, was still on offer, when the reality was that Muller's anecdotal and illustrative treatment of the historical subject was no more than the thin end of Courbet's wedge:

> Dans l'ouvrage de M. C. Müller l'appareil dramatique fait encore briller une lueur de pensée qui intéresse l'âme; mais il n'en est plus ainsi dans les productions des peintres purement *naturalistes*. Alors il ne s'agit plus comme on l'a cru jusqu'ici, d'élever l'esprit en lui présentant les idées revêtues des formes les plus belles, les plus délicates que la vue puisse saisir. Non; l'intelligence et l'œil du peintre *naturaliste* sont transformés en une espèce de daguerréotype qui, sans volonté, sans goût, sans conscience se laisse pénétrer par l'apparence des objets, quels qu'ils soient, et en rend mécaniquement l'image. L'artiste, l'homme renonce à lui-même; il se fait instrument, il s'aplatit en miroir et son principal mérite est d'être bien uni et d'avoir reçu un bon tain. Ce système de peinture sauvage, ce résultat d'un art avili et dégradé, ont été présentés, développés avec une témérité presque cynique par un homme doué d'ailleurs heureusement par la nature, M. Courbet. (pp. 230–31, Delécluze's italics)

Delécluze used the same analogy of the daguerreotype that Gautier had used in his preliminary remarks, but the resemblance between the two critics ended there.[19] Delécluze would not negotiate with an artist who displayed such a cynical disregard for painting's accepted procedures. Gautier's commentary, on the other hand, showed at every turn that negotiation, however unpleasant, could not be avoided with a painter of Courbet's force. In his preliminary remarks he had spoken of him as the leader of a dissident realist faction and in his article he attempted to define this dissidence, to neutralize it within broader, more familiar categories and, where necessary, to explain to Courbet and his own readers what the painter had to do to correct the error of his ways. By 1851 Gautier could cope with the idea that genre subjects could be painted in the dimensions of history painting.

Courbet was hardly an innovator in that respect, and the initiative, 'déjà tentée par MM. Lessore et Duveau, l'un dans sa *Pauvre famille* [the painting was in fact by Antigna],[20] l'autre dans son *Noyé breton*', had 'un côté humain qui séduit'. After all, if certain subjects were timeless, it stood to reason that the modern genre scene could aspire legitimately to the values of history painting.[21] If the pain of widowhood was universal, why should Andromaque be allowed to weep for Hector in a painting of vast dimensions, but a modern widow be expected to confine her grief to a few centimetres? Besides, from a purely tactical point of view, Courbet had demonstrated in 1849 how effective it could be to adopt the scale of history painting for genre subjects. As Gautier put it, who would have noticed *Une après-dînée à Ornans* had it been painted in the normal dimensions of genre?[22] It was hardly surprising, therefore, if in 1850–51 the painter had taken the same liberties a stage further.[23] But for Gautier the freedom to take liberties of this kind brought responsibilities, and he had no doubt that, in the *Enterrement* at least, Courbet had refused to recognize his. The key responsibility was to 'rester dans la généralité', and Courbet had clearly gone out of his way to do the opposite.

For Gautier the *Enterrement*, far from generalizing, emphasized the particular, the local. It was a collection of separate portraits knowable only to those of their immediate community. The burial's location in a provincial backwater negated the aspiration to universality. Gautier even advised Courbet to drop the *à Ornans* from the title (and, as if to underline the point, Delécluze, who had obviously never heard of the place, repeatedly misspelled it as Ornus).[24] The painting showed 'non pas les amis, le prêtre, les parents, les enfants, la veuve, mais bien M. un tel, Mme une telle, que tous les Francs-Comtois du département peuvent reconnaître'. Such an exaggerated emphasis on the individual at the expense of the general only served to tip the work into farce:

> Une pauvre femme, pleurant son enfant mort, peut être traitée en peinture avec la même importance que Niobé, parce qu'elle symbolise un fait humain, qu'elle est la représentation collective des douleurs maternelles; si vous peignez sous des proportions épiques Mme Baboulard, déplorant la perte de Dodolphe, son petit dernier, vous exaltez l'individualisme outre mesure, et lui faites prendre une valeur ridicule.

The only explanation Gautier could find was the political one, and he took it for granted.[25] Courbet was attempting to take the Salon Carré for his own kind ('faire entrer dans le salon carré ses personnages de la vie réelle en compagnie des prophètes, des dieux et des héros'). It is perhaps a measure of his unease at what he saw as Courbet's audacity that Gautier was prepared to resort, in a barely subliminal way, to anxieties about the *partageux* invading French art's sacred sites. Memories of the invasion of the Tuileries Palace in 1848 and the destruction of art works in the king's collection contained there were still fresh.

Faced with a work as challenging as *Un Enterrement à Ornans*, Gautier turned to art history's bigger picture and, as usual for his readers in *La Presse*, he kept it simple. The history of art was that of the idealists versus the realists, the Greeks and the masters of the Italian Renaissance versus the Flemish and Spanish, the transformation of nature versus its representation. Courbet belonged with the second group in the sense that, like them, he was 'plus soucieux de la vérité que de la beauté', but he did not belong with them in the sense that he painted according to an ideal of nature but one in which nature was transformed in the opposite direction to that of the idealists. Courbet was, in short, a mannerist, the François Boucher of the ugly:

> Boucher est un maniériste en joli, M. Courbet est un maniériste en laid; mais tous deux sont des maniéristes, chacun *flatte* la nature à sa façon; l'un lui prête des grâces, l'autre des disgrâces qu'elle n'a pas [...] Tous deux dépassent le but, car la manière est une sorte d'idéal manqué: qu'on reste en deça ou en delà, il n'importe.[26]

Courbet's mannerism was to Boucher's as his realism was to Leleux's. In both we were dealing, said Gautier, with a dissident version of a familiar category. Furthermore, Courbet's dissidence was obviously an affectation, for, as his self-portrait in *L'Homme à la pipe* showed, he could paint very well when it suited him. For that work, 'M. Courbet s'est départi de son système; il s'est idéalisé, embelli et traité d'un pinceau très fin et très adroit, selon les procédés ordinaires'. It only underlined the extent to which in the *Enterrement* he had, as far as Gautier was concerned, deliberately misused his talent.

We can only wonder whether Gautier's readers in *La Presse* were convinced by this explanation, but there is reason to believe that he himself was not. It did not begin to explain what he called 'l'absence résolue de toute composition' and left far too many questions unresolved: the arrangement of the figures in a single line, men to one side, women the other, flattened on the picture surface by the horizontality, the lack of perspective and modelling; the absence of all the usual signs of a cemetery (headstone, cross, immemorial yew-tree), and in their place merely a hole hewn out of the ground, of which only one edge was visible and on which was perched a single tiny skull thrown up by the digging in what could only be a tasteless note of the macabre; the beadles, who looked like crown court judges in their bright-red robes and ribbed caps and whose faces, as rudimentary as shop signs and apparently stained with the marks of a life's devotion to the local wine, ruined the dignified bearing of the priest and women and were so grotesque in their 'étrangeté caraïbe du dessin et de la couleur' that they could have come from a Daumier caricature.[27] In a work in which Gautier had expected to see the artist's reflection on 'ce fatal pèlerinage que nul n'évite', the most successful feature was the white dog, 'peint de main de maître'. Wherever he looked, to whichever area of pictural practice he turned his attention, he found excellence ruined by wilful nonsense. The only analogies he could find for such shocking discordances were Monnier's *Scènes populaires* and, inevitably, the gravedigger scene in *Hamlet*, with which it was possible to imagine the thematic links of cliché ('à la mélancolique pensée de la mort l'insouciante grossièreté de la vie'); but however many of these reassuring categorizations Gautier tried on, none of them fitted the *Enterrement* anything like closely enough. His support, albeit conditional, in 1849 for the painter of *Une après-dînée à Ornans* was impossible in the case of *Un Enterrement à Ornans*.[28]

Faced with these difficulties, Gautier took heart from the fact that at least the *Casseurs de pierres* was comprehensible. Everyone could see it was a painting of hard work poorly paid but at least it was not a socialist tract.[29] The men were too busy for that sort of thing. Turned away from the spectator they let their torn, threadbare clothes make their silent protest against rural poverty. They were, as he put it, 'comme des nègres, ou, ce qui est bien pis, comme des blancs', implying with some unease that in the countryside of the Republic, they were the reality of the slavery that it prided itself on having abolished in the colonies. At this point Gautier turned to less sombre subjects. The young man's body had the grace and strong articulations which not even poverty destroyed, his clothes were masterful in tone and texture. The old man, however, was less amenable to this hidden beauty of the poor. His clogs were the main problem, for in Gautier's view they were insufficiently differentiated from the ground. Sharing its solidity, they summed up his unease that everything in the painting was 'également solide'. He also found the overall dark-green tone, the 'localité verdâtre générale', disagreeable but at least that could be easily remedied by discreet glazing. He thought that the *Autoportrait* was the best painting of those submitted by Courbet that year but that the *Paysans de Flagey* was unspeakable, literally, triggering a volley of clauses introduced by the 'que dire de?' of the critic lost for words at such a provocative disregard for the methods of the Flemish masters who had secured noble status for these menial subjects.

Fearing perhaps that his readers might be put off by an attack whose severity was unusual by his standards, Gautier sought to reassure them. Courbet, he said, was made of stern stuff and could cope with a few harsh truths. Fearing perhaps that they might be concerned that he was trying to resist the forward march of progress in art, he launched into a vintage piece on the theme of 'le laid ne nous fait pas peur', a 250-word defence of his record for defending the strongest forms of realism. Murillo's beggars, Velasquez's drunks, Ribera's scoundrels, Delacroix, Préault, 'tous les violents, tous les féroces, tous les barbares', Gautier had defended them all. Adopting his friend of the people pose, he asked how any painter with republican or socialist sympathies could portray them in such unflattering terms when he himself had seen among workers and peasants 'de très beaux types, de tournures carrées et pleines de style, des torses bien assis', and so on. He ended with a short paragraph which proposed yet another category for the wayward artist to consider:

> Nous concevrions plutôt qu'un peintre socialiste fît sur le peuple de France le travail que Léopold Robert a fait sur les types rustiques d'Italie, dont il a idealisé la beauté par son style élégant et pur. Il y aurait, dans nos provinces du Nord et du Midi, de quoi faire des *Moissonneurs*, des *Vendangeurs* et des *Pêcheurs* égaux à ceux de ce peintre *populaire* dans la vraie acception du mot. (Gautier's emphasis)

With our hindsight we may well imagine what Courbet thought of this invitation to become the Léopold Robert of the French provinces and produce idealized types of the rural poor, but what does it indicate about Gautier's response to Courbet's work in 1851? A sign of desperation perhaps on the part of a critic who cannot or does not wish to work out what is going on in Courbet's realism? Or a serious piece of advice, evidence of a residual optimism that no cause was ever completely lost, that it was still early days in the painter's career, that there was always next year, by which time Courbet might have matured, come to his senses, and reflected on the errors of his ways? Though, in this case, all the resources of Gautier's experienced and flexible interpretation of contemporary French painting appeared to have failed him, his condemnation was rarely final, rarely so harsh that the artist on the receiving end could not be retrieved.[30]

Gautier returned indirectly to Courbet's work the following month in his eighth article, in which he discussed the realists. One after another their work served as a *repoussoir* for the unintelligibility of Courbet's painting. In Antigna's *Incendie* (Figure 6.2), the poor are 'populaires sans être bas', for Antigna paints 'la misère et non l'abjection, la trivialité et non la laideur, le peuple et non la canaille'. In his *Enfants dans les blés*, the children of the rural poor are transformed by the sunlight of July, the great leveller, and nature's answer to social inequality: 'le beau temps du pauvre, le mois indulgent et doux, où la misère ne se sent pas, où l'enfant qui n'a rien peut se couronner comme un fils de roi, avec les bleuets et les coquelicots'. By implication, the subject was another opportunity that Courbet had declined. Compared to Riesener's shepherd in *Un berger et une bergère*, Courbet's *Casseurs de pierre* and *Paysans qui reviennent de la foire* 'sont de petits-maîtres poupins, mignons et jolis' but, however realistic the shepherd's hideous appearance, clothes, and bestial expression, 'dont on retrouverait plus d'un type dans nos campagnes', Riesener created familiar visual types (the 'Polyphême de village' and 'Caliban de campagne') and set up with the young shepherdess 'le piquant contraste de beauté et de laideur, de rusticité et de délicatesse'. Millet's *Semeur* was Gautier's favourite peasant in the Salon that year: 'Il y a du grandiose et du style dans cette figure au geste violent, à la tournure fièrement délabrée, et qui semble peint avec la terre qu'il ensemence.' In Lacoste's *Premier travail après l'insurrection*, showing carpenters making coffins, the philosophical intention was laudable and the lesson clear ('des discordes civiles il ne résulte que des malheurs'), which was more than could be said for some of the details (what exactly were the old man, young women, and *garde mobile* doing there? was the coffin an order or was it for one of the family? was the episode based on historical fact and had the June Days really led to increased activity for coffin-makers, since Gautier had always assumed that the funeral services always had a plentiful supply of coffins in advance for just such occasions as revolutions and epidemics?)[31] Despite these unresolved issues and the shortcomings in execution ('son dessin est quelquefois lourd, sa couleur terne et grisâtre'), Gautier had to applaud the effort 'pour donner du style et de la noblesse à des figures d'ouvriers qu'il a représentés avec la taille d'Ajax ou d'Agamemnon'.

These worthy realists only underlined how little Courbet went in for saving graces but when Gautier came to the Courbet portraits in his twelfth article, his ambivalence returned. The Fourierist Jean Journet 'était une nature robuste, naïve et carrée qui devait inspirer M. Courbet', he tells us, and, sure enough, Courbet's portrait of Journet had 'le ton local et la franchise de brosse' characteristic of 'le talent rude et mâle du peintre des *Casseurs des pierres* et de l'*Enterrement à Ornans*': the fine portrait, the admirable stonebreakers, and the unfathomable burial reunited in unexpected praise of Courbet's rough, naive, and virile talent.

As for representations of contemporary history, the Salon of 1850–51 confirmed for Gautier what that of 1849 had shown, that Meissonier and Adolphe Leleux were

FIG. 6.2. Alexandre Antigna, *Incendie*, 1850
Orleans, Musée des Beaux-Arts.
© The Bridgeman Art Library

the two great artists of the events of June 1848. As we saw (above, p. 106), Meissonier had withdrawn the earlier version of his *Barricade* from the Salon of 1849 shortly before it opened. In 1850–51 he showed the finished version. Gautier considered it even more sinister than the *ébauche* which had made such an impression on him two years earlier.[32] The heightened precision of the paving-stones made the confusion of tangled bodies even more shocking. Noting that between the earlier and later versions the painter had replaced the solitary boot in the bottom left-hand corner with a cap, he assumed that the head had been removed with it: 'ce n'est plus le pied, c'est la tête que le boulet a prise', its victim no longer maimed but decapitated. He urged that this *Souvenir de guerre civile*, as it was now called, be put permanently on display in the Luxembourg, not because he thought it would serve as a lesson to radical thugs and criminals (which was how many commentators chose to see the painting),[33] but because, art being more important than politics in Gautier's scheme of things, it demonstrated what realism in art, applied to a contemporary political subject, could achieve in the hands of a painter who succeeded in purging compositional elements of all forms of declamation. It showed the unspeakable history of June 1848 — the vanquished rebels reduced to the state of refuse littering the streets — with exemplary, indispensable impartiality:

> C'est une page d'histoire exacte comme un procès-verbal, sans emphase, sans rhétorique, un spécimen de cette vérité vraie que personne ne veut dire, pas plus les peintres que les écrivains; la Morgue de l'émeute prise au daguerréotype, le détritus d'une révolution sur le pavé de la ville, du sang, des haillons et de maigres cadavres vides.

In stating that the work had the authenticity of the daguerreotype, he did not mean that Meissonier had painted a real scene (as the artist had witnessed it, or even taken part in it, on 25 June 1848), for Gautier knew perfectly well that he had reworked the original scene in his studio using models.[34] He meant that Meissonier's composition *d'après le modèle* had produced an enhanced, more authentic and expressive realism, all the more powerful for its neutrality. Of course this 'admirable et navrante peinture' was a warning about the horrors of civil war. That was obvious to everyone. Where Gautier was unusual was in stressing its refusal to take sides, insisting that its 'actualité si saignante' was 'sans malédiction pour les vaincus, sans *hosannah* pour les vainqueurs'.[35]

Impartiality was also what characterized for him Adolphe Leleux's second major painting of the June insurrection, *La Sortie*. Introducing it, Gautier returned briefly to *Le Mot d'ordre*, shown in 1849 (see above, pp. 106–08). At that time he had drawn attention to the impartiality of Leleux's treatment of the three rebels, describing them as 'malheureux et coupables'.[36] In 1851 he saw this impartiality directed instead towards the larger issues that Leleux had not represented but which for Gautier his three rebels had evoked, namely 'les causes de cette triste bataille, où les deux armées parlaient la même langue: malheur, misère et vice'. No longer simply an account of who the three men were and how their pose, dress, and actions were to be understood, his commentary now focused on the conditions and responsibilities common to both sets of combatants. This change of emphasis served as a preliminary to his commentary on *La Sortie*, in which Leleux presented what T. J. Clark described 'as a modern equivalent to David's *Intervention of the Sabine Women*, as a plea for home and family against the strife of factions'.[37] After a short paragraph in which he explained that the cropping of the male figure by the picture frame was designed to show that women had been unable to restrain their men from rushing off to the fight, Gautier developed at much greater length the 'idée touchante' manifested by this formal device and by the 'quelque chose de violent, de troublé, de turbulent' in the painting's compositional elements. Where men on both sides were divided 'par le fanatisme des partis', women on both sides shared the impartiality of suffering and death, even if it was clear for which group of women the consequences were more far-reaching:

> Pour la femme, une émeute, une révolution, c'est un mari, un amant, un fils apporté, informe et sanglant, sur une civière, ou laissé mort sur le pavé de la rue, trois heures de queue aux portes de la Morgue, pour aller reconnaître un cadavre mutilé, et, plus tard, si elle est pauvre et du peuple, le déshonneur pour ses filles, la famine pour ses petits.

For Gautier, therefore, Meissonier and Leleux demonstrated that the artist painting a modern political subject had to allow the pictorial means to create the event if the work was to function as art at all, that to select and compose formal elements in such a way as to subordinate them to a political idea was to render the work inarticulate. Visual form had an intrinsic impartiality — 'Le peintre a en outre [...] cet avantage [...] qu'il peut avoir une impartialité impossible à l'écrivain' — which, if fully employed, not only gave the idea its true dimension and impact but also might direct the spectator away from less impartial verbalized responses generated by the painting's subject. Whether Gautier really believed this idea that the visual form had an inherently greater potential for impartiality than the verbal is not the point. More important is that he felt the need to say it in 1850–51 in response to these two paintings. Evidently three years had given time for reflection in some quarters on the reasons for which impartiality had been so thin on the ground in June 1848.[38] By 1851, in the context of new polarizations created by the ascendancy of the Catholic reaction — on 15 March 1850 the *loi Falloux* had been adopted — and uncertainty about Louis Napoleon's longer-term political agenda, sober warnings no doubt seemed again to be the order of the day. Gautier's response to the work of Meissonier and Leleux in April 1851 belongs in that context, and we can be fairly sure that he was not only concerned about the radicals (and the future for their women). His distaste for the church militant had never left him. As we have seen, he had had a sharp reminder of its intransigence only the previous month, when Chenavard's Panthéon project and his own account of it had been the object of vitriolic attacks in *L'Ami de la religion*.

After taking his readers through these disturbing works and their sober warnings, Gautier changed the mood. He decided that it was time to cheer everyone up with a painting no one could fail to enjoy. 'Pour nous débarrasser de ces funestes images', as he put it in article 15, Bonvin's work was ideal. It was 'un Chardin logé chez un Granet', in which familiar and much-admired eighteenth- and early-nineteenth-century models, assimilated in an appropriate manner, were emulated with due respect. Bonvin's *Intérieur d'école de petites orphelines* (Figure 6.3) gave a more

Fig. 6.3. François Bonvin, *Intérieur d'école de petites orphelines*, 1850
Langres, Musée des Beaux-Arts
© The Bridgeman Art Library

reassuring image of Catholicism and a calm, graceful view of childhood which left the spectator 'pénétré d'un sentiment de tranquilité, de douceur et d'onction'. His still lifes of kettle and candlestick prompted Gautier into sentimental evocations of cosy winter evenings and reading by the light of a flame. He followed Bonvin with Penguilly L'Haridon for what Gautier called his realism 'presque fantastique', with its echoes of Dürer and the German primitives.

That left only landscape, enjoying in the mid-nineteenth century its golden age. 'Jamais le paysage n'a été traité d'une façon si supérieure qu'aujourd'hui.'[39] The reasons were for Gautier obvious. At a time of declining faith and advancing, overcrowded urban civilization, landscape was solitude, refuge, and religious observance. He began by repeating his now familiar history lesson: from the mid-1830s Cabat had led a new generation out of the neoclassical wilderness into the *paysage naturel* whose key practitioners at the midpoint of the century were Théodore Rousseau and Corot.[40] The jury's persecution of Rousseau during the July Monarchy had forced his talent to flower in isolation, with the strengths (originality, determination) and weaknesses (lack of exposure to critical comparison of peers) that this implied.[41] Like other critics, Gautier had reservations about the artist's *Paysage*, but where others criticized its disorderly composition and lack of finish, Gautier found the arrangement of the trees unusually theatrical by Rousseau's standards ('défaut rare chez l'artiste'). The *Lisière de forêt: effet du matin* (Figure 6.4) had the 'manière rembrunie, robuste et sauvage [...] habituelle au peintre' and the smaller *Effet de printemps*, though 'peu conforme aux descriptions des poètes qui copient sur les classiques les printemps de Grèce et d'Italie', was 'très ressemblant à l'atroce saison qui porte ce nom chez nous, et que personne avant M. Théodore Rousseau n'avait eu le courage de représenter sous ses véritables couleurs': an authentic, original naturalism *à la parisienne*. Rousseau's execution was, admittedly, unorthodox ('tantôt molle, tantôt violente, négligée comme une esquisse ou brutalement surchargée') but the energy and truth of his representation of nature swept all before it.

Corot's landscapes were the antithesis of Rousseau's grandiose, brutal, and impenetrable vegetation. Where Rousseau was dramatic, Corot was lyrical. What they had in common was authenticity. Corot's *Une matinée, danse des nymphes* (Figure 6.5) was both natural and antique. It reconciled landscape's ancient and modern virtues, breathing new life into a form of idealized landcape widely thought to be defunct.[42] For Gautier it was a painted idyll of gentle light and tender harmonies, of discreet brushstrokes which allowed the feeling of nature to shine through: 'Personne n'a mis plus d'âme dans le paysage.' Likewise for Clément de Ris, there were in Corot's work none of the historical landscape's pedantic reconstructions, no Greek or Roman erudition and the trees were more Fontainebleau than Arcadia or Sicily, but in its impression and effect it had the universality of the antique.[43] Only Delécluze resisted its spell.[44] The painting was a turning-point in Corot's career, ushering in the series of antique scenes which would mark the later stages of his career. In 1851, on the third anniversary of the revolution of 1848, it chimed with a deeply felt desire to achieve reconciliation between present and past, truth and beauty, progress and tradition. For Gautier, Corot's achievement in assimilating

FIG. 6.4 (above). Théodore Rousseau, *Lisière de forêt: effet du matin*, 1850, London, Wallace Collection. © The Bridgeman Art Library
FIG. 6.5 (below). Jean-Baptiste Camille Corot, *Une Matinée, danse des nymphes*, 1850, Paris, Musée d'Orsay. © Patrice Schmidt, Musée d'Orsay

antique subjects with modern sensibility was underlined by Cabat's belated but welcome recognition that he had failed to achieve it. In 1851 he reappeared in the Salon 'prèsque tout à fait guéri', as Gautier put it, from the disabling effects of his Italian phase, with its failed emulation of Poussin's austere historical landscapes. His return to the inspiration of the landscapes of the Paris region was proof that 'il ne doit pas aller plus loin que la Normandie; les voyages ne vont pas à toutes les natures'. Paul Huet's work illustrated the same danger. Raised on the work of Gainsborough, Constable, and Turner, he too was unsuited to the *paysage de style* and, like Cabat's, his work had benefited, as far as Gautier was concerned, from his return to what he knew best.[45]

After the painting, the sculpture reserved the odd surprise and a number of reassuring continuities. Coming at the end of such a long review, it inevitably appears relegated in relation to the issues with which the painting engaged that year and it may have been in an effort to freshen up the final stages of his commentary that Gautier began the sculpture section with the return to the Salon of the animal sculptor Antoine Barye, after an absence of fourteen years and with a subject out of keeping with his normal production.[46] Unusually for this sculptor whose lions, tigers, panthers, and eagles presented in their long series of massacres 'cette immolation perpétuelle du faible au fort' and the sombre, Shakespearean fatality of their lesson — 'manger ou être mangé, voilà la question' — Barye had submitted a plaster of a human and hybrid figure, *Thésée [et le centaure Biénor]*, which Gautier hailed as the representation of the superiority of human thought over animal brutality:

> Une impassible sérénité, un calme marmoréen règnent sur le front du héros dix fois plus faible physiquement que son ennemi; c'est le courage moral, le sang-froid, l'intelligence domptant la force stupide, la fureur aveugle de la brute; c'est le triomphe de l'esprit sur la matière.[47]

The centaur's defeat represented the end of his reign and, with it, that of 'tout ce qui est bestial et violent', and the emergence of the gods in the image of man, the next stage of the historical process as Gautier had described it in his commentary on Chenavard. 'Du premier coup', Barye 'arrive à l'idéal grec', and in a striking summary of Barye's change of subject, 'on le croyait repu de chair saignante [...] il se nourrissait de Phidias'.

Barye's powerful restatement of the enduring relevance of the antique ideal took precedence for Gautier that year over the work of Préault, who, relieved henceforth of the obligation to submit his work to the jury following his medal at the Salon of 1849, began to exhibit works from different periods of his career in what amounted to a small private exhibition within the Salon.[48] In 1850–51 he showed a bronze bas-relief of *Tuerie*, whose inclusion in the Salon of 1834 had helped to trigger the Institute's intolerance of the new sculpture,[49] the 1843 bas-relief *Ophélie*, refused in 1849, a bust of Poussin, and a version in bronze of his *Christ*, accepted the same year (see above, pp. 100–01). Gautier began his commentary on Préault's submission with a long description of *Tuerie*, which had in his view lost none of its power to 'horripiler les Philistins débonnaires et positifs' and whose 'verve sauvage' and 'emportement féroce' more than compensated for its imperfections. *Ophélie*, of

whom 'on ne saurait imaginer rien de plus noyé', was the antithetical representation
of death to that of the *Tuerie*, suicide chosen rather than slaughter inflicted, and
demonstrated for Gautier Préault's exceptional range. 'Faire de la transparence, du
flou, du vaporeux avec la sculpture, le plus opaque de tous les arts, c'est un vrai
tour de force.' Her pose was that of a dead Christ, which linked her to *Christ*, on
which Gautier repeated his approval of what he had called in 1849 Préault's Spanish
treatment of the subject, adding only that the authenticity of his 'très chrétienne,
très catholique' interpretation had now been enhanced by the presence opposite
of an unspecified academic 'Christ en cuivre jaune, à formes molles et d'aspect
douceâtre, qui n'avait pas l'air de souffrir du tout'.

The religious subject was the occasion for Gautier of the second surprise of the
sculpture section in 1850–51 and on which he began his second article. Clésinger had
abandoned his provocative nudes shown in the Salons of 1848 and 1849 in favour of
a *Pietà* of three figures (Christ, Mary, and Mary Magdalene). Having explained the
origins of the *Pietà* tradition for those readers unfamiliar with it and the relationship
of Clésinger's version to this tradition, he attributed the originality of the work
to the same modern interpretation of Mary that he had found in Lehmann's
painting of the subject shown at the Salon of 1848 and in which human feeling
had taken precedence over divine mission (see above, p. 52): 'La mère l'emporte en
ce moment sur la Vierge'. He attributed minor technical faults to a desire on the
sculptor's part to recreate what he called the rigidity of ancient Catholic sculpture
but was more critical of the fact that the work had not been executed in marble,
for which he censured the authorities who had not supplied it free of charge.[50] Yet
the real interest of the *Pietà* was the change of direction it appeared to represent in
Clésinger's output.

Gautier was convinced that the sculptor had produced a religious work in response
to the scandal created by his earlier Salon exhibits: 'cette fois on ne l'accusera
pas de paganisme et de volupté'. He was sympathetic — 'Nous comprenons ces
incertitudes; dans la vie de l'artiste le mieux trempé, il y a des momens où l'on
donne raison à la première critique venue, fût-elle inepte' — but urged Clésinger
to have the courage of his convictions, to read Plutarch advising Cicero to be true
to his temperament (he helpfully quoted the extract) and to resist the temptation to
censor his own nature:

> Il faut se perfectionner dans le sens de sa nature, et non pas essayer d'en changer,
> et c'est là toujours ce que la critique recommande; vous êtes brun, on vous
> conseille d'être blond; vous avez la gaîté, on vous demande la mélancolie; vous
> dessinez comme Holbein, on vous vantera le coloris de Rubens, et ainsi de
> suite.

Having turned the attacks against their authors by replacing issues of morality with
a series of oppositions based on natural, emotional, and artistic attributes and by
opposing censorship with common sense, he justified his advice to the artist to
return to his female subjects writhing in agony or ecstasy by quoting the familiar
Platonic refrain that the beautiful could not be immoral. The defence of Clésinger
became self-referential in this return to the issue of censorship, as Gautier had
attacked it in his preface to *Mademoiselle de Maupin*:

> Est-ce donc impie de représenter la santé, l'épanouissement, le bonheur, tout
> ce qui peut faire aimer Dieu? La Nature, cette forme visible de la pensée
> éternelle, n'est-elle pas belle et souriante? Tout en préconisant la violence
> superbe du contour, la splendeur des formes, la volupté rayonnante, sommes-
> nous insensibles pour cela aux graces chastes, à l'onction et aux délicatesses de
> l'art religieux?

The defence of Clésinger again suggests Gautier's fears that the forces of moral order
were in 1851 threatening to turn the clock back to the mid-1830s.

Only after his comments on Barye, Préault, and Clésinger did Gautier turn to
Pradier's exhibit that year, *Atalante à sa toilette*. It was a sign that for him too the
Salon of 1850-51 represented more of the same as far as Pradier was concerned.
Certainly the critical debate contained nothing new, turning as before on the
question whether Atalante was an antique or a modern nude. Was she dressing or
undressing, was she modest or indecent? In Ovid's version of the legend, Atalanta
was an athletic huntress who challenged suitors to a race in which the loser was
punished with death, but could Pradier's nude possibly be an athlete with a bosom
that size?[51] Gautier, as always, stressed the classical purity of her feet, arms, and
legs and, for the instruction of his readers, made the connection between her
pose and that of the traditional representations of the crouching Venus, but he too
acknowledged that 'la gorge seule nous a paru un peu forte pour une jeune fille
aussi *entraînée* que devait l'être Atalante' (Gautier's italics). The sense that Gautier
was doing little more than going through the motions on Pradier's submission that
year is compounded by his comical paragraph on the sculptor's bust of Maxime
du Camp. We saw earlier Du Camp's description of Gautier counting his travel
miles in lines of copy (p. 34, n. 55) so he will no doubt have appreciated, if he ever
received, the greetings telegram that Gautier sent him via his commentary on the
bust and which he concluded by expressing the hope: 'Que ces lignes, s'il n'est pas
dévoré ou mis en pièces dans quelque coin de l'Inde ou de l'Afrique [Du Camp
was in Egypt with Flaubert], aillent lui présenter notre salutation amicale'.[52] The
paragraph is 250 words long and appears designed to fill up the remainder of the
article *en égayant la matière* for the pleasure of his readers. What Pradier thought of
this use of his sculpture is not recorded.

The third and final article on the sculpture followed his usual practice of
sweeping up with brief comments the remaining works (of eighteen artists in this
case) of interest to him before signing off with his familiar complaint about the
impossibility of squeezing three thousand items into a little over twenty articles.
Having done so, it only remained for him to write up the awards ceremony, and
here readers who had taken note of his commentary on Courbet may have been
surprised to find the painter's name on the list of those who should, according to
Gautier, have received a medal that year:

> Pourquoi Courbet a-t-il éte passé sous silence? Il a fait événement au Salon;
> il mêle à des défauts, sur lesquels nous l'avons vertement tancé, des qualités
> supérieures et une incontestable originalité; il a remué le public et les artistes; il
> a ses enthousiastes et ses détracteurs. — On aurait dû lui donner une médaille
> de première classe, comme à M. Antigna.

We cannot be sure that these comments are not tongue-in-cheek, but it seems more likely that in the period between mid-February, when he published his article on Courbet, and the first week of May, Gautier had recognized the strength of the opinion that 1850–51 was the Courbet Salon and that he was seeking to find an accommodation with it. Gautier had himself, after all, conceded that technically the painter possessed 'superior qualities', that no one could dispute his originality and that, as he had said many times, even eccentricity was better than blandness. Perhaps he really did think that Courbet, having been on the receiving end of the well-deserved telling off that Gautier had administered, might be persuaded more easily by another medal to return to the fold. Admittedly, to pair him with Antigna seems to be a deliberate provocation on Gautier's part but since, as we have seen, he respected Antigna's work and considered it a more acceptable form of realism, we must assume that he had decided to end his review on the optimistic note that Courbet might yet be reconciled with a less extreme approach to the modern subject. If so, it is difficult to avoid the conclusion that Gautier was clutching at straws.

The Salon of 1850–51 was an essential one in Gautier's trajectory because it was there that he was forced to confront for the first time the serious possibility that his entire *système des beaux-arts* might be displaced by a form of painting of which it could give no account. In the space of three years Courbet had imposed himself on Gautier's attention to such an extent that he made special arrangements within the sequence of his review to rebut the work of an artist whom he had ignored in 1848 and patronized in 1849. The appeal to Delacroix to reassert his authority and retrieve the Salon event for the safe keeping of the previous generation's legacy seems to me to reflect an underlying panic in Gautier that the foot soldiers whose broken ranks he had observed in the Salon of 1850–51 might regroup behind Courbet's leadership and threaten what was for Gautier the ultimate hierarchy of the arts, that which maintained the subordination of what he called 'le fait' to what he called 'l'idée' and without which art ceased.

With the closure of the Salon, Gautier produced only two further articles of art journalism in 1851, both published during the summer period when the Parisian theatres were closed and Gautier needed to plug the gap in earnings resulting from this forced interruption to his weekly theatre review. The first article was a review of Eugène Piot's monthly series of photographs published under the title of *L'Italie monumentale*.[53] The second was devoted to Préault's statue of Marceau, 'l'une des plus jeunes et des plus pures gloires de la République', as Gautier called him, which had been sited temporarily in front of the Louvre's Cour Carrée and facing the Pont des Arts, in advance of its transfer to Chartres, Marceau's birthplace, where local officials had commissioned the work by means of a public subscription.[54] In the first article Gautier rubbished the view that photography would prove 'fatale à l'art, en accoutumant les peintres à ne plus consulter directement la nature' and argued that, far from being merely a useful tool for the artist by making available 'une foule de documents d'une certitude incontestable', photography should be considered an art in its own right:

> Et qu'on n'aille pas s'imaginer, pour humble qu'elle se fasse, qu'il n'y ait pas d'art dans la photographie. Outre le choix du point de vue, du jour, de l'heure, de

l'incidence des ombres et des clairs, qui exigent une grande entente pittoresque,
la photographie sur papier offre parfois des effets inattendus.

Once again he invoked his own travels in Italy to confirm the visual authenticity
of the illustrations and the power of the aesthetic effects derived from the camera's
ability to embrace in a single image what the human eye could grasp only
successively.

After this newest art, Gautier returned to the oldest. As we saw, on 6 March 1848,
in his review of Auber's *La Muette de Portici*, Gautier had urged artists to develop
an original republican iconography for the new historical phase ushered in by the
collapse of the July Monarchy. By then Préault's bronze of Marceau had already
been commissioned for over a year (with Gautier no doubt involved in the choice
of Préault for the work),[55] and Gautier's commentary on it suggests that Préault had
responded successfully to this injunction. Abandoning conventional representations
of apotheosis in which the hero was presented as a Greek nude draped only in the
peplum, Préault presented Marceau in the military uniform of the general of the
Republican army of 1792.[56] In the statue's 'beauté chevaleresque toute nouvelle', in
Marceau's pose and expression, Gautier found 'quelque chose de [...] sereinement
impérieux' that corresponded to his vision of the ideal republic, just as the latest
republican phase was about to be consigned to history. By the time the next Salon
opened in April 1852, the coup d'état of December 1851 had raised some new issues
which his art journalism would need to take into account but in which the challenge
raised by Courbet's form of modernity in 1850–51 would continue to resonate.

Notes to Chapter 6

1. The proposal for a dual system of exhibitions was put by Fernand Boissard in two articles
   entitled 'De la condition des artistes et des moyens de l'améliorer', published in *L'Artiste* of 1
   February and 1 March 1850 (pp. 100–02 and 136–39 respectively). As we saw above (Chapter 2,
   note 13), Boissard here reformulated the idea of the dual exhibition put forward by the sculptor
   David d'Angers in *L'Artiste* of 11 April 1847 but, unlike David d'Angers, Boissard did not support
   abolition of the jury.
2. In 1854 the Salon was cancelled in order to encourage maximum participation in the 1855
   Exposition Universelle on the part of those artists selected to represent France in the fine arts
   section but the effect of the cancellation was to introduce the biennial Salon. That of 1855 was
   replaced by the Exposition Universelle and the next Salon took place in 1857.
3. Reporting the Commission's findings, *Le Moniteur universel* stated on 17 January 1850: 'En
   exécution de la loi du 7 avril 1849 l'exposition s'est faite l'année dernière au palais des Tuileries,
   mais les résultats n'ont pas été complètement heureux; car si les ouvrages de sculpture ont été
   placés dans des conditions assez favorables, ceux de peinture ont eu à souffrir de l'insuffisance
   du local et de la mauvaise disposition du jour.'
4. In *L'Artiste*, Clément de Ris considered it 'déplorable', on the grounds that painting needed the
   light of spring and early summer and that the snow and rain were unlikely to encourage the
   Salon public to venture out (15 November 1850, p. 187).
5. The correspondence contains invitations from Riesener and Lehmann (IV, 264–65) but no doubt
   they are merely the tip of the iceberg.
6. 'Je travaille à mon Salon que je commencerai irrévocablement mardi' (*Corr.*, IV, 288; letter dated
   '23? janvier 1851' by the editor).
7. The previous longest was the first, that of 1837, which contained sixteen articles. Where the
   1849 articles had appeared in the space of three weeks, those of 1850–51 were spread over three

months, the final eight appearing only after the Salon had closed its doors on 15 April. The reason for the large number of articles may well have been the obvious one. In January 1851 Gautier's financial problems, aggravated by his Italian trip, were even worse than usual and 'la littérature alimentaire' was back with a vengeance. 'J'ai un besoin absolu d'argent', he wrote that month to Claude Rouy, the financial manager of *La Presse* (see below, Appendix, pp. 181–82). Now that he was being paid on the basis of articles delivered instead of a fixed monthly salary, the only way out of debt was to increase the number. The twenty-five he published on his Italian travels only paid off the money he had borrowed from the newspaper to pay for the trip, together with the balance still outstanding on earlier advances. Notwithstanding these cries of poverty, Gautier earned 3174 francs (138 × 23) for his Salon of 1850–51, a handsome sum for a Salon review in 1850.

8. Early in the tenth article he notes: 'Dans une revue composée d'éléments si divers, il faut se décider à passer sans transition aux objets les plus disparates.'

9. 'Mais cette liste ne se fermerait jamais, et il est temps, cependant, d'arriver aux tableaux de genre et aux paysages si nombreux, si variés et si pleins de mérite qui attendent depuis onze feuilletons d'être appréciés à leur tour, sans compter la sculpture, qui nous fait ses yeux blancs et nous menace de son geste de marbre, se croyant à tort négligée.'

10. On Alphonse Toussenel, whose *L'Esprit des bêtes* had been published in 1847, see Ceri Crossley, *Consumable Metaphors: Attitudes towards Animals and Vegetarianism in Nineteenth-Century France* (Oxford and Berne: Peter Lang, 2005), pp. 133–60.

11. In a letter to Gautier at the end of December 1850, Riesener drew a diagram of the layout of the galleries and commented: 'Je sors du palais royal et réellement on ne saurait trop en louer l'architecte qui a bien voulu que notre exposition fut favorable aux tableaux et qui a tout fait dans ce but' (*Corr.*, IV, 276–77).

12. By way of examples, among the landscape artists, Gautier placed Cabat and Théodore Rousseau with the *coloristes*, Corot and Aligny with the *dessinateurs*; among the sculptors he placed David d'Angers and Préault with the *coloristes* and Pradier and Simart with the *dessinateurs*. As an example of the turncoat there was Scheffer, who, with his *Eberhard, comte de Wurtemberg* (known as *Le Larmoyer*), shown at the Salon of 1834, was accused of having deserted the *coloristes*. See '*Le Larmoyeur*' *d'Ary Schefer* (Paris: Éditions Paris-Musées, 1989), pp. 42–43, and Leo Ewals, 'La Carrière d'Ary Scheffer: ses envois aux Salons parisiens', in *Ary Scheffer 1795–1858: dessins, aquarelles, esquisses à l'huile* (Paris: Institut néerlandais, 1980), pp. 7–31 (p. 19).

13. Gautier firmly believed that his attacks on Delaroche in his Salons of 1833, 1834, and 1836 (he did not review the Salon of 1835) had contributed to the painter's decision to withdraw from the Salon from 1837. As we see, by 1848 Gautier had mellowed and was slowly but surely changing his tone in relation to the painter.

14. Thanking Gautier for his 'appréciation grave et amicale', which had calmed 'les mille blessures que m'a si largement distribuées la majorité des journaux', Muller asked: 'Qu'ai-je donc fait à tous ces gens, bon Dieu! pour exciter à ce point leurs violences hargneuses!' (*Corr.*, IV, 299–300).

15. 'On oublie presque que l'on a devant soi une prison. On croirait plutôt voir un salon dans lequel viendrait éclater une nouvelle fâcheuse.' Clément de Ris thought that 'ses personnages sont si régulièrement placés, qu'on les croirait disposés pour une fin d'acte. On s'attend presque à voir le rideau tomber devant ces acteurs' ('Le Salon de 1851, II', *L'Artiste*, 15 January 1851, pp. 241–44 (pp. 241–42)).

16. 'La figure d'André Chénier est habilement composée: ressemble-t-elle? Les uns disent oui, les autres non. Les quelques vieillards qui peuvent avoir vu le poète sont d'avis différens.'

17. E. J. Delécluze, *Exposition des artistes vivants, 1850* (Paris: Comon, 1851), p. 230.

18. As Gustave Planche put it the following year: 'la plupart des artistes ne voient, dans les expositions annuelles, qu'une occasion de placer les produits de leur industrie: l'activité mercantile a remplacé l'émulation [...] les expositions annuelles suppriment la renommée et ne laissent debout que la soif du gain' ('Salon de 1852', *Études sur l'école française*, 2 vols (Paris: Michel Lévy, 1855), II, 287–88).

19. On responses to Courbet's work on show in the Salon of 1850–51 see Clark, *Image of the People*, pp. 130–54; on Gautier's response see Moulinat, 'Théophile Gautier et Gustave Courbet'.

20. See Girard, *Théophile Gautier, Critique d'art*, p. 141, note 7.
21. Gautier considered the *Exilés de Tibère* by Barrias the best history painting on show in 1850–51. Noting the similarities in theme and details between it and Muller's *Appel des dernières victimes*, he regretted that the public was more interested in the latter and stated: 'Ce qu'il y a de toujours actuel, de toujours humain, c'est la souffrance, c'est l'exil, c'est l'adieu suprême, ce sont les yeux humides, les mains qui s'étreignent, les sanglots soulevant la poitrine [...] et, à ce titre, la barque de M. Barrias nous impressionne comme la charrette de M. Muller.'
22. 'Traités dans un petit cadre, sa *Soirée à Ornans* n'eût pas été remarquée et se fût confondue avec la méritante école des Leleux parmi les Hedouin, les Chaplin, les Luminais, les Fortin et autres réalistes.' Gautier does not blame Courbet for not wishing to see his artistic personality lost within the 'worthy realist school' but he must therefore find another form of categorization for him.
23. As he put it: 'Un *Enterrement à Ornans* occupe tout un pan du grand salon, donnant ainsi à un deuil obscur le développement d'une scène historique ayant marqué dans les annales de l'humanité.'
24. To be fair, so had the catalogue. For other examples of Ornus see Clark, *Image of the People*, p. 140.
25. On the socialist reading of Courbet, see Clark, ibid., p. 134.
26. We remember his quite different defence of mannerism in his Salon of 1848, when he defended Gérôme against this charge (see above, p. 47).
27. 'Le *Charivari* ne donne pas à ses abonnés de plus bizarres pochades'.
28. As Moulinat succinctly put it, 'Gautier, au sortir du Salon de 1850–51, se sentit très certainement incertain', in 'Théophile Gautier et Gustave Courbet', p. [12].
29. It was, he implied, taken from Francis Wey's rural novel *Biez de Serine*, which Gautier describes as 'la plus fine étude de paysans que nous ayons vue depuis Balzac', serialized in *Le National* from January 1850. In fact Courbet's stonebreakers, painted in November 1849, are the main characters of Wey's novel, but whether Gautier's implied reversal of authorship would have helped to make Courbet's stonebreakers seem less threatening is uncertain. On the one hand, Wey's novel had a happy ending, on the other, the same could hardly be said of Courbet's painting.
30. Clément de Ris, who, as we have seen on a number of occasions, was associated with progressive opinion in the fine arts, delivered a definitive rejection of Courbet that puts Gautier's hesitations in a clearer light. Alleging respect for his readers, he refused to grant Courbet's painting the credibility of a serious commentary. Coming to it only in the fifth of his seven articles, he stated: 'Quelques personnes ont bien voulu nous demander notre avis et nous reprocher notre silence, à propos des autres tableaux de M. Courbet [other than the *Autoportrait*], et surtout de son *Enterrement à Ornans*; notre réponse a été bien simple: nous ne regardons pas ce tableau comme une œuvre sérieuse. [...] Nous pourrions, à tout prendre, y voir une réclame, une manière adroite d'attirer l'attention sur son nom; mais discuter de semblables choses, indiquer pourquoi elles sont mauvaises, et pourquoi elles sortent du domaine de l'art et de la critique, ce serait revenir à des notions tellement élémentaires, que nos lecteurs pourraient aussi penser que nous abusons de leur bonne foi et que nous nous moquons d'eux' ('Le Salon de 1851, V', *L'Artiste*, 1 March 1851, pp. 34–35).
31. The catalogue commentary made explicit the moral and political lesson — 'Inhumer les victimes après l'insurrection, tel est le premier devoir. Pauvres et riches, citoyens et soldats, tous confondus dans la mêlée, le sont bientôt après sur le pavé sanglant où ils ont reçu la mort. Triste et terrible drame, résultat de ces combats de frères, que la raison publique, l'honneur national et la religion doivent bannir à jamais de nos cœurs' — but hardly answered Gautier's questions. In *Ernest Meissonier: rétrospective*, Hungerford notes that Lacoste's painting 'se rapproche un peu de celui [*Souvenir de guerre civile*] de Meissonier' (p. 164). Not more than just 'un peu'? It was commissioned by the government and could have been designed to neutralize the political implications of Meissonier's *Souvenir*, also shown in 1850–51 but presented all too clearly by Gautier's commentary eighteen months earlier.
32. 'Le tableau a conservé les qualités de l'ébauche, et peut-être par le fini impitoyable, le rendu minutieux de l'horreur est-il devenu encore plus sinistre. L'on a froid dans les os en regardant cette toile pâle et morte, où la tuerie s'exprime par de petits tons gris et fins comme une chair dont le sang a coulé, où la bouche livide des blessures bâille en touches imperceptibles' ('Salon de 1850–51 (14e article)' *La Presse*, 10 April 1851).

33. To give but one example, Clément de Ris began his commentary on the painting with a description of its street as 'un de ces sales égouts de Paris dont les honteuses maisons suent la débauche et le crime' ('Le Salon de 1851, III', *L'Artiste*, 1 February 1851, pp. 3–9 (p. 5)).

34. As Gotlieb points out in *The Plight of Emulation*, much positive nineteenth-century commentary on the work was based on the view that Meissonier's naturalism derived in this case from the fact that he had actually witnessed this scene. Not having invented it, he had avoided the inauthenticity that resulted in his genre painting from his devotion to the model (p. 232, n. 64). Gautier was one of the very few critics in the nineteenth century to recognize that the naturalistic effects in *Souvenir* were directly and intimately linked to the painter's use of the model. Some of Meissonier's preparatory drawings of the insurgents are reproduced in *Ernest Meissonier: rétrospective*, pp. 181–83.

35. Clark stated that Meissonier's intention was clear: 'to paint a picture of civil war as a sober warning to the rebels of the future'. 'Sober' is right, but if, as Hungerford suggests, 'cette leçon ne s'adressait pas simplement aux rebelles éventuels' (*Ernest Meissonier: rétrospective*, p. 165), Gautier was likely to have been aware of this.

36. 'Et maintenant quel est l'effet moral qui résulte du tableau? Est-ce la pitié ou l'horreur? Est-ce un jugement ou une protestation qu'a voulu faire l'artiste? Ni l'un ni l'autre; il a vu et il a peint, comme c'était son droit; la peinture a l'impartialité de la nature.'

37. See *The Absolute Bourgeois*, p. 27. Clark also quotes (p. 23) the comments of one reviewer who believed that Leleux's women in *La Sortie* were urging their menfolk to join the battle, not pleading for it to stop. He adds in a footnote (p. 191, n. 63) that the 'well-informed critics in 1851 (such as Gautier) were clear that his intentions were pacific'.

38. Forty years later, the extent to which 'dans ces épouvantables guerres des rues, les esprits sont hors d'eux-mêmes' was Meissonier's abiding memory of June 1848. The example he gave was that of an officer in the *garde républicaine*, not an *insurgé*. See Hungerford (*Ernest Meissonier: rétrospective*, p. 164) and in the same work (p. 181) the reproduction of Meissonier's letter to Alfred Stevens in 1890.

39. 'Salon de 1850–51 (18e article)', *La Presse*, 24 April 1851.

40. This tandem of Rousseau and Corot at the head of French landscape art was a commonplace in the writing on the Salon of 1851 by the time Gautier employed it in his review. Clément de Ris had stated it two months earlier ('Le Salon de 1851, IV', *L'Artiste*, 15 February 1851, pp. 17–21 (pp. 18–19)).

41. In 1850–51, Rousseau exhibited *Paysage*, *Effet de matin*, *Lisière*, *Trouée de forêt*, and *Effet de printemps*. Other critics also felt that, after two decades of exclusion from the Salon, Rousseau had not yet adjusted to its requirements. Clément de Ris, for example, though a great admirer, thought that the vegetation of *Paysage* needed a few days' more work in the studio and reminded the painter that 'la solennité des Salons annuels ne comporte pas le laisser-aller d'une exposition particulière ou d'une vente publique' ('Le Salon de 1851, IV', p. 18).

42. On *Une matinée*, see *Hommage à Corot* (Paris: Éditions des Musées Nationaux, 1975), pp. 81–83, *Le Musée de Luxembourg en 1874* (Paris: Éditions des Musées Nationaux, 1974), pp. 54–56. Of the opposition Rousseau–Corot, Clément de Ris wrote: 'Devant les tableaux de M. Rousseau, on est tenté d'admirer bruyamment; devant ceux de M. Corot, au contraire, on regarde et on jouit en paix. L'un est magnifique, l'autre est beau' ('Le Salon de 1851, IV', p. 18).

43. 'M. Corot a su y mettre non pas une vérité de détail peu importante, mais une vérité plus vraie, celle du sentiment, celle de l'impression, celle que l'on explique difficilement, mais dont tout le monde se rend compte parce que tout le monde a pu la ressentir ou l'éprouver'.

44. Delécluze included Corot in his condemnation of the genre, which was 'menacé de déchoir par l'abus de la facilité et souvent de dévergondage avec lesquels on commence à le traiter' (*Exposition des artistes vivants*, p. 238).

45. Gautier praised his *Étude de rochers*, *Lisière de bois*, and *Enfants au milieu de la forêt de Fontainebleau*, but of his *Rives enchantées* he had only this plea: 'Mais, pour dieu! plus de petits amours et plus de nymphes!'.

46. On Barye see *La Griffe et la Dent: Antoine Louis Barye (1795–1875), sculpteur animalier* (Paris: RMN, 1996).

47. 'Salon de 1850–51 (20e article)', *La Presse*, 1 May 1851.

48. See Charles W. Millard's biographical section on the sculptor in *Auguste Préault, sculpteur romantique*, pp. 11–75 (p. 48).

49. *Tuerie* was the only one of the five works submitted by Préault to be accepted. Millard quoted Silvestre's suggestion that the jury had accepted *Tuerie* only to serve as a warning about the danger that the Romantic revolution represented for sculpture (ibid., p. 19).

50. 'Quoi! N'y avait-il pas, dans les magasins du gouvernement [...] un bloc de Carrare pour Clésinger? Ce n'est ni la pierre, ni le bronze qu'il faut à Clésinger, c'est le marbre: le marbre lui fond sous les mains comme de la neige; cette brillante et rebelle matière a pour lui la ductilité de la cire.' Clésinger, unlike Pradier in the case of *Nyssia*, had been unwilling to take on the cost of the marble without a buyer lined up in advance.

51. See Caso, in *Statues de chair*, p. 166.

52. Gautier transformed Du Camp into a Dumas hero, one of the staple diets of the *feuilleton* in *La Presse*: 'Pour se perfectionner à la nage il remonte les cataractes et il s'exerce à l'équitation sur les montagnes de la lune, comme les savans; il ne se laisse pas manger par les crocodiles, il les mange, et quant aux tigres, il leur met le bras dans la gueule, plus inquiet de son gant que de sa main, comme ce héros d'un prologue d'Alexandre Dumas.'

53. 'Photographie: *L'Italie monumentale*, par M. Eugène Piot', *La Presse*, 26 July 1851.

54. 'La Statue de Marceau par M. Auguste Préault', *La Presse*, 15 September 1851.

55. See *Corr.*, II, 211–12 (letter from Gautier to Hugo, February 1845), and III, 11–12 (letter from Préault to Gautier, 26 January 1846), and the detailed commentary on the statue by Catherine Chevillot in *Auguste Préault, sculpteur romantique*, pp. 166–71.

56. Gautier presented this modernity in a characteristically more accessible form for a readership less versed in French sculpture's academic tradition: 'Auguste Préault a pensé que [...] la température de notre climat de pluie et de neige ne permettait pas d'exposer dans ce déshabillé un héros à des rhumatismes inconnus sous le ciel bleu de la Grèce.' Charles Blanc made the same point but in a more distinguished idiom: 'Il fallait y apporter, en effet, ce sentiment passionné, cet accent de la vie moderne, qui dans ce genre de sculpture, doit remplacer la gravité calme, la rigide immobilité de l'art antique', quoted by Chevillot in *Auguste Préault, sculpteur romantique*, p. 168.

CONCLUSION

Beyond Description

We saw earlier (p. 110) that in his review of the Salon of 1849 Gautier had welcomed Daumier's arrival as a Salon artist. The terms in which he did so are of some interest as far as his own art journalism is concerned:

> Célébrons l'avènement au Salon de M. Daumier, une de ces immenses organisations qui s'éparpillent en des milliers de petits chefs-d'œuvre sans façon, qu'on n'admire pas parce qu'ils sont nombreux et qu'il s'amuse: l'estime étant réservée en France, comme nous l'avons déjà dit bien des fois, pour les talens stériles et ennuyeux.[1]

It is difficult not to read an autobiographical grievance in this statement of support for Daumier, in the sense of injustice that it expresses on behalf of the 'immense organizations' whose vast creative efforts, channelled into allegedly less serious work in the so-called minor genres, appeared to merit only condescension. It was, as Gautier rightly said, a point he had made frequently. The expertise and range of skills he had described in the planned prospectus for his *Salon de 1847* warranted as far as he was concerned the same consideration as that which he believed was due to Daumier's talents and serious moral purpose, but in French hierarchies of cultural forms, prolixity and humour appeared to be frowned upon in equal measure. In his art journalism he had committed his energies to the cause of what he considered to be an elevated ideal of art, but he had no illusions that the medium in which he had done so would do very much to smooth his path to literary immortality.

We have seen in the foregoing pages some of the forms of cultural exchange in which Gautier's art journalism participated. We have, for example, seen him share subjects with painters and sculptors (in the the case of *Nyssia*), provide insights into the visual arts to which artists themselves turned for their own work (Spanish art for Préault), and actively support artists in their efforts to achieve the professional advancement of commissions and honours. But for his employer these were primarily side effects, the perks in a sense, of his art critic's central responsibility to address the cultural aspirations of the public for which *La Presse* had been founded in the first place. In this respect, entertaining instruction and accessible expertise were the remit. Gautier could empathize closely with Daumier's situation because he too was working in a medium which had still to establish its cultural credentials, acquire its *titres de noblesse*.

Gautier was well aware that his knowledge of the technical issues in painting and sculpture, of the language of the studio and the tricks of the trade, gave him an important competitive advantage in art journalism, 'aujourd'hui surtout que les peintres sacrifient tout à l'exécution', as he put it.[2] The modern painter's emphasis on execution was, he said, understandable as a 'réaction nécessaire après les tendances abstraites et philosophiques de l'ancienne école française [i.e. the neoclassicists], où tout était subordonné à l'idée' (ibid.). A certain level of technical analysis was essential in any case for his specialist readership of artists, fellow critics, and real or would-be connoisseurs, while for lay readers it presumbly inspired confidence that he at least knew what he was talking about, even (especially?) if they did not. Yet Gautier also knew that the art journalist could not fill a three-thousand-word article with technical analysis, not if he wanted to retain his 'average' reader's attention and not with an employer like Girardin reading over his shoulder. Sentiment, instruction, entertainment, and Parisianisms on the meaning of life were also requirements of the genre. By 1848 Gautier had achieved the position he had in art journalism because, in the process of juggling his personal, professional, and aesthetic commitments with the obligations that the newspaper imposed, he developed forms of writing on the visual arts which made most effective use of the possibilities the medium made available to him. I should like to conclude this study by returning briefly to these forms of art writing and, to introduce them, I shall summarize what I see as the essential features of his engagement with the visual arts during the Second Republic.

Hitherto I have argued that from February 1848 Gautier supported much of the Second Republic's programme for the visual arts (with the notable exception of the arrangements adopted for the open competition to create new symbols of the Republic) and that he did so because by 1848 he had already supported important elements of this programme for over a decade, not because he decided that he had better jump on the bandwagon before it left him behind. It is true of course that the first reason does not exclude the second, and it is reasonable to assume that Gautier recognized that it would not be in his personal and professional interests to withhold his support from the new regime. The evidence suggests, however, that he continued to support the Republican programme when others within the artistic community who had initially been supportive had given up on it (broadly speaking, within weeks rather than months of the revolution). In the closing months of the Second Republic, he returned to the themes with which he had embraced its arrival three years earlier. In September 1851, visiting the Universal Exhibition in Crystal Palace, he reiterated his faith that industrial progress would set humanity free and, in doing so, democratize the pleasures of reflection, study, and art.[3] The following month, in the first editorial of the newly resurrected *Revue de Paris*, edited by Houssaye, Du Camp, Louis de Cormenin, and himself, he celebrated in terms directly taken from his Salon of 1848 the new horizons opened up to art in the modern age, and once again dismissed art for art's sake as a false problem.[4] He reasserted the artist's place in the world — 'Nous n'avons nulle envie de nous enfermer, même dans une tour d'ivoire, hors du mouvement contemporain' (ibid., p. 11) — and in a transparent reference to the supporters of 'l'art social', he rejected their misrepresentation of poets as 'des espèces de fakirs absorbés dans la contemplation d'eux-mêmes, insensibles à tout ce qui se passe autour d'eux'. Citing the involvement of poets in the conflicts of ancient and modern history (Aeschylus,

Dante, Byron, Béranger), he reminded them, in a reference that two months before Louis Napoleon's coup d'état was distinctly unfashionable, of Lamartine's role in the revolution of February 1848.

It is true that all this hardly amounted on Gautier's part to an ideal of republican art. Even if he had had such a thing in February 1848 and it had enjoyed a consensus within the art community, he could soon see for himself that the new Republican administration was in no position to deliver it, for it already had quite enough to do to get a grip on the short-term funding crisis in the arts. At the outbreak of the revolution, Gautier already had a long-standing ideal in art, one which he evidently considered to be as compatible in principle with the art of a republic as with that of any other political regime. It was an ideal based on what he thought of as the timeless values of art's ideal beauty, which, if they could be made available to all, would usher in a new age of moral, social, and spiritual instruction and fulfilment, and, with it, 'le bonheur', which, as we saw, he had described in his preface to *Mademoiselle de Maupin* as 'la seule chose utile au monde'. That this might be the age of the republic created no intrinsic problem for him any more than he had a problem proposing that Ingres, the painter of the *Vénus anadyomène*, should be invited to create a figure of the Republic, or stating that Delacroix's *La Liberté guidant le peuple* and Meissonier's *Souvenir de guerre civile* were two of the great paintings of the century. Gautier undoubtedly considered himself uniquely qualified to provide the education into art necessary to enable the new wider public of the mid-nineteenth century to access the values of ideal beauty. By the mid-1830s, however, the notion of 'le beau idéal' was under attack from the proponents of social romanticism and on both sides this opposition overlaid others (Ingres–Delacroix, line–colour, 'l'art pour l'art'–'l'art pour l'homme', and so on). For social romantics, the polemical brilliance of the preface to *Mademoiselle de Maupin* appeared to show where the main threat from the other side lay. Disparaging Gautier with the facile label of art for art's sake was a response to this threat, and was complemented by foisting the same label onto the art of Ingres. Gautier's well-known devotion to Ingres's work served to reinforce the idea of the Ingres–Gautier tandem as metonymic of conservative resistance to art's forward march in the modern age.

For Gautier the obligation to ensure that the legacy of the art of Ingres and Delacroix was handed on successfully to the following generation of artists was by the mid-century the crucial issue. The annual Salon was the essential occasion on which this obligation had to be assumed, and in this respect, those of 1848, 1849, and 1850–51 had not made his task any easier. The continued absence of Ingres, the relatively low-key presence of Delacroix, and the fact that no single follower of either of these two towering figures had by that stage succeeded in imposing an undisputed authority on contemporary French art had resulted in what appeared to Gautier to be a vacuum of leadership, one in which talented individuals jostled for position in a growing, more diverse, and more open marketplace. This situation increased the pressure on the art journalist, for whom the Salon review was, as much as for the artist, the decisive annual competition in which he had to demonstrate once more his capacity to inform and direct public debate on the visual arts. In this respect the emergence of Courbet was, from Gautier's point of view, a complication, for he was baffled as well as attracted by the work and could see the success with which Courbet was himself promoting it. Gautier's position on *La Presse* depended on Girardin's continuing confidence in his art critic's ability to determine and lead artistic debate in ways appropriate to its readership.[5] While looking at his analyses of the major fine art events during the Second Republic, we have seen some examples of the range of forms that his art writing took in response to the resources and constraints that his position on *La Presse* implied. I shall conclude this study with a few more, in the hope of underlining the type of issues that need to be addressed if we are to achieve a fuller understanding of Gautier's art journalism than has been hitherto the case.

The issue of the visual artist's technique is a good place to begin, and his commentary on *La Tentation* by Célestin Nanteuil and *La Mal'aria* (Figure 7.1) by Ernest Hébert, both shown in the Salon of 1850–51, provide an interesting contrast in this respect. Gautier's friendship with Nanteuil went back almost two decades to the *Jeunes-France* days of their shared youth.[6] We have seen examples of his loyalty to his friends and support for their work, and though he could pose as well as the next critic as a model of integrity unwilling to allow friendship to cloud his judgement, harsh words on such occasions were the exception which proved the rule.[7] Nanteuil's case was similar to that of Daumier in the sense that he too had spent much of his career up to that point working in what was generally considered to be the minor visual art of book illustration, following the critical acclaim which had greeted his frontispieces for the 1832 Renduel edition of Hugo's work. As with Daumier, Gautier deplored the public's lack of appreciation for the skills and productivity of this 'Alexandre Dumas de la vignette',[8] with the result that *La Tentation* was guaranteed to be the occasion of a vintage Gautier performance:

> La *Tentation* nous fait voir une Madeleine toute fraîche repentie et installée de la veille au désert, avec l'ameublement obligé de la tête de mort, de chapelets à grains noirs, de grands bouquins à couverture jaune, de cruche de grès, de pain bis et de légumes crus.
>
> La sainte de date récente n'a pas encore eu le temps de se macérer beaucoup. La pénitence n'a rien enlevé à ses charmes. Sa gorge opulente, ses bras ronds, ses joues roses, à qui le soleil libertin donne amicalement un petit soufflet lumineux à travers les découpures des feuilles, la draperie de velours, jetée sur ses genoux, montrent qu'elle vient de quitter sa folle vie de courtisane dans Jérusalem ou dans Paris, et cependant déjà la tentation a trouvé le chemin de sa solitude; un essaim de petits amours, de petits diables, voulons-nous dire, dansent la sarabande autour d'elle en faisant luire à ses yeux des cassettes pleines de colliers de perles, de pièces d'or et de billets doux, des flacons empourprés, où scintille en rubis le généreux sang de la vigne, des fleurs en couronnes et en bouquets, des miroirs, des étoffes chatoyantes, toutes les damnations de la femme. Il ne faut pas être un très grand sorcier pour prévoir que cette Madeleine-là retournera bientôt aux boudoirs tendus de rose, aux petits coupés, aux cabinets de la Maison-d'Or et aux avant-scènes des théâtres de vaudeville les soirs de première représentation.

Here Gautier dispenses altogether with issues of execution. There is no attempt, for example, to manufacture a position for Nanteuil as a 'revelation' of the Salon of 1850–51 on the basis of technical skills hitherto hidden under a bushel. This lack of

FIG. 7.1. Ernest Hébert, *La Mal'aria*, 1848–49, Paris, Musée d'Orsay.
© Patrice Schmidt, Musée d'Orsay

commentary on execution already makes clear the limits of the work's achievement as far as Gautier is concerned, but there are other ways in which to execute his duty of friendship. In this case Nanteuil's original treatment of the subject would do nicely, and in the company of his very modern and Parisian repentant, Gautier went to town. Traditionally Mary Magdalene was represented in one of two ways, either before or after her conversion, and with one of two corresponding sets of attributes (the vanities of the world or the symbols of renunciation). In *La Tentation* Nanteuil brought them together in an original way by depicting her in the immediate aftermath of conversion and showing her torn between pleasures renounced (on the right) and duty embraced (on the left). Most critics chose to see the painting as a morally uplifting representation of a familiar spiritual dilemma, with duty resisting temptation's renewed attacks,[9] but Gautier knew Nanteuil better than that. From his first comment the tone is unmistakeable. This Madeleine, he tells us, has only just 'set herself up' in the desert with renunciation's mandatory 'fixtures and fittings' but the vanities of the world are back with a vengeance (their charms evident in the *lists* of items, one of the staple elements of Gautier's description of paintings) and the sun itself connives to thwart penitence's threat to her physical charms. With the scene set in this way, there is only one outcome possible. *La Tentation* is renunciation renounced, a celebration of the worldly pleasures to which this Madeleine will soon return in Parisian theatres, boudoirs, and horse-drawn carriages, and a slap in the face for the Catholic spoilsports of the *parti de l'ordre*. In Gautier's account, Nanteuil's biblical subject is the pretext for a display of very Parisian pleasures.

Hébert's *La Mal'aria*, on the other hand, engaged modern Parisian anxieties about contamination and mortality but it did so in ways in which the painter's technical performance gave it for Gautier a different dimension from *La Tentation*. In 1850–51 Hébert became the latest painter to be enrolled in the group of young artists who Gautier hoped would reinvigorate the tradition discredited by what he saw as the exhausted remnants of the Davidian school, and *La Mal'aria* would join the list of works to which he dedicated a poem.[10] He began the short opening paragraph of his commentary with a characteristic eye-catching announcement of the painter's achievement that year: 'La *Malaria*, de M. Hébert, est sinon le meilleur tableau du Salon, du moins celui qui a le plus de charme.' He then justified the claim with a series of oppositions — between given and acquired talent, grace and effort, feeling and idea — which, for Gautier, Hébert had transcended with his demonstration of the complementarity of the sister arts which set the born painter apart. In *La Mal'aria*, 'l'habilité du peintre n'y nuit en rien à la pensée du poète'.

Having begun his article with a statement designed to impose Hébert on public opinion, Gautier put art criticism to one side and, turning to the painting's subject, padded out his article with four paragraphs (almost five hundred words) on the subject of malaria. In 1850 Parisians were understandably interested in and fearful of contagious diseases. There had been another outbreak of cholera in the city the previous year, and the idea that it was becoming urgent to address the problem of 'Paris, ville malade' was by then well established.[11] In this sense Hébert's choice of subject was well timed and, for Gautier, too good to miss. A disease which was, he said, 'quelque chose d'incompréhensible' for 'les gens du Nord' would now no longer be so for readers of *La Presse*, since his recent travels in Italy had evidently made him as much an authority on the ravages of malaria as he was on the accomplishments of the Quattrocento. So in another list he explained for their benefit the whole story of which Hébert's painting was one carefully crafted moment: the glorious landscapes of the Italian summer whose serene beauty only made more incomprehensible the mysterious and lethal poison that lurked there, the shock at the first symptoms of illness, the mournful spectacle of sick villages, the rueful philosophico-religious reflection on malaria the great leveller, which apparently spared Rome's filthy ghettos but decimated the inhabitants of its most luxurious villas.

It seems unlikely that Gautier's readers in 1850–51 would have regarded this mixture of travelogue and contemporary epidemiology as a digression from the task of evaluating Hébert's painting, rather than as a legitimate extension of its moral, scientific, and cultural implications. Knowing from experience that Gautier would soon return to *La Mal'aria*, they presumably recognized that he was preparing them for this larger subject:

> Est-ce la nature qui veut reprendre cette terre que l'homme a trop fatiguée et la reposer par une jachère de mort? Est-ce au contraire le sol abandonné qui distille dans le silence les poisons de la solitude, pour montrer que là où la communauté humaine étend sa famille, là sont la vie et la santé? Ce n'est pas ici le lieu d'approfondir ce mystère; revenons au tableau de M. Hébert.

With the familiar sign that the account of the bigger picture is now complete ('Ce n'est pas ici le lieu'), Gautier returns, as expected, to Hébert's work, to demonstrate how subject and execution underpin the relationship between the particular painting and the bigger picture, which is itself the relationship between exotic, picturesque genre painting and the culturally more prestigious *grande peinture*. At the level of subject, Hébert's boat contains a family escaping the plague, and in Gautier's description each figure is allotted a particular type of signification. The father, symbol of authority and responsibility and, as such, the only one standing, has his back to the spectator in a simple and strong bearing that is a silent reproach to Courbet.[12] The same art historical lesson of the nobility of poverty is true of the young woman in the brown cape who shivers from the illness 'qui attaque sa vie en respectant sa beauté'. With the young man, whose thin yellow body is drained by the disease, the realist reference makes way for local colour and tourist guide vernacular guaranteed to interest Parisian readers; he wears 'un de ces chapeaux pointus comme en portent les pifferari et les pâtres des Abruzzes', which gives Gautier another opportunity to use his foreign travel to authenticate the artist's representation.[13] A beautiful young woman, sitting with her back to the spectator in a relaxed pose (she is untouched by the disease and her golden hair shimmers in the light) presents the simple parable of the bloom of life in the midst of death. In the prow of the boat a few vegetables form a simple provision for the family and a discreet but eloquent still life for the artist, critic, and connoisseur. The image of the Madonna on the seat next to the caped woman and the blessed amulet worn by the seated young man provide the spiritual counterpart of this terrestrial sustenance.

In terms of execution, Gautier draws attention to the poetic realism which would subsequently characterize much of Hébert's work, with its combination of sharply highlighted figures and *sfumato*, transitions of tone from light to dark by stages so gradual as to be imperceptible: 'tout nage dans le *flou* d'une exécution invisible [...] l'art a disparu, et le sentiment seul reste'. As if to demonstrate the pertinence of Gautier's advice to Courbet the same year to become the Léopold Robert of the modern French peasantry, Hébert had, according to Gautier, achieved the same idealization of Italian peasants as Robert but by means of an execution diametrically opposed to that of his predecessor:

> Autant le peintre des *Moissonneurs* a été ferme, arrêté, laborieux dans son style, autant le peintre de la *Malaria* s'est montré naïf, simple, attendri et plein de *vaghezza* et de *morbidezza* pour employer deux termes italiens qui nous manquent et qu'on devrait bien franciser.[14]

Making visible the execution on which the artist himself had exercised such discretion, Gautier gave readers the sense that, having grasped the philosophical and art historical implications of Hébert's treatment of the subject, they were now being given a deeper understanding of the secrets of the painter's craft and its technical language, both vouched for by his own expertise. By the end of the exercise, he had situated Hébert in a tradition and defined the painter's originality in relation to it as the author of a poetic realism, superior technically and intellectually to that of Courbet. In 1850–51 a new artist had emerged and Gautier had identified and positioned him, forging another of the alliances with painters through which he would speculate on the future of French art and reassert the role of his own art journalism in shaping and directing this future.

The subjects of *La Tentation* and *La Mal'aria* were cases in which, with Gautier, the boundary between the *feuilleton d'art* and the *roman feuilleton* could become blurred. He knew well enough that Nanteuil's Madeleine was the sort of heroine who had given the serial novel a bad name, and his description of malaria would make little sense if Hébert's painting had not touched on the sort of deep, anxiety-laden 'medicalizing tropology' which Eugène Sue had used to such effect in *Les Mystères de Paris*.[15] Sculpture too lent itself to such extensions. When, introducing his commentary on Lescorné's marble statue *Clytie*, shown in the Salon of 1848, Gautier excused in an elegant and light-hearted way his readers' lack of classical education by saying that 'en ce temps où l'on a bien le droit d'avoir oublié sa mythologie, nous rappellerons en peu de mots l'histoire de cette infortunée', he presented the sculptor's subject in terms of a character (the young woman who, forsaken in love, wastes away while remaining unswerving in her devotion) and a plot (jealousy, revenge, and a happy ending) that were the food and drink of the *roman feuilleton*. To do so he took Lescorné's own account of the Greek myth given in the Salon catalogue and embroidered the sculptor's treatment of Clytie and Apollo as a tender narrative of love triumphant: 'La tête de Clytie est charmante, elle semble baigner dans la lumière et s'enivrer d'un rayon comme d'un baiser. Le soleil, moins cruel peut-être à ce moment-là, oublie qu'il est un astre pour se souvenir qu'il était un amant.'[16] In this way, he gave due consideration to the artist's intentions, took advantage of the fact that part of his commentary had in effect been written for him in advance, and presented a Greek legend in a manner quickly recognizable in terms of the horizons of experience and expectation of his readers. He then enlarged this account of Clytie's doomed love for Apollo into a sort of case study of Antiquity's 'idée singulière et touchante' of metamorphosis, extending this horizon back towards classical sources before delivering to the artist his expert assessment and advice:

> Cette statue pleine de grace et de sentiment, ne laisse rien à désirer, qu'un peu plus de rendu et d'accent. Certaines attaches sont trop mollement indiquées; l'exécution, çà et là, est un peu ronde; mais c'est un défaut qui peut être réparé par huit jours de travail.

Addressing a smaller and socially less heterogeneous readership than that of *La Presse*, Malitourne in *L'Artiste* and de Mercey in the *Revue des deux mondes* could dispense with most of this. Malitourne did not mention the work's source in the Greek legend, and de Mercey referred to 'l'amante délaissée d'Apollon' only as an alternative to repeating her name. Similarly, both analysed the female figure's anatomy, pose, and expression with reference to procedures of idealization which formed the nineteenth-century sculptor's classical training and with which their readers could be assumed to have at least a basic familiarity.[17] Gautier, on the other hand, kept the technical analysis shorter and more general, acknowledging perhaps that for his readers these issues were likely to figure less prominently in their cultural *acquis* in the case of sculpture than in that of painting.

We could add to these three examples any number of others from the art journalism Gautier produced during the four-year period which we have been following. What they illustrate, together with those we have seen in the course of this study, is the need to consider how the relationship between the different types of discourse that made up each of his evaluations of an art work was composed and targeted. Though the essential elements of his value system as far as the visual arts were concerned were in place from an early stage in his career and remained quite stable throughout it, his journalism was designed to be a highly flexible response to an artistic environment that was busy, complex, and constantly changing. Each article was the result of a series of decisions, each a response to specific factors, about which artist to discuss, at what length, in which order, and in relation to which wider issues. Central to this activity was the description of the art work itself, its subject, form, and in most cases the relationship between the two. We began this study with the serious reservations which Delacroix expressed about Gautier's performance in this area but, as Marie-Hélène Girard reminded us, his comments failed to appreciate 'le parti qu'un écrivain pouvait légitimement tirer de cette tradition de l'*ekphrasis* héritée de Philostrate'.[18] Hitherto discussion of this issue in the Gautier literature has centred on his use of art description in his creative writing (and here there has been greater emphasis on his short fiction than on his travel writing, for example).[19] Yet the specificity and originality of his adaptation of the ekphrastic tradition in his art journalism following his recruitment to *La Presse* have barely begun to be studied, despite the fact that it was his credentials and status as an art journalist which authenticated for his readers these types of literary production. Here again, it is essential to remember that Gautier was in on the revolution of the French press from the very beginning in 1836 and that his art descriptions were therefore designed to enable him to target its new reading public in ways that the more established forms of art description in the established press would not.[20]

Landscape painting is an obvious case in point. It was clearly recognized during the Second Republic that the move from historical to natural landscape was both a response to and an agent of changing public taste. We saw Gautier's account of this development both in general terms (its history) and in some of its details (Cabat's role). In 1850–51 he celebrated Cabat's return to natural landscapes after a period during which he had sought — wrongly in Gautier's view — to assimilate some of the features of the *paysage de style* (see above, p. 159). Gautier expressed his satisfaction in the following terms:

> Cabat, qui s'était un peu alangui et attristé dans ses recherches du style de Poussin, qu'il avait la modestie d'imiter comme s'il n'était pas lui-même un grand maître, a reparu presque tout à fait guéri. Ses *Disciples d'Emmaüs* témoignent seuls qu'il a été malade. Mais ses *Chèvres dans un bois*, sa *Prairie près de Dieppe*, sa *Ferme à Bercenay*, son *Bois au bord d'une rivière*, témoignent qu'il est en pleine santé. Il peint comme autrefois: les chaumières aux toits verdis de mousse, à la cheminée qui fume dans le feuillage, les blés piqués de coquelicots, les petits sentiers parfumés d'aubépine, les ruisseaux qui courent à travers le cresson, les mares où les canards nagent par escadres, les pommiers dont les branches ploient, les prés herbus, les rivières bordées de joncs, tout ce petit monde rustique et charmant des environs de Paris qu'il a découvert et que nul n'a peint comme lui, humbles motifs qu'il eut tort de dédaigner plus tard pour les grands sites italiens. Enfin, le voilà revenu avec ses eaux limpides, ses lointains légers, ses détails fins et sobres, sa touche nette et son talent individuel: pour le garder, il ne doit pas aller plus loin que la Normandie; les voyages ne vont pas à toutes les natures.

Cabat who had been pining away in a foreign land had been restored to health by the return to his roots. In this secular parable of the prodigal son, his recovery was just reward for his virtuous modesty. Gautier pronounced him 'almost' cured, and the note of caution is a reminder of where the authority for the clean bill of health lay. Naming the artist's latest works prompts Gautier's topography of the urban myth of nature, each element of which drips with emotional resonance in Parisians uprooted from the land like Gautier himself and deposited in the city. The list of subjects culminates in the double superlative of 'tout' and 'nul', which underline Cabat's failure to recognize the riches that were contained in these humble scenes on the Parisian's doorstep. Reference to their motifs is Gautier's signal that landscape's restorative power can be accessed through the forms of its representation, the water, distant skies, and all the other details bearing the personal signature of the brushstroke. It only remained to write out the simple prescription for preventing relapse and the lesson it contained, the nugget of common sense that travelling did not suit everyone.

These forms of eloquence and their effects may be obvious and we can well imagine what Delacroix (and perhaps Cabat himself) might have thought of them, but what is important is what they tell us about how Gautier proceeded in order to bring a public into contact with a work of art which he admired and to educate that public into reaching what he regarded as the proper conclusions about that art. Each art work created the task anew, and Gautier's choice of materials was pragmatic, based on his sense, derived from his vast experience, of what worked. Just as his empathetic approach was the key to his interpretations of art (what Baudelaire had called Gautier's capacity, when faced with British art, to 'britanniser son génie'; see above, p. 10 n. 15),[21] so also was it the key to his account of this work to the readers of his art journalism. However great or small their knowledge and experience of art might be, they shared the capacity to respond imaginatively to the stories that art works told and through which Gautier could lead them to an understanding of the painterly or sculptural means by which they told them. His art descriptions and the other types of discourse within which he enclosed them show us the changing forms of urban bourgeois culture in mid-nineteenth-century France.

The examples that we have seen represent only a small part of those that Gautier produced in the course of the forty-nine articles in which he reviewed the Fine Art Salons of the Second Republic, which were themselves only three of the thirty Salons that he reviewed during his long career. Gautier's production of art descriptions therefore needs to be analysed as it developed in the course of his career in much greater detail than has hitherto been the case. It also needs to be seen in conjunction with that of other art journalists of the period, for it is quite clear that the Salon review, for example, was in mid-nineteenth-century France an intertextual activity in which judgements and the forms in which they were expressed were the result of a collective activity of discussing, reading, copying, and adapting the opinions of others and that Gautier's originality as an art journalist cannot be fully assessed outside this intertextual framework.[22] At the micro level, the constituent elements of Gautier's descriptions would also need to be charted, and again in relation to those of other art critics, in order to determine more precisely the specific features of his contribution.[23] Such investigation went far beyond the scope of this study, in which Gautier's art journalism has been considered in its relationship to a series of specific events during a brief historical period, but we must hope that the forthcoming publication of his complete Fine Art Salon reviews will make it easier to carry out this long-overdue study of his contribution in an area which, taken in association with his creative writings, may finally help to give him the place that he deserves as one of the central and most creative figures in French nineteenth-century culture.

Notes to the Conclusion

1. 'Salon de 1849', *La Presse*, 8 August 1849. Referring the previous year to history painting of the Empire and Restoration, he stated that 'les Français, ce peuple léger, n'ont jamais admiré que ce qui les ennuyait' ('Salon de 1848', 26 April 1848).
2. Gautier made the comment in the context of his commentary on Hébert's painting *La Mal'aria* ('Salon de 1850–51 (neuvième article)', *La Presse*, 22 March 1851).
3. 'La machine relève l'homme et l'animal d'un labeur, d'une fatigue ou d'un ennui [...] et chaque jour, le temps pour la pensée, la rêverie, l'étude, devient plus large et plus long' ('Le Palais de Cristal: les barbares, I', *La Presse*, 5 September 1851).
4. 'De nouveaux horizons s'ouvrent de toutes parts; des races inconnues se révèlent tout à coup. L'Orient mystérieux, qui garde dans son immobilité de sphinx le secret de bien de civilisations disparues, l'Égypte, qui était déjà vieille quand notre Europe émergeait à peine des eaux du déluge, consentent à se laisser pénétrer et déchiffrer. Nous puiserons souvent dans cette mine d'où Goëthe et Victor Hugo ont tiré tant de pierres précieuses. Nous nous arrêterons pas à la vieille querelle de l'objectif et le subjectif, de l'idée et de la forme; nous ne concevons pas plus

le corps sans l'âme que l'âme sans le corps' ('Liminaire', *Revue de Paris* (October 1851), 5–11 (p. 9)).

5. Gautier was grateful for the resources that Girardin made available to him and the freedom that he was granted in their use. He acknowledged them at the beginning of his review of Piot's *L'Italie monumentale* with his comment that 'la direction de la *Presse* a bien voulu nous confier, outre le théâtre, tout ce qui touche à l'art, sculpture, peinture, dessin, et nous abandonner, pour ces hautes questions, une liberté complète d'initiative' (*La Presse*, 26 July 1851). But he can have had no illusions about the responsibilities that came with such favours.

6. See Gautier's *Histoire du romantisme* (Paris: Charpentier, 1854), pp. 45–53.

7. 'Malgré la longue amitié qui nous lie à Louis Boulanger, amitié formée au sein du cénacle romantique dans le temps des beaux enthousiasmes et des grandes fraternités d'art, nous ne pouvons nous empêcher de trouver la *Douleur d'Hécube* un très mauvais tableau et de le dire' ('Salon de 1850–51 (10e article)', *La Presse*, 28 March 1851).

8. 'Quelle inépuisable fécondité, quel esprit toujours éveillé, quelle main toujours prête, quelle compréhension rapide de tous les styles et de toutes les époques! Célestin Nanteuil est l'Alexandre Dumas de la vignette. Que de force il lui a fallu pour suffire à cet effroyable gaspillage que notre temps inattentif et cruel demande à tous les talens, et dont il ne leur tient aucun compte!' (ibid.).

9. The following account by Clément de Ris was typical: 'Elle est là, tristement penchée, écoutant les deux voix qui parlent en elle, ses beaux seins nus livrés aux caresses du soleil qui se joue sur le satin de sa peau, ses longs cheveux dénoués, en butte aux obsessions, mais ferme cependant à sa place; image des ces âmes courageuses qui ne reculent pas lâchement devant les charmes de la séduction, et qui ont trouvé dans l'aride sentier du devoir assez de force pour y résister ('Salon de 1851, III', p. 7).

10. See 'A Ernest Hébert, sur son tableau *La Malaria*', *PC*, III, 151.

11. This pathology of Paris was of course a key element in the Second Empire's decision to demolish and rebuild the city centre from 1852. See Louis Chevalier, *Classes laborieuses et classes dangereuses à Paris pendant la première moitié du XIXe siécle* (Paris: Plon, 1958), David H. Pinkney, *Napoleon III and the Rebuilding of Paris* (Princeton University Press, 1958) and Colin Jones, *Paris: Biography of a City* (London: Penguin/Allen Lane, 2004), pp. 344–95.

12. 'Nos peintres rustiques si amoureux de l'ignoble et du difforme apprendront par cette figure que la rusticité a son élégance et la misère sa noblesse'.

13. Spain and the Orient provide particularly fertile ground for this hybridization of art description and travel writing. Defending Gérôme against the charge of mannerism on the grounds that it was an authentic feature of the natural world, he wrote: 'Jamais maja andalouse suivie de son majo et de ses attentifs n'a, dans l'alanuda, sous ce feu de mille prunelles, manégé plus savamment qu'une biche solitaire dans la forêt d'Ardennes' ('Salon de 1848', *La Presse*, 27 April 1848). The following year, he had described the eighth article of his Salon of 1849 as 'ce voyage d'Afrique dont l'idée nous a été inspirée ce matin par un rayon de soleil, une hirondelle qui passait et un lambeau de ciel bien entrevu pardessus les maisons'. Its centrepiece was a description of his experience, four year earlier, of a djinn dance in the very courtyard in Constantine in which Adolphe Leleux had painted his *Danse de Djinns* shown in the Salon of 1849. Here the painting's achievement was to compensate 'avec bien plus de force, de réalité et de couleur' for the limitations of the writer's description, which was the least the artist deserved for enabling Gautier to re-use an extensive piece of travel literature written in advance. In the Salon of 1850–51, in Hédouin's *Vue de Constantine* 'nous pourrions certifier conforme la place des Grains à Constantine pour en avoir traversé nous-même le trapèze en tous sens'; and of Giraud's Sierra Nevada landscape: 'Nous qui avons passé dans la Sierra-Nevada par l'étroit sentier où M. Giraud fait cheminer son arriero ayant pour contrepoids une brune Andalouse à la basquine rose, tandis que le mozo de mulas, renversé sur son bat, gratte insoucieusement de la guitare, nous comprenons parfaitement l'effroi de la jeune femme' (both in 'Salon de 1850–51 (16e article)', *La Presse*, 19 April 1851).

14. We have here a characteristic of Gautier's art journalism which was repeatedly held against it, the apparent inconsistency of praising an artist/stylistic feature in one article and attacking him/it in the next. We saw him earlier praising mannerism in Gérôme and attacking it in Courbet;

here he criticizes Léopold Robert as a means to promote Hébert after using the same Robert as a stick with which to beat Courbet. Again the importance of the ends no doubt justified for Gautier the flexibility of the means, especially since the means would be more subject than the ends to the newspaper's short shelf-life.

15. The phrase is that of Christopher Prendergast in *For the People by the People?*, p. 47.

16. 'Salon de 1848', *La Presse*, 23 April 1848.

17. Malitourne: 'L'attitude de la tête est expressive [...] mais le masque n'est pas arrivé à un suffisant modelé. Certaines parties du torse n'ont pas assez d'élégance et de finesse. Dans les jambes, assez habilement traitées, les plans ne sont pas assez sentis' ('La Sculpture en 1848', 1 June 1848, pp. 141–42); de Mercey: 'Le ventre, cet écueil de l'art de la statuaire, contre lequel tout le talent du sculpteur vient souvent échouer, est lourd, pendant, sans grace. C'est la nature sans doute, mais la nature vulgaire, fatiguée, vieillie' ('Le Salon de 1848', 15 May 1848, p. 595).

18. See *Théophile Gautier, Critique d'art*, pp. 21–22. Picking up and enlarging Girard's comment, Francis Moulinat has outlined in general terms the issues that it raises (see his 'Gautier et l'ekphrasis', *BSTG*, 21 (1999), 133–47).

19. It is not a coincidence in this respect that, in addition to being the most prolific art journalist of the mid-nineteenth century in France, Gautier inscribed the visual art work in his fiction 'avec une fréquence qui n'est apparemment égalée par aucun de ses contemporains', as Marc Eigeldinger put it in 'L'Inscription de l'œuvre plastique dans les récits de Gautier' (in *Théophile Gautier: l'art et l'artiste* (= *BSTG*, 4.1–2 (1983)), II, 297–309). See also Pascale Auraix-Jonchière, 'Ekphrasis et mythologie dans la *Toison d'or* de Théophile Gautier (1839): la Madeleine prétexte', in *Écrire la peinture: entre XVIIIe et XIXe siècles*, ed. by Pascale Auraix-Jonchière (Clermont-Ferrand: Presses universitaires Blaise Pascal, 2003), pp. 451–63, and Lisette Thome-Jarrouché, 'L'Art descriptif de Théophile Gautier: la description d'un critique d'art', *BSTG*, 20 (1998), 125–41. For a more general discussion of this issue see the important article by Bernard Vouilloux, 'La Description des œuvres d'art dans le roman français au XIXe siècle', in *La Description de l'œuvre d'art: du modèle classique aux variations contemporaines* (Paris: Sogomy/Académie de France à Rome, 2004), pp. 153–84. For the poetry see David Scott, *Pictorialist Poetics: Poetry and the Visual Arts in Nineteenth-Century France* (Cambridge University Press, 1988).

20. As Moulinat states, Gautier's use of ekphrasis placed him in 1837 in a position of 'contre-critique' ('Gautier et l'ekphrasis', p. 135).

21. See Wolfgang Drost, 'L'Esthétique de l'empathie et les prétendues contradictions de Gautier', in *Théophile Gautier: exposition de 1859*, pp. 462–65.

22. To take just one obvious example, Gautier's comments on Millet's *Le Vanneur* quoted above (p. 53) reproduce very closely, albeit in a more enthusiastic tone, those of Clément de Ris, published three weeks earlier: 'Ses tableaux semblent être faits plutôt par un maçon que par un peintre, et la couleur paraît y avoir été jetée plutôt par une truelle que posée par une brosse' ('Salon de 1848, V', p. 69). Given Gautier's connections with *L'Artiste*, it would be surprising if he had not read this article. Similarly, commenting on the realistic rendering of the dust produced by the winnower's action of sifting the grain, Gautier said that it made the spectator sneeze and de Mercey that it made it hard to see the rest of the scene ('Le Salon de 1848', 15 April 1848, p. 287). Each case is more likely to be an example of both critics using descriptive elements circulating widely about the work in question among artists and critics during the Salon period, rather than of one critic borrowing from another.

23. Patrick Berthier has looked at Gautier's use of metaphor in the art descriptions contained in his first four Salons, noting particularly those related to food. See 'L'Humour chez Théophile Gautier critique d'art 1833–1837', *BSTG*, 23 (2001), 153–63.

APPENDIX

'J'ai un besoin absolu d'argent'

(23? Janvier 1851)

Mon cher Maitre

Je travaille à mon Salon que je commencerai irrévocablement mardi. Je vous préviens que je désire qu'il me soit fait aucune retenue sur ces articles. J'ai un besoin absolu d'argent; comme je ne touche plus maintenant les 833 fr 33 centimes par mois qui faisaient la somme de dix mille fr par an convenue sur mon traité j'ai toutes les peines du monde à vivre avec ce qui me revient par semaine la dividende de février qui me sera retenue cette année comme les autres sans doute, paiera ce qui me reste dû sur le voyage; j'ai fait 12 articles soit deux mois de ma rédaction au prix ordinaire. 6 articles par mois font 833 fr 33 centimes. 12 articles font donc 1666 fr 66. – Je ne dois donc plus que 134 fr. – puisque vous m'avez donné 1.800 fr: ma part au bénéfice de la presse couvrira cela très bien: pour le reste de ma dette je la payerai en roman de cinq ou dix feuilletons: je vous écris cela je pourrais vous le dire mais rien ne me répugne comme ces discussions d'argent. J'ai souffert sans me plaindre mais ce Salon qui me donne quelques centaines de francs à la fois me permet de payer des loyers et des dettes que je ne puis satisfaire avec 138 fr sur lesquels il faut prélever la nourriture de 5 personnes.

Tout à vous

Théophile Gautier

Écrivez-moi un mot pour savoir si je dois ou non continuer ces articles.

Paris le 24 janvier 1851

A Mr Th. Gautier

Mon cher maitre,

J'ai l'autorisation de vous accorder ce que vous demandez, c'est-à-dire le paiement intégral de votre salon, mais à la condition expresse que vous nous remettrez dans le cours de l'année, mais *le plus tôt possible*, treize feuilletons qui termineront votre Voyage en Italie, et sur lesquels vous ne réclamerez rien de nous, les abandonnant pour terminer votre compte qui ne s'élève plus maintenant qu'à F 1713,06, déduction faite de 693, qui vous sont revenus sur votre participation aux bénéfices des Propriétaires de la Presse en 1850. Ces 13 feuilletons donnés et éteignant votre compte, vous n'aurez plus de retenue à subir, et vous pourrez vendre votre voyage à un éditeur. Vous aurez donc double profit.

Par simple renseignement et par pure curiosité, tant de votre part que de la mienne, je vous remets ci derrière le relevé par année de ce que la Presse, cette bonne mère nourrice vous a remis jusqu'à présent, tout en conservant l'espoir de vous en donner encore bien plus et bien longtemps.

Votre tout dévoué

C. Rouy

Mr Théophile Gautier

1836	770	
37	2216	80
38	5575	
39	5650	
40	3423	75
41	1774	75
42	2050	50
43	5000	
44	7633	33
45	9945	15
46	9805	59
47	11724	38
48	13680	66
49	9384	
50	9990	
	1713	06 redu en avances
	100336	97

(25 janvier 1851)

Mon cher Maitre

J'accepte la condition de faire 13 feuilletons de voyage sur lesquels je ne toucherai rien pour finir mon arriéré et je commence mon Salon qui me sera payé intégralement je vous remercie de l'intéressant relevé que vous m'avez envoyé il m'a fait beaucoup de plaisir et je le garde comme un curieux document

Tout à vous

Théophile Gautier

Monsieur
Monsieur Rouy
administrateur de la Presse

(*Corr.*, IV, 288–91)

SELECT BIBLIOGRAPHY

Primary Sources

(1) Works by Gautier and editions of his work

(a) Books

Abécédaire du Salon de 1861 (Paris: Dentu, 1861)
L'Art moderne (Paris: Michel Lévy, 1856)
Les Beaux-Arts en Europe, 2 vols (Paris: Michel Lévy, 1856)
Bonjour, Monsieur Corot: ensemble des articles de 1836 à 1872, ed. by Marie-Hélène Girard (Paris: Séguier, 1996)
Caprices et zigzags (Paris: Lecou, 1852)
Correspondance générale, ed. by Claudine Lacoste-Veysseyre, 12 vols (Geneva and Paris: Droz, 1985–2000)
Courbet, le Watteau du laid, ed. by Christine Sagnier (Paris: Séguier, 2000)
Critique d'art: extraits de Salons (1833–1872), ed. by Marie-Hélène Girard (Paris: Séguier, 1994)
Exposition de 1859, ed. by Wolfgang Drost (Heidelberg: Carl Winter, 1992)
Fusains et eaux-fortes (Paris: Charpentier, 1880)
Les Grotesques (Paris: Desessart, 1844)
Histoire de l'art dramatique en France depuis vingt-cinq ans, 6 vols (Paris: Hetzel, 1858–59)
Histoire du romantisme (Paris: Charpentier, 1874)
Italia (Paris: Lecou, 1852)
Œuvres, ed. by Paolo Tortonese (Paris: Coll. Bouquins, 1995)
Œuvres de Gavarni (Paris: Hetzel, 1846)
Paris et les Parisiens (Paris: La Boîte à Documents, 1996)
Poésies complètes, ed. by René Jasinski, 3 vols (Paris: Nizet, 1970)
Portraits contemporains (Paris: Charpentier, 1874)
Romans, contes et nouvelles, dir. by Pierre Laubriet, 2 vols (Paris: Gallimard, Bibliothèque de la Pléiade, 2002)
Salon de 1847 (Paris: Hetzel, 1847)
Souvenirs de théâtre, d'art et de critique (Paris: Charpentier, 1883)
Tableaux à la plume (Paris: Charpentier, 1880)
Voyage en Espagne suivi de Espana, ed. by Patrick Berthier (Paris: Gallimard, Coll. Folio, 1981)

(b) Articles

'Arts: buste de Victor Hugo', *Mercure de France au XIXe siècle*, 35 (October 1831), 95–96
'Le Musée Colbert', *Le Cabinet de lecture*, 29 May 1832, pp. 12–14
'De l'originalité en France', *Le Cabinet de lecture*, 14 June 1832, p. 11
'Examen critique des écoles de Rome et de Paris en 1832', *La France littéraire*, 4 (October 1832), 74–86

'Salon de 1833', *La France littéraire*, 6 (March 1833), 139–66

'Salon de 1834', *La France industrielle*, April 1834, 17–22

'Salon de 1836', *Ariel: journal du monde élégant*, 5 March, 9 March, 19 March, 2 April, 15 April, 20 April, 30 April 1836

'Exposition de 1836, premier article: Sculpture religieuse', *Le Cabinet de lecture*, 19 March 1836; 'Exposition de 1836, deuxième article: Sculpture historique et de genre', 9 April 1836

'Peintures de la Chambre des Députés: Salle du Trône', *La Presse*, 26 August 1836

'Envois de Rome', *La Presse*, 30 August 1836

'Concours pour le prix de sculpture et de peinture', *La Presse*, 27 September 1836

'Nouvelles statues des Tuileries', *La Presse*, 11 October 1836

'Des beaux-arts et autres', *Le Figaro*, 16 October 1836

'Statues du Jardin des Tuileries', *La Presse*, 18 October 1836

'Projets d'embellissements pour les Champs-Élysées et la Place de la Concorde', *La Presse*, 25 October 1836

'Progrès dans les arts', *Le Figaro*, 27 October 1836

'Les Beaux-Arts et l'industrie', *Le Figaro*, 31 October 1836

'Travaux de Notre-Dame-de-Lorette', *La Presse*, 1 November 1836

'Le Passage de Thermidon', *La Presse*, 8 November 1836

'Chronique des beaux-arts', *Le Figaro*, 11 November 1836

'Illustrations pour Notre-Dame de Paris et le théâtre de M. Victor Hugo', *La Presse*, 15 November 1836

'De la composition en peinture', *La Presse*, 22 November 1836

'Les Rubens de la cathédrale d'Anvers', *La Presse*, 29 November 1836

'Beaux-Arts' [on portraiture], *La Presse*, 6 December 1836

'Chronique', *Le Figaro*, 7 December 1836

'De l'application de l'art à la vie usuelle', *La Presse*, 13 December 1836

'Chronique' [Travaux de Notre-Dame-de-Lorette], *Le Figaro*, 16 December 1836 (see above, *La Presse*, 1 November 1836)

'Applications de l'art', *La Presse*, 27 December 1836

'Sculpteurs contemporains: M. Antonin Moine', *La Charte de 1830*, 2 February 1837 (repr. *Fusains et eaux-fortes*, pp. 55–65)

'Salon de 1837', *La Presse* [16 articles, 1 March — 1 May 1837]

'Vente de la Galerie de l'Élysée-Bourbon', *La Charte de 1830*, 8 May 1837 (repr. *Fusains et eaux-fortes*, pp. 109–19)

'Copie du *Jugement dernier* de Michel Ange', *La Charte de 1830*, 17 May 1837 (repr. *Fusains et eaux-fortes*, pp. 121–31)

'Statues de Michel-Ange', *La Charte de 1830*, 22 May 1837 (repr. *Fusains et eaux-fortes*, pp. 133–43)

'Les Concours de 1837, I: Concours pour le Grand Prix de Paysage Historique', *La Charte de 1830*, 10 September 1837 (repr. *Fusains et eaux-fortes*, pp. 155–63)

'Les Concours de 1837, II: Concours de sculpture', *La Charte de 1830*, 23 September 1837 (repr. *Fusains et eaux-fortes*, pp. 164–75)

'Collection de tableaux espagnols', *La Presse*, 24 September 1837

'Le Chemin de fer', *La Charte de 1830*, 15 October 1837 (repr. *Fusains et eaux-fortes*, pp. 185–95)

'Illustrations de *Paul et Virginie*', *La Charte de 1830*, 11 December 1837 (repr. *Fusains et eaux-fortes*, pp. 197–205)

'Salon de 1838', *La Presse*, 16 March 1838

'Salon de 1840. Sculpture. VIII', *La Presse*, 3 April 1840

'Salon de 1841', *Revue de Paris*, 18 April 1841, pp. 153–71; 25 April 1841, pp. 255–70

'Revue des arts', *Revue universelle*, May 1841, pp. 384–94

'Salon de 1842', *Cabinet de l'amateur et de l'antiquaire* (1842), 119–28

'Salon de 1846', *La Presse*, 2 April 1846

'Exposition de 1847', *La Presse*, 31 March 1847

'Salon de 1847, *La Presse* [11 articles, 30 March–10 April 1847]

'Une visite à M. Ingres', *La Presse*, 27 June 1847

'Du beau dans l'art: *Réflexions et menus propos d'un peintre genevois*, ouvrage posthume de M.Töpffer', *RDM*, 1 September 1847 (repr. *L'Art moderne*, pp. 129–66)

'Chronique des arts: copies de Raphaël, par les frères Balze, exposées au Panthéon', *La Presse*, 20 November 1847

'Troisième exposition de l'Association des Artistes, Bazar Bonne Nouvelle', *La Presse*, 13 February 1848

'Théâtre de la Nation (Opéra): *La Muette de Portici*', *La Presse*, 6 March 1848 (repr. *Histoire de l'art dramatique*, v (1859), 239–41)

'Théâtre de la République (Français): *Rentrée de mademoiselle Rachel — La Marseillaise*', *La Presse*, 20 March 1848 (repr. *Histoire de l'art dramatique*, v (1859), 241–44)

'Salon de 1848', *La Presse* [14 articles, 22 April — 10 May 1848]: 1, 22 April; 2, 23 April; 3, 25 April; 4, 26 April; 5, 27 April; 6, 28 April; 7, 29 April; 8, 2 May; 9, 3 May; 10, 5 May; 11, 6 May; 12, 7 May; 13, 9 May; 14, 10 May

'L'Art en 1848', *L'Artiste*, 15 May 1848, pp. 113–15

'Concours pour la figure de la République', *La Presse*, 21 May 1848

'École Nationale des Beaux-Arts: symbolisme de la République', *L'Artiste*, 15 June 1848, pp. 160–61) [reprise of the first 14 paragraphs of 'Concours pour la figure de la République']

'Marilhat', *RDM*, 1 July 1848, pp. 56–75 (repr. *L'Art moderne*, pp. 95–128)

'La Nyssia de Pradier', *L'Artiste*, 1 July 1848, pp. 185–86

'La Bacchante de Clésinger', *L'Artiste*, 15 July 1848, pp. 185–86

'La République de l'avenir', *Le Journal*, 28 July 1848 (repr. *Fusains et eaux-fortes*, pp. 227–38)

'L'Atelier de M. Ingres en 1848', *L'Événement*, 2 August 1848 (repr. *Fusains et eaux-fortes*, pp. 239–50)

'Plastique de la civilisation: du beau antique et du beau moderne', *L'Événement*, 8 August 1848 (repr. *Souvenirs de théâtre, d'art et de critique*, pp. 197–204)

'Le Panthéon: peintures murales, par Chenavard', *La Presse* [7 articles, 5–11 September 1848] (repr. *L'Art moderne*, pp. 1–94)

'A propos de ballons', *Le Journal*, 25 September 1848 (repr. *Fusains et eaux-fortes*, pp. 251–64)

'De l'obésité en littérature', *L'Artiste*, 1 October 1848, pp. 49–50

'Voyage dans le bleu', *L'Artiste*, 1 November 1848, pp. 72–74

'École Nationale des Beaux-Arts: exposition des figures du concours pour la République: envois de Rome', *La Presse*, 5 December 1848

'Vaudeville: *La Propriété c'est le vol*', *La Presse*, 11 December 1848 (repr. *Histoire de l'art dramatique*, vi (1859), 22–30)

'Palais du Quai d'Orsay: peintures murales de M. Théodore Chassériau', *La Presse*, 12 December 1848

'Le Musée ancien', *La Presse*, 10 February 1849 (repr. *Tableaux à la plume*, pp. 1–30)

'La Galerie française, I', *La Presse*, 13 February 1849 (repr. *Tableaux à la plume*, pp. 30–46)

'La Galerie française, II', *La Presse*, 17 February 1849 (repr. *Tableaux à la plume*, pp. 46–64)

'En Chine', *La Presse*, 25 June 1849

'Salon de 1849', *La Presse* [12 articles, 26 July — 11 August 1849]: 1, 26 July; 2, 27 July; 3, 28 July; 4, 31 July; 5, 1 August; 6, 3 August; 7, 4 August; 8, 7 August; 9, 8 August; 10, 9 August; 11, 10 August; 12, 11 August

'Manufactures nationales de Beauvais et des Gobelins', *La Presse*, 10 September 1849

'Fonte de la Sapho de Pradier', *La Presse*, 9 December 1849

'Exposition des manufactures nationales de porcelaine, vitraux et émaux de Sèvres, de tapis et de tapisseries des Gobelins et de Beauvais, faite au Palais-National', *La Presse*, 1 June 1850

'Le Musée des Antiques', *La Presse*, 27 July 1850 (repr. *Tableaux à la plume*, pp. 65–79)

'Le Musée français de la Renaissance', *La Presse*, 24 August 1850 (repr. *Tableaux à la plume*, pp. 80–92)

'Le Musée espagnol, I', *La Presse*, 27 August 1850 (repr. *Tableaux à la plume*, pp. 93–103)

'Le Musée espagnol, II', *La Presse*, 28 August 1850 (repr. *Tableaux à la plume*, pp. 103–14)

'La Galerie du Luxembourg', *La Presse*, 2 September 1850 (repr. *Tableaux à la plume*, pp. 115–30)

'Le Musée de Tours', *La Presse*, 7 September 1850 (repr. *Tableaux à la plume*, pp. 131–43)

'Salon de 1850–51' *La Presse* [23 articles, 5 February — 7 May 1851]: 1, 5 February; 2, 6 February; 3, 14 February; 4, 15 February; 5, 21 February; 6, 1 March; 7, 8 March; 8, 15 March; 9, 22 March; 10, 28 March; 11, 5 April; 12, 8 April; 13, 9 April; 14, 10 April; 15, 11 April; 16, 19 April; 17, 23 April; 18, 24 April; 19, 25 April; 20, 1 May; 21, 2 May; 22, 6 May; 23, 7 May

'Salon de 1850–51: distribution des récompenses', *L'Artiste*, 15 May 1851, pp. 116–17 [repr., with some variants, of article 23, 7 May]

'Photographie: *L'Italie monumentale*, par M. Eugène Piot', *La Presse*, 28 July 1851

'La Galerie française au Musée du Louvre, I', *L'Artiste*, 1 August 1851, pp. 6–9 [see above, *La Presse*, 13 February 1849]

'La Galerie française au Musée du Louvre, II', *L'Artiste*, 15 August 1851, pp. 17–20 [see above, *La Presse*, 17 February 1849]

'Le Palais de Cristal: les barbares' [on the Indian pavilion], *La Presse*: I, 5 September 1851; II, 7 September 1851; III, 11 September 1851

'Études sur Rembrandt', *L'Artiste*, 15 September 1851, pp. 50–53

'La Statue de Marceau par M. Auguste Préault', *La Presse*, 15 September 1851

'Liminaire', *Revue de Paris* (October 1851), 5–11

'Ceux qui seront connus', *L'Illustration*, 8 June 1872

(2) Other primary sources

ANON., *De l'exposition et du jury* (Paris: F. Sartorius, 1848)

ANON., 'Le Salon de 1848', *Revue nationale*, 23 March 1848, pp. 345–46

ANON., 'Concours: figure symbolique de la République', *L'Artiste*, 30 April 1848, pp. 108–09

ANON. [letter on the competition for the figure of the Republic], *L'Artiste*, 30 April 1848, p. 112

ANON. [letter on the four inspectors of provincial museums], *L'Artiste*, 1 June 1848, p. 152

ANON. [on poverty in the studios and on closure of the Salon of 1848], 'Revue de la quinzaine: beaux-arts', *L'Artiste*, 15 June 1848, p. 172

ANON. [response to letter on the inspectors of provincial museums], *L'Artiste*, 1 July 1848, pp. 190–91

ANON. [petition of the Société libre des Beaux-Arts], *L'Artiste*, 15 July 1848, p. 208

ANON., 'Courrier de Paris' [on Ingres's studio exhibition, August 1848], *L'Illustration*, 12 August 1848, p. 363

ANON. [on Ingres's *Vénus anadyomène*], *L'Artiste*, 15 August 1848, p. 239

ANON. [on the location of the Salon of 1849], *L'Artiste*, 1 November 1848, p. 83

ANON. [on the date of the Salon of 1849], *L'Artiste*, 15 January 1849, p. 164

Anon., 'Salon de 1849', *La Tribune des artistes*, 1 (1849), 5–6, 17–23, 33–36, 65–68, 81–85, 97–102

Anon. [on unsuitability of the Tuileries Palace for the Salon], *Le Moniteur universel*, 17 January 1850

Anon. [on the Louvre's refurbished rooms for sculpture], *L'Artiste*, 1 February 1850, p. 108

Artiste qui n'a pas exposé, Un, 'Salon de 1849: critique de la critique', *L'Artiste*, 15 September 1849, pp. 177–80

B., Ch. de, 'Exposition des ouvrages d'art aux Tuileries en 1849', *L'Union*, 23 June, 24 June, 26 June 1849

Balzac, Honoré de, *La Comédie humaine*, ed. by Pierre-Georges Castex, 12 vols (Paris: Gallimard, Bibliothèque de la Pléiade, 1976–81)

Banville, Théodore de, 'Salon de 1848', *La Sylphide*, 10 March 1848, pp. 113–16; 30 March 1848, pp. 148–51; 10 May 1848, pp. 220–23

Barbier, Auguste, *Iambes et poèmes*, 5th edn (Paris: Masgana, 1845)

Baudelaire, Charles, *Lettres inédites aux siens*, ed. by Philippe Auserve (Paris: Grasset, 1966)

—— *Œuvres complètes*, ed. by Claude Pichois, 2 vols (Paris: Gallimard, Bibliothèque de la Pléiade, 1976)

—— *Salon de 1846*, ed. by David Kelley (Oxford: Clarendon Press, 1975)

Charles Baudelaire–Théophile Gautier: Correspondances esthétiques sur Delacroix, ed. by Stéphane Guégan and Karine Marie (Paris: Éditions Olbia, 1998)

Blanc, Charles, *Histoire des peintres français au dix-neuvième siècle* (Paris: Cauville, 1845)

—— 'Rapport au citoyen ministre, sur les arts du dessin et sur leur avenir dans la République', *Le Moniteur universel*, 10 October 1848, p. 2763

Blanc, Louis, *Histoire de la Révolution française* (Paris: Langlois and Leclercq, 1847)

Boissard [de Boisdenier], Fernand, 'De la condition des artistes et des moyens de l'améliorer, I', *L'Artiste*, 1 February 1850, pp. 100–02; II, 1 March 1850, pp. 136–39

Carrière, C. de, 'Sur un tableau de M. Ingres', *L'Artiste*, 19 March 1848, pp. 40–42

Champfleury [Jean Husson, *dit*], *Œuvres posthumes: Salons 1846–1851* (Paris: Alphonse Lemerre, 1894)

Chennevières, Philippe de, *Lettres sur l'art français en 1850* (Argentan: Barbier, 1851)

—— *Souvenirs d'un Directeur des Beaux-Arts* (Paris: Arthena, 1979)

—— 'Musée de Cherbourg', *L'Artiste*, 26 December 1847, pp. 115–18

—— 'Le Musée d'Amiens', *L'Artiste*, 15 December 1849, pp. 55–57

Clément de Ris, Louis, *De l'oppression dans les arts et de la composition d'un nouveau jury d'examen pour les ouvrages présentés au salon de 1847* (Paris: Masgana, 1847)

—— *Les Musées de province*, 2 vols (Paris: [n. pub.], 1859)

—— 'Salon de 1847: le jury', *L'Artiste*, 14 March 1847, pp. 17–18

—— 'Les Refus du jury', 27 June 1847, pp. 218–21

—— 'Le Musée de Tours', *L'Artiste*, 17 December 1847, pp. 103–06

—— 'Troisième exposition de l'Association des artistes', *L'Artiste*, 23 January 1848, pp. 177–80

—— 'Remarques sur le Musée du Louvre', *L'Artiste*, 20 February 1848, pp. 248–50

—— 'Le Musée du Louvre', *L'Artiste*, 19 March 1848, pp. 29–30

—— 'L'École française au Louvre', *L'Artiste*, 26 March 1848, pp. 39–40

—— 'Salon de 1848, III', *L'Artiste*, 26 March 1848, pp. 35–36; IV, 2 April, pp. 58–60; V, 9 April, pp. 68–70; VI, 16 April, pp. 86–89; VII, 30 April 1848, pp. 102–04 [for articles I and II, see Houssaye, Arsène]

—— 'Le Musée du Luxembourg', *L'Artiste*, 9 April 1848, pp. 72–74

—— [as C.R.] 'Distribution de prix aux artistes: Salon de 1848', *L'Artiste*, 1 September 1848, p. 15

——— 'Nouvelle Galerie française du Musée du Louvre', *L'Artiste*, 1 December 1848, pp. 110–12

——— 'Musée du Louvre: Grande galerie', *L'Artiste*, 15 January 1849, pp. 149–52

——— 'Le Musée de Rouen', *L'Artiste*, 15 June 1849, pp. 90–94

——— 'Le Musée de Rennes', *L'Artiste*, 15 August 1849, pp. 150–53

——— 'Le Musée de Nantes', *L'Artiste*, 15 September 1849, pp. 180–85

——— 'Des Musées de province, I', *L'Artiste*, 1 November 1849, pp. 6–8; II, 15 November 1849, pp. 22–25; III, 1 December 1849, pp. 38–41

——— 'Mouvement des arts', *L'Artiste*, 15 November 1850, pp. 187–90

——— 'Le Salon de 1851, I', *L'Artiste*, 1 January 1851, pp. 225–26; II, 16 January, pp. 241–44; III, 1 February, pp. 3–9; IV, 15 February, pp. 17–21; V, 1 March, pp. 33–37; VI, 15 March, pp. 49–52; VII, 15 April 1851, pp. 81–83

——— 'Musée de Luxembourg', *L'Artiste*, 1 July 1851, pp. 161–63

DAVID D'ANGERS [Pierre-Jean David *dit*], 'Le Jury', *L'Artiste*, 11 April 1847, pp. 92–94

DELACROIX, EUGÈNE, *Journal 1822–1863*, ed. by André Joubin, rev. by Régis Labourdette (Paris: Plon, 1996)

——— *Eugène Delacroix, Nouvelles lettres*, ed. by Lee Johnson and Michèle Hannoosh (Bordeaux: William Blake, 2000)

DELAUNAY, A. H., 'Lettres sur le Salon de 1847, III', *Journal des artistes*, 28 March 1847, pp. 121–25

——— [on Chenavard's nomination for the Panthéon project], *Journal des artistes*, 21 April 1848, pp. 93–96

DELÉCLUZE, ÉTIENNE-JEAN, *Exposition des artistes vivants, 1850* (Paris: Comon, 1851)

——— 'Salon de 1848', *Journal des débats*, 21 March, 5 April, 16 April, 31 May 1848

——— 'Exposition des ouvrages d'art aux Tuileries en 1849', *Journal des débats*, 25 June, 5 July, 17 July, 31 July, 22 August 1849

DESNOYER, LOUIS, 'Le Salon', *Le Siècle*, 9 February 1851, 13 March 1851

DESPLACES, AUGUSTE, *Galerie des poëtes vivans* (Paris: Didier, 1847)

DU BOYS, ALBERT, 'Rapport fait au nom de la commission d'enquête nommée par la Société française pour la conservation des monuments', *L'Ami de la religion*, 4 March 1851, pp. 530–32

DU CAMP, MAXIME, *Souvenirs littéraires*, 2 vols (Paris: Hachette, 1882–83)

ÉMERIC-DAVID, TOUSSAINT-BERNARD, *Recherches sur l'art statuaire, considéré chez les anciens et les modernes* (Paris: Vve Nyon aîné, an XIII-1805)

ESQUIROS, ALPHONSE, *Histoire des Montagnards* (Paris: Lecou, 1847)

Explication des ouvrages de peinture, sculpture, architecture, gravure et lithographie des artistes vivants, exposés au Musée national du Louvre le 15 mars 1848 (Paris: Vinchon, 1848)

Explication des ouvrages de peinture, sculpture, architecture, gravure et lithographie des artistes vivants, exposés au Palais des Tuileries le 15 juin 1849 (Paris: Vinchon, 1849)

Explication des ouvrages de peinture, sculpture, architecture, gravure et lithographie des artistes vivants, exposés au Palais National le 30 décembre 1850 (Paris: Vinchon, 1850)

FEU DIDEROT, 'Salon de 1849, Préface', *L'Artiste*, 15 June 1849, pp. 81–85; I, 1 July, pp. 97–100; II, 15 July, pp. 113–17; III, 1 August, pp. 129–32; IV, 15 August, pp. 145–50; V, 1 September 1849, pp. 161–63

GEOFROY, L. DE [= L.G. = L. DE GEFFROY = LAGENEVAIS, F. DE?], 'Vénus anadyomène: portrait de Mme de Rothschild, par M. Ingres', *RDM*, 1 August 1848, pp. 441–49

GIRARDIN, DELPHINE DE, *Lettres parisiennes du vicomte de Launay par Madame de Girardin*, ed. by Anne Martin-Fugier, 2 vols (Paris: Mercure de France, 2004)

GIRARDIN, ÉMILE DE [letter to Gautier on the Salon jury], *La Presse*, 30 March 1847

——— 'Confiance! Confiance!', *La Presse*, 25 February 1848

——— 'Éditorial', *La Presse*, 7 August 1848

GUINOT, EUGÈNE, 'Revue de Paris' [on Ingres's studio exhibition, August 1848], *Le Siècle*, 7 August 1848

H[AUSSARD], PR[OSPER], 'Salon de 1848', *Le National*, 23 March, 2 April, 14 April, 20 May, 15 June 1848

—— 'Salon de 1849', *Le National*, 26 June, 10 July, 7 August, 28 August, 4 September, 18 September 1849

HAUSSARD, PROSPER, 'Revue des beaux-arts' [Musée Espagnol, Musée Standish], *Le National*, 26 November 1850

—— 'Les Peintures murales de M. P. Chenavard, au Panthéon', *Le National*, 9 March 1851

HOUSSAYE, ARSÈNE, 'Salon de 1848, I', *L'Artiste*, 12 March 1848, pp. 1–4; II, 19 March 1848, pp. 17–20

—— 'Revue de la semaine', *L'Artiste*, 9 April 1848, pp. 75–76

—— 'Les Musées de province', *L'Artiste*, 16 April 1848, pp. 89–90

—— 'République des arts: Le Panthéon – Chenavard – Lettre au ministre', *L'Artiste*, 30 April 1848, pp. 106–08

Lettres d'Ingres à Gilibert, ed. by Marie-Jeanne and Daniel Ternois (Paris: Champion, 2005)

Lettres d'Ingres à Marcotte d'Argenteuil, ed. by Daniel Ternois (Nogent-le-Roi: Librairie Jacques Laget, 1999)

ISNARD, CHARLES, 'De la peinture la veille et le lendemain de la République', *L'Artiste*, 1 October 1848, pp. 46–49

—— 'Les Concours et les envois de Rome à l'école des Beaux-Arts', *L'Artiste*, 15 October 1848, pp. 59–61

L., 'M. Ingres: Portrait de Mme La Baronne de Rothschild, Vénus sortant de la mer', *Le Constitutionnel*, 18 August 1848

LAGENEVAIS, F. DE [PSEUD. FRÉDÉRIC DE MERCEY], 'M. Ingres', *RDM*, 1 August 1846, pp. 514–41

—— 'Le Salon de 1848', *RDM*, 15 April 1848, pp. 283–99; 15 May 1848, pp. 591–606

—— 'Le Salon de 1849', *RDM*, 15 August 1849, pp. 559–93

LAMARTINE, ALPHONSE DE, *Histoire des Girondins* (Paris: Furne, 1847)

LORD PILGRIM, 'Mouvement des arts', *L'Artiste*, 15 December 1848, pp. 125–27

—— 'Mouvement des arts', *L'Artiste*, 1 January 1849, pp. 146–48

—— 'Mouvement des arts', *L'Artiste*, 15 February 1849, pp. 188–91

—— 'Mouvement des arts', *L'Artiste*, 1 April 1849, pp. 14–15

—— 'Mouvement des arts', *L'Artiste*, 15 April 1849, pp. 26–27

—— 'Mouvement des arts', *L'Artiste*, 1 May 1849, pp. 33–36

M..., 'Histoire de l'oppression dans les arts', *L'Artiste*, 20 February 1848, pp. 243–48

MALITOURNE, PIERRE, 'La Sculpture en 1848', *L'Artiste*, 1 June 1848, pp. 141–45

—— 'La Sculpture en 1849', *L'Artiste*, 1 October 1849, pp. 193–95; 15 October 1849, pp. 209–11

—— 'Salon de 1851: sculpture', *L'Artiste*, 15 April 1851, pp. 83–87

MALLARMÉ, *Œuvres complètes*, ed. by Bertrand Marchal, 2 vols (Paris: Gallimard, Bibliothèque de la Pléiade, 1998–2003)

MANTZ, PAUL, 'Les Cérémonies de la République', *L'Artiste*, 12 March 1848, pp. 7–9

—— 'Le Musée de Toulouse', *L'Artiste*, 15 August 1848, pp. 225–29

—— 'Les Salles du Louvre', *L'Artiste*, 15 June 1851, pp. 145–48

MERCEY, FRÉDÉRIC DE, see de Lagenevais, F. de

MICHELET, JULES, *Histoire de la révolution française*, 7 vols (Paris: Chamerot, 1847–53)

P.M. [PAUL MANTZ?], 'Assemblée générale des peintres à l'Institut', *L'Artiste*, 15 January 1849, pp. 163–64

P[ILLET], FAB[IEN], 'Exposition de 1849, au Palais des Tuileries', *Le Moniteur universel*, 17 June 1849, pp. 2088–89; 21 June, p. 2115; 29 June, pp. 2198–99; 4 July, p. 2235; 10 July, pp. 2302–03; 19 July, pp. 2386–87; 24 July, pp. 2443–44; 31 July, pp. 2532–33; 7 August, pp. 2603–04; 12 August 1849, p. 2687

PLANCHE, GUSTAVE, *Études sur l'école française*, 2 vols (Paris: Michel Lévy, 1855)

—— *Portraits d'artistes, peintres et sculpteurs* (Paris: Michel Lévy, 1853)

—— 'Les Cartons de M. P. Chenavard', *RDM* (January 1852), 363–77

PRADIER, JAMES, *Correspondance*, ed. by Douglas Siler, 3 vols (Geneva: Droz, 1984–88)

SAINT JOHN, BAYLE, *The Louvre, or Biography of a Museum* (London: Chapman Hall, 1855)

THORÉ, THÉOPHILE, *Salons de 1844, 1845, 1846, 1847, 1848* (Paris: Librairie internationale, 1868)

TOUSSENEL, ALPHONSE, *L'Esprit des bêtes* (Paris: Librairie sociétaire, 1847)

VALENCIENNES, PIERRE-HENRI DE, *Élémens de perspective pratique à l'usage des artistes* (Paris: Desenne, an VIII-1799)

VALETTE, E. DE [letter from Paul Chenavard], *L'Ami de la religion*, 15 March 1851, pp. 604–05

VAPEREAU, GUSTAVE, *Dictionnaire universel des contemporains*, 4th edn (Paris: Hachette, 1870)

ZOLA, ÉMILE, *Documents littéraires, études et portraits* (Paris: Charpentier, 1881)

Secondary Sources

Note: An asterisk denotes a catalogue of an exhibition, whose location and date follow the title of the publication. In the case of multiple international locations and dates, only those of the French exhibition are given; in the case of multiple French locations, only the first is given.

(1) On Gautier

AMELINCKX, FRANS, 'Théophile Gautier et Marilhat: peintures, textes et contextes', in *Théophile Gautier: l'art et l'artiste* (= *BSTG*, 4.1–2 (1983)), I, 1–9

AURAIX-JONCHIÈRE, PASCALE, '*Ekphrasis* et mythologie dans la *Toison d'or* de Théophile Gautier (1839): la Madeleine prétexte', in *Écrire la peinture: entre XVIIIe et XIXe siècles*, ed. by Pascale Auraix-Jonchière (Clermont-Ferrand: Presses universitaires Blaise Pascal, 2003), pp. 451–63

BANN, STEPHEN, 'Entre philosophie et critique: Victor Cousin, Théophile Gautier et l'art pour l'art', in *L'Invention de la critique d'art*, ed. by Pierre-Henry Frangne et Jean-Marc Poinsot (Presses Universitaires de Rennes, 2002), pp. 137–44

BERTHIER, PATRICK, 'Gautier journaliste', in *Relire Théophile Gautier: le plaisir du texte*, ed. by Freeman G. Henry (Amsterdam and Atlanta, GA: Rodopi, 1998), pp. 49–70

—— 'L'Humour chez Théophile Gautier critique d'art 1833–1837', *BSTG*, 23 (2001), 153–63

—— 'Théophile Gautier journaliste: de quelques pratiques d'écriture', in *Presse et plumes*, ed. by Marie-Eve Thérenty and Alain Vaillant (Paris: Nouveau monde Éditions, 2004), pp. 443–55

COGMAN, PETER, 'Le Triangle de la mort: du *Roi Candaule* à *Jettatura*', *BSTG*, 18 (1996), 239–54

DOUPHIS, PIERRE-OLIVIER, 'Le Poète et l'artiste-philosophe: une collaboration retrouvée entre Gautier et Chenavard en 1848', *BSTG*, 23 (2001), 21–36

DROST, WOLFGANG, 'Rodolphe Töpffer et Charles Baudelaire esthéticiens — affinités et influences — et le rôle de Théophile Gautier', in *Propos töpfferiens*, ed. by Danielle Buyssens and others (Geneva: Société d'études töpfferiennes, 1998), pp. 173–88

—— 'Der Blick der Frau auf den Voyeur: zu Gautiers Roi Candaule', in *Die Ästhetik des Voyeur/L'Esthétique du voyeur*, ed. by Lydia Hartl and others (Heidelberg: Winter, 2003), pp. 135–45

—— 'Pour une réévaluation de la critique d'art de Gautier', *Cahiers de l'Association Internationale des Études françaises*, 55 (2003), 401–21

—— 'Le Sens de l'antique et le sentiment moderne dans la critique d'art de Théophile Gautier', in *Panorama Gautier*, ed. by Sarga Moussa and Paolo Tortonese (= *Revue des Sciences Humaines*, no. 277 (2005)), 135–53

—— 'Les Poètes critiques d'art devant la facture en liberté', in *Les Pas d'Orphée: scritti in onore di Mario Richter* (Padua: Unipress, 2005), pp. 191–201

—— and MARIE-HÉLÈNE GIRARD, eds, *Gautier et l'Allemagne* (Siegen: UniverSi-Verlag, 2005)

EIGELDINGER, MARC, 'L'Inscription de l'œuvre plastique dans les récits de Gautier', in *Théophile Gautier: l'art et les artistes* (= *BSTG*, 4.1–2 (1983)), II, 297–309

GIRARD, MARIE-HÉLÈNE, 'Gautier et les sculpteurs romantiques', *48/14: la revue du Musée d'Orsay*, 7 (Autumn 1997), 51–57

GUÉGAN, STÉPHANE, 'Le Théâtre idéal de Théophile Gautier', *Regards d'écrivains au Musée d'Orsay* (Paris: RMN, 1992), 8–14

—— 'Gautier et l'art pour l'art 1830–1848', *48/14: la revue du Musée d'Orsay*, 5 (1993), 63–68

—— 'Le Regard de Gygès', in *Théophile Gautier: la critique en liberté* (Paris: RMN, 1997), pp. 17–37

GUILLAUMIE-REICHER, GILBERTE, *Théophile Gautier et l'Espagne* (Paris: Hachette, 1935)

HAMBLY, P. S., 'Théophile Gautier et le fouriérisme', *Australian Journal of French Studies*, 11 (1974), 210–36

HAMRICK, CASSANDRA, 'The *feuilleton artistique*: On the Margins of Nineteenth-Century Texts (with Théophile Gautier)', in *On the Margins*, ed. by Freeman G. Henry, French Literature Series, 20 (Amsterdam and Atlanta, GA: Rodopi, 1993), pp. 71–85

—— '"L'Art robuste seul a l'éternité": Gautier et la sculpture romantique', *BSTG*, 18 (1996), 439–67

—— 'Repression and Non-Expression: The Case of Gautier', in *Repression and Expression: Literary and Social Coding in Nineteenth-Century France*, ed. by Carrol F. Coates (New York: Peter Lang, 1996), pp. 247–58

—— 'Gautier et l'anarchie de l'art', in *Relire Théophile Gautier: le plaisir du texte*, ed. by Freeman G. Henry (Amsterdam and Atlanta, GA: Rodopi, 1998), pp. 91–118

HENRY, FREEMAN G., ed., *Relire Théophile Gautier: le plaisir du texte* (Amsterdam and Atlanta, GA: Rodopi, 1998)

JASINSKI, RENÉ, *Les Années romantiques de Gautier* (Paris: Vuibert, 1929)

—— 'Théophile Gautier et la politique', in *Actes du Quatrième Congrès international d'histoire littéraire moderne* (Paris: Boivin, 1948), pp. 119–33 (repr. René Jasinski, *A travers le XIXe siècle* (Paris: Minard, 1975), pp. 229–48)

JUNOD, PHILIPPE, 'Théophile Gautier ou les paradoxes de la modernité', *Histoire de l'art*, 50 (June 2002), 49–54

KEARNS, JAMES, 'Gautier et la peinture allemande à L'Exposition Universelle de 1855', in *Gautier et l'Allemagne*, ed. by Wolfgang Drost and Marie-Hélène Girard (Siegen: UniverSi-Verlag, 2005), pp. 217–39

—— 'From Store to Museum: The Reorganisation of the Louvre's Painting Collections in 1848', *MLR*, 102 (2007), 60–76

LACOSTE, CLAUDINE, 'Théophile Gautier juge de lui-même', *BSTG*, 11 (1989), 156–60

LACOSTE-VEYSSEYRE, CLAUDINE, *La Critique d'art de Théophile Gautier* (Montpellier: Université Paul Valéry, 1985)

LAVAUD, MARTINE, *Théophile Gautier militant du romantisme* (Paris: Champion, 2001)

LEDUC-ADINE, JEAN-PIERRE, 'Théophile Gautier et le réalisme: Courbet, Millet, Manet', *Théophile Gautier: l'art et l'artiste* (= *BSTG*, 4.1–2 (1983)), I, 21–33

MATORÉ, GEORGES, *Le Vocabulaire et la société sous Louis-Philippe* (Geneva: Slatkine, 1967)

MOULINAT, FRANCIS, 'Théophile Gautier et Gustave Courbet', *Les Amis de Gustave Courbet*, 83 (1990) [unpaginated], pp. [5–31], repr. *BSTG*, 11 (1989), 85–107

—— 'Gautier et l'ekphrasis', *BSTG*, 21 (1999), 133–47

—— 'Gautier, Pradier, hellénisme', *BSTG*, 24 (2002), 45–52

RICHER, JEAN, *Une collaboration inconnue: la description du Panthéon de Paul Chenavard par Gautier et Nerval*, Archives des lettres modernes, 48 (Paris: Minard, 1963)

ROSSITER, ANDREW, 'Gautier et le "Livre du peuple" de Lamennais', *Histoire politique et histoire des idées (XVIIIe–XIXe siècles)* (Paris: Les Belles Lettres, 1976), pp. 181–207

RUBY, FRANCK, 'Théophile Gautier et la question de l'Art pour l'Art', *BSTG*, 20 (1998), 3–13

SCHICK, CONSTANCE GOSSELIN, 'Le Donner à voir de Gautier ou pour un Candaule', in *Relire Théophile Gautier: le plaisir du texte*, ed. by Freeman G. Henry (Amsterdam and Atlanta, GA: Rodopi, 1998), pp. 243–63

SENNEVILLE, GÉRARD DE, *Théophile Gautier* (Paris: Fayard, 2004)

SENNINGER, CLAUDE-MARIE, *Théophile Gautier, une vie, une œuvre* (Paris: SEDES, 1994)

SNELL, ROBERT, *Théophile Gautier: A Romantic Critic in the Visual Arts* (Oxford: Clarendon Press, 1982)

SPENCER, MICHAEL CLIFFORD, *The Art Criticism of Théophile Gautier* (Geneva: Droz, 1969)

SPOELBERCH DE LOVENJOUL, CHARLES VTE DE, *Histoire des œuvres de Théophile Gautier* (Paris: Charpentier, 1887; repr. Geneva: Slatkine, 1968)

★*Théophile Gautier: la critique en liberté*, Paris: Musée d'Orsay, 1997; ed. by Stéphane Guégan (Paris: RMN, 1997)

Théophile Gautier: l'art et l'artiste, Actes du colloque international, Montpellier, Université Paul Valéry, septembre 1982 (= *BSTG*, 4.1–2 (1983))

THOME-JARROUCHÉ, LISETTE, 'L'Art descriptif de Théophile Gautier: la description d'un critique d'art', *BSTG*, 20 (1998), 125–41

TORTONESE, PAOLO, 'Gautier classique, Gautier romantique: considérations en marge de l'exposition Gautier au musée d'Orsay', *BSTG*, 19 (1997), 75–93

VOISIN, MARCEL, 'Gautier et la politique', *BSTG*, 15 (1993), 323–39

—— 'La Pensée de Théophile Gautier', in *Relire Théophile Gautier: le plaisir du texte*, ed. by Freeman G. Henry (Amsterdam and Atlanta, GA: Rodopi, 1998), pp. 73–89

WHYTE, PETER, 'État présent des études sur Théophile Gautier', in *Relire Théophile Gautier: le plaisir du texte*, ed. by Freeman G. Henry (Amsterdam and Atlanta, GA: Rodopi, 1998), pp. 11–34

—— 'Théophile Gautier, poète-courtisan', in *Art and Literature of the Second Empire/Les Arts et la littérature sous le Second Empire*, ed. by David Baguley (University of Durham, 2003), pp. 129–47

(2) Literary history, art history and criticism (including exhibition catalogues)

ACKERMAN, GERALD M., *The Life and Work of Jean-Léon Gérôme* (London: Sotheby's, 1986)

ADAMS, STEVEN, *The Barbizon School and the Origins of Impressionism* (London: Phaidon, 1994)

★*Les Années romantiques: la peinture française de 1815 à 1850*, Nantes: Musée des Beaux-Arts, 1995–96 (Paris: RMN, 1995)

ARMAGNAC, LÉO, *Bonnassieux, statuaire, membre de l'Institut, 1810–1892* (Paris: Picard, 1897)

Artistic Relations: Literature and the Visual Arts in Nineteenth-Century France, ed. by Peter Collier and Robert Lethbridge (New Haven and London: Yale University Press, 1994)

AUBRUN, MARIE-MADELEINE, *Henri Lehmann: catalogue raisonné de l'œuvre*, 2 vols (Nantes: Les Amis de Henri Lehmann, 1984)

★*Auguste Préault, sculpteur romantique, 1809–1879*, Paris: Musée d'Orsay, 1997 (Paris: Gallimard/RMN, 1997)

BANN, STEPHEN, *The Clothing of Cleo: A Study of the Representation of History in Nineteenth-Century Britain and France* (Cambridge University Press, 1984)

—— *Paul Delaroche: History Painted* (London: Reaktion Books, 1997)

—— *Parallel Lines: Printmakers, Painters and Photographers in Nineteenth-Century France* (New Haven and London: Yale University Press, 2001)

BATICLE, JEANNINE and CRISTINA MARINAS, *La Galerie espagnole de Louis-Philippe au Louvre 1838–1848* (Paris: RMN, 1981)

BÉNICHOU, PAUL, *Le Sacre de l'écrivain* (Paris: José Corti, 1973)

—— *L'École du désenchantement* (Paris: Gallimard, 1992)

BENOIST, LUC, *La Sculpture romantique*, ed. by Isabelle Leroy-Jay Lemaistre (Paris: Gallimard, 1994)

BERALDI, H., *Les Graveurs du XIXe siècle*, 12 vols (Paris: Conquet, 1885–92)

BOIME, ALBERT, *The Academy and French Painting in the Nineteenth Century* (London: Phaidon, 1971)

—— *Hollow Icons: The Politics of Sculpture in Nineteenth-Century France* (Kent, OH, and London: Kent State University Press, 1987)

—— 'The Second Republic's Contest for the Figure of the Republic', *Art Bulletin*, 53 (March 1971), 68–83

BOURDIEU, PIERRE, *Les Règles de l'art: genèse et structure du champ littéraire* (Paris: Éditions du Seuil, 1992)

—— 'The Link between Literary and Artistic Struggles', in *Artistic Relations: Literature and the Visual Arts in Nineteenth-Century France*, ed. by Peter Collier and Robert Lethbridge (New Haven and London: Yale University Press, 1994), pp. 30–39

BRUNEL, GEORGES, 'Peintures commandées pour les églises de Paris', in *Les Années romantiques: la peinture française de 1815 à 1850* (Paris: RMN, 1995), pp. 61–75

BRYSON, NORMAN, *Tradition and Desire: From David to Delacroix* (Cambridge University Press, 1984)

BURTON, RICHARD, *Baudelaire and the Second Republic: Writing and Revolution* (Oxford: Clarendon Press, 1991)

CASO, J. DE, 'Prix de Rome, sculptures exposées aux Salons et projets pour de grandes statues' in *Statues de chair, sculptures de James Pradier (1790–1852)* (Paris: RMN, 1985), pp. 109–78

CASSAGNE, ALBERT, *La Théorie de l'art pour l'art en France* (Paris: Lucien Dorban, 1959)

*Chassériau: un autre romantisme, Paris: Grand Palais, 2002; ed. by Stéphane Guégan, Vincent Pomarède, and Louis-Antoine Prat (Paris: RMN, 2002)

CHAUDONNERET, MARIE-CLAUDE, *La Figure de la République: le concours de 1848* (Paris: RMN, 1987)

—— *L'État et les artistes: de la Restauration à la Monarchie de Juillet (1815–1833)* (Paris: Flammarion, 1999)

—— 'Historicism and "Heritage" in the Louvre, 1820–1840: From the Musée Charles X to the Galerie d'Apollon', *Art History*, 14 (1991), 488–520

—— 'L'Aube d'une République des arts: un programme pédagogique de David d'Angers', in *Les Collections: fables et programmes*, ed. by Jacques Guillerme (Seyssel: Champ Vallon, 1993), pp. 265–74

—— 'Le Décor inachevé pour le Panthéon', in *Paul Chenavard: le peintre et le prophète* (Paris: RMN, 2000), pp. 67–79

CHU, PETRA TEN-DOESSCHATE and GABRIEL P. WEISBERG, eds, *The Popularization of Images: Visual Culture under the July Monarchy* (Princeton University Press, 1994)

CLARK, T. J., *The Absolute Bourgeois* (London: Thames and Hudson, 1973)

—— *Image of the People* (London: Thames and Hudson, 1973)

COFFINIER, MARGUERITE, *Jean-Claude Ziegler, 1804–1856: sa vie, son œuvre* (Beauvais: GRECB, 1978)

Les Collections: fables et programmes, ed. by Jacques Guillerme (Seyssel: Champ Vallon, 1993)

★*Constable to Delacroix: British Art and the French Romantics*, London: Tate Britain, 2003 (London: Tate, 2003)

CONSTANS, CLAIRE, 'Versailles: les grandes commandes', in *Les Années romantiques: la peinture française de 1815 à 1850* (Paris: RMN, 1995), pp. 86–97

★*Corot, 1796–1875*, Paris: Grand Palais, 1996 (Paris: RMN, 1996)

Corot, un artiste et son temps, ed. by Chiara Stefini, Vincent Pomarède, and Gérard de Vallens (Paris: Klincksieck, 1998)

CROSSLEY, CERI, *Consumable Metaphors: Attitudes towards Animals and Vegetarianism in Nineteenth-Century France* (Oxford and Berne: Peter Lang, 2005)

★*Daumier 1808–1879*, Paris: Grand Palais, 1999 (Paris: RMN, 1999)

La Description de l'œuvre d'art: du modèle classique aux variations contemporaines (Paris: Sogomy/ Académie de France à Rome, 2004)

★*Les Élèves d'Ingres* (Montauban: Musée Ingres, 1999)

★*Ernest Meissonier: rétrospective*, Lyons: Musée des Beaux-Arts, 1993 (Paris: RMN, 1993)

EWALS, LEO, 'La Carrière d'Ary Scheffer: ses envois aux Salons parisiens', in *Ary Scheffer 1795–1858: dessins, aquarelles, esquisses à l'huile* (Paris: Institut Néerlandais, 1980), pp. 7–31 (p. 19)

★*Exigences de réalisme dans la peinture française entre 1830 et 1870* (Chartres: Musée des Beaux-Arts, 1984)

FOSCA, FRANÇOIS, *De Diderot à Valéry: les écrivains et les arts visuels* (Paris: A. Michel, 1960)

FOUCART, BRUNO, *Le Renouveau de la peinture religieuse en France (1800–1860)* (Paris: Arthena, 1987)

FOUCHÉ, JEAN-LOUIS, 'L'Opinion d'Ingres sur le Salon: procès-verbaux de la Commission permanente des beaux-arts (1848–1849)', *La Chronique des arts et de la curiosité*, 14 March 1908, pp. 98–99; 4 April 1908, pp. 129–30

GALASSI, PETER, *Corot in Italy: Open-Air Painting and the Classical-Landscape Tradition* (New Haven and London: Yale University Press, 1991)

GARNIER, G., 'La Carrière d'un artiste officiel à Paris', in *Statues de chair: sculptures de James Pradier (1790–1852)* (Paris: RMN, 1985), pp. 77–96

GEORGEL, CHANTAL, *1848: la République et l'art vivant* (Paris: Fayard/RMN, 1998)

GEORGEL, PIERRE, 'Les Transformations de la peinture vers 1848, 1855, 1863', *Revue de l'art*, 27 (1975), 66–77

GOTLIEB, MARC J., *The Plight of Emulation: Ernest Meissonier and French Salon Painting* (Princeton University Press, 1996)

GREEN, NICHOLAS, *The Spectacle of Nature: Landscape and Bourgeois Culture in Nineteenth-Century France* (Manchester University Press, 1990)

—— 'Dealing in Temperaments: Economic Transformation of the Artistic Field in France during the Second Half of the Nineteenth Century', *Art History*, 10 (1987), 59–78

GREENBERG, SUSAN, 'Reforming *Paysage historique*: Corot and the Generation of 1830', *Art History*, 27 (2004), 412–30

★*La Griffe et la Dent: Antoine Louis Barye (1795–1875), sculpteur animalier*, Paris: Musée du Louvre, 1996–97 (Paris: RMN, 1996)

GUÉGAN, STÉPHANE, 'Ziegler dans l'œil des critiques', *Bulletin des musées et monuments lyonnais*, 4 (1990), 12–21

—— 'From Ziegler to Courbet: Painting, Art Criticism and the Spanish Trope under Louis-Philippe', in *Manet/Velasquez: The French Taste for Spanish Painting* (New Haven and London: Yale University Press, 2003), pp. 191–201

—— 'Rouge Venise', in *Venise en France: du romantisme au symbolisme* (Paris: École du Louvre, 2006), pp. 147–66

—— and LOUIS-ANTOINE PRAT, eds, *Chassériau, 1819–1856: un autre romantisme* (Paris: La Documentation Française, 2002)

★*Gustave Courbet (1819–1877)*, Paris: Grand Palais, 1977–78 (Paris: Éditions des Musées Nationaux, 1977)

HARGROVE, JUNE, ed., *The French Academy: Classicism and its Antagonists* (Newark, DE: University of Delaware Press, 1990)

★*Henri Lehmann, 1814–1882*, Paris: Musée Carnavalet, 1983 (Paris: Les Musées de la Ville de Paris, 1983)

HÉRAIN, FRANÇOIS DE, *Les Grands Écrivains critiques d'art* (Paris: Mercure de France, 1943)

★*Hommage à Corot*, Paris: Orangerie des Tuileries, 1975 (Paris: Éditions des Musées Nationaux, 1975)

HUNGERFORD, CONSTANCE CAIN, ' "Les choses importantes": Meissonier et la peinture d'histoire', in *Ernest Meissonier: rétrospective* (Paris: RMN, 1993), pp. 162–87

IMBERT, D., 'La Sculpture aux Champs-Élysées', *Monuments historiques*, no. 172 (1991), 76–81

★*Ingres 1780–1867*, Paris: Musée du Louvre, 2006 (Paris: Gallimard/Musée du Louvre Éditions, 2006)

★*In the Light of Italy: Corot and Open-Air Painting*, Washington: National Gallery of Art, 1996 (New Haven and London: Yale University Press, 1996)

L'Invention de la critique d'art, ed. by Pierre-Henry Frangne et Jean-Marc Poinsot (Presses Universitaires de Rennes, 2002)

★*Jean-François Millet*, Paris: Grand Palais, 1975–76 (Paris: Éditions des Musées Nationaux, 1975)

★*La Jeunesse des musées*, Paris: Musée d'Orsay, 1994 (Paris: RMN, 1994)

JOHNSON, LEE, *The Paintings of Eugène Delacroix*, 6 vols (Oxford: Clarendon Press, 1981–89)

KEARNS, JAMES, ' "Niera-t-on le pouvoir des arts?" Revisiting Jacques-Louis David at the 1846 Exhibition at the *Bazar Bonne-Nouvelle*', *MLR*, 102 (2007), 672–86

KELLEY, DAVID, 'Transpositions', in *Artistic Relations: Literature and the Visual Arts in Nineteenth-Century France*, ed. by Peter Collier and Robert Lethbridge (New Haven and London: Yale University Press, 1994), pp. 178–91

LACAMBRE, GENEVIÈVE, 'Introduction', *Le Musée du Luxembourg en 1874* (Paris: Éditions des Musées Nationaux, 1974), pp. 7–11

—— 'Les Achats de l'État aux artistes vivants: le musée du Luxembourg', in *La Jeunesse des musées* (Paris: RMN, 1994), pp. 267–77

LACAMBRE, J., 'Les Élèves d'Ingres et la critique du temps', *Actes du colloque Ingres* (Montauban: Dupin, 1969)

★*'Le Larmoyeur' d'Ary Schefer*, Paris: Musée de la Vie Romantique, 1989 (Paris: Éditions Paris-Musées, 1989)

LEROY-JAY LEMAISTRE, ISABELLE, ' "Ses œuvres sont les strophes en pierre, en marbre, en bronze, en bois, du poème de la douleur humaine" ', in *Auguste Préault, sculpteur romantique, 1809–1879* (Paris: Gallimard/ RMN, 1997), pp. 79–88

LICHTENSTEIN, JACQUELINE, *La Couleur éloquente: rhétorique et peinture à l'âge classique* (Paris: Flammarion, 1989)

MCWILLIAM, NEIL, *A Bibliography of Salon Criticism in Paris from the July Monarchy to the Second Republic, 1831–1851* (Cambridge University Press, 1991)

—— *Dreams of Happiness: Social Art and the French Left, 1830–1850* (Princeton University Press, 1993)

—— 'Art, Labour and Mass Democracy: Debates on the Status of the Artist in France around 1848', *Art History*, 11 (1988), 64–87

—— 'Opinions professionnelles: critique d'art et économie de la culture sous la Monarchie de Juillet', *Romantisme*, 71 (1991), 19–31

MAINARDI, PATRICIA, *The End of the Salon: Art and State in the Early Third Republic* (Cambridge University Press, 1993)

★*Manet/Velasquez: The French Taste for Spanish Painting*, New York: Metropolitan Museum of Art, 2003 (New Haven and London: Yale University Press, 2003)

MARRINAN, MICHAEL, *Painting Politics for Louis Philippe: Art and Ideology in Orléanist France, 1830–1848* (New Haven and London: Yale University Press, 1988)

—— 'Historical Writing and the Writing of History at Louis-Philippe's Versailles', in *The Popularization of Images: Visual Culture under the July Monarchy*, ed. by Petra ten-Doesschate Chu and Gabriel P. Weisberg (Princeton University Press, 1994), pp. 113–43

MILLARD, CHARLES W., 'La Vie d'Auguste Préault', in *Auguste Préault, sculpteur romantique, 1809–1879* (Paris: Gallimard/RMN, 1997), pp. 11–75

MIQUEL, PIERRE, *Le Paysage français au XIXe siècle*, 3 vols (Maurs-la-Jolie: Éditions de la Martinelle, 1975)

MITCHELL, CLAUDINE, 'What is to be done with the Salonniers?', *Oxford Art Journal*, 10.1 (Fall 1987), 106–14

MORIARTY, MICHAEL, 'Structures of Cultural Production in Nineteenth-Century France', in *Artistic Relations: Literature and the Visual Arts in Nineteenth-Century France*, ed. by Peter Collier and Robert Lethbridge (New Haven and London: Yale University Press, 1994), pp. 15–29

MOVER, D., 'A. A. Préault', *Art Bulletin*, 63 (1981), 288–307

★*Le Musée de Luxembourg en 1874*, Paris: Grand Palais, 1974 (Paris: Éditions des Musées Nationaux, 1974)

OCKMAN, CAROL, *Ingres's Eroticized Bodies: Retracing the Serpentine Line* (New Haven and London: Yale University Press, 1995)

ORWICZ, MICHAEL R., *Art Criticism and its Institutions in Nineteenth-Century France* (Manchester University Press, 1994)

★*Paul Chenavard: le peintre et le prophète*, dir. by Marie-Claude Chaudonneret, Lyons: Musée des Beaux-Arts, 2000 (Paris: RMN, 2000)

★*Paul Delaroche: un peintre dans l'histoire*, dir. by Claude Allemand-Cosneau and Isabelle Julia, Nantes: Musée des Beaux-Arts, 1999–2000 (Paris: RMN, 1999)

★*Paysages d'Italie: les peintres du plein air (1780–1830)*, Paris: Grand Palais, 2001 (Paris: RMN, 2001)

PELTRE, CHRISTINE, *Théodore Chassériau* (Paris: Gallimard, 2001)

★*Portraits by Ingres: Image of an Epoch*, ed. by Gary Tinterow and Philip Conisbee (New York: Metropolitan Museum of Art, 1999)

PRENDERGAST, CHRISTOPHER, *Napoleon and History Painting: Antoine Gros's 'La Bataille d'Eylau'* (Oxford: Clarendon Press, 1977)

—— *Paris and the Nineteenth Century* (Oxford: Blackwell, 1992)

—— *For the People by the People? Eugène Sue's 'Les Mystères de Paris'* (Oxford: Legenda, 2003)

RECHT, ROLAND, ed., *Le Texte de l'œuvre d'art: la description* (Strasbourg: Presses universitaires, 1998)

ROSENBERG, MARTIN, *Raphael and France: The Artist as Paradigm and Symbol* (University Park: Pennsylvania State University Press, 1995)

ROSENTHAL, LÉON, *Du Romantisme au réalisme* (Paris: Laurens, 1914; repr. Paris: Éditions Macula, 1987)

ROUSSEAU, MADELEINE, *La Vie et l'œuvre de Philippe-Auguste Jeanron: peintre, écrivain, directeur des Musées nationaux 1808–1877*, completed and ed. by Marie-Martine Dubreuil (Paris: RMN, 2000)

RUBIN, JAMES H., 'Delacroix and Romanticism', in *The Cambridge Companion to Delacroix*, ed. by Beth S. Wright (Cambridge University Press, 2000), pp. 26–47

SAGNIER, CHRISTINE, *Courbet: un émeutier au Salon* (Paris: Séguier, 2000)

SANCHEZ, PIERRE and XAVIER SEYDOUX, *Les Catalogues des Salons*, 12 vols (Dijon: L'Échelle de Jacob, 1999–2006), V [1846–50] (2001)

SANDOZ, MARC, *Théodore Chassériau 1819–1858: catalogue raisonné des peintures et estampes* (Paris: Arts et Métiers Graphiques, 1974)

SCHULMAN, MICHEL, *Théodore Rousseau: catalogue raisonné de l'œuvre peint* (Paris: Les Éditions de l'Amateur, 1999)

SCOTT, DAVID, *Pictorialist Poetics: Poetry and the Visual Arts in Nineteenth-Century France* (Cambridge University Press, 1988)

★*La Sculpture française au XIXe siècle*, Paris: Grand Palais, 1986 (Paris: RMN, 1986)

SÉRULLAZ, ARLETTE and VINCENT POMARÈDE, *Eugène Delacroix, 'La Liberté guidant le peuple'* (Paris: RMN, 2004)

SESMAT, PIERRE, 'Le Musée historique de Versailles: la gloire, l'histoire et les arts', in *La Jeunesse des musées* (Paris: RMN, 1994), pp. 115–21

SHELTON, ANDREW CARRINGTON, *Ingres and his Critics* (Cambridge University Press, 2005)

—— 'The Critical Reception of Ingres's Portraits (1802–1855)', in *Portraits by Ingres: Image of an Epoch*, ed. by Gary Tinterow and Philip Conisbee (New York: Metropolitan Museum of Art, 1999)

—— 'Ingres versus Delacroix', in *Fingering Ingres*, ed. by Susan Siegfried and Adrian Rifkin (Oxford: Blackwell, 2001), pp. 76–92

—— 'Ingres et la critique moderne', in *Ingres 1780–1867* (Paris: Gallimard/Musée du Louvre Éditions, 2006), pp. 21–31

SIEGFRIED, SUSAN and ADRIAN RIFKIN, eds, *Fingering Ingres* (Oxford: Blackwell, 2001)

SILER, D., 'Documentation', in *Statues de chair: sculptures de James Pradier (1790–1852)* (Paris: RMN, 1985), pp. 329–78

SLOANE, JOSEPH CURTIS, *Paul Chenavard, Artist of 1848* (Chapel Hill: University of North Carolina Press, 1962)

★*Statues de chair: sculptures de James Pradier (1790–1852)*, Paris: Musée du Luxembourg, 1986 (Paris: RMN, 1985)

TEYSSÈDRE, BERNARD, *Roger de Piles et les débats sur le coloris au siècle de Louis XIV* (Paris: Bibliothèque des arts, 1965)

THOMAS, GREG M., *Art and Ecology in Nineteenth-Century France: The Landscapes of Théodore Rousseau* (Princeton University Press, 2000)

TINTEROW, GARY and PHILIP CONISBEE, *Portraits by Ingres: Image of an Epoch* (New York: Metropolitan Museum of Art, 1999)

TOUSSAINT, HÉLÈNE, *'La Liberté guidant le peuple' de Delacroix* (Paris: RMN, 1982)

VAISSE, PIERRE, *La Troisième République et les peintres* (Paris: Flammarion, 1995)

—— 'Le Conseil supérieur de perfectionnement des manufactures nationales sous la deuxième république', *Bulletin de la Société de l'Histoire de l'Art français* (1974), 153–71

—— 'Considérations sur la Seconde République et les beaux-arts', *Bulletin de la Société d'histoire de la révolution de 1848 et des révolutions du XIXe siècle* (1985), 59–85

VIGNE, GEORGES, *Ingres* (Paris: Citadelles & Mazenod, 1995)

VOUILLOUX, BERNARD, 'La Peinture dans l'écriture: esquisse d'une typologie', in ★*Balzac et la peinture*, Tours: Musée des Beaux-Arts, 1999 (Tours: Farrago, 1999), pp. 133–51

—— 'La Description des œuvres d'art dans le roman français au XIXe siècle', in *La Description de l'œuvre d'art: du modèle classique aux variations contemporaines* (Paris: Sogomy/Académie de France à Rome, 2004), pp. 153–84

WHITE, HARRISON C. and CYNTHIA A., *Canvases and Careers: Institutional Changes in the French Painting World* (New York: John Wiley, 1965)

WHITELEY, JON, 'Exhibitions of Contemporary Painting in London and Paris, 1760–1860', in *Saloni, gallerie, musei et loro influenza sulla sviluppo dell'arte dei secoli XIX e XX*, ed by Francis Haskell (Bologna: CLUEB, 1981), pp. 69–87

WRIGHT, BETH S., ed., *The Cambridge Companion to Delacroix* (Cambridge University Press, 2000)

(3) General history

AGULHON, MAURICE, *1848 ou l'apprentissage de la république* (Paris: Éditions du Seuil, 1973)

APRILE, SYLVIE, *La IIe République et le Second Empire, 1848–1870* (Paris: Pygmalion, 2000)

BELLANGER, CLAUDE and others, eds, *Histoire générale de la presse française*, 5 vols (Paris: PUF, 1969)

CHEVALIER, LOUIS, *Classes laborieuses et classes dangereuses à Paris pendant la première moitié du XIXe siècle* (Paris: Plon, 1958)

GIRODET, RAOUL, 'Les Trois Couleurs', in *Les Lieux de mémoire*, ed. by Pierre Nora, 3 vols (Paris: Gallimard, 1984–92), I: *La République*, pp. 5–35

JONES, COLIN, *Paris: Biography of a City* (London: Penguin/Allen Lane, 2004)

MAGRAW, ROGER, *France 1815–1914: The Bourgeois Century* (London: Fontana, 1983)

—— *France, 1800–1914: A Social History* (Harlow: Longman, 2002)

MARTIN, MARC, 'Journalistes parisiens et notoriété (vers 1830–1870): pour une histoire sociale du journalisme', *Revue historique*, no. 539 (July–September 1981), 31–74

OZOUF, MONA, 'Le Panthéon', in *Les Lieux de mémoire*, ed. by Pierre Nora, 3 vols (Paris: Gallimard, 1984–92), I: *La République*, pp. 139–66

Le Panthéon: symbole des révolutions: de l'Église de la Nation au Temple des grands hommes (Paris: Caisse national des monuments historiques, 1989)

PELLISSIER, PIERRE, *Émile de Girardin, prince de la presse* (Paris: Denoël, 1985)

PILBEAM, PAMELA M., *Republicanism in Nineteenth-Century France, 1814–1871* (Basingstoke and London: Macmillan, 1995)

PINKNEY, DAVID H., *Napoleon III and the Rebuilding of Paris* (Princeton University Press, 1958)

★*La Presse dans le centre de Paris 1830–1851*, Paris: Mairies Annexes des IIe et XIIe Arrondissements, 1981 (Paris: Délégation à l'Action Artistique de la Ville de Paris et Société d'Histoire du Ier et IIe Arrondissement, 1981)

★*Quand Paris dansait avec Marianne*, Paris: Petit Paris, 1989 (Paris: Éditions Paris Musées, 1989)

THÉRENTY, MARIE-ÈVE and ALAIN VAILLANT, *1836: l'an I de l'ère médiatique: analyse littéraire et historique de 'La Presse' de Girardin* (Paris: Nouveau monde Éditions, 2001)

—— eds, *Presse et plumes* (Paris: Nouveau monde Éditions, 2004)

INDEX

For Product Safety Concerns and Information please contact our EU
representative GPSR@taylorandfrancis.com Taylor & Francis Verlag GmbH,
Kaufingerstraße 24, 80331 München, Germany

Printed and bound by CPI Group (UK) Ltd, Croydon, CR0 4YY
01/05/2025
01858359-0010